The (M)other Tongue

THE
(M)other Tongue

Essays in Feminist
Psychoanalytic Interpretation

EDITED BY

Shirley Nelson Garner
Claire Kahane
Madelon Sprengnether

Cornell University Press

ITHACA AND LONDON

First published 1985 by Cornell University Press.
Published in the United Kingdom by
Cornell University Press Ltd., London.

International Standard Book Number (cloth) 0-8014-1693-0
International Standard Book Number (paper) 0-8014-9299-8
Library of Congress Catalog Card Number 84-17560

Printed in the United States of America

*Librarians: Library of Congress cataloging information
appears on the last page of the book.*

*The paper in this book is acid-free and meets the guidelines
for permanence and durability of the Committee on Production
Guidelines for Book Longevity of the Council on Library Resources.*

For our families

Contents

Preface　　　　　　　　　　　　　　　　　　　　9

Introduction　　　　　　　　　　　　　　　　　15

PART I.　FEMINISTS ON FREUD

1. The Father's Seduction　　　　　　　　　　33
   Jane Gallop

2. Enforcing Oedipus: Freud and Dora　　　　51
   Madelon Sprengnether

3. The Hand That Rocks the Cradle:
   Recent Gender Theories and Their Implications　　72
   Coppélia Kahn

4. Hysteria, Psychoanalysis, and Feminism:
   The Case of Anna O.　　　　　　　　　　89
   Dianne Hunter

PART II.　REREADING PATRIARCHAL TEXTS

5. "This Is and Is Not Cressid":
   The Characterization of Cressida　　　　119
   Janet Adelman

6. Difference and Silence: John Milton and the
   Question of Gender　　　　　　　　　　142
   Jim Swan

7. The Mother Tongue: *Christabel* and the
   Language of Love   169
   Margery Durham

8. Mrs. Hawthorne's Headache: Reading
   The Scarlet Letter   194
   David Leverenz

9. *Eugénie Grandet*: Mirrors and Melancholia   217
   Naomi Schor

PART III. WOMEN REWRITING WOMAN

10. A Map for Rereading; or, Gender and the
    Interpretation of Literary Texts   241
    Annette Kolodny

11. Class, Gender, and Family System:
    The Case of George Sand   260
    Wendy Deutelbaum and Cynthia Huff

12. Women and Men in Doris Lessing's *Golden Notebook*:
    Divided Selves   280
    Gayle Greene

13. Writing as Difference in Violette Leduc's Autobiography,
    La Bâtarde   306
    Martha Noel Evans

14. "Women Together" in Virginia Woolf's *Night and Day* 318
    Shirley Nelson Garner

15. The Gothic Mirror   334
    Claire Kahane

16. Writing and Motherhood   352
    Susan Rubin Suleiman

Contributors   378

Index   383

8

Preface

This book takes its point of departure from the editors' perception that in recent years a new genre of criticism has begun to emerge, one that combines feminist and psychoanalytic analysis. This is of necessity a complex and to some people even a contradictory phenomenon, given feminist opposition to patriarchal systems of organization, including those that structure or support Freud's thought. At the same time, Freud himself, in his speculations about the significance of preoedipal stages of development as well as the complexity of oedipal socialization, has provided clues to feminists who seek nothing less than a transformation of the root metaphors of Western culture.

It is no secret that we are, as a culture, primarily androcentric and phallocentric. Feminism challenges this fundamental orientation of our social system, seeking not only to reveal its partiality, its limited application, but also to disrupt it, to propose alternate models of understanding and behavior. We believe that the role of literature in this process is crucial. The stories we tell ourselves about who we are or hope to be play a primary role in creating and sustaining our identities as we move through our uncertain world. To explore, to question, to interpret these stories (whether literary or psychoanalytic) is to take a position in relation to them, as well as to reveal one's own assumptions. It makes a difference, we maintain, where one stands as reader as well as writer, and whether one constructs or responds to a mother-based or father-based fiction. On the whole, oedipally organized narrative (as well as interpretation) that is based on the determining role of the father and of patriarchal discourse tells a different story from preoedipal narrative, which locates the source of movement and conflict in the figure of the mother.

The essays in this volume, in dealing with the meanings of gender, not only raise questions about the psychosymbolic resonance of preoedipal and oedipal narratives but also illustrate its effects in their own narrative emphasis. It is possible, and perhaps inevitable, that mother-based and father-based stories coexist in the same narrative (as they do in Freud's theories), the emphasis shifting as one co-opts or is set in opposition to the other. We are thus also interested in the silences of discourse, in what a culture chooses to obscure, to deny, or to render mute in its hegemonic fictions. While the silent and the obscure have long been associated with the feminine, this book is intended to encourage the silent subjects to speak. These essays point to the following topics as inhibited or absent in dominant cultural expression: relationships among women as mothers and daughters, as sisters, friends, and lovers; aspects of specifically female experience, such as menstruation and childbirth; explorations of women's sexuality and eroticism; and portrayals of motherhood as a source of cultural as well as biological creativity.

It is clear that fascination by the preoedipal period and a corresponding focus on the figure of the mother in theories of human development have had a profound impact on the discipline of psychoanalysis and on the feminist interpretation of literature. Out of differing aims and desires, both feminism and psychoanalysis focus our attention on a female subject. What this focus will mean ultimately for our culture is as yet uncertain, though it seems difficult to imagine a return to a purely androcentric awareness. Given the specific failures of our mythos of aggressive masculinity, along with our tendencies as a culture to glamorize fictions of murderous rivalry among men, it may well be in the interest of our survival as a species to herald the end of the androcentric era.

We thank Bernhard Kendler of Cornell University Press for helping us in a variety of ways as we prepared our manuscript for publication. Shirley Nelson Garner and Madelon Sprengnether are grateful to their friend and colleague Toni A. H. McNaron for her encouragement and support over the long period of time when we were in the process of

Preface

imagining and creating this book. They thank as well the secretarial staff of the English Department at the University of Minnesota, particularly Catherine Aunan, Dorothy Conlan, and Gregory Holupchinski, for providing us with clerical assistance. Claire Kahane thanks her former colleague Norman Holland for helping to fund the conference "The Creative Use of Difference" at the State University of New York at Buffalo in 1980, where some of these essays were first presented as papers; Joan Cipperman for her invaluable secretarial services; and Gwen Ashbaugh for her research assistance.

SHIRLEY NELSON GARNER

Minneapolis, Minnesota

CLAIRE KAHANE

Buffalo, New York

MADELON SPRENGNETHER

Minneapolis, Minnesota

The (M)other Tongue

Introduction

Freud understood the power of story, whether in the form of a Dickens narrative or of one of his own case histories. Poets, he believed, with their intuitive understanding of the workings of the unconscious, were capable of conveying psychic truths. Fascinated as he was by forms of symbolic representation and by the process of interpretation, Freud in turn has engaged the imagination of literary critics seeking guidance in their own hermeneutic wanderings. Contemporary critics especially regard Freud less as the founder of a science that provides keys to psychic mysteries than as a theorist of the imagination engaged in a lifelong study of the relationships among psyche, language, and symbol, who generated through this process (perhaps necessarily) his own influential stories.

Regarding Freud as a narrator as well as an analyst of narrative raises questions outside the range of his own considerable introspection. Freud, for instance, did not view his own stories as in any way arbitrary or culturally determined, much less influenced by gender. Feminists, who are acutely aware of the shaping power of myth, specifically as it relates to male and female socialization, are understandably skeptical of Freud as a storyteller when his narratives concern gender.

Freud's most common story, of course, is a borrowed one, that of *Oedipus*. In this drama by Sophocles Freud saw a reflection, a magnification, and a codification of his own archaic desire for his mother, his murderous wishes directed against his father, and his fears of paternal retaliation.[1] From this moment of empathic recognition, Freud ventured a series of daring interpretations about the primacy of the father, the belatedness of the son, and the competition among men for access to a woman, perceived alternately as maternal and sexual object. Needless to say, Freud's private *Bildungsroman*, his account of growing up male in the latter half of the nineteenth century, caught the imagination of his culture—and ours. One can read this remarkable instance either as a validation of his subjective insight about male psychic development or as a demonstration of the paradigmatic fit between individual psychic structure, both male and female, and the essential features of partriarchial society. Juliet Mitchell has argued the latter interpretation, maintaining that Freud is valuable to feminism precisely because of his power to elucidate the unconscious underpinnings of patriarchy.[2] Everywhere in our society, in our legal, economic, and sexual arrangements, we see the effects of the Oedipus complex and its corollary, the castration complex, writ large. Where Mitchell and other feminists differ from Freud is in their assumption that the patriarchal structure of relations can be dislocated, that other social and psychic structures are not only possible but desirable.

The relation between Freud and feminism is, however, not a recent phenomenon. It begins as early as Freud's own engagement with hysteria, an encounter that led him to explore the interrelation of sexual desire and its representation in the psychic life of women. Bertha Pappenheim, Josef Breuer's famous patient described in the case of Anna O., provided Freud with both a name and a method for understanding hysteria—the "talking cure."[3] In the symbolism of her cure Freud discovered the unconscious poetics of her malady. Restated by Jacques Lacan, himself obsessed by the role of language, the endless play of signifiers in the representation of desire, this perception takes

1. On Freud's discovery of the Oedipus complex through his own self-analysis, see his letters to Wilhelm Fliess, especially that of October 15, 1897, in *The Standard Edition of the Complete Psychological Works of Sigmund Freud*, ed. and trans. James Strachey et al. (London: Hogarth, 1953–74), I, 265. Subsequent references to Freud's complete works will be to *Standard Edition*.

2. Juliet Mitchell, *Psychoanalysis and Feminism* (New York: Random House, 1974).

3. For a comprehensive discussion of Anna O.'s contribution to psychoanalytic theory, see Dianne Hunter's article in this volume, reprinted from *Feminist Studies*, 9 (1983), 465–88.

the following form: "It is the truth of what this desire has been in his history that the patient cries out through his symptom."[4]

But reading symptoms is a difficult process, one from which Breuer himself, shocked by a demonstration of Bertha's erotic attachment to him, fled. She, on the other hand, released from the prison of her illness, and presumably less squeamish than her physician, went on to lead a productive life in the world, committed to the cause of social justice and in particular to the rights of women. Freud, in his own famous case history of a female hysteric, Dora, differs from Breuer in two important ways.[5] Here it is the physician that doggedly pursues his path of inquiry, regardless of the "dirty secrets" he must confront, and the patient that flees, her treatment regarded as incomplete, finally unsuccessful. While Breuer ultimately left Bertha to her own devices, Freud could not, at least in imagination, let Dora go. If we examine the interpretation he wished her to accept, we may also see some of the fault lines in his representation of femininity.

In the melodrama that unfolds through Freud's case history, two men are exchanging a woman in return for sexual favors: Dora's father attempts to hand her over to Herr K. in return for the services of Frau K., Dora's choice being the passive one (if only in fantasy) of accepting the outcome. Freud's early assumption that heterosexual desire is natural leads him to conclude that a healthy response on the part of Dora would involve desire for Herr K., a desire for the virile male that would repeat her childhood desire for her father. Having constructed the object of Dora's desire as phallic, both in the fantasy of fellatio he attributes to her and in his assumption of her arousal by the advances of Herr K., Freud presses Dora to confirm the pattern of social expectation for a girl of her class, to admit her desire for and to accept the man of her father's choosing. But given the particularly seamy version of this plot in Dora's case, in which an admission of heterosexual desire means complicity in a sordid sexual circuit, Dora's

4. Jacques Lacan, "The Agency of the Letter in the Unconscious or Reason since Freud," in *Ecrits*, trans. Alan Sheridan (New York: Norton, 1977), 167.

5. "Fragment of an Analysis of a Case of Hysteria" (1905), in *Standard Edition*, VII, 7–112; rpt. as *Dora: An Analysis of a Case of Hysteria*, ed. Philip Rieff (New York: Crowell Collier, 1963). Of the numerous reevaluations of the case and of the function of sexual difference in Freud's narrative, see especially *Diacritics*, 13 (Spring 1983), and the collection of articles edited by Charles Bernheimer and Claire Kahane, *In Dora's Case: Freud, Hysteria, Feminism* (New York: Columbia University Press, forthcoming).

stubborn rejection of the plot and her flight are not surprising. What is surprising is Freud's blindness to another plot that he assigns to the margins of his story: Dora's desire for Frau K., a preoedipal desire for the sexual mother, which disrupts Freud's oedipal plot. Although the maternal figure is relegated to an aside, her absent presence points to a fluidity of sexual aim, an indeterminacy of object that undermines Freud's construction of a normal female desire for the phallic male.

Whatever the character of Dora's desire (homosexual, heterosexual, bisexual), Freud's reading of her text is consistent with his conservative view of marriage as the appropriate conclusion to the narrative of feminine development. Yet his very failure led him to recognize the aberrant vicissitudes of sexuality itself and compelled him to rewrite repeatedly the story of the ordering of sexual desire.[6] That he constantly stumbled over the question of the nature of female desire testifies to the precariousness of that ordering. While his continued elaboration of the Oedipus complex made sense of the position of the male child in relation to the parents in a conventionally structured patriarchal family, the story Freud tells about femininity is essentially a broken one, a hysterical narrative, uncertain and fragmentary, as though he himself, while aware of its insufficiency, were unable to revise it.[7] The mistake, monumentally obvious yet so deeply inscribed in Freud's own culture as to be invisible, is in its premise: that for both sexes desire is phallic. At the beginning, he maintains, the little girl is a little boy, actively desiring her mother but ill equipped, her clitoris an inferior penis. In the oedipal stage she recognizes her condition of lack, from which there is no reprieve, and, repudiating her mother, is precipitated into the feminine position, a desire for the penis, and thus for a series of substitute phallic objects, ultimately a baby, preferably a boy. The pleasure she has known in masturbation, now understood as inappropriately phallic and aggressive, she must renounce in order to achieve the receptive goal of femininity—at best

6. Freud's first and in many ways most radical formulation of the ordering of sexuality is *Three Essays on a Theory of Sexuality* (1905), in *Standard Edition*, VII, 125–244 (rpt. New York: Basic Books, 1975).

7. For Freud's evolving narrative of oedipal sexuality, see in *Standard Edition*, "The Dissolution of the Oedipus Complex" (1924), XIX, 173–83; "Some Psychical Consequences of the Anatomical Distinction between the Sexes" (1925), XIX, 241–61; "Female Sexuality" (1931), XXI, 221–47; all rpt. in *Sexuality and the Psychology of Love*, ed. Philip Rieff (New York: Collier, 1963). Freud's final narrative of female desire is "Femininity" (1933), in *Standard Edition*, XXII, 112–36; rpt. in *New Introductory Lectures on Psychoanalysis*, ed. James Strachey (New York: Norton, 1965).

a consolation prize, hardly a joy. Despite the pains Freud takes to soften the impact of this story, he does not alter its basic message. However threatening the story of Oedipus, the drama of castration, it is better to face this potential tragedy (masculinity) than its certainty (femininity).

In his continued revisions of the story of sexual difference, Freud never gave up his attempt to understand femininity as a problematic and necessarily inferior version of masculinity. Directing his gaze at the penis, whose primacy in the order of gender he never questioned, Freud concluded that castration was the pivotal threat in the development of both sexes. This privileging of the male aroused great controversy in the mid-1920s, and the theoretical debate sparked by Freud opened the possibility of an alternate basis for stories about female desire.[8] Such a basis would begin to appear, however, only through a shift of focus from father to mother, a shift that has led to more complex and flexible narratives of female desire.

Excavating that shadowy Minoan culture, the domain of the mother that Freud had discovered to precede the oedipal phase, object-relations theory describes the preoedipal period as an interpersonal field of relationships internalized by the infant and thus constitutive of the self.[9] In this story the early relationship between mother and child is symbiotic, a dual unity from which the child must separate. Both sexes in this account assume their primary identity from this mirroring relation. Both make use of transitional objects (mediating between self and other) to separate from this dyadic matrix, and both turn from mother to father on a developmental journey toward individuation.

While this new attention to the mother essentially colonized what had been a dark continent for psychoanalysis, like a colony, the mother in object-relations theory remains an object of service—a "good enough mother," in the influential phrase of D. W. Winnicott—whose desire is shaped by the child's need and whose subjectivity remains unexamined.[10] More significant, this reorientation has tended to evade the

---

8. For a history of this controversy, see Juliet Mitchell, "Introduction I," in *Feminine Sexuality*, ed. Mitchell and Jacqueline Rose (New York: Norton, 1982). See also Zenia Odes Fliegel, "Feminine Psychosexual Development in Freudian Theory," *Psychoanalytic Quarterly*, 52 (1973), 385–408.

9. For a full discussion of preoedipal dynamics, see Margaret Mahler, *The Psychological Birth of the Human Infant* (New York: Basic Books, 1975), and D. W. Winnicott, *Playing and Reality* (New York: Basic Books, 1971).

10. See Winnicott, "The Mirror-Role of Mother and Family in Child Development," in *Playing and Reality*, 111–18.

question of gender and to neglect the issue of sexual difference by focusing on the relation between a mother and a sexually undifferentiated child.

The feminist revision of this narrative inserts gender into this crucible of identity by locating its origin at the point of differentiation, and by insisting on the difference the mother makes as a woman in her relations with sons and daughters. Nancy Chodorow, perhaps the most influential feminist theorist of object relations, explores the way culture reproduces in girls the desire to mother by tracing the consequences of the female monopoly over child rearing.[11] Constructing a new narrative of feminine development, Chodorow proposes an essential continuity in the mother-daughter relation that is unavailable to the male child. Mothers treat sons as more separate beings, encouraging them toward autonomy. Sons in turn define their maleness in opposition to their primary sense of oneness with a mother-woman. But mothers identify with female infants, and by treating daughters as extensions of themselves, create in them through that mirroring both an ambivalence about separation and a deep emotional bonding that is never surrendered. Even at the oedipal period daughters retain their preoedipal attachment to their mothers as their primary love objects. On the basis of this distinction Chodorow accounts for several gender-related phenomena: for more flexible, fluid ego boundaries in women, for the female tendency to perceive reality in relational terms, for a fundamental bisexual orientation underlying heterosexual development.

Although relatively unknown in Europe, Chodorow's analysis has offered a paradigm that many American feminists have found useful both in interpreting patterns of relationship among women in writings by women authors and in locating traces of the maternal imago as a subtext in works by male authors. What is lacking in the narrative Chodorow offers is the particular consideration of the relation between gender as she describes it and representation, between the effect of gender on symbolic expression and the effect of a preexisting system of representation on the emergence of gender. These considerations have been at the center of a growing body of feminist thought that

11. Chodorow's discussion, which is fully developed in *The Reproduction of Mothering: Psychoanalysis and the Sociology of Gender* (Berkeley: University of California Press, 1978), has been extremely influential among American feminist critics, but European critics take issue with her sociological use of psychoanalysis and its premise of an unproblematized concept of reality.

has produced a sea change in feminist literary criticism, a virtual vortex of discourse stemming from France and directed by Jacques Lacan's rereading of Freud.

While Anglo-American theories and their feminist revisions proceed from an assumption of unmediated presence embodied in the mother, French psychoanalysis constitutes its myth of origin from absence. Where Anglo-American theorists conjure or invoke the preoedipal mother, Lacanians insist on her loss. Taking up Freud's representation of the ego as an elegiac concept, as the "precipitate of lost object cathexes," Lacanians translate maternal loss into the more generalized concept of originary loss, of a lack in the subject, displaced and veiled by language but persisting as unconscious desire.[12] Desire, Lacan's key concept, challenges the unity of the subject, and thus any fixed unitary sexual identity.

Whereas the self in object-relations theory is constituted as a unity through the process of differentiation, for Lacanians that self is a fiction, a creation of desire, organized around a fantasy of wholeness and integration, reflected in the mirror image.[13] The mirror stage thus represents the moment when the subject is alienated, located within an order outside itself, and subject to that order. In Lacan's complex narrative of mirror relations, the child desires to be what the mother desires. But both mother and child are themselves already located within the Symbolic order of language and culture, in which the mother's desire is governed by the "law of the Father." Unlike Freud's natural father, Lacan's Father is the figure of a function that breaks the Imaginary dual relation between mother and child, between self and other-as-image-of-self. The Father's law enjoins the subject to line up according to an opposition, man/woman, to assume its place as "he" or "she" in a preexisting order of language and culture. For Lacan, the phallus is the mark of this division (having or not having it) as well as the ultimate signifier of desire, or a lack-in-being, because of its status as potentially missing. Recognition of this lack, castration, begins

---

12. The elegaic concept of the ego is presented in Freud, "The Splitting of the Ego in the Defensive Process" (1940), in *Standard Edition*, XXIII, 271–79. For Lacan's discussion of the relation between language and desire, see especially "The Agency of the Latter in the Unconscious" and "The Function and Field of Speech and Language in Psychoanalysis," both in *Ecrits*, 146–78 and 30–113.

13. Lacan, "The Mirror Stage as Formative of the Function of the I," in *Ecrits*, 1–7.

the endless process of signification and exchange, which is culture.[14] Thus a patriarchial structuring of desire and prohibition determines the limits within which sexual life can be experienced.

While some feminists criticize Lacan's totalizing equivalence of the Symbolic and the law of the Father and his privileging of the phallus, Lacanian feminists defend his phallocentrism by arguing that psychoanalysis is phallocentric because the human order into which the subject is born is phallocentric.[15] What they find liberating in Lacan's father-dominated narrative is his uncovering of "sexual identity" as a fiction, an unnatural division into man and woman constructed in language. It is the Lacan who exposes desire as ubiquitous and undefined, who thus exposes the phallus as an empty signifier, a sham, that Lacanian feminists appropriate in order themselves to expose the illusory terms of female desire as represented in discourse.[16]

Yet the problem remains: however revolutionary in emphasizing the fictive nature of identity and its basis in alienation, Lacan's rewriting of Freud's story is nonetheless conservative in its virtual closure to women of a relation to the Symbolic and to themselves which is not dominated by the Father's word. If woman is nothing but a category within language, constructed by male desire, where and what are women? If language structures sexuality around the male term, is there no female sexuality that is other? Can women be retrieved from the dominance of the phallic term? If women are beyond the phallus, where are they?

In response to such questions, several French feminists have turned to the preoedipal relation between mother and daughter for a narrative of female desire that emerges from the relation to the maternal body, exploring the possibilities for interpretation in the realm of the Imaginary.[17] Although this shift to the mother has brought some degree of

14. Lacan, "The Signification of the Phallus," in *Ecrits*, 281–91.

15. This position is most clearly represented by Juliet Mitchell in *Psychoanalysis and Feminism* and in "On Freud and the Distinction between the Sexes," in *Women and Analysis*, ed. Jean Strouse (New York: Viking, 1974), 27–38.

16. Lacan's fictionalization of sexual identity is discussed by Jacqueline Rose in her "Introduction II" to *Feminine Sexuality*, ed. Mitchell and Rose. See also Jane Gallop, "The Ladies' Man," *Diacritics*, 6 (Winter 1976), 28–34.

17. Among those French feminists concerned with placing women in a privileged relation to the preoedipal mother, the most familiar to English-speaking readers are Hélène Cixous, Luce Irigaray, and Chantal Chawaf. For a sampling of the diversity of positions among French feminists, see the ground-breaking anthology *New French Feminisms*, ed. Elaine Marks and Isabelle Courtivron (Amherst: University of Massachusetts Press, 1980).

rapprochement between this line of French feminist concern and Anglo-American theory, the French detour through Lacan results in a
difference. The insertion of the question of language introduces the
notion of a form of expressivity outside the dominant discourse, a
discourse closer to the body, an *"écriture feminine."*[18] Repudiating
the inevitability of the division instituted by the phallus and rejecting
Lacan's concept that a lack compels women to renounce their mothers,
such French feminists as Hélène Cixous and Luce Irigaray seek to
formulate a female poetics that would allow mother and daughter,
once locked in a symbiotic fusion and plenitude, to become women
and subjects, in and through language.

Irigaray, feminist, psychoanalyst, writer, and rebel Lacanian (whose
expulsion from Lacan's academy can itself figure the volatile and still
seductive relation between Father and Daughter), asserts with Lacanian ingenuity that Western discourse follows a male morphology,
analogous in its linearity, unity, and visible form to the phallus. Lacking a language that can articulate their experience, women are left
mutes or mimics. Indicting psychoanalysis as a representative of this
discourse for its repression/exclusison of the female subject and her
desire, Irigaray writes to open language to a different analogy, a female
morphologic figured by the female genitals—the two-lipped vulva "in
touch . . . joined in an embrace" and the diffuse, multiple structure
of female pleasure.[19] Like Cixous, Irigaray attempts to map a new
geography of female relations along the lines of the child's sensual
pleasure in the mother's body, a pleasure prohibited and repressed
by the fathers of psychoanalytic theory. Woman's language as Irigaray
and Cixous write it is fluid, autoerotic, diffuse. By subverting the
referentiality of language, by constantly pushing against the limits of
discourse, they make reading a dizzying activity.

In this project Irigaray finds an ally in Jacques Derrida, himself a

18. The term derives from Hélène Cixous and is amplified in "The Laugh of the
Medusa," in *New French Feminisms*, ed. Marks and Courtivron, 245–64. See also Ann
Rosalind Jones, "Writing the Body: Toward an Understanding of *L'Ecriture Feminine,*"
Feminist Studies, 7 (1981), which presents an introductory overview of the positions
of Julia Kristeva, Hélène Cixous, Luce Irigaray, and Monique Wittig.

19. "Women's Exile: Interview with Luce Irigaray," *Ideology and Consciousness*,
no. 1 (May 1977), 75. See also Irigaray, "When Our Lips Speak Together," trans.
Carolyn Burke, *Signs*, 6 (1980), 69–79. which is preceded by an illuminating introduction by Burke.

critic of what he calls the "phallogocentrism" of Lacan's thought.[20] Derrida shares with Lacan a view of the self as an illusory construct, but like Irigaray, he does not share Lacan's adherence to the phallus as master term, as the Logos, the "signifier of signifiers." For Derrida the privileging of the phallus is as misguided as the assumption of an original fullness of Being, rather than the condition of lack out of which, male and female, we create ourselves daily. Derrida's strategy of deconstruction dismantles the opposition male/female in order to demonstrate the inequality of the terms locked into this dualism, overthrow its disguised conceptual hierarchy, and reinscribe the terms in another way. While Derrida thus refuses to privilege either father or mother, male or female, in his myth of self-invention, in a fruitful paradox he does often choose female over phallic metaphor in his writing, as in his construction of a "hymeneal" fable to represent the creation of meaning.[21] Feminist critics seeking examples of nonhierarchal modes of analysis to both men and women have found Derrida's hymeneal fable, like Irigaray's vulval analogy, appealing in its assumption that female anatomy may provide its own ground for metaphor.

At this juncture, then, the tendency of Anglo-American psychoanalytic feminism to focus on the drama of the preoedipal relationship between mother and daughter intersects with French feminist dreams of another mode of discourse, another side of language whose authority is the mother. In *Civilization and Its Discontents* Freud reproduces the conventional association of women with nature, men with culture, attributing that division to woman's maternal instinct, which causes her to resist the demands of culture as a disruption of the family.[22] When women claim authorship, they not only subvert this paradigm, in which women may be spoken of, spoken through, but may not bespeak themselves, they also raise questions about priority and the stories by which it is maintained or conferred. It is hardly surprising that in feminist fables mother goddesses, representations of female authority, are displacing the authority of the father god of Judeo-Christian tradition. From a less hierarchical classic mythology, American feminists invoke the figures of Demeter and Persephone or Kore,

20. For an excellent discussion of the relation between Irigaray and Derrida, see Carolyn Burke, "Irigaray through the Looking Glass," *Feminist Studies*, 7 (Summer 1981), 288–306.

21. See Gayatri Spivak's "Translator's Preface" to Jacques Derrida, *Of Grammatology* (Baltimore: Johns Hopkins University Press, 1976), lxxi.

22. Freud, *Civilization and Its Discontents* (New York: Norton, 1962), 50–52.

revealing their need for a mother-daughter story, while French feminists supplant Oedipus with Antigone, the rebellious daughter who becomes a hero by defying the patriarchal state.[23]

So far we have traced the ways in which feminism has reacted to psychoanalysis, adapting psychoanalytic insights to its own examination of the unconscious organization of patriarchy, taking clues from the drama of the preoedipal period to construct alternate plots, exploring the possibilities of female metaphor and maternal authority. But there may be another story here, that of the response of psychoanalysis to feminism. Without resolving questions of gender difference, this story may even suggest some new narratives. Psychoanalysis, whether it posits in the beginning maternal presence or absence, has yet to develop a story of the mother as other than the object of the infant's desire or the matrix from which he or she develops an infant subjectivity. The mother herself as speaking subject, as author, is missing from these dramas. If feminism has learned from psychoanalysis to respect the ways in which the individual unconscious responds to the social order and hence the deep-rooted character of resistance to change, psychoanalysis may learn from feminism to move with a more open-minded awareness into areas in which it has traditionally shown the least sensitivity. It is particularly in the area of the female subject that psychoanalysis, fulfilling Freud's prophecy concerning the insight of poets into the unconscious, may enrich its understandings of women from women themselves, writers and interpreters.

The first four essays in this anthology confront Freud himself, in his patriarchal and heterosexual biases, in his anxieties about female otherness, in the degree to which his preoccupation with oedipal constructs obscures the figure of the mother and her importance for the daughter as well as the son. Jane Gallop, reading Freud through Luce Irigaray's interpretation of his essays on femininity, demonstrates an essential technique of feminist analysis, subjecting Freud to his own psychoanalytic method, thereby revealing the blind spots in his theorizing. The feminist reader, she argues, must act as an interrogator

23. The use of the Demeter myth as an empowering paradigm is reflected in the emphasis on mothers and daughters in American feminist criticism, and is perhaps most creatively exploited by Adrienne Rich in *Of Woman Born* (New York: Norton, 1976). A stimulating instance of Antigone as a figure in a French feminist narrative is Josette Feral's "Antigone or the Irony of the Tribe," *Diacritics*, 8 (Fall 1978), 2–15.

of Freud, rejecting the complicity of the daughter in her submission to the father's desire, opting instead for the disruptive role of the "wild analyst." Madelon Sprengnether, reading Freud's case history of Dora as the product of his own unconscious needs, sees Freud himself as a player in the psychic melodrama he outlines for his patient. In his insistence on a heterosexual interpretation of Dora's desire, she claims that Freud reveals his need to sustain an aggressive view of masculinity as well as his anxieties about feminine identification.

While both of these essays focus on the father/daughter relationship, Coppélia Kahn turns her attention to recent feminist texts concerning the figure of the mother and their implications for psychoanalysis. The science of the preoedipal, she maintains, actually subverts the oedipal by revealing the matriarchal substratum of all psychic development. With this understanding, she reveals the ways in which the tendencies of men to idealize and degrade women derive from a fundamental ambivalence about maternal power. Dianne Hunter, giving new consideration to the role of Bertha Pappenheim in the development of psychoanalysis, argues that she performed her own cure with Breuer as audience. Hunter, moreover, sees Bertha's "multilingual regression" as the implicitly preoedipal strategy of her illness, as a subversion of the patriarchal order of her family, and hence as an aspect of her feminism. In hysteria, Hunter argues, "the body signifies what social conditions make it impossible to state linguistically." Taken together, these four essays not only constitute a critique of the oedipal and patriarchal bias of Freud's thought, they also point toward preoedipal theory as a more fruitful ground for feminist writing and interpretation.

The next five essays explore the preoedipal grounding of some classic texts in the patriarchal tradition: Shakespeare's *Troilus and Cressida*, Milton's *Samson Agonistes*, Coleridge's *Christabel*, Hawthorne's *Scarlet Letter*, and Balzac's *Eugénie Grandet*. Janet Adelman and David Leverenz both deal with ways in which plot may be structured by conflicts involving women. Both see a central female character "sacrificed" in her development to principles of psychic need. For Janet Adelman, Cressida diminishes in psychic credibility as a result of Troilus' fantasy of union with her, which arouses in him fears of engulfment by a maternal figure and anxieties about soiling her through sexual contact. The plot, by transforming Cressida into a unidimensional character, a whore, defends against this fantasy, allowing Troilus to preserve an idealized maternal imago. It is Hawthorne's emphasis on Hester's asexual mothering that diminishes her as a character in

The Scarlet Letter, according to David Leverenz. Here the narrator's retreat from intimacy (in the form of anger or desire) causes a shift of focus in the plot from Hester's autonomy to the idealized male bonding of Dimmesdale and Chillingworth. In both texts, these critics maintain, some splitting of motherhood from sexuality, necessitated by male anxiety, shapes the narrative.

Margery Durham reads the structuring of narrative somewhat differently. She sees evidence in *Christabel* of the struggle undergone by every infant to deal with its ambivalence regarding the originally all-powerful mother. Culture, she argues in opposition to Freud, begins at the mother's breast, and though it may encode the infant's archaic strategy of splitting the mother into good and bad objects, it need not simply denigrate women.

Jim Swan and Naomi Schor examine the impact of gender difference in the movement from the preoedipal to oedipal periods, from the Imaginary to the Symbolic. Jim Swan approaches the question of misogyny in Renaissance literature from an analysis of Milton's poetry. Here he sees the Miltonic hero's betrayal of a silence, his fall into language, as an outgrowth of his need to define his gender difference in relation to a woman, thus divorcing himself from a state of undifferentiated identity—the condition of his creativity. If for Milton the acknowledgment of gender difference is destructive of male poetic identity, for Balzac, in Naomi Schor's view, it is fatal to femininity. Eugénie Grandet's movement from the Imaginary, where a state of near fusion exists between mother and daughter, to the Symbolic, where she is subject to the law of the father, leaves no room for her autonomy. This process in fiction parallels the phallocentric theory elaborated by Lacan, in which the only avenue of development for the girl away from her mother involves her subjection to phallic rule and the erasure (as Luce Irigaray has demonstrated) of her sexual desire. Schor interprets Eugénie's melancholic retreat into narcissism as the only form of autonomy available to her.

In treating texts by women authors, feminist critics whose readings are informed by the insights of psychoanalysis adopt a variety of strategies. Annette Kolodny, in her ground-breaking essay, "A Map for Rereading; or, Gender and the Interpretation of Literary Texts," offers one explanation for the reluctance of feminist critics simply to accept the prevailing paradigms for literary interpretation. Because of the difference between the experiences of men and women in social and economic terms, she argues, the encoding of female meaning in texts by women authors may be inaccessible to male interpretation. As an example of unconscious male bias in the theory of poetic meaning, she analyzes Harold Bloom's oedipally based paradigm of literary influence, arguing that the shared tradition of meaning he assumes does not historically include women. As an example of the kind of awareness she calls for, she offers a reading of Susan Glaspell's story "A Jury of Her Peers," which requires an understanding of the influence of gender in the creation of meaning.

Wendy Deutelbaum and Cynthia Huff, who are sensitive to the kinds of difficulty Kolodny delineates, approach the work of George Sand from at least two directions. By combining the insights of Marxism into the nature of class conflict with those of psychoanalysis into family dynamics, they construct an explanation of Sand's ambivalent feminism. Her apparent inability to bond with other women, they argue, derives from her adoption of the mediating role of her father in the class rivalry between her mother and her grandmother.

The feminism of Violette Leduc and Doris Lessing, according to the authors of the next two essays, goes further than that of George Sand, whose vision of women was compromised by internal and external conflict. In *The Golden Notebook*, Gayle Greene argues, Lessing examines male and female gender roles as crippling adjustments to an intolerable world. Greene charts the journey of Lessing's heroine through destructive relationships with men who need and regard her as a mother, through personal fragmentation and breakdown toward a new integration of self. Martha Noel Evans, making use of Derrida's insights about writing and difference, interprets Leduc's autobiography, *La Bâtarde*, as an account of her liberation from both paternal and maternal definitions of selfhood and origin. Leduc deconstructs the mythology of gender, revealing through the process of her autobiography the "illegitimate birth of the subject in the speech of the Other." Both essays, though employing different strategies, describe a liberating gesture on the part of a woman from constricting definitions of her identity.

Each of the final three essays in this collection deals with the relations of women to other women or to themselves. Shirley Nelson Garner, in her interpretation of *Night and Day*, shows how Virginia Woolf's portrayal of female friendship and attraction alters the conventions of romantic love in literature by male authors. Woolf transforms the patterns of idealization and debasement of women so familiar in this literature by focusing on the nature of women's love for one another, a subject illuminated by the work of Nancy Chodorow. Claire Kahane, whose work is also indebted to Chodorow's account of female development, examines the conventions of gothic literature in terms of the heroine's encounter with a spectral mother who threatens to dissolve the boundaries of her identity. The figure of the mother in this genre appears as the original Other, against whom the heroine struggles to establish a self. Finally, Susan Rubin Suleiman, who criticizes psychoanalysis as a theory of childhood, offers a plea for the discourse of the mother. The concept of an ideally selfless mother, accepted rather uncritically by psychoanalysis in both its oedipal and preoedipal constructs, creates its own anxiety of influence on writers who are mothers, effectively alienating them from participation in the creation of culture. Invoking the work of Julia Kristeva, Chantal Chawaf, and others who seek to integrate biological with cultural creativity, Suleiman calls for feminist interpretations of the fictions of motherhood that include the mother as subject rather than object, offering as examples her own analyses of two works by Rosellen Brown.

To link the potential for reproduction in all women with the capacity for cultural production is to transform not only the figure of the mother but the very bases of psychoanalytic theories in their preoedipal orientation. Feminists working from a number of critical approaches are concluding that it is time to learn, to begin to speak our mother tongue.

PART I

Feminists on Freud

1

The Father's Seduction

JANE GALLOP

The following is part of a reading of "The Blind Spot of an Old Dream of Symmetry," the first section of Luce Irigaray's book *Speculum de l'autre femme*.[1] "The Blind Spot of an Old Dream of Symmetry" is itself a reading of Freud's essay "Femininity," one of the *New Intro-ductory Lectures on Psychoanalysis*.[2] The rest of *Speculum* is a reading of the history of Western philosophy from Plato to Hegel. The importance of the encounter with philosophy is based on an understanding that the exclusion of women from history, commerce, discourse is grounded in philosophical suppositions, such as that truth, logic, identity should be stable, serene, free from desire, sexually indifferent. As long as these suppositions and their maintenance of various struc-

  1. Luce Irigaray, *Speculum de l'autre femme* (Paris: Minuit, 1974), published in English as *Speculum of the Other Woman*, trans. Gillian Gill (Ithaca: Cornell University Press, 1985); referred to hereafter as *Speculum*. Translations are my own. I first presented this paper at "The Creative Use of Difference: A Conference on Feminism," sponsored by the Center for the Psychological Study of the Arts, State University of New York at Buffalo, March 1980. The complete reading of this section of *Speculum* is chap. 5 of *The Daughter's Seduction*.
  2. Sigmund Freud, *New Introductory Lectures*, in *the Standard Edition*, XXII; referred to subsequently as *NIL*.

tures oppressive to women go unquestioned, feminism remains a regional rather than a radical upheaval. But before she goes out to meet philosophy, Irigaray spends a third of her book reading Freud.

In *Speculum*, Freud has at least a double function—oppressive authority and yet also beloved father—which reflects his double position in relation to metaphysical ideology. Irigaray writes in her second book, *Ce Sexe qui n'en est pas un*, that "if Freudian theory offers what is necessary to shake up the philosophical order of discourse, it paradoxically remains subject to that order as regards definition of the difference of the sexes."[3] Irigaray is indebted to psychoanalysis for the techniques of her disruption, disarming, unsettling of the philosophical order. Psychoanalysis has taught her to hear the libidinal investments of supposedly objective theory. At the same time she turns on Freud, exposing the metaphysical prejudices that structure his theory of female sexuality, reading him as he has taught her to read.

Speculum (and feminism) must always keep at least a double relation to psychoanalysis. While it is necessary and urgent to criticize the way psychoanalysis always reduces the otherness, the specificity of woman's sexuality, to masculine models, it is also important to hold on to psychoanalysis as the place where the reappropriation of otherness by an economy of sameness (the economy of systematic philosophy, market exchange value, and imperialist foreign policy, among other examples) becomes blatant, readable, where the claim to exclusively male standards for gauging sexuality is loud and clear.

Freud might mark the end of the phallocentric rule of metaphysics because, although participating in that rule, he exposes it. And it must remain implicit in order to be most effective (*Speculum*, p. 29). The privilege of the intelligible over the sensible, of the idea over matter: those binary formulations have historically had great power to intimidate any would-be questioners. But the domination of the phallus over nonphallic bodies—which Freud theorizes and Irigaray shows as solidary with the above-mentioned "neutral" hierarchies—elicits rebellion and cries of injustice. Reading Freud, who is unseemly enough to expose his phallocentrism, Irigaray learns to see what is inside the metaphysician's robe. *Speculum* begins with the reading of Freud as training for the more austere, more modest texts that follow.

This encounter between Irigaray's feminist critique and Freud's final

---

3. Luce Irigaray, *Ce Sexe qui n'en est pas un* (Paris: Minuit, 1977), 70; subsequent references will be to *Ce Sexe*.

text on woman is an important training ground for a new kind of battle, a feminine seduction/disarming/unsettling of the positions of phallocratic, metaphysical ideology. Irigaray's tactic is a kind of reading: close reading, which separates the text into fragments of varying size, quotes it, and then comments with various questions and associations. She never sums up the meaning of Freud's text, or binds all her commentaries, questions, associations into a unified representation, a coherent interpretation. Her commentaries are full of loose ends and unanswered questions. As a result, the reader does not so easily lose sight of the incoherency and inconsistency of the text. So "the philosophical order of [Freud's] discourse is shaken up" and reduced to an unredeemed disorder.

That could be seen as a victory for feminism. The Man's order is disturbed by the woman with the impertinent questions and the incisive comments. But as with all seductions, the question of complicity poses itself. The metaphysical dichotomy active/passive is always equivocal in seduction; that is what distinguishes it from rape. So Freud might have been encouraging Irigaray all along, "asking for it." Irigaray writes, "By exhibiting this 'symptom,' this crisis point in metaphysics where the sexual 'indifference' which assures metaphysics its coherence and 'closure' finally exposes itself, Freud proposes it to analysis: his text asking to be heard, to be read" (*Speculum*, p. 29).

Freud might have seduced Irigaray. It might be psychoanalysis that won over feminism. The very strategy of reading with which Irigaray works Freud over is presented by Freud himself earlier in these *New Introductory Lectures*, where he writes,"We ask the dreamer, too, to free himself from the impression of the manifest dream, to divert his attention from the dream as a whole on to the separate portions of its content and to report to us in succession everything that occurs to him in relation to each of these portions—what associations present themselves to him if he focuses on each of them separately" (*NIL*, pp. 10–11).

Freud's text asks for analysis. Not just any analysis, but the peculiar technique developed in psychoanalysis for dealing with dreams and other "symptoms." Irigaray's dream analysis does not offer a final latent thought, but merely presents the abundance of associations, not editing those that "lead nowhere."

Yet Irigaray's encounter with Freud is not a psychoanalysis. Freud is not there to associate. Irigaray both asks questions (the analyst's role) and supplies associations (the dreamer's role). And inasmuch as many questions go unanswered, they seem to be directed to the reader, who thus becomes the dreamer. She does not aim to decipher Freud's peculiar psyche, but rather to unravel "an old dream," everyone's dream, even Irigaray's dream. The dream is everyone's inasmuch as everyone is within "the metaphysical closure," inasmuch as any reader is a "subject," which is to say has been philosophically reduced as consumer of discourse to a unified, stable, sexually indifferent subject, trapped in the old dream of symmetry. (" 'Symmetry', from the Greek *summetros*—'of like measure'; from *sun*—'like, same', and *metron*— 'measure'." Symmetry is appropriating two things to measure by the same standard; for example, the feminine judged by masculine standards. Judged by masculine measures, woman is inadequate, castrated.)

On the first page of *Speculum*, Irigaray interrupts Freud's text with the attributive indicator: "he says, they (masculine plural) say." She repeatedly does that, attributing Freud's words to both a masculine singular and a masculine plural subject pronoun. The old dream belongs to any subject, to anyone speaking and therefore in the position of subject. "Every theory of the 'subject' [Every theory about the subject as well as every theory produced by a subject] will always have been appropriate(d) to the 'masculine' " (*Speculum*, p. 165). The neutral "subject" is actually a desexualized, sublimated guise of the masculine sexed being. Women can be subjects by fitting male standards that are not appropriate to, cannot measure any specificity of femininity, any difference. Sexual indifference is not lack of sexuality, but lack of any different sexuality, the old dream of symmetry, the other, woman, circumscribed into woman as man's complementary other, his appropriate opposite sex.

But what of "*the blind spot* of an old dream of symmetry"? What is the blind spot? What cannot be seen, what is excluded from the light? According to Freud, the sight of woman's genitalia horrifies the young boy because he sees an absence. Mark that he doesn't see what is there (vulva, clitoris, *mons veneris*, vagina, etc.—Irigaray stresses the plurality of woman's sex organs. *Ce Sexe qui n'en est pas un* means "This sex [organ] that isn't one"), he sees the absence of a phallus. Nothing to see, nothing that looks like a phallus, nothing of like measure (*summetros*), no coherent visual representation in a familiar form. Nothing to see becomes nothing of worth. The metaphysical privileging of sight over other senses, oculocentrism, supports and unifies phallocentric sexual theory (theory—from the Greek *theoria*, from *theoros*, "spectator," from *thea*, "a viewing"). *Speculum* (from *specere*, "to look at") makes repeated reference to the oculocentrism of theory, of philosophy. "Every theory of the 'subject' will always have been appropriate(d) to the 'masculine.' " Every *theoria*, every viewing of the subject will have always been seen according to phallomorphic standards. Hence there is no valid representation of woman, but only a lack.

The female sex organs are the blind spot. Freud's theory must occult female sexuality in order to manifest symmetry. But a blind spot can also be thought of as the locus of greatest resistance in a dream, the least easily interpretable point and thus the most tantalizing. To call a text a dream in a Freudian context is not like calling it an illusion. To point to the blind spot of a dream is *not a moral condemnation*. For it to be a moral condemnation, it would have to be grounded in an ethic of absolute *luc*idity and en*light*enment. The etymology of such words implies the morality of oculocentrism. Dreams are the "royal road to the unconscious" and ask for the feminist reading, destructive of unified "phallomorphic" representation, that Irigaray gives. The locus of greatest resistance, "the blind spot," is the heart of the dream, the crisis point crying, begging for analysis.

Blind also as Oedipus is blinded. Freud is assimilated by Irigaray to Oedipus. Freud, man, is never really out of the Oedipus complex, never resolves his oedipal phase. According to Freud, the end of the Oedipus complex marks the end of the boy's phallic phase. The phallic phase is characterized by the opposition phallic/castrated. In that phase there is no representation of an other sex—the vagina, for example, is "unknown." Supposedly, the difference between the phallic phase and adult sexuality is that the dichotomy phallic/castrated gives way to the opposition masculine/feminine. But if, as Irigaray finds in her reading of Freud, the boy, the man, never resolves his oedipal complex, then he never leaves the phallic phase, and the opposition masculine/feminine merely masks the opposition phallic/castrated. We read in "Femininity": "A boy's mother is the first object of his love, and she remains so too during the formation of his Oedipus complex and, *in essence, all through his life*" (*NIL*, p. 118; my italics). Woman's destiny Irigaray discovers, is to become her husband's mother. According to Freud, "a marriage is not made secure until the wife has succeeded in making her husband her child as well and in acting as a mother to him" (*NIL*, pp. 133–34). Woman must mold herself to become man's lifelong object, his own mother. Then a marriage is "secure"—stable, serene, impassive, not some locus of encounter with sexual difference. The blind spot is the price of man's inability to escape his oedipal destiny. Theory cannot see woman, but can only represent, re-present, make present again endlessly, "all through his life," Mother, the subject's *own* original complementary other.

Although Freud begins his lecture "Ladies and Gentlemen," a few pages later he says, "Nor will *you* have escaped worrying over this problem, because *you* are men; as for the *women among you* this will not apply, *they* are themselves this riddle" (my italics). When he explicitly addresses the audience as sexed beings, he reserves the second-person pronoun for men, and refers to women with the third-person pronoun. Freud talks *to* men *about* women. I have provided my own translation because Strachey's translation (*NIL*, p. 113) covers over this telling inequity in Freud's text, using the second-person pronoun for both sexes. Irigaray's "impertinence" is her assumption of the place of Freud's interlocutor, an exclusively male position. As she is a woman, this lecture does not speak to her, only about her. But she speaks up, responds, breaking the homosexual symmetry.

Irigaray impertinently asks a few questions, as if the students, the woman, the reader were not merely a lack waiting to be filled with Freud's knowledge, but a real interlocutor, a second viewpoint. And in her questions a certain desire comes through for an encounter, a hetero-sexual dialogue. Not in the customary way we think of heterosexual—the dream of symmetry, two opposite sexes complementing each other. In that dream the woman/student/reader ends up functioning as mirror, giving back a coherent, framed representation to the appropriately masculine subject. There is no real sexuality of the *heteros*. "Will there ever be any relation between the sexes?" asks Irigaray (*Speculum*, p. 33).

Irigaray's reading of Freud seeks that "relation between the sexes." Her aggression is not merely some man-hating, penis-envying urge to destroy the phallocentric oppressor. She lays fiery siege to the Phallus, yearning to get beyond its prohibitiveness and touch some masculine body. It is the rule of the Phallus, as standard for any sexuality, that denigrates women and makes any relation between the sexes impossible, makes unthinkable any relation between two modalities of desire, between two desires. The rule of the Phallus is the reign of the One, of Unicity. In the "phallic phase," according to Freud, "only *one* kind of genital organ comes into account—the male."[4]

4. Freud, *Standard Edition*, XIX, 142.

Freud, man, is arrested in the phallic phase, caught in the reign of the One, obsessively trying to tame otherness in a mirror image of sameness.

In her second book, Irigaray says: "What I desire and what I am waiting for is what men will do and say if their sexuality gets loose from the empire of phallocratism" (*Ce Sexe*, p. 134). The masculine exists no more than does the feminine. The specificity of both is suppressed by the reign of the Idea, the Phallus. The difference, of course, is that men by giving up their bodies gain power—the power to theorize, to represent oneself, to exchange women, to reproduce themselves and mark their offspring with their name. All those activities ignore bodily pleasure in pursuit of representation, reproduction, production. "In this 'phallocratic' power, man is not without loss: notably in regard to the enjoyment of his body" (*Ce Sexe*, p. 140).

Irigaray's reading of Freud's theory continually discovers an ignoring of pleasure. The theory of sexuality is a theory of the sexual function (ultimately the reproductive function), and questions of pleasure are excluded because they have no place in an economy of production. Commenting on Freud's discussion of breast-feeding, Irigaray remarks: "Every consideration of pleasure in nursing appears here to be excluded, unrecognized, prohibited. That, certainly, would introduce some nuances in such statements" (*Speculum*, p. 13). A consideration of pleasure would introduce a few nuances into the theory ("nuance," from *nue*, cloud). A consideration pleasure might cloud the theory, cloud the view, reduce its ability to penetrate with clarity, to appropriate. The distinction of active and passive roles becomes more ambiguous when it is a question of pleasure. And it is the distinction active/passive that is in question in Freud's discussion of nursing.

Freud writes: "A mother is active in every sense towards the child; the act of nursing itself may equally be described as the mother suckling the baby or as her being sucked by it" (*NIL*, p. 115). The sentence seems contradictory. If a mother is so clearly "active in every sense," why is the only example chosen so easily interpretable as either active or passive? The difficulty is symptomatic of one of the most insistent problems for Freud—the relation of the dichotomies active/passive and masculine/feminine. According to Freud, the opposition active/passive characterizes the phase of anal erotism, whereas masculine/feminine is the logic of adult sexuality. In this discussion of the mother Freud is trying to show how improper it is to identify feminine with passive, masculine with active, since a mother is clearly feminine and clearly active. Again and again in books and articles over a span of twenty years, Freud will try to differentiate and articulate the anal dichotomy and the adult sexual opposition.[5] Without much success.

In "Femininity" Freud refers to the confusion of these two oppositions as "the error of superimposition." The footnote to the English translation indicates that such an error consists in "mistaking two different things for a single one" (*NIL*, p. 115). Thus "the error of superimposition" is emblematic of what Irigaray finds as the general "error" of Freud's sexual theory—mistaking two different sexes for a single one. Phallocentrism is the primacy of the One, and "the error of superimposition" is *the* phallocentric mechanism.

In the French translation of the text, "*Überdeckungsfehler*" ("error of superimposition") becomes "*l'erreur de raisonnement analogique*" ("the error of analogical reasoning").[6] The specific superimposition in this text is both analogical and anal-logical. Anal logic organizes everything according to the opposition active/passive. The phrase "analogical reasoning" ties the whole problematic of defining sexual difference in a non-anal logic to another persistent embarrassment. For Freud, analogy is dangerously seductive. In 1905 he writes: "Shall we not *yield to the temptation* to construct [the formation of a joke] on the analogy of the formation of a dream?" In 1937: "I have not been able to *resist the seduction* of an analogy."[7] Is not the guilty compulsion to analogy symptomatic of Freud's inability to escape anal logic?

An accusation of contradiction could be leveled at this point. Earlier in the present text Freud has been deemed to be arrested in the phallic phase. Now he is judged to be arrested in the anal phase. It is not a question of resolving this contradiction, of fixing the diagnosis of Freud's personal pathology. Freud himself acknowledged that the stages of development are not clearly separate and distinct. The attempt to isolate each stage could be considered an effort to reduce

---

5. The most glaring of these symptomatic attempts to disengage the anal definitions from the genital can be found in a 1915 footnote to the third of Freud's *Three Essays on the Theory of Sexuality*; a footnote to chap. 4 of *Civilization and Its Discontents* (1930); and here in "Femininity" (1933).

6. *Nouvelles Conférences sur la psychanalyse*, Collection Idées (Paris: Gallimard, 1936). This is the edition Irigaray uses.

7. The first quotation is from *Jokes and Their Relation to the Unconscious*, the second from "Constructions in Analysis." The italics in both are mine.

sexuality to only one modality at any given moment, symptomatic of the rule of the One.

The investment in unicity, in one sexuality, shows itself in Freud's description of the little girl "in the phallic phase." (Of course the very assimilation of the girl into a *phallic* phase is already a sign of an "an error of superimposition," analogical reasoning.) Freud insists that in the phallic phase, little girls get pleasure only from their clitoris and are unfamiliar with the rest of their genitalia. (Remember the phallic phase is characterized as recognizing only one kind of sexual organ.) Yet others have found girls at this stage aware of vaginal sensations. Freud dismisses this finding peremptorily as well as somewhat contradictorily: "It is true that there are a few isolated reports of early vaginal sensations as well, but it could not be easy to distinguish these from sensations in the anus or vestibulum; *in any case they cannot play a great part*. We are *entitled to keep our view* that in the phallic phase of girls the clitoris is the leading erotogenic zone" (*NIL*, p. 118; italics mine). Why can they not play a great part? Because then "we" would not be "entitled to keep our *view*," keep our *theoria*. Entitled by what or whom? The blind spot is obvious; what must be protected is "our view," appropriate to the masculine.

Irigaray adds to this discussion the opinion that the little girl "could not have not" discovered the sensitivity of her labia, her vulva, "through her mother's attentions, through the rubbing of diapers or pants, through the hand in search of the 'little penis' " (*Speculum*, p. 30). Contrary to any possible experience, Freud insists on reducing the little girl's genitalia to her clitoris because that organ fits "our view," is phallomorphic, can be measured by the same standard (*summetros*). "We are now obliged to recognize that the little girl is a little man" (*NIL*, p. 118), declares Freud, making the phallocentric, anal logical economy clear. The girl is assimilated to a male model, male history, and "naturally" found lacking. The condition of that assimilation is the reduction of any possible complexity, plural sexuality, to the one, the simple, in this case to the phallomorphic clitoris.

Once reduced to phallomorphic measures, woman is defined as "really castrated" by Freud/man. As such she is the guarantee against man's castration anxiety. She has no desires that don't complement his, so she can mirror him, provide him with a representation of himself which calms his fears and phobias about (his own potential) otherness and difference, about some "other view" that might not support his

41

narcissistic overinvestment in his penis. "As for woman, *on peut se demander* [one could wonder, ask oneself] why she submits so easily. . . to the counterphobic projects, projections, productions of man relative to his desire" (*Speculum*, p. 61).

The expression for wondering, for speculation, which Irigaray uses above is the reflexive verb *se demander*, "to ask oneself." Most of her "impertinent questions" in *Speculum* seem to be addressed to Freud, or men, or the reader. But this question of woman's easy submission she must ask herself. And the answer is not so obvious. A little later she attempts to continue this line of questioning: "And why does she lend herself to it so easily? Because she's suggestible? Hysterical? But one can catch sight of the vicious circle" (*Speculum*, p. 69). The vicious circle here is, first of all, that to explain woman's complicity with phallocentrism by the characteristics attributed to woman inside phallocentric theory is to explain nothing, is tautology. But this question of the complicity, the suggestibility of the hysteric who "finally says in analysis [what is not] foreign to what she is expected to say there" (*Speculum*, p. 64) leads us to the contemplation of another vicious circle—the (hysterical) daughter's relationship to the father (of psychoanalysis).

The daughter's desire for her father is desperate: "the only redemption of her value as a girl would be to seduce the father, to draw from him the mark if not the admission of some interest" (*Speculum*, p. 106). If the phallus is the standard of value, then the father, possessor of the phallus, must desire the daughter in order to give her value. But the father is a man (a little boy in the anal, the phallic phase) and cannot afford to desire otherness, an other sex, because that opens up his castration anxiety. The father's refusal to seduce the daughter, to be seduced by her (seduction wreaking havoc with anal logic and its active/passive distribution), gains him another kind of seduction (this one more one-sided, more like violation) in the form of the law. The daughter submits to the father's rule, which prohibits the father's desire, the father's penis, out of the desire to seduce the father by doing his bidding and thus pleasing him.

That is the vicious circle. The daughter desires a hetero-sexual encounter with the father, and is rebuffed by the rule of the homological choosing the homo over the hetero, the logical over the sexual, decreeing neither the hetero nor the sexual worthy of the father. Irigaray would like to really respond to Freud, provoke him into a

42

real dialogue. But the only way to seduce the father, to avoid scaring him away, is to please him, and to please him one must submit to his law, which proscribes any sexual relation.

Patriarchal law, the law of the father, decrees that the "product" of sexual union, the child, shall belong exclusively to the father, be marked with his name. Also that the womb which bears that child should be a passive receptacle with no claims on the product, the womb "itself possessed as a means of (re)production" (*Speculum*, p. 16). Irigaray understands woman's exclusion from production via a reading of Marx and Engels which she brings in as a long, intrusive association near the end of her reading of Freud's dream. That exclusion of the woman is inscribed in her relation to the father. Any feminist upheaval, which would change woman's definition, identity, name, as well as the foundations of her economic status, must undo the vicious circle by which the desire for the father's desire (for his penis) causes her to submit to the father's law, which denies his desire/penis but operates in its place and, according to Irigaray, even procures for him a surplus of pleasure.

The question of why woman complies must be asked. To ask that question is to ask what woman must not do anymore, what feminist strategy ought to be. Only a fool would wait for an answer, deferring the struggle against phallocentrism until a definitive explanation were found. In lieu of that "answer," I would like to trace slowly a reading of a section of *Speculum* which concerns the father and the daughter, in this case specifically the father of psychoanalysis and his hysterics, but also the father of psychoanalytic theory and his daughter Irigaray.

Irigaray reads in Freud an account of an episode from the beginnings of psychoanalysis which "*caused (him) many distressing hours*" (her italics): "In the period in which the main interest was directed to discovering infantile sexual traumas, almost all my woman patients told me that they had been seduced by their father. I was driven to recognize in the end, that these reports were untrue and so came to understand that hysterical symptoms are derived from phantasies and not from real occurrences" (*NIL*, p. 120; *Speculum*, p. 40). Irigaray suggests that the reader "imagine that x, of the masculine gender, of a ripe age, uses the following language, how would you interpret it: 'it caused me many distressing hours,' 'almost all *my* woman patients told *me* that they had been seduced by their *father*.'" Irigaray invites her reader to interpret Freud. She does not offer a definitive reading, closing the text, making it her property, but only notes those phrases that seem interpretable, drawing the rebus but not giving the solution, so as to induce her reader to play analyst.

"And let us leave the interpretation up to the discretion of each analyst, even if she/he be improvised for the occasion. It would even be desirable if she/he were, otherwise he/she would risk having already been seduced, whatever her/his sex, or her/his gender, by the *father* of psychoanalysis" (pp. 40–41; Irigaray's italics). The reader is considered an analyst and capable of his/her own interpretation. But Irigaray recognizes that "the analyst" in question may not "really" be a psychoanalyst, but rather the recipient of a sort of battlefield promotion, prepared only by the experience of reading Freud with Irigaray. *Speculum* becomes a "training analysis," the reading of it preparing the reader to make her/his own interpretations. And the analyst trained by *Speculum* is likely to be a better analyst of Freud than a proper psychoanalyst, for any analyst—male or female, masculine or feminine, *Irigaray herself*—is likely to have been seduced by Freud, seduced by his theory.

There is a contrast here between two different kinds of analysts. The one privileged by Irigaray is an amateur, a "wild analyst,"[8] not "entitled" to analyze, but simply a reader, who can catch symptoms and make her/his own interpretations. The other sort of analyst is a professional, which is to say has investments in analysis as an identity and an economically productive system, and a transference onto Freud, that is, a belief in Freud's knowledge. The analyst is likely to "see" according to Freud's theory, having been seduced into sharing "our view," giving a predictable "Freudian" interpretation, one that always hears according to the same standards, returning every text to preexistent Freudian models, "bringing definitions into a discourse from outside." Irigaray as an analyst is perhaps not as likely to give an attentive, specific interpretation as is her reader. So that she proceeds to some sort of overthrow of a certain hierarchy between theoretical writer as distributor of knowledge and reader as passive, lacking consumer.

But certain questions pose themselves to this reader at this point. Can Irigaray really overthrow the pedagogic relation, or is this merely a ruse to flatter the reader into less resistance (to seduce her reader)? For she *does* go on to interpret, simply having deferred interpretation

8. The term is Freud's from his " 'Wild' Psychoanalysis," in *Standard Edition*, XL.

for a few sentences. As in an artificial, Socratic (pederastic) dialogue, if she asks the reader to think for him/herself, that reader will produce an answer that the teacher expected all along, the right answer. Irigaray is fantasizing a reader, one who will make the same associations that she does, one created in her own image.

It is thus interesting that at this point Irigaray is reasoning by analogy: Freud : hysteric :: father : daughter :: Freud : any other psychoanalyst. Analogy, as Irigaray has said, is one of the "eternal operations that support the defining of difference in function of the a priori of the same" (*Speculum*, p. 28). The analogy of analyst to father is the analytic analogy par excellence, the fact of transference. Transference is the repetition of infantile prototype relations, of unconscious desires, in the analytic relation. Without transference, psychoanalysis is simply literary criticism by an unimplicated, discriminating reader.

Her use of analogy as well as her projection of a reader in her own image, a narcissistic mirror, means she has acceded to a certain economy of the homo . . . and the auto . . . , the economy that men have and women are excluded from. Of course the "answer" is not to set up another homosexual economy, but that may be necessary as one step to some hetero-sexuality. "Of course, it is not a question, in the final analysis, of demanding the *same* attributions. Still it is necessary that women arrive at the same so that consideration be made, be imposed, of the differences that they would elicit there" (*Speculum*, pp. 148–49). The specific feminist problem is a balancing act: "How to articulate the double 'demand': for equality and difference?" (*Ce Sexe*, p. 78).

Yet having posed these questions of Irigaray's own imaginary economy, I might also say that she was right about her reader. Her fantasized reader would be the impertinent questioner she is. I am asking Irigaray Irigarayan questions, reopening the interrogation when Luce becomes too tight, when she seems to settle on an answer. I have been seduced into a transference onto her, into following her suggestion, into saying what is not "foreign to what I am expected to say," into playing "wild analysis."

"This seduction," she continues, "is covered of course, in practice or theory, by a normative statement, by a *law*, which denies it." Which seduction? The hysteric by her father or the analyst by Freud? In this context the seduction is deliberately ambiguous, but a new element is introduced by Irigaray and emphasized: the law. This term, foreign to the Freud passage she is reading, not suggested by him, is Irigaray's

45

own association, her remaining in excess of the Freudian seduction. "Law" is a political term, refers to patriarchy, the law of the father, and here will refer to Freud's legislative control of his theory, his normative prescriptions.

Her text continues with another sentence from Freud: "It was only later that I was able to recognize in the phantasy of being seduced by the father *the expression of the typical Oedipus complex* in women" (*NIL*, p. 120; *Speculum*, p. 41; Irigaray's italics). The seduction by the father is not only a mere fantasy but is the manifestation of a typical complex, one that is supposed to be universal, and therefore a law of Freudian theory. Given Irigaray's introduction to this passage, we read that the Oedipus complex, the incest taboo, the law forbidding intercourse between father and daughter, covers over a seduction, masks it so it goes unrecognized. Also covered over is a seduction in the theory, whereby psychoanalysts through their transference onto Freud (their unfulfillable desire for his love and approval) accept his immutable theoretical laws.

"It would be too risky, it seems, to admit that the father could be a seducer, and even eventually that he desires to have a daughter *in order* to seduce her. That he wishes to become an analyst in order to exercise by hypnosis, suggestion, transference, interpretation bearing on the sexual economy, on the proscribed, prohibited sexual representation, *a lasting seduction upon the hysteric*" (*Speculum*, p. 41; Irigaray's italics). Freud is a father who must deny the possibility of being seductive. Patriarchy is grounded in the uprightness of the father. If he were devious and unreliable, he could not have the power to legislate. The law is supposed to be just—that is, impartial, indifferent, free from desire.

"It is necessary to endure the law that exculpates the operation. But, of course, if under cover of the law the seduction can now be practiced at leisure, it appears just as urgent to interrogate *the seductive function of the law itself*" (*Speculum*, p. 41; Irigaray's italics). For example, the law that prohibits sexual intercourse between analyst and patient actually makes the seduction last forever. The sexually actualized seduction would be complicitous, nuanced, impossible to delineate into active and passive roles, into the anal logic so necessary for a traditional distribution of wealth and power. But the "lasting seduction" of the law is never consummated and as such maintains the power of the prohibited analyst. The seduction that the daughter

46

desires would give her contact with the father as masculine sexed body. The seduction that the father of psychoanalysis exercises refuses her the body and asks her to embrace his law, his indifference, his phallic uprightness.

Psychoanalysis works because of the transference, which is to say because the hysteric transfers her desire to seduce her father, to be seduced by him, onto her analyst. But since the fantasy of seducing the father is produced in analysis, then it is produced for the analyst. In order to please him, in order to seduce him, in order to give him what he wants. The installation of the law in psychoanalysis, the prohibition of the analyst's penis by the doctor in a position to validate the hysteric, to pronounce her healthy, sets up the desperate situation outlined by Irigaray: "the only redemption of her value as a girl would be to seduce the father" (*Speculum*, p. 106).

"Thus is it not simply true, nor on the other hand completely false, to claim that the little girl fantasizes being seduced by her father, because it is just as pertinent to admit that *the father seduces his daughter* but that, refusing to recognize and realize his desire—not always, it is true—*he legislates to defend himself from it*" (*Speculum*, p. 41; Irigaray's italics). The father's law is a counterphobic mechanism. He must protect himself from his desire for the daughter. His desire for the feminine threatens his narcissistic overvaluation of his penis. It is so necessary to deny his attraction for the little girl that Freud denies her existence: "We must admit that the little girl is a little man." If the father were to desire his daughter, he could no longer exchange her, no longer possess her in the economy by which true, masterful possession is the right to exchange. If you cannot give something up for something of like value, if you consider it nonsubstitutable, then you do not possess it any more than it possesses you. So the father must not desire the daughter, for to do so would threaten to remove him from the homosexual commerce in which women are exchanged between men, for the purpose of power relations and community for the men.

Also: if the father desires his daughter as daughter, he will be outside his oedipal desire for his mother, which is to say also beyond "the phallic phase." So the law of the father protects him and patriarchy from the potential havoc of the daughter's desirability. Were she recognized as desirable in her specificity as daughter, not as son ("little man") or as mother, there would be a second sexual economy besides the one between "phallic little boy" and "phallic mother"; an economy in which the stake might not be a reflection of the phallus, the phallus' desire for itself.

"In place of the desire for the sexed body of the father there thus comes to be proposed, to be imposed, his law, that is to say an institutionalizing and institutionalized discourse. In part, defensive (think of those 'distressing hours' . . .)" (*Speculum*, pp. 41–42; Irigaray's italics). The father gives his daughter his law and protects himself from his body. For it is only the law—and not the body—that constitutes him as patriarch. Paternity is corporeally uncertain, without evidence. But patriarchy compensates for that uncertainty with the law that marks each child with the father's name as his exclusive property.

"That is not to say that the father *should* make love with his daughter—from time to time it is better to state things precisely—but that it would be good to call into question this mantle of the law with which he drapes his desire, and his sex (organ)" (p. 42; Irigaray's italics). The strategic difference between a prescriptive "should" and a suggestive "it would be good" is emphasized by this sentence. But suggestion may always have been a more devious, more powerful mode of prescription.

"It would be good" to question the law's appearance of indifference, as Irigaray questions it, and find the phallic stake behind it. "It would be good" to lift "the mantle of the law" so that the father's desire and his sex were exposed. But that does not mean the "answer" is for the father to make love to his daughter. Irigaray, above all, avoids giving an answer, a prescription such as "the father *should* make love with his daughter." Not that he might not, not that it might not be a way to lift the law and expose the sexed body. The "should" is underlined, because that is what Irigaray will not say. She will not lay down a law about how to lift the law.

If she did lay down such a law—"that the father should make love with his daughter"—it would, like all laws, mask and support a desire, her desire for the father's body. The negated appearance of this law suggests the mechanism Freud called denegation—"a process by which the subject, although formulating one of his until now repressed desires, thoughts, feelings, continues to defend himself from it by denying that it belongs to him."[9] What surfaces that Irigaray needs to

9. Jean Laplanche and Jean-Baptiste Pontalis, *The Language of Psychoanalysis,* trans. Donald Nicholson-Smith (London: Hogarth, 1973), 201.

deny is her desire to impose the law upon the father, her desire for a simple reversal rather than an overthrow of patriarchy.

This sentence is marked as symptomatic, asking for analysis, by the parenthetical remark, "from time to time it is better to state things precisely." "From time to time" pretends that this is a random moment; it just happens to be at this moment that she will be precise. But this is the only such remark in all of her reading of Freud; this is the point where she is most afraid of a misunderstanding. Her desire to be precise is in direct contradiction to something she says later in *Speculum* about feminist strategies of language: "No clear or univocal statement can in fact dissolve this mortgage, this obstacle, all of them being caught, trapped, in the same reign of credit. It is as yet better to speak only through equivocations, allusions, innuendos, parables ... even if you are asked for some *précisions* [precise details]" (*Speculum*, p. 178). All clear statements are trapped in the same economy of values, in which clarity (oculocentrism) and univocity (the One) reign. Precision must be avoided if the economy of the One is to be unsettled. Equivocations, allusions, and the like are all flirtatious; they induce the interlocutor to listen, to encounter, to interpret, but defer the moment of assimilation back into a familiar model. Even if someone asks for *précisions*, even if that someone is oneself, it is better for women to avoid stating things precisely.

Yet on one point Luce Irigaray tightens up, prefers to be precise, to return to an economy of clarity and univocity. The locus of her conservatism, her caution, her need to defend herself, is the question of making love with the father. To lift the mantle of the law and encounter the father's desire is frightening. What if in making love the father still remained the law, and the daughter were just passive, denied? The father's law has so restructured the daughter and her desires that it is hard, well-nigh impossible, to separate the Father (that is to say, the Law) from the male sexed body. What if making love with the father were merely a ruse to get the impertinent daughter to give up her resistance to the law?

Irigaray clutches for something stable, something precise, because she too is a "subject," with a stake in identity. And the law of the father gives her an identity, even if it is not her own, even if it blots out her feminine specificity. To give it up is not a "simple" matter. It must be done over and over.

Later she will say of her method in *Speculum*, "what was left for me to do was to *have an orgy with the philosophers*" (*Ce Sexe*, p. 147;

49

Irigaray's italics). Intercourse with the philosophers, the father of psychoanalysis included, is her method of insinuation into their system, of inducing them to reveal the phallocentrism, the desire cloaked in their sexual indifference. Perhaps these are merely two different moments in her inconsistency: a brave, new, loose moment—"have an orgy with the philosophers"—and a defensive, cautious moment— refusal to make love with the father.

But perhaps these are not merely two moments. The two situations are *analogous but not the same*. Some terms may be more frightening, more sensitive than others. "Father" may be more threatening than "philosophers." She writes in *Ce Sexe*: "As far as the family is concerned, *my answer will be simple* and clear; the family has always been the privileged locus of the exploitation of women. Thus, as far as familialism is concerned, there is no ambiguity" (pp. 139–40; my italics). Yet earlier in the same text she says she cannot give a "simple answer." Also: *"faire l'amour"* (make love) may be more threatening than *"faire la noce"* (have an orgy). Maybe what frightens her is not seduction of the father or by the father but "making love." "Love" has always been sublimated, idealized desire, away from the bodily specificity and toward dreams of complementarity, the union of opposites, difference resolved into the One. "Love" is entangled with the question of woman's complicity; it may be the bribe that has persuaded her to agree to her own exclusion. It may be historically necessary to be momentarily blind to father love; it may be politically effective to defend—tightly, unlucidly—against its inducements, in order to have a "relation between the sexes," in order to rediscover some feminine desire, some desire for a masculine body that does not re-spect the Father's law.

2

Enforcing Oedipus: Freud and Dora

MADELON SPRENGNETHER

Philip Rieff, in his introduction to *Dora*, his edition of Freud's "Fragment of an Analysis of a Case of Hysteria," refers to the intricately structured love life of Dora's family as a "group illness." More specifically, he points out that "the sick daughter has a sick father, who has a sick mistress, who has a sick husband, who proposes himself to the sick daughter as her lover. Dora does not want to hold hands in this charmless circle—although Freud does, at one point, indicate that she should." At another point he comes close to admitting that Freud himself participates in the "neurotic eroticism" of this domestic scene. Having noted Freud's nonlinear, novelistic technique, he speculates briefly that "Freud's own therapeutic habits—spinning out beautiful and complicated lines of argument—meet all the requirements of neurotic brilliance," but chooses not to pursue this line of reasoning.[1] More recent readers of *Dora* point to the elements of countertransference in this case history, revealing the extent of Freud's subjective involvement in his construction of Dora's responses.[2] In my own read-

1. Sigmund Freud, *Dora: An Analysis of a Case of Hysteria*, ed. Philip Rieff (New York: Crowell-Collier, 1963), 10, 19. References to the Dora case history are hereafter documented in the text by page number both in this edition and in *Standard Edition*, VII. Rieff's edition is cited first.
2. There is an extremely rich body of commentary on *Dora*. Many readers who have found themselves entangled in this case history have pointed to areas of Freud's own unacknowledged entanglement in Dora's dilemma. The following readers find

51

ing of *Dora*, I want to consider first the relationship between illness and seduction, then the degree of Freud's complicity in this structure, and finally the ways in which Freud's narrative style may be viewed as symptomatic or hysterical.

Playing Doctor

I. THE POLITICS OF NAMING

Freud himself, in his passion for significance, reveals the genesis of the pseudonym Dora.

> Who else was there called Dora? I should have liked to dismiss with incredulity the next thought to occur to me—that it was the name of my sister's nursemaid; . . . I had seen a letter on my sister's dining-room table addressed to 'Fräulein Rosa W.' I asked in surprise who there was of that name, and was told that the girl I knew as Dora was really called Rosa, but had had to give up her real name when she took up employment in the house, since my sister could take the name "Rosa" as applying to herself as well. "Poor people," I remarked in pity, "they

---

varying degrees of sexual interest on the part of Freud toward his young and attractive patient and corresponding feelings of anger and pain at her noncooperation with the treatment and her subsequent departure. See Jerre Collins, J. Ray Green, Mary Lydon, Mack Sachner, and Eleanor Honig Skoller, "Questioning the Unconscious: The Dora Archive," in *A Fine Romance: Freud and Dora*, ed. Neil Hertz, *Diacritics*, 13 (Spring 1983), 37–42; Karl Kay Lewis, "Dora Revisited," *Psychoanalytic Review*, 60 (1973), 519–32; Janet Malcolm, "Aaron Green," pt. 2 *New Yorker*, December 1, 1980, pp. 54–152; Steven Marcus, "Freud and Dora: Story, History, Case History," in *Representations: Essays on Literature and Society* (New York: Random House, 1976), 247–309; Toril Moi, "Representation of Patriarchy: Sexuality and Epistemology in Freud's Dora," *Feminist Review*, October 1981, 60–73; Hyman Muslin and Merton Gill, "Transference in the Dora Case," *Journal of the American Psychiatric Association*, 26 (1978), 311–28; Arnold Rogow, "A Further Footnote to Freud's 'Fragment of an Analysis of a Case of Hysteria,'" *Journal of the American Psychoanalytic Association*, 26 (1978), 331–56; Jacqueline Rose, " 'Dora—Fragment of an Analysis," *m/f*, 2 (1978), 5–21. While these readers stress Freud's implicit alliance with Herr K. in his libidinal involvement with Dora, other commentators suggest an identification with Dora herself—with her hysteria. See Suzanne Gearhart, "The Scene of Psychoanalysis: The Unanswered Questions of Dora," in *The Tropology of Freud, Diacritics*, 9 (1979), 114–26; Neil Hertz, "Dora's Secrets, Freud's Techniques," in *A Fine Romance*, 65–76; and Maria Ramas, "Freud's Dora, Dora's Hysteria: The Negation of a Woman's Rebellion," *Feminist Studies*, 6 (1980), 472–510.

cannot even keep their own names!" . . . When next day I was looking
for a name for someone *who could not keep her own*, "Dora" was the
only one to occur to me.[3]

To this piece of intimate information Steven Marcus adds the association with David Copperfield's invalid child-wife, Dora.[4] Both lines
of association seem relevant, inasmuch as nearly everyone in Dora's
family circle occupies the role of nurse or invalid, and sometimes both.

Notable among the ill are Dora's father, who suffers from tuberculosis, syphilis, a detached retina, partial paralysis, confusional mental states, and a nervous cough; Frau K., the victim of some form of
paralysis, which renders her unable to walk; Dora's mother, afflicted
with a vaginal discharge, presumably gonorrhea contracted from her
husband; Dora's aunt, dying from a wasting disease; her uncle, a
"hypochondriacal bachelor"; and Dora herself, prey to shortness of
breath, coughing, loss of voice, an apparent attack of appendicitis,
catarrh, and a vaginal discharge of undetermined origin. In this atmosphere of real and imagined illness, Dora's mother, about whom
we know very little, accepts expensive presents of jewelry from her
husband, ignores the relationship between her husband and Frau K.
as well as the attentions paid by Herr K. to her daughter, locks doors,

---

3. Freud, "The Psychopathology of Everyday Life," in *Standard Edition*, VI, 241.
4. Marcus, "Freud and Dora," 309. Exploring the implications of the choice of the
name Dora, Marcus reminds us that

> Dora, of course, was David Copperfield's first love and first wife. She is at once
> a duplication of David's dead mother and an incompetent and helpless creature,
> who asks David to call her his "child-wife." She is also doomed not to survive,
> and Dickens kills her off so David can proceed to realize himself in a fuller way.
> One could go on indefinitely with such analogies, but the point should be suf-
> ficiently clear: in the very name he chose, Freud was true to his method, theory,
> and mind, expressing the overdeterminations and ambivalences that are so richly
> characteristic of this work as a whole.

I have taken Marcus' essay, in which he regards the writing of a case history as an
instance of modern narrative and Freud himself as a typical "unreliable narrator," as
a model for my own mode of investigation, treating both Freud and Dora as characters
in a novella authored by Freud himself. While I recognize the necessary distance
between any author and his or her self-representations, I am taking the liberty psychoanalytic critics usually allow themselves of exploring the psychological implications
of certain narrative and rhetorical forms. More precisely, I have taken Freud's own
theoretical pronouncements about Dora and used them to illustrate his portrait of
himself.

and otherwise spends her time in obsessive housecleaning.[5] Significantly, she refuses the role of nurse; that role falls first to Dora, whose attachment to her father is based in part on her attentions to him during his various ailments. The extent to which the role of nurse involves service or more specifically caretaking links it with that of nursemaid or governess, both positions of subordination and even exploitation in this story. While Dora's governess betrays the affection of her charge in her pursuit of the elusive love of Dora's father, the K.s' governess suffers a worse fate, being first seduced and then abandoned by Herr K. The position of nurse/nursemaid/governess offers only the illusion of control, and it is no accident that Freud associates the position of Ida Bauer in her family with that of his sister's nursemaid, a role that confers seeming maternal power firmly fixed within the context of patriarchal control.[6]

---

5. Rogow, in "Further Footnote," provides some interesting historical information about the Bauer household, including some details of Kathe Bauer's concern for cleanliness. The most extensive treatment of the background of the Bauer family that I have encountered, however, is provided by Ramas in "Freud's Dora." Iza Erlich discusses the difference between Freud's vivid treatment of the men in this case history and that of Dora's mother, whom he dismisses rather summarily. She concludes that

> it is as if Freud could not bring himself to look closely at the mother, the figure his theory proclaims to be so central. Be it Dora's madly cleaning mother, Little Hans's beautiful, seductive mother, or the Rat Man's absentee mother, they all appear as silhouettes against the rich background of other relationships; other entanglements. ["What Happened to Jocasta," *Bulletin of the Menninger Clinic*, 41 (1977), 284]

Freud's subordination of Dora's mother may be related to his sketchy treatment of the homosexual element in Dora's affectional life, an element that embraces not only her avowed love for Frau K. but also her apparently conflicted feelings toward her mother. Among critics who touch on this subject are Lewis, "Dora Revisited"; Moi, "Representation of Patriarchy"; Rieff, ed., *Dora*; and Ramas, "Freud's Dora."

6. The figure of the nursemaid, whose position as servant, surrogate mother, and sexual object in the Victorian household makes her the locus of exploitation, regressive fantasy, and desire, is central to this case history. Critics who have commented on the family structures and erotic implications of the inclusion of such a figure in the Victorian family are Leonore Davidoff, "Class and Gender in Victorian England: The Diaries of Arthur J. Munby and Hannah Cullwick," *Feminist Studies*, 5 (1979), 87–141; Sander Gilman, "Freud and the Prostitute: Male Stereotypes of Female Sexuality in Fin-de-Siècle Vienna," unpublished manuscript; Theresa McBride, "As the Twig Is Bent: The Victorian Nanny," in *The Victorian Family: Structure and Stresses*, ed. Anthony S. Wohl (New York: St. Martin's Press, 1978), 44–58; and Ramas, "Freud's Dora." Jim Swan, in a remarkable essay titled "*Mater* and Nannie: Freud's Two Mothers and the Discovery of the Oedipus Complex," *American Imago*, 31 (1974),

Frau K., moreover, repeats Dora's pattern of nursing her father, displacing her in the process. From occupying the privileged position of nurse in relation to her father, Dora is abruptly shifted to that of nursemaid or governess, disappointed in her love for the master. Frau K., in the meantime, trades the role of invalid for that of nurse, and in doing so reveals the extent to which both giving and receiving attention are predicated on illness. Dora's option for the role of invalid might be seen in this light as both a desperate bid for affection and a means of avoiding, temporarily at least, the nurse/governess role, associated in both households with betrayal. Dora's situation is complicated by her role as nursemaid of the K.s' children and her intimacy with Frau K., based on the exclusion of Herr K., until her father's affair with Frau K. shatters those relationships. Deprived of the role (involving for her maternal rather than sexual ministrations) on which she had counted to elicit the affections and attentions of members of both families, Dora, now excluded by her father and Frau K., is offered only one position, that of Herr K.'s mistress—a role that renders her powerless and vulnerable to further rejection. Freud's choice of a name for Dora seems to fix her in her dilemma.

Freud performs another significant act of naming in regard to Dora, attributing to her the specific sexual fantasy of fellatio. The choice of this fantasy is central, I believe, not only to Freud's subsequent interpretations of Dora's unconscious wishes but also to the stance he adopts toward her in his narrative.

If there is a "primal scene" in this narrative, it is not the classic one in which the child imagines a sadistic father inflicting pain on the mother. The scene of seduction focuses rather on Dora's father and Frau K. engaged in a sexual act that Freud himself imagines, names, and then at length defends. On the basis of a backward pun (assuming that the phrase "ein vermögender Mann" for Dora means "ein unvermögender Mann"), Freud concludes that Dora's father is impo-

---

1–64, explores the origin in Freud's own infancy of the image of the woman split into the idealized mother and the debased object of desire. Kenneth Griggs points out the ways in which the figure of Freud's nursemaid and his mother are conflated in some of his dreams in "All Roads Lead to Rome: The Role of the Nursemaid in Freud's Dreams," *Journal of the American Psychoanalytic Association*, 21 (1973), 108–26. Jane Gallop argues that class difference (as well as sexual difference) prevents Freud from identifying with the figure of the governess. See *The Daughter's Seduction: Feminism and Psychoanalysis* (Ithaca: Cornell University Press, 1982), 132–150.

tent.[7] "Dora confirmed this interpretation," he claims, "from her conscious knowledge" (64; 47), though he does not inquire into the source of such knowledge. Moving quickly, Freud presses Dora to admit that she knows of "more than one way of obtaining sexual gratification" (64; 47). Freud concludes that fellatio is the primary means of sexual gratification employed by Dora's father and Frau K., and that it is precisely this fantasy that preoccupies Dora, giving rise to one of her hysterical symptoms, the state of irritation of her throat and mouth. What is curious here is that Freud imagines a scene in which a woman gives sexual solace to a man, but not the reverse. If it is true that Dora's reading of Paolo Mantegazza's *Physiology of Love* has given her knowledge of the practice of fellatio, then it would make sense to suppose that she had equal knowledge of cunnilingus.[8] If it is also true that Frau K. has shared with Dora intimacies about her sexual life with her husband (from whom she withholds herself, preferring to share her bedroom with Dora), and that they have read Mantegazza together, then it would make even more sense to suppose that if Dora's fantasy life includes fellatio, it also includes cunnilingus. Supposing the impotence of Dora's father, moreover, full sexual gratification is more easily imaginable for the woman with this fantasy than it is with the one Freud proposes. At this important juncture in his interpretation of Dora's hysterical symptoms, Freud chooses, despite her unwillingness to confirm his theory, to maintain that Dora fantasizes fellatio. This fantasy then becomes the cornerstone of his

7. The line of reasoning here is that Dora's use of the word *vermögender* (capable, powerful), which has connotations of sexual potency, reveals the true nature of her thought, which is just the opposite. It doesn't seem to occur to Freud to wonder how Dora might have come by such knowledge of her father's prowess or lack of it. Here, as elsewhere, Freud's verbal preoccupations are evident.

8. While the subject of Dora's and Frau K.'s reading may never be fully elucidated, it seems clear to me from my reading of Mantegazza's book that Dora could not have obtained knowledge of specific sexual practices from it. *The Physiology of Love* (published in 1877), one of three books by Mantegazza dealing with human sexuality, is largely a romantic and sentimental paean to human reproduction. See *The Physiology of Love*, trans. Herbert Alexander, ed. Victor Robinson (New York: Eugenics, 1936). If, on the other hand, Dora had read Mantegazza's more explicit text, *The Sexual Relations of Mankind*, she would have discovered a full sexual vocabulary, including references to lesbian lovemaking. Critics who have noted the oddness of Freud's choice of fellatio over cunnilingus are Hertz ("Dora's Secrets") and Moi ("Representation of Patriarchy") as well as Sharon Willis ("A Symptomatic Narrative," in *A Fine Romance*, ed. Hertz, 46–60). Willis relates Freud's "blindness" in this instance to the phallocentrism of his discourse.

subsequent interpretations of Dora's repressed love for Herr K. Let us look, then, at some of the determinants of this crucial choice.

The fantasied scene of seduction in Dora's family, according to Freud, is one in which Dora gives sexual satisfaction, in the form of fellatio, to her impotent father (83; 48). This fantasy is remarkable not only for its incestuous character but also in the way in which it reproduces the structure of the nurse/invalid relationship. Dora's father, by occupying the role of invalid, a curiously passive stance in relation to Freud's orthodox notions of male heterosexuality, compels his partner into the role of nurse, so that the act of fellatio appears as one more ministration to his need. At the same time, the figure of the nursemaid, ever present in this case history, recurs oddly in Freud's defense of his discussion of this "perversion" (67; 51). In a brilliant series of analogies, Freud relates fellatio regressively to thumb-sucking and ultimately to breast-feeding. The passage culminates in the following observation:

It then needs very little creative power to substitute the sexual object of the moment (the penis) for the original object (the nipple) or for the finger which does duty for it, and to place the current sexual object in the situation in which gratification was originally obtained. So we see that this excessively repulsive and perverted phantasy of sucking at a penis has the most innocent origin. It is a new version of what may be described as a prehistoric impression of sucking at a mother's or a nurse's breast—an impression which has usually been revived by contact with children who are being nursed. In most instances a cow's udder has aptly played the part of an image intermediate between a nipple and a penis. [69–70; 52]

By the end of this passage there is no clear line of demarcation between the nurser and the nurse. In her sexual activity with Dora's father Frau K. may be said to "nurse" him in two senses, both of which "feminize" her partner through identification with either the figure of the passive invalid or that of the nursemaid who breast-feeds her charge. The image of the cow's udder, in shape midway between the nipple and the penis, marks the ground of this indeterminacy.

Freud's choice of a name and of a fantasy for Dora lock her into an apparently subordinate relationship to the object of her love. The conjunction of love and illness in the scene of seduction, however, creates a paradoxical source of power in the figure of the nurse. The primary figure in this fantasy is female, just as the primary organ may be said to be the nipple rather than the penis. Against this image of fluid gender identity, Freud constructs a more conventional scene of heterosexual seduction, which he then presses Dora to accept. Freud's "interpretation" of Dora's repressed love of Herr K. serves at least two functions. It permits the nurse/invalid structure of sexual relations to survive as a fantasy along with the surrender of an aggressive male role at the same time that it denies the power of the nurse by asserting the more culturally sanctioned role division in the structure of Herr K.'s relation to Dora. If the first structure may be described as preoedipal, focusing as it does on a maternal figure, the second is clearly oedipal. The oedipal overlay is the one with which Freud himself identifies, effectively preventing him from exploring the extent to which he also identifies with the figure of the nurse, or with the feminine position generally, which he tends to associate with homosexuality.[9] The power of the nurse to disrupt Freud's oedipal interpretation persists however through refusal which Freud understands as rejection and ultimately as "revenge." The conflict between the two levels of fantasy in this case history repeats itself in the form of the narrative, appearing symptomatically as Freud's anxiety about filling gaps and completeness.

While Freud displays, from time to time, a skeptical attitude toward Dora's father, admitting to the validity of some of Dora's claims about his lack of straightforwardness, he is remarkably uncritical of Herr K., whom he considers to be an attractive lover (44; 28–29).[10] In the two instances in which Herr K. forces his attentions on Dora, Freud clearly sympathizes with him, regarding her behavior rather than his as inappropriate. When Herr K. maneuvers Dora into a situation in which he can embrace her without fear of observation, Freud comments: "This was surely just the situation to call up a distinct feeling of sexual excitement in a girl of fourteen who had never before been approached" (43; 28).[11] Freud interprets her failure to experience excitement as evidence of her hysteria.

9. Others have proposed different reasons for Freud's avoidance of the feminine position. See in particular Gallop, *Daughter's Seduction*; Hertz, "Dora's Secrets"; Collins et al., "Questioning the Unconscious."

10. It is perhaps not surprising that Freud was predisposed in favor of Herr K., given the fact that it was Herr K. that introduced Dora's father to him for the treatment of syphilis.

11. Several critics have commented on the inappropriateness of Freud's expectation that Dora should have been aroused. Erik Erikson, Mark Kanzer, Steven Marcus,

In this scene—second in order of mention, but first in order of time— the behavior of this child of fourteen was already entirely and completely hysterical. I should without question consider a person hysterical in whom an occasion for sexual excitement elicited feelings that were preponderantly or exclusively unpleasurable; and I should do so whether or no the person were capable of producing somatic symptoms. [44; 28]

Later, referring to the scene by the lake in which Herr K. propositions Dora, Freud observes: "Her behaviour must have seemed as incomprehensible to the man after she had left him as to us, for he must long before have gathered from innumerable small signs that he was secure of the girl's affections" (63; 46). Freud sees both incidents through the eyes of Herr K., going as far as to provide Herr K. with an erection at the scene of the kiss.[12] The origin of this fantasy, however justified, is clearly signaled in the following passage: "I have formed in my own mind the following reconstruction of the scene. I believe that during the man's passionate embrace she felt not merely his kiss upon her lips but also the pressure of his erect member against her body" (47; 30). On the basis of this fantasy, Freud concludes that Dora's feeling of disgust represents a displacement upward of a sensation on the lower part of her body. While we have no information about the reasons for Frau K.'s preference for Dora's father as a lover,

---

Toril Moi, and Philip Rieff all signal Freud's failure to take into account the full complexity of Dora's dilemma, including the fact of her adolescence. See Erikson, "Reality and Actuality," *Journal of the American Psychoanalytic Association*, 10 (1962), 451–74; Kanzer, "The Motor Sphere of the Transference," *Psychoanalytic Quarterly*, 35 (1966), 522–39. I find Marcus' statement describing Dora's situation in many ways the most poignant and acute.

> The three adults to whom she was closest, whom she loved the most in the world, were apparently conspiring—separately, in tandem, or in concert—to deny Dora her reality and reality itself. This betrayal touched upon matters that might easily unhinge the mind of a young person; for the three adults were not betraying Dora's love and trust alone, they were betraying the structure of the actual world. ["Freud and Dora," 256]

Ramas, in "Freud's Dora," calls the process by which Dora's version of events was either undermined or denied "gaslighting." If subsequent accounts of Dora's life are true (see, for example, Felix Deutsch, "A Footnote to Freud's 'Fragment of an Analysis of a Case of Hysteria,'" *Psychoanalytic Quarterly*, 26 [1957], 159–67), the "success" of Freud's treatment may be gauged by Dora's inability either to throw off her neurosis or to accept the terms within which Freud offered cure.

12. Moi states: "It is little wonder that he [Freud] feels the need to defend himself against the idea of fellatio, since it is more than probable that the fantasy exists, not in Dora's mind, but in his alone" ("Representation of Patriarchy," 66).

it is interesting that Freud chooses a virile construction of Herr K.'s advances. Herr K. represents in this story "normal"—that is to say aggressive—male heterosexuality. By representing Dora's refusal of Herr K.'s courtship as abnormal or "hysterical," Freud protects the oedipal as opposed to the preoedipal fiction. By attempting to coerce Dora verbally into an acceptance of this structure, he further identifies with Herr K., masking his identification with Dora's father. Dora's perception that she is being handed from one man to another would seem to be accurate. The extent to which Freud occupies the role of father/seducer in this analysis appears at the end of a chain of his associations linking the idea of smoke with the longing for a kiss and Dora's thumb-sucking to a desire for a kiss from him. "I came to the conclusion that the idea had probably occurred to her one day during a session that she would like to have a kiss from me" (92; 74).

If we examine Freud's line of argument as the product of *his* unconscious needs and wishes, applying his own interpretive rules to his narrative, we arrive at a view of this case history as an attempted seduction via interpretation. From this point of view, moreover, many of Freud's digressions and overstatements make sense as expressions not of his scientific neutrality but of his anxiety.

II. THE RIGHTS OF THE GYNECOLOGIST

It is axiomatic for Freud, in his analysis of Dora's motives, that "there is no such thing at all as an unconscious 'No' " (75; 57). Denial, from this vantage point, may be interpreted as affirmation. "If this 'No,' instead of being regarded as the expression of an impartial judgement (of which, indeed, the patient is incapable), is ignored, and if work is continued, the first evidence soon begins to appear that in such a case 'No' signifies the desired 'Yes' " (76; 58–59). Freud's rule for interpreting accusations, moreover, is to look for self-reproaches. "A string of reproaches against other people leads one to suspect the existence of a string of self-reproaches with the same content. All that need be done is to turn back each particular reproach on to the speaker himself" (51; 35).

With these two principles in mind, one may interpret Freud's furious denial of the charge of titillating his patient with sexual language, coupled with his anxiety about being so reproached, as an indication that he is doing just that.[13] Freud's attempts to disarm such criticism

13. Collins et al. also make this point in "Questioning the Unconscious."

tend, moreover, only to make matters worse. In anticipating the astonishment and horror of his readers at his attribution of the fantasy of fellatio to Dora, he first appeals to the analogy of the gynecologist. Claiming that it is possible for a man to speak to young women about sexual matters "without doing them harm and without bringing suspicion on himself," he argues that "a gynaecologist, after all, under the same conditions, does not hesitate to make them submit to uncovering every possible part of their body" (65; 48), thus introducing new associations concerning nudity.[14] Next, in defense of the use of technical language to describe sexual matters, he falls into a syntactical slip whereby he seems to be saying that if a woman is ignorant of certain physiological processes, he instructs her concerning them. "I call bodily organs and processes by their technical names, and I tell these to the patient if they—the names, I mean—happen to be unknown to her" (65; 48). As if to compound this error, he concludes, appealing to the euphemistic idiom of another language: "J'appelle un chat un chat" (65; 48). Continuing in this vein, and introducing another set of unwanted associations, he argues that "pour faire une omelette il faut casser des oeufs" (66; 49).[15] If something is to be broken, it would seem to be Dora's innocence. "There is never any danger of corrupting an innocent girl," Freud affirms. "For where there is no knowledge of sexual processes even in the unconscious, no hysterical symptom will arise; and where hysteria is found there can no longer be any question of 'innocence of mind' in the sense in which parents and educators use the phrase" (66; 49).

Having metaphorically undressed and violated Dora, Freud then declares her to be experienced already, a kind of Victorian Lolita, whose early pleasure in thumb-sucking is cited as evidence of her predisposition to the fantasy of "sucking at the male organ" (68; 51).[16]

14. Mary Daly has also noticed the intrusive and prurient implications of this statement. See GynlEcology (Boston: Beacon, 1978), 256.

15. "I call a cat a cat"; "to make an omelet one must break eggs." Gallop presents a particularly witty discussion of this resort to euphemism in Daughter's Seduction, 140.

16. Gilman finds ample evidence in nineteenth-century Vienna of the stereotype of female children as sexually precocious. In "Freud and the Prostitute" he links this attitude to the prevalence of adolescent prostitutes, the exploitation of lower-class women generally, and the need of their male clients to "blame the victim." He speculates that Freud's ideas concerning the seductiveness of children may derive in part from prevailing stereotypes of female sexuality and in part from his own need to deny parental seduction of female children. From this point of view one may well ask to what extent Freud projects his own sexual desires onto Dora.

Freud's own ambivalence about this fantasy, reflected in part in his indulgence in this digression, appears as well in his classification of fellatio as one of the "aberrations of the sexual instincts" and in his need to defend himself for not taking "every opportunity of inserting into the text expressions of his personal repugnance at such revolting things" (67; 50). The question may well be not what Dora wanted from Freud but what he wanted from her.

While Freud attributes Dora's unwillingness to continue therapy with him to a desire for revenge, arguing on the basis of her identification with the rejected governess, he does not perceive the extent to which he stands in the position of the spurned lover or the extent to which he may share her feelings of betrayal and consequent desire for retaliation.[17] At the same time, he feels the need to defend himself from the reproach of betraying her by writing her history.

> I shall not escape blame by this means. Only, whereas before I was accused of giving *no* information about my patients, now I shall be accused of giving information about my patients which ought not be given. I can only hope that in both cases the critics will be the same, and that they will merely have shifted the pretext for their reproaches. [21; 7]

Reading this statement, once again, in the context of Freud's interpretations of Dora's reproaches and denials, one arrives at a self-reproach on Freud's part for wishing to expose and humiliate his client. Such a desire—to pain Dora—appears at the end of a statement assuring the reader of her anonymity. "I naturally cannot prevent the patient herself from being pained if her own case history should accidentally fall into her hands. But she will learn nothing from it that she does not already know: and she may ask herself who besides her could discover from it that she is the subject of this paper" (23; 8–9). The callousness of this remark immediately supplemented by Freud's other invocation of the rights of the gynecologist suggests that he fully intends to bare Dora's secrets and to reveal her intimacies in a manner that would hurt her. Anticipating a reproach concerning his frank discussion of sexual matters, he says:

> Am I, then, to defend myself upon this score as well? I will simply claim for myself the rights of the gynaecologist—or rather, much more

17. For Moi, Freud's revenge consists in part of his giving Ida Bauer the name of his sister's servant.

modest ones—and add that it would be the mark of a singular and perverse prurience to suppose that conversations of this kind are a good means of exciting or of gratifying sexual desires. [23; 9]

In view of Freud's understanding of writing as a supplement for Herr K.'s absence, it does not seem unreasonable to consider the supplementary functions of either conversation or the writing of a case history.[18]

The interpretation of Dora's two dreams serves at least two functions, that of oedipal camouflage for a preoedipal fantasy based on the figure of the nurse and that of revenge. It is the combination of these two elements that accounts, I believe, for the coercive quality of Freud's interpretations and for the uneasy tone of the narrative. In his relentless pursuit of a heterosexual interpretation of Dora's desire, Freud often substitutes his own train of associations for hers, a tactic that reveals the extent to which he idealizes the figure of Herr K. in order to blame Dora for her refusal. On an interpretive level, he subjects her to a process of defloration, impregnation, and parturition in an aggressively oedipal fashion at the same time that he invalidates her rejection by naming it hysteria. Metaphorically, Freud seems to accomplish what he cannot in fact, neatly turning the tables on Dora by seducing and abandoning her, revealing in the process her "dirty secrets"—her habit of masturbation and her catarrh. Thus discredited and shamed, the nurse/nursemaid/governess is deprived of her power.

The logic Freud pursues in his interpretation of Dora's first dream leads him to accuse her of childhood masturbation (hardly a remarkable discovery), the repudiation of which then provides him with evidence of her repressed desire for Herr K. "For if Dora felt unable to yield to her love for the man, if in the end she repressed that love instead of surrendering to it, there was no factor upon which her decision depended more directly than upon her premature sexual enjoyment and its consequences—her bedwetting, her catarrh, and her disgust" (107; 87). As if to underscore this point, Freud repeats:

18. I am using "supplement" in the Derridean sense, both as an attempt to fill a void, to create a presence, and as an inevitable reminder of a void or an absence. I am guided here by Freud's own observation that Dora took up her pen when Herr K. was absent. Moi, discussing the "supplementary" status of Freud's text, states: "Freud's text oscillates endlessly between his desire for complete insight or knowledge, and an unconscious realization (or fear) of the fragmentary, deferring status of knowledge itself" ("Representation of Patriarchy," 64).

There was a conflict within her between a temptation to yield to the
man's proposal and a composite force rebelling against that feeling. This
latter force was made up of motives of respectability and good sense,
of hostile feelings caused by the governess's disclosures (jealousy and
wounded pride, as we shall see later), and of a neurotic element, namely,
the tendency to a repudiation of sexuality which was already present
in her and was based on her childhood history.   [108; 88]

The reasoning by which Freud arrives at this conclusion is highly
questionable, based as it is on his own verbal conversions and the
presumption of causal relationships between masturbation, bed-wetting, and vaginal discharge.

It is of course the element of fire in Dora's first dream that leads
to the speculations about bed-wetting, through Freud's own associations to the phrase "something might happen in the night so that it
might be necessary to leave the room" (82; 65) and his folkloristic
explanation of the parental prohibition against playing with matches,
an explanation of which Dora, by the way, seems to be ignorant. "She
knew nothing about it.—Very well, then; the fear is that if they do
they will wet their bed. The antithesis of 'water' and 'fire' must be at
the bottom of this. Perhaps it is believed that they will dream of fire
and then try and put it out with water. I cannot say exactly" (89; 71–
72).

Having established his own conviction that where there is fire there
must be water, Freud presumes a history of bed-wetting in Dora's
family. While adapted to his dream theory, which he wishes to elucidate by means of Dora, this piece of information would seem to be
irrelevant to her present condition were it not for the spurious connection between bed-wetting and masturbation, subsequently affirmed by Freud. "Bed-wetting of this kind has, to the best of my
knowledge, no more likely cause than masturbation, a habit whose
importance in the aetiology of bed-wetting in general is still insuffi-
ciently appreciated" (92; 74). Masturbation itself would seem to be
equally irrelevant were it not for Freud's medically unsupported notion of a causal relation between masturbation and vaginal discharge.

I met her half-way by assuring her that in my view the occurrence of
leucorrhoea in young girls pointed primarily to masturbation, and I
considered that all the other causes which were commonly assigned to
that complaint were put in the background by masturbation. I added
that she was now on the way to finding an answer to her own question

of why it was that precisely she had fallen ill—by confessing that she had masturbated, probably in childhood. [94; 76]

Dora's discharge is then cited as further evidence of the preferred fantasy of fellatio: "it came to represent sexual intercourse with her father by means of Dora's identifying herself with Frau K." (102; 83). If Freud seeks to win an admission from Dora that she masturbated in childhood, moreover, it is because such an admission constitutes a preliminary surrender to the heterosexual solution proposed for hysteria.[19]

> Hysterical symptoms hardly ever appear so long as children are mas-
> turbating, but only afterwards, when a period of abstinence has set in;
> they form a substitute for masturbatory satisfaction, the desire for which
> continues to persist in the unconscious until another and more normal
> kind of satisfaction appears—where that is still attainable. For upon
> whether it is still attainable or not depends the possibility of a hysteria
> being cured by marriage and normal sexual intercourse. [97–98; 79]

Within this interpretive frame, Freud construes Dora's melancholy dream of rescue (in which the very man to whom she appeals for protection is in the act of betraying her) as a statement of repressed desire. If she perceives her jewel case to be in danger not only of being wetted but of being contaminated by the venereal diseases that seem to circulate in this domestic daisy chain, neither her father nor her analyst is likely to help her, as both are driving her into the arms of Herr K. It is hardly surprising that her second dream seems to be

---

19. Freud's views on the relationship between masturbation and hysteria were not unusual for his time, nor was his assumption that heterosexual intercourse offered a cure. Richard Krafft-Ebing, whom Freud most assuredly read, was unequivocal in his conviction that masturbation posed an obstacle to heterosexual relations. See *Psychopathia Sexualis*, trans. Harry E. Wedeck (New York: Putnam, 1965). While less virulent on this subject, Freud was entirely conventional in his assumption that normal female development required women to abandon masturbation and turn to heterosexual intercourse. Mantegazza, perhaps not incidentally, adopted the same view in *Sexual Relations of Mankind*. For feminist critiques of the compulsory and institutionalized nature of heterosexuality in patriarchal culture, see Ramas, "Freud's Dora," and Adrienne Rich, "Compulsory Heterosexuality and Lesbian Existence," *Signs*, 5 (1980), 631–59. For speculations about the social environment that defined nineteenth-century conceptions of hysteria, see Roberta Satow, "Where Has All the Hysteria Gone?" *Psychoanalytic Review*, 66 (1979–80), 463–73, and Carol Smith Rosenberg, "The Hysterical Woman: Sex Roles and Role Conflict in 19th-Century America," *Social Research*, 39 (1972), 652–78.

dominated by a mood of confusion, and that the figure eliminated in this dream is that of the father.

As Dora stiffens against Freud's attempts to persuade her of her desire to be violated by Herr K., Freud becomes more entrenched in his insistence that she fantasizes not only fellatio and intercourse but also impregnation, following once again his own train of association. It is for Freud that the words *bahnhof* (railway station), a place of commerce, and *friedhof* (cemetery), a place of death, are suggestive of female genitals, and it is he that supplies the additional term *vorhof* (vestibule) as the link with *nymphae*, a term uncommon even among physicians for the labia minora. Instead of questioning the capacity of an eighteen-year-old girl to reproduce this series, he argues backward that she must have derived such arcane knowledge from books, "and not from popular ones either, but from anatomical text-books or from an encyclopaedia—the common refuge of youth when it is devoured by sexual curiosity" (120; 99). He concludes, ignoring the implications of his own intrusiveness, that her dream represents a "phantasy of defloration, the phantasy of a man seeking to force an entrance into the female genitals" (120; 100). A truly ingenious argument follows in which Freud manages to convert a presumed attack of appendicitis accompanied by fever and an injury to Dora's foot into hysterical symptoms representing a "phantasy of childbirth" (124; 103). Triumphantly, then, he concludes: "If it is true that you were delivered of a child nine months after the scene by the lake, and that you are going about to this very day carrying the consequences of your false step with you, then it follows that in your unconscious you must have regretted the upshot of the scene" (124–25; 103–4). All paths lead to Herr K., whom Freud fantastically imagines as an appropriate suitor with honorable intentions (108). Trapped in this interpretive labyrinth, "Dora disputed the fact no longer" (125; 104).

Given Freud's bias in favor of Herr K. as an unconventional though perfectly acceptable lover, he can interpret Dora's resistance only as "a morbid craving for revenge" and her rejection of her treatment as an "unmistakable act of vengeance." Revealing his own wounded feelings, however, he describes the effect of Dora's "breaking off so unexpectedly, just when my hopes of a successful termination of the treatment were at their highest," as "bringing those hopes to nothing" (131; 109). If Dora, in the one gesture permitted the figure with whom she has been identified (the governess), wishes to injure Freud, she seems to have been successful. "For how could the patient take a more effective revenge than by demonstrating upon her own person the helplessness and incapacity of the physician?" (142; 120).

Dora's flight leaves Freud to wrestle with the specters of self-doubt and impotence, an implicit identification not with the supposedly virile Herr K. but with the invalid father. Freud's attempted camouflage of this figure through his aggressively heterosexual interpretation of Dora's desire is unmasked by her noncooperation. In the face of this refusal, he can only insist repeatedly that she is in error. His own self-justification, as well as his revenge, takes the form of a lonely monologue in which he exposes and shames the lost object of his desire— her absence providing both the animus for his narrative and its ultimate irresolution.[20]

Hysterical Narrative

Among the symptoms of hysteria, Freud points to the patient's inability to produce a "smooth and precise" history.

> They can, indeed, give the physician plenty of coherent information about this or that period of their lives; but it is sure to be followed by another period as to which their communications run dry, leaving gaps unfilled, and riddles unanswered; and then again will come yet another period which will remain totally obscure and unilluminated by even a single piece of serviceable information. [30; 16]

From this point of view, it is the goal of analysis to restore or to construct "an intelligible, consistent, and unbroken case history" (32; 18). Given this understanding, Freud's "Fragment of an Analysis of a Case of Hysteria" appears to be structured around a central irony— the attempt to complete a story and to achieve a narrative closure rendered forever impossible by Dora's deliberate rupture. Freud's claim that the case would have been fully elucidated had Dora stayed only underscores its actual state of incompletion.

> The treatment was not carried through to its appointed end, but was broken off at the patient's own wish when it had reached a certain point.

20. I am indebted to Sara Eaton for this insight. Sharon Willis describes Dora's disruptive status as a refusal "to enter the system of circulation governed by the phallus as master signifier" ("Symptomatic Narrative," 47).

At that time some of the problems of the case had not even been attacked and others had only been imperfectly elucidated; whereas if the work had been continued we should no doubt have obtained the fullest possible enlightenment upon every particular of the case. In the following pages, therefore, I can present only a fragment of an analysis. [26; 12]

Not only does Freud begin his case history with a statement about its "ungratifying conclusion" but he also finds occasion periodically to remind the reader of its deficiences. "I should like to be able to add some definite information as to when and under what particular influence Dora gave up masturbating; but owing to the incompleteness of the analysis I have only fragmentary material to present" (98; 79). The gaps in Freud's own narrative cause him to resort to "guessing and filling in what the analysis offers him in the shape of hints and allusions" (58; 42). Yet, he assures the reader, "it is only because the analysis was prematurely broken off that we have been obliged in Dora's case to resort to framing conjectures and filling in deficiencies. Whatever I have brought forward for filling up the gaps is based upon other cases which have been more thoroughly analysed" (104; 85). Freud's anxiety about filling gaps coupled with his awareness of the impossibility of constructing a seamless case history reveal the extent to which he participates in the phenomenon he describes as hysterical narrative. As if to emphasize his failure to achieve closure, he writes the last section as a "postscript," beginning it with yet another statement of inadequacy: "It is true that I have introduced this paper as a fragment of an analysis; but the reader will have discovered that it is incomplete to a far greater degree than its title might have led him to expect" (133; 112).

In a structural sense, Freud's insistence on the fragmentary nature of his narrative, and in particular on his inability to fill all the gaps, points to the failure of his interpretation, to the failure of his verbal seduction of Dora, whom he imagines at one point as a wholly intractable subject and whose behavior he views as a rejection of all men. "Men are all so detestable that I would rather not marry. This is my revenge" (142; 120). Freud, in his pursuit of a phallic interpretation of Dora's desire, urging her toward a heterosexual pact in which her gap will be filled and his case history brought to a suitable conclusion, does not perceive the way in which phallic aggressiveness itself acts as a symptom. If writing may be viewed as a supplement, as an attempt to substitute presence for absence, then the fragmentation of Freud's narrative attests not only to the impossibility of this task but also to the anxiety it generates in him. Freud's interpretive choices—fellatio over cunnilingus, the virility of Herr K. in contrast to the impotence of Dora's father, and an identification with the master rather than with the governess—all point to the source of this anxiety as female identification.

Many critics, both feminist and nonfeminist, have found conspicuously wanting in this case history any consistent portrayal of Dora's dilemma from her point of view. Standing in the way of Freud's ability to identify with Dora, I believe, are two sets of associations: one that equates femininity with castration, so that a man who occupies a passive, submissive, or feminine position in a sexual relation is subject to the anxiety of castration, and another that equates female sexuality in its clitoral manifestations with the rejection of heterosexual intercourse.[21] These two sets of associations appear symptomatically in Freud's references to bisexuality and homosexuality, which he mentions as asides, never integrating them with his main arguments concerning Dora.[22] The reference to bisexuality, the most threatening to Freud's concept of aggressive male heterosexuality, occurs at the end of a list of topics that he declines to develop: "But, once again, in the present paper I have not gone fully into all that might be said to-day about 'somatic compliance,' about the infantile germs of perversion, about the erotogenic zones, and about our predisposition toward bisexuality" (135; 113–14). When Freud refers to the possibly homosexual element in Dora's relationship with Frau K., he does so as an afterthought at the end of a chapter—making a significant association, moreover, between female homosexuality and masculinity: "These masculine or, more properly speaking, *gynaecophilic* currents of feeling are to be regarded as typical of the unconscious erotic life of hysterical girls" (81; 63). The most notable reference to female hom-

21. Freud's insistence that the clitoris is a masculine organ and that the little girl's pleasure in it is phallic creates an insuperable barrier to his understanding of female sexuality as anything but an obstacle to the achievement of heterosexual intercourse. He must at some level have understood that he was fighting a losing battle in trying to persuade his female patients to abandon this obvious source of pleaure. Mantegazza, who seems on the whole less conflicted about this subject, nevertheless clearly assumes that a woman who has become accustomed to clitoral stimulation will require her lover to learn how to satisfy her in this way.

22. Alternate explanations of Freud's nervous treatment of bisexuality and homosexuality may be found in Collins et al., "Questioning the Unconscious"; Gallop, "Daughter's Seduction"; and Willis, "Symptomatic Narrative."

osexuality appears oddly in a footnote: "I failed to discover in time and to inform the patient that her homosexual (gynaecophilic) love for Frau K. was the strongest unconscious current in her mental life" (142; 120).

The allusions to both bisexuality and homosexuality, on the margins of the narrative, as it were, and hence only partially repressed, raise again the question of what is accomplished by Freud's rather shrill insistence on Dora's love for Herr K. The fantasy of vaginal penetration functions, I think, in two ways in this case history: it both allays and maintains the anxiety of castration, as it both permits and denies a fantasy of male passivity. It functions on the one hand as a sign of virility and a means of filling a gap, of confronting and defeating the fear provoked by the sight of a woman's genitals, at the same time that it establishes a dominant/submissive relation in which a woman's "masculine" autoerotic power is denied. While Freud wishes to maintain the sexually indeterminate position of a Herr K. in the fantasy of fellatio, he simultaneously wants to divorce it from associations with male homosexuality and to eliminate the power of the nurse. In order to do so, however, he must win Dora's assent. By withholding that gratification, Dora not only holds out for the possibility of another interpretation of femininity but also stands as a silent witness to the anxieties and repressions of Freud's narrative.

Freud's attempt to enforce an oedipal interpretation on Dora's desire, coupled with his repeated attempts to achieve narrative closure, points finally to a fear associated with that of castration, though not identified with it: that of not being in control. Above all, perhaps, he wishes not to *be* Dora, the victim of multiple betrayals and subject to everyone's desire but her own. Against her silence, his simulated conversations sound awkward, a manic insistence on the power of *his* voice to create her reality. Finally, however, he does not even have the power of a Pygmalion to make a woman who will love him. She is more like Spenser's False Florimell, a seductive but empty image, composed literally of dead metaphors. Surely at least the misunderstandings of female sexuality prevalent at the turn of the century, the misnamings of the sources of female pleasure, are by now dead metaphors. Freud's own anxieties and confusions regarding the nonreproductively oriented nature of female sexuality, though not unusual for his time, provide, however, an insuperable barrier to a noncoercive representation not only of heterosexual intercourse but of any kind of adult sexual encounter. What he repeatedly misses is the other clue tantalizingly offered in his choice of a name for Dora, a clue that haunts and eludes him throughout his distraught narrative—the vision of sexual relations as open to vulnerability and to risk.[23] If the indeterminacy of sex roles, like the indeterminacy of narrative form, represents a state of not being in control, then it is no surprise that Freud is unable to imagine love as something not taken but given.

Still at the heart of his naming of Dora lies another possibility, that of a love not bound by the conventions of comic narrative (which traditionally closes with marriage), a love mutually desired and mutually gratifying, revealed in the Greek root of her name—like an open secret, perhaps, but as yet an unopened gift.

23. Janet Malcolm's suggestion in "Aaron Green" that "Dora" refers ultimately to the Pandora of mythology is altogether convincing, I think. I would only add that in its simplest form "Dora" refers to the "gift" that Freud could neither acknowledge nor accept. For him the encounter with this attractive and intelligent woman was always a power struggle of sorts, never an exchange of vulnerabilties. In this sense "Dora" stands for all that Freud could neither understand nor simply allow to *be* on its own terms in the other sex.

3

The Hand That Rocks the Cradle: Recent Gender Theories and Their Implications

COPPÉLIA KAHN

The question is breathtakingly basic, yet so novel that it might seem to be no question at all: Why do women mother children as well as give birth to them? Why is it women who assume responsibility for children after they are born and weaned, who spend hours and years as their constant companions, nurturing them emotionally and physically, and making them fit for adult society? What authorizes this universal division of labor which makes women, no matter how much time they spend away from home, what other work they do, or how much "help" their husbands give them, the persons on whom we all depend not only for survival at first, but ultimately for the bedrock of existence, a sense of self? And what effect does this arrangement have on gender, the way in which we define and live our maleness and femaleness? Finally, how can understanding the phenomenon of mothering extend psychoanalytic theory, and how does it lead to the reinterpretation of texts, both psychoanalytic and literary?

These questions are suggested by the works of four well-known feminist writers: Jean Baker Miller, Adrienne Rich, Dorothy Dinner-

A portion of this essay, in an earlier version, appeared in "Excavating 'Those Dim Minoan Regions': Maternal Subtexts in Patriarchal Literature," *Diacritics*, 12 (Summer 1982), 32–41. Reprinted by permission of the publisher, The Johns Hopkins University Press.

stein, and Nancy Chodorow.[1] As a group, they argue that the institution of motherhood is the root cause of the oppression of women and the sexual malaise experienced by men and women. I mean "cause" in an atemporal sense, for of course we don't know whether mothering by women ever "began" at a certain point in history. Rather, motherhood (these authors suggest) is the "cause" of the oppression of women in the sense that it is necessary for that oppression, and the oppression of women is inevitable given the institution of motherhood. In this essay I intend to examine the ideas put forth by these four authors, and in order to suggest how they may sustain and expand the enterprise of feminist criticism, to interpret some texts by Freud in the light of those ideas.

Let me first state briefly what these authors have in common, without trying to do justice to the range and complexity of their respective arguments. To begin with, they all regard gender less as a biological fact than as a social product, an institution learned through and perpetuated by culture. And they see this gender system not as a mutually beneficial and equitable division of roles, but as a perniciously symbiotic polarity that denies full humanity to both sexes while meshing—and helping to create—their neuroses. Second, they describe the father-absent, mother-involved nuclear family as creating the gender identities that perpetuate patriarchy and the denigration of women. In Chodorow's account, women as mothers produce daughters with mothering capacities and the desire to mother which itself grows out of the mother-daughter relationship. They also produce sons whose nurturant capacities and needs have been systematically curtailed in order to prepare them for their future as fathers. Third (and most important), because a woman is the first significant other through whom both girls and boys realize subjectivity, women in general become charged with the ambivalence of fear and desire which is the inevitable by-product of that process. The child's love for the mother doesn't come under the sway of the reality principle, in that the child doesn't at first recognize that the mother exists or has interests apart from it. Selfhood at first consists largely of the hard-won recognition

1. Jean Baker Miller, *Toward A New Psychology of Women* (Boston: Beacon Press, 1976); Adrienne Rich, *Of Woman Born: Motherhood as Experience and Institution* (New York: Harper & Row, 1976); Nancy Chodorow, *The Reproduction of Mothering: Psychoanalysis and the Sociology of Gender* (Berkeley: University of California Press, 1979); Dorothy Dinnerstein, *The Mermaid and the Minotaur: Sexual Arrangements and Human Malaise* (New York: Harper & Row, 1976).

that such separateness does exist. Thus the mother, and all women perceived in her shadow, are tainted with the grandiose expectations and bitter disappointments of a necessarily alienated subjectivity. In contrast, the child tends to perceive its father from the beginning as a separate being, and thus love and hate for the father, including that of the Oedipus complex, *does* fit under the reality principle. The father stands outside the charmed preoedipal dyad while, "for children of both genders, mothers represent regression and the lack of autonomy."[2]

A focus on the primacy of the mother's role in ego formation is not in itself new. It follows upon the attempts of such theorists as Melanie Klein, Michael and Alice Balint, and John Bowlby to cast light on that dim psychic region that Freud likened to the Minoan civilization preceding the Greek, "grey with age, and shadowy and almost impossible to revivify."[3] But, as Susan Suleiman has noted, "it is as if, for psychoanalysis, the only self worth worrying about in the mother-child relationship were that of the child."[4] What distinguishes these recent accounts of the mother-child relationship from previous ones is their insistence on historical contingency rather than biological destiny. According to these authors, psychoanalytic theory makes several questionable assumptions about the role of gender and family in the formation of the ego. First, the assumption that the sexual division of labor, gender personality, and heterosexuality rest on a biological and instinctual basis. Second, that proper ego development requires a nuclear family with authority vested in the father and "an inevitable and necessary single mother-infant relationship."[5] Third, that (as Adrienne Rich says), "the two-person mother-child relationship is by nature regressive, circular, unproductive, and that all culture depends on the father-son relationship. . . . Through the resolution of the oed-

2. Chodorow, *Reproduction of Mothering*, 181.

3. Freud uses these words to describe the first attachment to the mother in "Female Sexuality" (1931), in *Standard Edition*, XXI, 225. For contributions to understanding of this phase, see Melanie Klein, "Love, Guilt, and Reparation," in *Love, Hate, and Reparation* by Melanie Klein and Joan Riviere (New York: Norton, 1964), 57–119; Alice Balint, *The Early Years of Life: A Psychoanalytic Study* (New York: Basic Books, 1954); Michael Balint, ed., *Primary Love and Psychoanalytic Technique* (New York: Liveright, 1965); John Bowlby, *Attachment and Loss*, 2 vols. (New York, Basic Books, 1969).

4. Susan Rubin Suleiman, "Writing and Motherhood," in this volume.

5. Chodorow, *Reproduction of Mothering*, 73.

ipal complex, the boy makes his way into the male world ... of patriarchal law and order."[6]

In contrast, these four authors believe that the breast is an institution sustained by patriarchal powers, and that in turn it reinforces that power. They present, in effect, a collective vision of how maternal power in the nursery defines gender so as to foster patriarchal power in the public world. Chodorow's book offers an incisive critique and revision of psychoanalytic theories of gender development. You will recall that Freud locates the beginning of our perception of gender in anatomical difference; centers it, with sublime phallocentrism, on the possession or lack of a penis; and portrays the establishment of gender as the product of the Oedipus complex. Chodorow, taking an object relations approach that stresses social rather than instinctual factors, argues that children realize their gender well before the Oedipus complex, by about the age of three, mainly through the identification and social ascription that occurs first and crucially in their relationships with their mothers. A mother is of the same gender as her daughter, and of a different gender from her son; thus she treats them differently. Mothers of daughters, Chodorow says, tend to experience them as physical and mental extensions of themselves, creating a deeper identification and more prolonged symbiosis with them than with their sons. Clinical evidence, she asserts, shows that girls simply do not, as Freud claimed, abandon their mothers as love objects at the inception of the Oedipus complex, nor do they perceive themselves as castrated.

Rather, they remain deeply identified with their mothers through adolescence, gaining their sense of femaleness first from this identification and not, as Freud would have it, from turning to their fathers as heterosexual objects and wishing to have babies from them. Thus Chodorow distinguishes two coexistent levels of gender identity: one oriented homosexually toward the mother, one heterosexually toward the father. She also recasts penis envy, that bugaboo which has justifiably angered many feminists and regrettably alienated them from psychoanalysis. Like the boy, the girl begins life psychically merged with her mother, and when she begins to separate from her, she longs for that primal oneness but also fears it as annihilation of self. Because she is of the same sex as her mother and thus is more profoundly

6. Rich, *Of Woman Born*, 196.

75

attached to her than the boy is, she desires a penis as a crucial sign of difference, to serve as a defense against the undertow of merger with the mother and, as a symbol of power, to establish herself against the woman she has known as all-powerful. She wants a penis, then, insofar as she wants to detach herself from her mother and become an autonomous person, not because she feels castrated without one.

Without seeking to do so, it seems, Chodorow reorients psychoanalytic theory with the feminist consciousness that has rejected the notion of woman as castrated man. She has discovered, in the mother-daughter relationship and in other relations among women, rich, various, and vital sources of feminine selfhood. She also provides "a context for understanding Freud's account of superego formation in women, without imposing the value judgments he insists on," by showing how it happens that women in general have a capacity for empathy built into themselves in a way that men do not.[7] Because of the lengthy identification with her mother, a girl's ego boundaries are less firmly, less defensively established than a boy's, and she experiences herself as less differentiated from, more continous with and related to the external object world than a boy. She tends, as Carol Gilligan has argued, to conceive ethical issues in particularized, relational ways rather than abstractly.[8] Chodorow's account of female development, then, gives Freud's famous description of the female superego a different context and tone. Indeed, it *is* "never so inexorable, so impersonal, so independent of its emotional origins as we require it to be in men."[9]

Chodorow's work is no less valuable for its account of masculine development than for its account of feminine development. If "the basic feminine sense of self is connected to the world, the basic masculine sense of self is separate," she holds.[10] This separateness arises because a boy must establish his gender identity in opposition to his mother's gender. To do so he must separate more firmly from his mother than does a girl, who can model her femaleness on her mother. Furthermore, mothers tend to treat their sons as objects separate from them, and to push them out of identification with themselves sooner

7. Chodorow, *Reproduction of Mothering*, 169.
8. Carol Gilligan, *In a Different Voice* (Cambridge: Harvard University Press, 1982).
9. Sigmund Freud, "Some Psychical Consequences of the Anatomical Distinction between the Sexes" (1925), in *Standard Edition*, XIX, 243–60.
10. Chodorow, *Reproduction of Mothering*, 169.

and harder into an oedipally toned relationship defined by gender difference. Very early, phallic-masculine self-definition becomes entwined with issues of object relations and separateness of self which have little connotation of gender for girls.[11] On the other hand, the boy's Oedipus complex is more decisively resolved than the girl's. Because his heterosexual oedipal love for the mother is an extension of his infantile love, it is more intense and thus more strenuously repressed. His rivalry with the father for the mother also intensifies his love for her and strengthens its repression. Thus the masculine personality tends to be formed through denial of connection with femininity and all relationships stemming from the crucial first one with the mother. Certain activities must be defined as masculine and superior to the maternal world of childhood, and women's activities must, correspondingly, be denigrated. In this sense, it is the boy and not the girl, as in the Freudian account, who must make a difficult switch—not a switch in love object from mother to father, from homosexual to heterosexual, but a switch in major identification, from identifying with the mother to identifying with the father.

Rich, Miller, and Dinnerstein in effect continue into adulthood Chodorow's account of the en-gendering of women. They elucidate the new symbiosis between male and female adult personalities which replaces the earlier one of mother and child. Rich and Dinnerstein are particularly eloquent and convincing on the ways in which woman's body becomes "the carnal scapegoat" for our fears of the flesh and mortality, or the idol in which we try to recreate our lost union with mother-as-flesh. Since, whether we are men or women, our earliest carnal interaction takes place with a woman, the female body becomes the locale par excellence of fleshly bliss. Men tend either to exalt its charms or to revile its functions. Women are encouraged to behave narcissistically as sex objects or masochistically as mothers, either position being a defense against the female body's resonance with primitive fears and needs.

Rich shows how male fears of woman's childbearing powers, and by extension her "transformative power" over nature (in cooking, pottery, and weaving, for example), have imprisoned women in motherhood. Patriarchal mythology, she holds, has used the ideal of maternal al-

11. See Robert J. Stoller, "Facts and Fancies: An Examination of Freud's Concept of Bisexuality," in *Women and Analysis: Dialogues on Psychoanalytic Views of Femininity*, ed. Jean Strouse (New York: Grossman, 1974), 343–64.

truism to deny the male fear and loathing of women's bodies. As mother and only as mother, woman is exonerated of Eve's crime. The mother's assumed capacity for unconditional love, uncontaminated by self-interest or anger, makes her sacred; her pain in childbirth, her self-sacrifice in childraising purify her sexuality. "Women who refuse to become mothers are dangerous," and men tend to perceive women either as mothers, purged of sexual taint, or antimothers, whores and witches. "Maternal altruism is the one quality universally approved and supported in women," Rich claims. [12]

What Rich describes as maternal altruism Miller elucidates as the principle on which the female ego, patterned by mothering, is built: selfhood achieved through serving others' needs and interests, as if women had none of their own. Women feel useful and worthy and function well, Miller explains, when they can regard their ambitious strivings as if they served others. Once a man has defined his masculinity by other than altruistic standards, he may choose to see himself as serving others, but women are not encouraged to satisfy their drives in a direct relation to reality as men are. Their egos, embedded in relationships, as Chodorow maintains, tend to mediate not their own drives but their drives in the service of another.

Miller poignantly describes the catch-22 quality of gender definition as both sexes experience it, a self-defeating complementarity of traits and frustrations. People of both sexes develop their selfhood by affiliation, by bonds with others, but women's sense of self tends to be founded on affiliation, while men direct themselves toward significant enterprise and starve inwardly for deeper affiliation. As infants, men enjoy affiliation with and through their mothers; but when they become men, they are encouraged to build their lives on self-aggrandizement, competition, and aggression. Rewarded for doing so, they must then struggle to redevelop the capacities for affiliation and nurturance they have previously denied. On the other hand, Miller says, women end up "doing good and feeling bad" when, after they altruistically pour their energies into the service of others, that service goes unrecognized and their own needs are frustrated. [13] For finally, despite the idealization of motherhood, it is men's work that really counts.

12. Rich, *Of Woman Born*, 164, 212.
13. Miller, *Toward a New Psychology*, 48–59.

The work of Chodorow, Dinnerstein, Miller, and Rich provides a basis for reading Freud's theory of gender as itself a patriarchal text. As such, it is all the more useful to feminist critics, I think, in their efforts to decipher the psychodynamics of other patriarchal texts. In 1926 Karen Horney noted, in "The Flight from Womanhood," that men in analysis revealed a surprisingly intense envy of pregnancy, childbirth, motherhood, and suckling, and suggested that the attribution of penis envy to women might be a way of denying what looked like womb envy.[14] She also argued that Freud's conception of feminine development matches the ideas he attributes to the four-year-old oedipal boy—that a girl once had a penis, was castrated, came to regard herself as inferior because of her loss, and was subject to lifelong envy of boys who had them.

The recent theory and research on which these four writers base their critiques of mothering as an exclusively feminine vocation enable us to find the subtext of Freud's account of femininity. These critiques suggest that it is only the penis that keeps a man from feeling like a woman, or being part of a woman as he once was. Men must insist on the superiority of the penis and their exclusive possession of it, or women will claim it, as they once claimed so much, for theirs. The impetus behind phallocentrism, then, is what Rich calls "matrophobia"—not the fear of one's mother or of motherhood, but of becoming like one's mother as in the original identification of the child with its mother, and thus losing one's gender identity as a male.[15]

In Freud, such matrophobia takes the form of a nearly lifelong reluctance to confront the child's, especially the male child's, early and close relationship to his mother. In the letters to Fliess in the 1890s, written as Freud stood on the brink of discovering his own Oedipus complex, he recounts a series of dreams that shadow forth his feelings about his experience of being mothered. Freud had, in effect, two mothers—his natural mother and the old Czech peasant woman who served as his nursemaid till he was two and a half. As Jim Swan shows, this circumstance encouraged Freud in maintaining a split between the internalized good and bad mothers that (psychoan-

---

14. Karen Horney, "The Flight from Womanhood," in *Feminine Psychology* (New York: Norton, 1967), 54–70.
15. Rich, *Of Woman Born*, 237; she takes the term from Lynn Sukenick.

alytic theory maintains) we all introject.[16] It helped him to preserve into his old age an idealized love for his natural mother, who died when he was seventy-four.[17]

According to Swan, in these early dreams the nursemaid appears ambivalently as both the young Freud's seductress and his punisher.[18] She is his "*Urheberin*"—in Swan's translation, the first to raise him up; that is, to give him an erection in the course of bathing or dressing him, to show him his maleness. But she is also the one who "scorns" or "shames" him for being clumsy and unable to do things for himself. When Freud recalls that this "Nannie" bathed him in reddish water in which she had previously washed herself, clearly an image of fusion with the mother, he strongly suggests—though without realizing it—that he identified himself with her. But his memory or fantasy that he stole coins and gave them to her is even more revealing. A few letters after recounting it, he tells Fliess that he was mistaken; he has learned that in fact it was the old woman who stole from him, and that she was arrested, convicted, and imprisoned for doing so. The mistake shows that he identified himself with her, and this time he seems to admit it: "I equals she," he writes to Fliess. But he thereby indicates transformation by the dreamwork, not the infant's deeper sense of "I *am* she" which survives in his unconscious. Swan argues that Freud fancied himself stealing and giving to his nurse because of this deeper kind of identification in which he does to her in reverse what he feels she has done to him: robbed him of that precious coin, his masculinity—the very masculinity she first gave him by arousing him, and then took away by shaming him.

Freud's early case histories reveal, Iza Erlich maintains, an "ironic discrepancy between his insistence on the importance of the mother in the oedipal love-hate triangle and the relatively pallid picture of

16. Jim Swan, "*Mater* and Nannie: Freud's Two Mothers and the Discovery of the Oedipus Complex," *American Imago*, 31 (1974), 1–64. I am much indebted to this brilliant, wide-ranging article.

17. Freud, the eldest of seven surviving children, once remarked, "A man who has been the indisputable favorite of his mother keeps for life the feeling of a conqueror, that confidence of his success that often induces real success" (quoted by Lionel Trilling in his introduction to the abridged edition of *The Life and Works of Sigmund Freud*, by Ernest Jones [New York: Doubleday, 1963]). When his mother died, he wrote, "I was not allowed to die as long as she was alive, and now I may. Somehow the values of life have notably changed in the deeper layers" (Jones, 470).

18. See Freud to Wilhelm Fliess, October 3, 1897, in *Standard Edition*, I, 261–62; Swan comments on this letter in "*Mater* and Nannie," 16–18.

the mother which he draws."[19] Looking at the stories of Dora (1905), Little Hans (1909), and the Rat Man (1909), she finds that Freud portrays the fathers in these family dramas as complex, interesting people and the mothers as drab, monochromatic creatures destined to play limited roles. I would add that in "Dora" he consistently swerves past clues that might lead toward Dora's relationship with her mother and pursues those that lead toward her father and Herr K.[20] His brilliant probing impels him to posit, behind her anger at her father, her disgust for Herr K., and her disillusionment with Frau K., that she is in some sense in love with each of them. But he never questions the feelings she expresses for her mother:

> I never made her mother's acquaintance. From the accounts given me by the girl and her father I was led to imagine her as an uncultivated woman and above all as a foolish one, who had concentrated all her interests upon domestic affairs, especially since her husband's illness and the estrangement to which it led. She presented the picture, in fact, of what might be called the "housewife's psychosis." She had no understanding for her children's more active interests, and was occupied all day long in cleaning the house with its furniture and utensils and keeping them clean—to such an extent as to make it almost impossible to use or enjoy them. . . . The relations between the girl and her mother had been unfriendly for years. The daughter looked down on her mother and used to criticize her mercilessly, and she had withdrawn completely from her influence.[21]

Freud finds no connection between this woman's obsessive cleanliness and the probability (which he mentions in a footnote) that her husband had infected her with venereal disease, which resulted in a vaginal discharge for which she sought treatment at a spa. Though he regards Dora's persistent cough as an upward displacement of her mother's illness, he links it to an identification with her father rather than with her mother. While he cleverly parallels Dora, the K.'s

---

19. Iza S. Erlich, "What Happened to Jocasta?" *Bulletin of the Menninger Clinic*, 41 (May 1977), 280–84.

20. For other kinds of swerves, see Steven Marcus, "Freud and Dora: Story, History, Case History," *Partisan Review*, 41 (1974), 12–23, 89–108, and Maria Ramas, "Freud's Dora, Dora's Hysteria: The Negation of a Woman's Rebellion," *Feminist Studies*, 6 (1980), 472–510, for a cogent feminist interpretation of the Dora case. Marcus comments on Freud's lack of clarity about female sexual development on 96–98.

21. Freud, "Fragment of an Analysis of a Case of Hysteria," in *Standard Edition*, VII, 20.

governess, and Frau K. because they have all served as mother substitutes for girl "children" and then betrayed them when their interest in a man required them to do so, he pursues the heterosexual connection to the exclusion of the homosexual, mother-identified dimension of these relationships. Finally, when Dora's second dream produces an association to the Sistine Madonna, before which she had once remained "rapt in silent admiration" for two hours, he links it to her identification with a certain young man rather than with her mother, the original madonna in everyone's life, boy or girl.[22] As Erlich comments, "It is as if Freud could not bring himself to look closely at the mother, the figure his theory proclaims to be so central."[23]

A comparison between Freud's two most extensive pieces of art criticism, "Leonardo da Vinci and a Memory of His Childhood" (1919) and "The Moses of Michelangelo" (1914), highlights his male-centered view of the mothering role and his preference for identifying with father figures. In these essays, written not long after the case histories discussed above, he addresses himself to two masterpieces powerfully resonant with traditional images of mothers and fathers. The Leonardo essay focuses on the riddle of the artist's career: the mysterious inhibition that caused him to forsake art for scientific investigation. In the course of answering the riddle, Freud elaborates on several topics that will become major psychoanalytic concerns: repression and sublimation in artistic creativity, the genesis of homosexuality, infantile theories of sexuality, and narcissism. The objects at the essay's center—Leonardo's brief description of a childhood memory and his paintings of the *Mona Lisa* and *St. Anne with the Madonna and Child*— are surrounded with a dense cloud of fascinating theory and speculation about that dim Minoan region of early mother-child relations. The *Moses* essay, in contrast, focuses on a single hard, clear object—the famous statue. Though Freud begins with a frank declaration of his own strong reactions to it, his approach is objective and empirical, involving detailed description of specific features and comparison of authorities. He spends only a paragraph on Michelangelo's life and the motives behind his portrayal of Moses, and confines himself to one specific question about the interpretation of the statue.

Broadly speaking, when Freud writes about Leonardo his language is often tender and impassioned. Though he doesn't allude to his own

22. Freud, "Fragment of an Analysis," 47–48, 96.
23. Erlich, "What Happened to Jocasta?" 284.

involvement in the subject, clearly it moves him. But when he writes about Michelangelo's *Moses*, even though he declares, "No piece of statuary has ever made a stronger impression on me than this," his dispassioned, objective stance serves to suppress that reaction. In the Leonardo essay he is moved by the maternal images he describes so vividly, but doesn't declare his feelings as his own; in the *Moses* essay he admits his feelings for the patriarchal image but then in effect denies them. The disparity is fully consonant with the ideas of mothers and fathers the two essays elaborate.

A conception of the mother as one who gives, then takes away; seduces, then shames, like the nurse of Freud's early memories, lies at the heart of the Leonardo essay. Making use of Leonardo's notebooks and of biographical data, Freud constructs a sentimental account of the artist's early development centered on his relationship to his mother, "Caterina, the poor peasant girl" who brought into the world an illegitimate son destined to become Leonardo, the great artist. Freud pictures Caterina as an unwed mother who compensates herself for the loss of a lover and her son for the absence of a father by taking her little boy in the place of a husband. Fondling and kissing him passionately, she robbed him, "by the too early maturing of his erotism," says Freud, "of a part of his masculinity" and set him on his course toward homosexuality.[24] But in the same paragraph he posits a notion of mothering which ultimately seems to encourage just this kind of robbery: "A mother's love for the infant she suckles and cares for is . . . in the nature of a completely satisfying love-relation, which not only fulfills every mental wish but also every physical need."[25] Here Freud presents mothering from the woman's point of view as he imagines it. The child is everything to its mother, as no adult love partner could be. The mother gets total satisfaction from her child, and the child gets the same from its mother. Such merging of needs and desires Freud portrays as unambivalently benign for *both* mother and child.

24. Freud, "Leonardo da Vinci and a Memory of His Childhood," *Standard Edition*, XI, 117. While it is the father's absence as well as the mother's excessive affection that, Freud maintains, is likely to fixate the son at a narcissistic stage of object relations and turn him toward homosexuality, throughout his essay he is much more concerned with the mother's role than with the father's. He does point out, however, that Leonardo's identification with his father had both negative and positive effects on his career.

25. Freud, "Leonardo da Vinci," 117.

When he examines mothering from the child's point of view, however, that child sees like a man, and it is a different story altogether. Turning to the *Mona Lisa's* smile, Freud argues that Leonardo found the model for it in Caterina's countenance, which held "the promise of unbounded tenderness and at the same time sinister menace," presumably the menace of robbing him of his masculinity. Both he and the critics he quotes at some length indulge their strikingly ambivalent feelings toward mothers and women as mothers by mystifying them and projecting them onto Mona Lisa. They endow her with both "tenderness and coquetry," with "the charm of deceit, the kindness that conceals a cruel purpose," and with "instincts of conquest, of ferocity, all the heredity of the species, the will to seduce and ensnare."[26]

Freud finds a more benign duality in Leonardo's *St. Anne with the Madonna and Child.* The artist composed the picture so as to melt the two women into a single form, with the virgin seated on her mother's lap, reaching toward the Christ Child. Grandmother and mother are equally young and beautiful, and "endowed with the blissful smile of the joy of motherhood." Thus Leonardo, Freud says, has synthesized "the history of his childhood," merging his true mother, Caterina, from whom he was separated before he reached five, and his father's young wife, who became his stepmother when he entered the paternal household.[27] It is not only Leonardo's two mothers we can see here, but Freud's and everyman's. In the letters to Fliess, amid his several recollections of the old woman who bathed, scolded, and stole from him, Freud mentions his own mother, but formally, in Latin, as *"matrem . . . nudam."*[28] Like the men whose sexual problems he discusses in two important essays written during the same period as the Leonardo essay, "A Special Type of Object Choice Made by Men" (1910) and "A Prevalent Form of Degradation in Erotic Life" (1912), Freud has split her into two images: the chaste, distant madonna and the ugly, sexual nursemaid. In these two essays Freud connects such a duality to the Oedipus complex. But in the light of the gender theories I discussed earlier, it seems more likely to originate in male preoedipal experience, which produces men who feel their gender endangered by a mother's love, and who therefore in

---

26. Freud, "Leonardo da Vinci," 109.
27. Freud, "Leonardo da Vinci," 113.
28. Freud to Fliess, October 4, 1897, in *Standard Edition*, I, 262.

one breath idealize that love and in the next call it deceitful and seductive.

If we look into Freud's associations with the figure of Moses, the topic of the second essay, we encounter a quite different constellation of feelings, concerning the father. Let us begin where Freud begins, after some general opening remarks, to look at the statue of the patriarch:

> For no piece of statuary has ever made a stronger impression on me than this. How often have I mounted the steep steps of the unlovely Corso Cavour to the lonely place where the deserted church stands, and have essayed to support the angry scorn of the hero's glance! Sometimes I have crept cautiously out of the half-gloom of the interior as though I myself belonged to the mob upon whom his eye is turned— the mob which can hold fast no conviction, which has neither faith nor patience and which rejoices when it has regained its illusory idols. [29]

The statue stands in Rome, a city of special meaning to Freud. In the original edition of *The Interpretation of Dreams* (1900) he recounts a revealing series of dreams based on a longing to visit Rome, and remarks that the longing must remain such. Then, in 1909, when his work has gained recognition, he adds in a footnote, "I discovered long since that it only needs a little courage to fulfill wishes which till then have been regarded as unattainable." [30] For him, Moses, Rome, and unattainable wishes are interconnected.

Moses, like Oedipus, is one of Freud's heroic images of himself in *The Interpretation of Dreams*. Both are entrusted with leading an imperiled people to safety, and both in the course of doing so bring back forbidden knowledge from realms considered sacred. Freud thought of Rome in connection with his boyhood hero Hannibal, who as a Carthaginian had challenged Roman superiority, but without being able to conquer the city. [31] Hannibal was thus akin to a Jew challenging the Gentile establishment—another forbidden act, attractive to Freud, who felt and fought anti-Semitism all his life. In his own oedipal dream, recounted piecemeal in the dream book, he feels ashamed of his father for not standing up for himself as a Jew when an anti-Semite humiliates him. That father shames him in a different way, however, by saying, "The boy will come to nothing," when Freud intrudes into his parents'

---

29. Freud, "The Moses of Michelangelo," in *Standard Edition*, XIII, 213.
30. Freud, *The Interpretation of Dreams*, in *Standrd Edition*, IV, 194.
31. Freud, *Interpretation of Dreams*, 196–97.

bedroom and urinates on the floor.[32] Thus when Freud, surpassing Hannibal, enters Rome and ferrets out the meaning of a statue of the first Jewish patriarch, the act symbolizes his attainment of manhood in a way best described by Freud's reaction when he reached the Acropolis: "It seems as though the essence of success were to have gotten farther than one's father, and as though to excel one's father were forbidden."[33] In the passage from the Moses essay quoted above, Freud casts himself in the role of a Moses climbing the steep steps of lonely self-analysis and professional isolation toward a Sinai of divine secrets. The statue that bends an angry glance on him is his masculine ego ideal, and the childish, fickle mob that Moses found worshiping the golden calf when he descended from the mountain is the weak, "womanish" part of himself that Freud feared giving in to. The passage springs from memories of self-reproaches arising from his fear of not being man enough for the great task he had set himself.[34]

The question of interpretation on which the essay centers concerns what action is implied by the pose of the patriarch, who sits holding the tables of the law entrusted to him by God on the mountain. Does Michelangelo depict a historical Moses just descended from Sinai, now about to "let loose his rage upon his faithless people," or an eternal "character-type . . . embodying an inexhaustible inner force

32. Freud, *Interpretation of Dreams*, 216. For an interpretation of the Rome dreams in the context of Freud's political and cultural experience, see Carl E. Schorske, "Politics and Patricide in Freud's *Interpretation of Dreams*," in Schorske, *Fin-de-Siècle Vienna* (New York: Random House, 1980), 181–207. Schorske suggests that for Freud, Rome ambivalently represented both an oedipal mother to be possessed and an oedipal father to be overcome.

33. Freud, "A Disturbance of Memory on the Acropolis," in *Standard Edition*, XXII, 247.

34. With regard to similar anxieties about conflicting male and female capacities within Freud, as expressed in the Irma dream, Erik H. Erikson comments:

> To overcome mankind's resistance, the dreamer had to learn to become his own patient and subject of investigation: to deliver free associations to himself; to unveil horrible insights to himself; to identify himself with himself in the double roles of observer and observed. . . . This, in view of the strong maleness of scientific approach cultivated by the bearded savants of his day and age . . . constituted an unfathomable division within the observer's self, a division of vague "feminine yielding" and persistent masculine precision: this, I feel, is one of the central meanings of the Irma dream. ["The Dream Specimen of Psychoanalysis," in *Psychoanalytic Psychiatry and Psychology: Clinical and Theoretical Papers*, Austen Riggs Center, vol. 1 (New York: International Universities Press, 1954), 164]

which tames the recalcitrant world?" In putting the question to his readers, Freud again interjects his own reactions:

> I can recollect my own disillusionment when, during my first visit to the church, I used to sit down in front of the statue in the expectation that I should now see how it would start up on its raised foot, hurl the Tables of the Law to the ground, and let fly its wrath. Nothing of the kind happened. Instead, the stone image became more and more trans-fixed, an almost oppressively solemn calm emanated from it, and I was obliged to realize that something was represented here that could stay without change: that this Moses would remain sitting like this in his wrath forever.[35]

I hear in this passage an echo of Freud's disappointment with the father who remained calm when a Gentile taunted him, and of his determination not to let a hostile world prevent him from reaching his promised land, the discovery of the unconscious.

But, not allowing personal feeling to interfere with the task at hand, Freud fixes his eyes on the statue and argues that, after all, the second view of a restrained and temperate Moses is the more nearly correct, given the evidence the statue offers. If Moses were to leap up in vindictive anger, the precious tables would slip from his grasp and shatter; the divine secret of the Law which God has given to his chosen people would be lost, and they would never reach the promised land. Rather, says Freud, the position of the leader's right hand and beard indicate that he has already felt but subdued a surge of wrath, precisely in order to keep the tables from harm, "so that the giant frame with its tremendous physical power becomes only a concrete expression of the highest mental achievement that is possible in a man, that of struggling successfully against an inward passion for the sake of a cause to which he has devoted himself."[36] "The highest mental achievement that is possible in a man"—that is, in a patriarch, the model for all men—is the opposite of the highest achievement, not exactly a mental one, he envisions for a woman: the "completely satisfying love-rela-tionship which fulfills not only every mental wish but every physical need"—mothering a child. Men have causes and women have babies. Men repress their feelings and thereby perform great tasks of lead-ership; women indulge their feelings and thereby produce women

35. Freud, "Moses of Michelangelo," 220.
36. Freud, "Moses of Michelangelo," 236.

who also indulge them, and men who repress them for fear of being like women.

Only in 1931 (interestingly, about a year after his own mother died) did Freud suggest, in "Female Sexuality," that the child *first* identifies with its mother—but with reference to a girl, not a boy. Long before that date he viewed a boy's identification with his mother as pathogenic; it could lead to homosexuality, an outcome of the negative resolution of the Oedipus complex in which a boy wants to be, like his mother, the passive object of his father's love. In fact, Freud characterizes identification in general as regressive (in "Mourning and Melancholia," 1917) and at the same time sex-types it; the passivity and loss of ego-boundaries identification it entails belong to a feminine mode and emanate from a time when all that an infant experienced came from a woman. As Jim Swan argues, for Freud

> maturity (that is, *masculine* maturity) means being well defended against one's past, which amounts to the same thing as having a strong capacity for resisting identification. . . . In effect, Freud's picture of maturity is of a man driven to outrun . . . identification with the body of his mother, the original unity of mother and infant.[37]

In *The Interpretation of Dreams* Freud says, "There is at least one spot in every dream at which it is unplumbable—a navel, as it were, that is its point of contact with the unknown."[38] For the first psychoanalyst, the "navel" of psychic development is identification with the mother.[39] It is "unknown" to him not because it is unknowable but because he is a man, because manhood as patriarchal culture creates it depends on denying, in myriad ways, the powerful ambivalence that the mother inspires. Part of our task as feminist critics, I suggest, is to excavate that gray, shadowy region of identification, particularly male identification with the mother, and trace its influence on perceptions and depictions of women in patriarchal texts.

37. Swan, "*Mater* and Nannie," 9–10.
38. Freud, *Interpretation of Dreams*, 111.
39. For a fascinating explication of the dream as maternal object and of interpretation as the oedipal act of penetrating the mother, see David Willbern, "Freud and the Inter-penetration of Dreams," *Diacritics*, 9 (Spring 1979), 98–110.

4

Hysteria, Psychoanalysis, and Feminism: The Case of Anna O.

DIANNE HUNTER

We [Breuer and I] had often compared the symptomatology of hysteria with a pictographic script which has become intelligible after the discovery of a few bilingual
inscriptions.

—Sigmund Freud, *Studies on Hysteria*

Hysteria is not a pathological phenomenon, and can, in
all respects, be considered as a supreme means of
expression.

—Louis Aragon and André Breton
"Le Cinquantenaire de l'hystérie"

The hysteric most often named and discussed by Freud, although he
never met her and never encountered a case like hers, was "Fräulein
Anna O.," the inventor of the "talking cure." She is introduced in the
first case history of *Studies on Hysteria*, published by Freud and
Breuer in 1895. Anna O.'s real name was Bertha Pappenheim. She
inspired what may be called the "legend" of the origin of psychoanalysis; later in her life, she became an important figure in the history

Reprinted from *Feminist Studies*, 9, no. 3 (1983), by permission of the publisher.

of the German Jewish women's movement and in the history of modern institutionalized social work. She lived from 1859 to 1936, and in 1954 was honored by the Republic of West Germany as a "Helper of Humanity." Although feminists have recognized Pappenheim for the philanthropic and political activities of her public life, we have given less attention to her role as a contributor to psychoanalytic theory and technique.[1]

The Anna O. described in psychoanalytic writings is an attractive, highly intelligent young woman. She suffered a hysterical collapse at the age of twenty-one, during a period when she had been responsible for prolonged day-and-night nursing of her father, Siegmund, who was dying of tuberculosis. For nearly two years, during and after her father's illness, Anna was a patient of the well-known and respected Viennese physician Josef Breuer, who described her case as "the germ cell of the whole of psychoanalysis."[2] Although Dr. Breuer never fully recognized the meaning of his encounter with Pappenheim, he found the case remarkable enough to report to his young friend and colleague Freud, who was profoundly impressed when he heard about Pappenheim's unusual treatment by verbalization and catharsis. That was in November 1882. Three years later, Freud was in Paris observing Jean-Martin Charcot's demonstrations of hypnosis and suggestion at the Salpêtrière Hospital. At that time, Charcot's lessons on hysteria were as fashionable as the tirades of Sarah Bernhardt, and for much the same reason. In the late nineteenth century, hysteria was a common subject in medical publications throughout Europe and in England. What Freud contributed to the work being done at this time in France was the idea of listening to what hysterics had to say. Bertha Pappenheim originated this technique, and another patient, "Elizabeth von R.," refined it by suggesting to Freud the method of free association.

Although Breuer edited the story of Bertha Pappenheim's hysteria and suppressed her identity, we know her biography from later sources.[3]

1. See Marion A. Kaplan, *The Jewish Feminist Movement in Germany: The Campaigns of the Jüdischer Frauenbund, 1904–1938* (Westport, Conn.: Greenwood, 1979).

2. Josef Breuer to August Forel, November 21, 1907, quoted in George Pollock, "The Possible Significance of Childhood Object Loss in the Josef Breuer-Bertha Pappenheim (Anna O.)–Sigmund Freud Relationship," *Journal of the American Psychoanalytic Association*, 16 (1968), 723.

3. Ernest Jones revealed Pappenheim's name. He writes: "Since she was the real discoverer of the cathartic method, her name . . . deserves to be commemorated" (*The Life and Work of Sigmund Freud*, 3 vols. [New York: Basic Books, 1953–57], I, 223–26). But Jones's account of Pappenheim and Breuer contains errors. More accurate

She was born in Vienna, the third child in a family that already had two daughters (the two sisters died in childhood). Her birth was followed by that of the family's only son, Wilhelm, whose privileges Pappenheim came to resent. She attended a Catholic school, although her home was traditionally Jewish. Her grandfather, Wolf Pappenheim, had been a prominent personality in the Pressburg ghetto. He devoted his fortune to the promotion of Jewish orthodoxy. Bertha's father was a wealthy grain merchant and a cofounder of the Jewish Schiffschul in Vienna. Bertha Pappenheim's mother, Recha, née Goldschmidt, has been described as rather authoritarian. Originally from Frankfurt-on-the-Main, she later returned there with her daughter. This city was a center of charitable activities among Bertha's relatives on her mother's side. That branch of the family included Heinrich Heine and was connected to artistic circles.

Breuer remarks that some of Anna's more distant relatives had been psychotic, but that she herself had been consistently healthy until her father's sickness in July 1880. She had received an education typical for girls of her class and family position. She spoke perfect English, read French and Italian, and practiced embroidery and lacemaking, which remained a lifelong passion. There was a certain modernism about her training, however: she rode horseback with her cousins. A photograph of Bertha in riding costume, dated 1882, Konstanz, Germany, bears little resemblance to the patient Breuer describes, although he does mention that she had once used a horsewhip in his presence when her pet dog attacked a cat. Breuer describes Anna as a willful, energetic, intuitive, and compassionate person who took pleasure in caring for the poor and the sick. According to Breuer, Anna could be obstinate, but "sympathetic kindness" was one of her essential character traits. Breuer reports that Anna had a "powerful instinct" for charity work; he does not mention that such work was one of the few forms of activity women were traditionally permitted outside the home.

During the time Bertha Pappenheim nursed her father, she stopped eating. She lost so much weight that she was forbidden to continue her nursing duties. She also developed a cough that resembled her

accounts of Pappenheim's life can be found in Dora Edinger, *Bertha Pappenheim— Freud's Anna O.* (Highland Park, Ill.: Congregation Solel, 1968); Henri Ellenberger, *The Discovery of the Unconscious* (New York: Basic Books, 1970), 480–84; Lucien Israël, *L'Hystérique, le sexe et le médecin* (Paris: Masson, 1980), 200–205; Kaplan, *Jewish Feminist Movement.*

father's. At this point, Dr. Breuer was called in for the first time. Over the next three months a very complex hysteria developed. Pappenheim suffered rigid paralyses of her arms and legs, paresis of the neck muscles, headaches, and somnambulism.

First her right arm, then her right side, then her entire body suffered contracture. She was intermittently deaf. She had a convergent squint and severe, inexplicable disturbances of vision. She had temper tantrums during which she would throw things about the room, tear the buttons off her bedclothes, and grow distressed when relatives appeared. In her hysteria Bertha experienced a profound disorganization of speech and, for a time, total aphasia.

It is Pappenheim's aphasia and her use of her body as a signifier with which I am particularly concerned. Although many of what Freud refers to as Pappenheim's "museum of monuments" to "hyperaesthetic memories" have been richly and repeatedly analyzed, no one has sufficiently studied her unique use of languages. When she regained her ability to talk, Bertha Pappenheim was unable to understand or speak her native tongue, although she proved surprisingly fluent in foreign languages, a circumstance Freud calls "strange" and other commentators call "bizarre." I would like to offer a psychoanalytic feminist reading of Bertha's speechlessness and her communication in translation, gibberish, and pantomime. I think it is possible to see a liberating motive implicit in Pappenheim's linguistic disruptions. Speaking coherent German meant integration into a cultural identity Bertha Pappenheim wanted to reject.

Pappenheim claimed to be divided into two selves, "a real one and an evil one which forced her to behave badly."[4] Two states of consciousness would alternate, one of which would interrupt while the other was speaking. Breuer refers to the pauses in Pappenheim's speech by the French term *absences*. This term suggests that for Breuer as well as for Pappenheim the abnormal states of consciousness represented foreign parts of the self. Parts of Anna O. were alien to signification in her native tongue.

In the afternoons Pappenheim would fall into a somnolent state. After sunset she would wake up, repeating the words "tormenting, tormenting." She was unable to speak a whole sentence, and her whole body was paralyzed. Breuer first noticed that she was at a loss for

4. Josef Breuer, "Fräulein Anna O.," *Studies on Hysteria*, in *Standard Edition*, II, 24.

words and then that she had lost her command of grammar and syntax as well. She no longer conjugated verbs, and eventually used only infinitives, which, says Breuer, were "for the most part incorrectly formed from weak past participles."[5] Although it is not apparent what Breuer means by infinitives "formed from weak past participles," it seems to be significant that neither infinitives nor participles specify a person; as Breuer notes, "tormenting" is an impersonal form. Pappenheim also omitted both the definite and the indefinite articles. In the course of time she became almost completely deprived of words. She would put them together laboriously out of four or five languages and became nearly unintelligible. Here is a reconstruction of Pappenheim's linguistic mélange: "Jamais acht nobody bella mio please lieboehn nuit."[6] She tried to write the same mumbo jumbo.

For two weeks Bertha Pappenheim was completely dumb, and at this point Dr. Breuer recognized for the first time the psychical mechanism of his patient's disorder: "She had felt very much offended over something and had determined not to speak of it."[7] When Breuer made this interpretation and obliged her to talk about it during hypnosis, Pappenheim's linguistic inhibition disappeared, but she spoke only in English. In moments of extreme anxiety, either her powers of speech deserted her entirely or she used a mixture of languages. At the times when she felt most free, Pappenheim spoke French and Italian. She had amnesia between these times and those when she spoke English. During her illness she baffled her family and servants with discourses in languages they did not understand and astonished her doctors by producing a rapid, fluent extemporaneous English translation of any text in French or Italian that she was asked to read aloud. Pappenheim also made up words—*gehäglich* for *behaglich*, meaning comfortable—and invented names in English for the process that she and Breuer had begun. She called it "chimney sweeping" when she was joking and "the talking cure" when she was being serious.

Freud and Breuer offer an inadequate explanation for Pappenheim's linguistic symptoms. We are told that one night while she was watching

5. Breuer, "Fräulein Anna O.," 25.

6. Ann Elwood, "The Beginning of Psychoanalysis," in *The People's Almanac*, ed. David Wallechinsky and Irving Wallace (Garden City, N.Y.: Doubleday, 1975), 502. Neither Breuer nor Freud quotes this sentence, although it is consistent with Breuer's description of Pappenheim's special use of languages.

7. Breuer, "Fräulein Anna O.," 25.

by her father's sickbed in a torment of anxiety, she fell into a twilight state and her right arm, which was hanging over the back of the chair, went to sleep. Pappenheim was so terrified to find her arm paralyzed that she tried to pray, but could find no words. At length she remembered a child's prayer in English. Therefore when her hysteria developed, she spoke and wrote English. This recollection of the child's prayer seems to bear no relation to Pappenheim's determination to keep silent. Nor does it explain her inventive nomenclatures, polylingual jargon, or amazing speeches in French and Italian. All it tells us is that Bertha was so upset that she forgot her mother tongue.

Although Breuer does not state what had offended Bertha, it is easy to infer that she resented and rejected her inferior position as a daughter in an orthodox Jewish family. Although her intellectual and poetic gifts were remarkable and she was a lively and charming person, Bertha Pappenheim at twenty-one was assigned routine and monotonous household tasks. Her brother, one year younger than she and not nearly so bright, had recently entered the University of Vienna, an institution closed to women at that time. Breuer writes, "This girl, who was bubbling over with intellectual vitality, led an extremely monotonous existence in her puritanically-minded family. She embellished her life in a manner which probably influenced her decisively in the direction of her illness, by indulging in systematic day-dreaming, which she described as her 'private theatre.' "[8] Speculating on the origin of "hypnoid" (dissociated, split) states, Breuer and Freud note that these conditions often seem to grow out of the daydreams that are common even in healthy people, "and to which needlework and similar occupations render women especially prone."[9] That is, people left to embroidery are bound to embroider fantasies.

Pappenheim's daydreaming and her illness were heavily influenced by the necessity of spending hours at her father's sickbed, a situation that cannot have failed to arouse erotic and aggressive wishes in such a lively and imaginative person, although Breuer makes no such suggestion and seems not to have thought of it. The squint developed while she was straining through her tears to see what time it was; she had waited up all night for a doctor who was late in arriving. In similar circumstances, Pappenheim hallucinated a black snake coming from the wall to bite the sick man. When she tried to drive it away, she

8. Breuer, "Fräulein Anna O.," 25.
9. Freud and Breuer, *Studies on Hysteria*, 13.

found her arm paralyzed and saw her hands turn into little snakes with death's-heads at the fingertips. Her cough developed when she heard dance music coming from a neighboring house, felt a sudden wish to leave her father's bedside, and was overcome by self-reproach. Thereafter she coughed nervously whenever she heard rhythmical music. Pappenheim hallucinated her father's face as a death's-head and then saw her own reflection in a mirror as the same image. Having lost her sisters to childhood deaths and apparently wishing for the termination of her father's agonizing illness, which she imitated with her cough, Pappenheim was preoccupied with skeletons. When Siegmund Pappenheim died, his daughter had to be removed to the country to protect her from suicidal impulses. Perhaps she wanted to join him in death, and perhaps she wanted to escape from guilt generated by what must have been a liberation and a relief. She had lost a patient "of whom she was passionately fond."

Pappenheim's hysteria arose from sources in her life history typical of her time. It was not uncommon in the nineteenth century for the potential of daughters to be sacrificed while sons were educated and privileged; it was also in keeping with prevailing customs for young women to be called upon to nurse aging and ill parents. Neither Pappenheim nor Breuer could consciously express the ambivalent emotions such situations would arouse. Although Breuer recognized Bertha's grief for her father's death as a cause of her symptoms, he overlooked the hostility, anger, guilt, and frustrated sexuality apparent to psychoanalysts.[10] Even a nonpsychoanalytic reading of the case indicates that Pappenheim found her existence lonely and tedious.

Late in her life Pappenheim thought of her lack of formal education as "defective spiritual nourishment," a reference that may illuminate the anorexic symptoms of her hysteria—her way of literalizing through her body her felt psychic condition.[11] Breuer uses a similar metaphor of undernourishment to describe Anna O.: "She possessed a powerful intellect which would have been capable of digesting solid mental

10. See Pollock, "Childhood Object Loss" and "Pappenheim's Pathological Mourning: Possible Effects of Childhood Sibling Loss," *Journal of the American Psychoanalytic Association*, 20 (1972), 476–93; Richard Karpe, "The Rescue Complex in Anna O.'s Final Identity," *Psychoanalytic Quarterly* 30 (1961), 1–27; and Marc Hollender, "The Case of Anna O: A Reformulation," *American Journal of Psychiatry*, 137 (1980), 797–800.

11. Ellen M. Jensen, "Anna O.—A Study of Her Later Life," *Psychoanalytic Quarterly*, 39 (1970), 277.

pabulum and which stood in need of it—though without receiving it after she had left school."[12] Once Dr. Breuer interrupted his visits to her for several days because he had to leave Vienna; Bertha went entirely without food during his absence.

At the time she fell ill Bertha Pappenheim must have wanted someone to talk with, someone to listen to her elaborate stories.[13] Breuer provided an audience for her mental creations. He increased by one the attendance at her "private theatre." Although Breuer had arrived as an old-fashioned physician with black bag in hand to treat Bertha Pappenheim's malady, she quickly changed the terms of the relationship by falling into autohypnosis and commencing to mutter in an apparently absentminded state. She was clearly intrigued by the good-looking and highly cultivated, successful doctor. Although Breuer does not say so, his account of Bertha Pappenheim's behavior suggests that she tried to seduce him, and that in a way she was successful. We are told about the various massages she received on her head and legs—standard treatments for paralysis. What was unusual, and the beginning of what developed into psychoanalysis, involved the long hours they spent in hypnosis together while Pappenheim told sad and fanciful stories and "talked herself out" until "she was clear in mind, calm, and cheerful." Breuer attributed her cheerfulness to the talking, not to his presence on the scene. During the course of their treatment Breuer spent a medically unprecedented amount of time in his patient's company, visiting her nearly every day between the end of 1880 and the middle of 1882, often more than once a day, listening to the most minute details of her present and past life, repeating set phrases from her stories to get her narratives started each session. Although Breuer states that Bertha Pappenheim was "astonishingly underdeveloped" sexually, every commentator has remarked on her physical attractions. There can be little doubt that Bertha fantasized a love affair with Breuer; and indeed, the infatuation seems to have been mutual, although unconscious on Breuer's part. Pappenheim refused to recognize her relatives and ignored all unwanted strangers, but she always had eyes for Breuer. According to Freud, her image of the treatment as "chimney sweeping" was a metaphor for sexual

12. Breuer, "Fräulein Anna O.," 21.

13. In 1890 Pappenheim published a book of short stories called *In the Rummage Store*, under the pseudonym Paul Berthold. The masculine name reverses her initials.

intercourse.[14] After many months of hearing reports of this fascinating patient, Mrs. Breuer finally grew jealous and angry. Surprised and probably feeling guilty as well, Breuer suddenly determined to end the treatment. He announced his intention to Pappenheim and prepared to depart on a trip to Venice with his wife. According to Freud, Pappenheim responded with an "untoward event."[15] She staged a hysterical childbirth to summon Breuer back for another session. He was shocked to find her in bed with abdominal cramps, which she explained with the words "Now Dr. Breuer's child is coming!"[16] He calmed her with hypnosis and then fled the house, abandoning her to a colleague. He never saw her again, and later when he heard that she was ill, he wished she would die and so cease to be miserable.[17] Breuer chose not to report the fantasy childbirth in the published version of the case history of Anna O., and he never acknowledged the erotic element in their attachment. This omission and repression might be explained by Breuer's fear of a scandal; and if he perceived that Pappenheim had been playing a role to allure him, he may have feared that publishing the story would not only compromise him but make him appear foolish as well. But his private obsession with the case after he had given it up, his reluctance to present any account of it publicly, and his ultimate rejection of psychoanalysis indicate that other causes contributed to the absence of the final scene from his report in *Studies on Hysteria*, which gives the false impression that Anna's hysteria had disappeared.

George Pollock traces Breuer's anxiety to the loss of his young and attractive mother in childbirth when he was three or four years old. She, as well as Breuer's oldest daughter, about eleven years old at the time of his relationship with the famous patient, was named Bertha.[18] When Freud began to uncover the role of transference love in hypnosis and psychoanalysis, and to stress the importance of sexuality in neuroses, Breuer dissociated himself from his controversial young col-

14. Freud to Carl Jung, November 21, 1909, quoted in Pollock, "Childhood Object Loss," 732.

15. *Standard Edition*, XIV, 12.

16. Reported by Freud in a letter to Stefan Zweig, 1932, quoted in Pollock, "Childhood Object Loss," 716.

17. Jones, *Life and Work*, I, 225.

18. Pollock, "Childhood Object Loss." In *The Story of Anna O.* (New York: Walker, 1972), 26, Lucy Freeman recounts that the two Berthas, patient and daughter, once went for a springtime carriage ride together with Breuer. Freeman depicts Pappenheim as unresponsive during the trip and depressed afterward.

league. Although Pappenheim had led the way to the unconscious through her invention of the "talking cure" and her dramatization of transference love in the doctor-patient relation, Breuer resisted the implications of their encounter. Freud reports that Breuer repeatedly read to him pieces of the case history during 1882 and 1883, but objected vehemently to publishing the story of the treatment. Freud decided to tell Charcot about what he saw as a great discovery. Charcot listened but showed no interest. Ten years later Breuer agreed to a joint publication because Freud convinced him that Pierre Janet's work in French anticipated some of his results, such as the tracing back of hysterical symptoms to events in the patient's life and their removal by means of hypnotic reproduction.

Although I think the evident oedipal configurations in Pappenheim's encounter with Breuer are significant, I want to focus for a moment on the oral dimension of their relationship. A recent discussion of transference wishes links the unconscious meanings of the doctor-patient relation to the universal craving for the omnipotent mother of early infancy. Summarizing Leo Stone, Janet Malcolm writes:

> This craving ... can be activated by doctors, politicians, clergymen, and teachers as well as by analysts. Stone draws a ... distinction between the meaning of the primary transference generated by the physician and that generated by the analyst. While the physician's direct physical and emotional ministrations correspond to those of the "omniscient, omnipotent, and unintelligible" mother of the earliest period of infancy, the analyst's activities resemble (in unconscious reverberation) the not so agreeable ones of the mother in the months when the infant is learning to talk and to separate from her—"that period of life where all the modalities of bodily intimacy and direct dependence on the mother are being relinquished or attentuated, *pari passu* with the rapid development of the great vehicle of communication by speech." It is in this state of "intimate separation," or "deprivation in intimacy," that analysis is conducted, deriving its mutative power from the tension between verbal closeness and emotional distance.[19]

In psychosexual development, linguistically constituted subjectivity ("I" versus "you," "he" versus "she," and syntactical relations) is superimposed on our rhythmical, corporeal rapport with the mother. Before we enter the grammatical order of language, we exist in a

19. Janet Malcolm, "The Impossible Profession," *New Yorker*, November 24, 1980, 104.

dyadic, semiotic world of pure sound and body rhythms, oceanically at one with our nurturer. Out of the infinite potential identities each newborn infant brings into the world, a single way of being is activated according to the way the mother behaves in oral symbiosis. The mother's style of relating communicates the unconscious significance the infant has for her. Through her body language—holding, nursing, caressing, bathing, dressing—and then through mirroring, through the image the child forms of itself as it sees itself reflected in the mother's face, especially in her eyes, the mother communicates an identity to the child. As Heinz Lichtenstein describes it, the mother "seduces the child into life" in the same way that the sun activates tropism in a plant and so shapes its form and direction.[20] Our sense of ourselves as separate beings, as "subjects," is bound up with our entry into the order of language, in which speech becomes a substitute for bodily connection. The world we as children enter is always already constituted and governed by language. When we accede to the world where communication in words allows both separation and intimacy, we are relinquishing the immediacy of semiotic and corporeal rapport with our nurturer, from whom we recognize our separation.

A child reared in a family such as Bertha Pappenheim's makes her transition to speech as part of the process according to which she recognizes the father's privileged relation to the mother. In the order of language, "I" and "you" conceptualize and mark separate persons, as "she" and "he," "mother" and "father" differentiate genders and roles. Although it is usually the mother who activates an infant's capacity for speech in the oral, semiotic stage, subjectivity in the sense of being a separate, syntactical agent, a grammatical "subject," comes later in childhood, when, in the patriarchal family, the father's role is being recognized. Discovery of the father's role in the primal scene and recognition of male dominance in the social world conjoin with the integration of the patriarchal child into the systematic organization of language. The interlocking of linguistic with cultural rules suggests an equation between the organization of language and the systematic organization of patriarchal culture and its sexually differentiated, oedipal subjectivity. In patriarchal socialization, the power to formulate

20. Heinz Lichtenstein, "Identity and Sexuality," *Journal of the American Psychoanalytic Association*, 9 (1961), 179–260. See also D. W. Winnicott, "Mirror-Role of Mother and Family in Child Development," in *The Predicament of the Family*, ed. Peter Lomas (London: Hogarth, 1972), 26–33.

sentences coincides developmentally with a recognition of the power of the father.

In this light, Bertha Pappenheim's linguistic discord and conversion symptoms, her use of gibberish and gestures as means of expression, can be seen as a regression from the cultural order represented by her father as an orthodox patriarch. Bertha Pappenheim was "unable" to speak her native language, but could be fluent in alien forms of expression. She failed to speak coherent German, but she succeeded in getting Dr. Breuer to speak her language and enter a world repressed by patriarchal consciousness. Breuer literally repeated Pappenheim's linguistic formulas and in this way came to an awareness of the unconscious. Bertha was twenty-one, on the brink of womanhood in a role that offered little in the way of satisfaction or development of her intellectual gifts. When she looked into the mirror she saw a death's-head. Rejecting the cultural identity offered her, she tried to translate herself into another idiom. She regressed from the symbolic order of articulate German to the semiotic level of the body and the unintelligibility of foreign tongues. Her communication in signs, mutterings, and made-up jargon indicates an attempt to recreate the special semiotic babble that exists between an infant and its mother.

Pappenheim reached the point of having to be fed by Breuer. She turned Breuer into a surrogate oral mother; in the sense that she took over his role as doctor, she turned him into an identity-giver as well. Her final birth fantasy can be read as a wish to bring a new identity and perhaps a new reality into the world.

Dr. Breuer was evidently not prepared for the idea that Pappenheim was giving birth to something. But he seems to have understood her situation admirably. Here is his analysis of the predisposing causes of her hysteria:

> (1) Her monotonous family life and the absence of adequate intellectual occupation left her with an unemployed surplus of mental liveliness and energy, and this found an outlet in the constant activity of her imagination.
> (2) This led to a habit of daydreaming (her private theatre), which laid the foundations for a dissociation of her mental personality.[21]

In other words, Bertha Pappenheim was schizoid because she was bored and needed to both watch and put on shows. She was alienated,

21. Breuer, "Fräulein Anna O.," 41.

split between what Breuer began to call "the unconscious" or "secondary" state and her "normal" state. Breuer adds that although her two states were sharply separated, not only did the "secondary" (or "hypnoid") state intrude into the first one, but also "a clear-sighted and calm observer sat, as she put it, in a corner of her brain and looked on at all the mad business." Pappenheim later confessed to Breuer the persistence of clear thinking in the midst of her madness. After her conversion symptoms had ceased and while she was passing through what Breuer called a temporary depression, Pappenheim told him that "the whole business had been simulated." He concludes:

> I have already described the astonishing fact that from the beginning to the end of the illness all the stimuli arising from the secondary state, together with their consequences, were permanently removed by being given verbal utterance in hypnosis, and I have only to add an assurance that this was not an invention of mine which I imposed on the patient by suggestion. It took me completely by surprise, and not until symptoms had been got rid of in this way in a whole series of instances did I develop a therapeutic technique out of it.[22]

Thus Pappenheim actually treated herself, with Breuer as her student.

One may well ask how it was that Bertha Pappenheim managed to achieve such a breakthrough. It seems that she was influenced by the widespread interest in catharsis which followed the publication of a book by the uncle of a friend of hers. This friend was Freud's future wife, Martha Bernays, whose uncle, Jacob Bernays, published a study of the Aristotelian concept of catharsis in 1880. Bernays' book was widely discussed by scholars and became an important topic of conversation in Viennese salons. Perhaps Pappenheim had been introduced to the concept of catharsis as a method of dramatizing and expelling emotions and then put it to use as a means of capturing and holding the attention of her scientifically minded physician.[23] Since women of Pappenheim's day remained outside the official cultural institutions that transmitted knowledge, as a teacher Pappenheim was limited in her form of discourse. She made a spectacle of herself in order to resolve the tension between her guilt and her desire to escape

---

22. Breuer, "Fräulein Anna O.," 46.
23. Ellenberger, *Discovery of the Unconscious*, 484; Hollender, "Case of Anna O.," 797.

familial exploitation.[24] Her knowledge of the unconscious (her "clouds") was expressed in a distressed and distressing way. This knowledge had then to be *theorized* by men. She presented a startling and engaging demonstration of the purely psychological, affective causes of hysteria, but Dr. Breuer went away still believing in the somatic foundation of hysterical phenomena. It was left to Freud to complete the shift from physiological to psychological study and to articulate in a scientific way the central role of eros in therapeutic relationships, a major transition in the history of psychiatry.

Bertha Pappenheim invented the "talking cure" in an epoch that needed to tell itself its troubles. An important figure in the history of consciousness, she expressed in the language of the body what psychoanalysis says in words. I think we can regard her in terms Erik Erikson has used to describe ideological leaders: "Individuals with an uncommon depth of conflict, they also have uncanny gifts, and uncanny luck with which they offer to the crisis of a generation the solution of their own crisis."[25]

In the process of talking herself out to Breuer, Pappenheim converted a nonverbal message, expressed in body language or pantomime and called a hysterical symptom, into a verbal language. That is, her narratives converted or translated a message from one language into another.[26] She was a psychodramatist, complete with appropriate scenic arrangements for the reproduction of crucial events; and she devised the method of narrating back piece by piece the story of each symptom to reach its source.[27] In a technique comparable to Shakespeare's in the play-within-the-play in *Hamlet*, Pappenheim put on a dumb show in distraction, muttered, and then spoke out the story behind the show. She restaged the origins of her symptoms in order to undo them. This is ritual as catharsis. Breuer's recognition that the patient's symptoms disappeared as soon as the event that had given

24. Compare Catherine Clément, *La Jeune Née* (Paris: Union Générale, 1975), 13, 22.

25. Erik H. Erikson, "Youth: Fidelity and Diversity," *Daedalus*, 91 (1962), 24.

26. Hollender, "Case of Anna O.," 798.

27. On the day Bertha Pappenheim regained her command of German, she rearranged the furniture to resemble her father's sickroom. Having decided in advance that the day of her cure was at hand, Bertha reproduced on schedule the original scene when snakes had appeared and she prayed in English. For this dramatic representation, she chose the anniversary of the day on which she had been moved to the country. Breuer reports that this ritual freed Bertha from "innumerable disturbances" ("Fräulein Anna O.," 40).

rise to them was reproduced in a trance enabled him "to arrive at a therapeutic technical procedure which left nothing to be desired in its logical consistency and systematic application." Each individual symptom in Bertha's museum of "hyperaesthetic" memories was taken up separately, and the occasions on which it had appeared were described in reverse order, starting before the time when she became bedridden and going back to the event that had led to its first appearance. According to Breuer, "when this had been described the symptom was permanently removed."[28] In dramatizing her past, Pappenheim was also dramatizing the unconscious, and she was engaging her audience in an oedipal repetition in the form of Breuer's countertransference.

I have said that Bertha turned Breuer into a substitute oral mother, audience, and identity-giver in order to escape the crisis of cultural identity occasioned by her father's terminal illness, and I have described her as a psychodramatist who enacted the birth to consciousness of a new psychic reality. Through her clever manipulations of languages, she managed to avoid the role of dutiful orthodox daughter and find an intelligent, stimulating, and sympathetic listener. Pappenheim's entry into public life remains to be discussed. She became a feminist in an epoch when women felt compelled to speak up against the abuses that paralyzed their development.

In the same year that Freud and Breuer published *Studies on Hysteria*, Pappenheim at the age of thirty-six became headmistress of an orphanage she founded in Isenburg, Germany, near her mother's birthplace. The orphanage became the central headquarters for her forty-year career in philanthropic social work, later commemorated by the West German government. She spent her life rescuing and sheltering abandoned and abused women and children.

She was particularly active in opposing the "white slave" trade, in which young girls were sold into prostitution. Well known as a caustic and formidable war-horse, she had many enemies among orthodox Jewish men who resented her exposure of Jewish complicity in the traffic in women. Organizations that pretended to secure identity papers for young Jewish girls and promised them safe-conduct to immigrate would meet the girls at train stations and then send them to work in houses of prostitution. To oppose this traffic, Pappenheim made numerous voyages of investigation and intervention. She trav-

28. Breuer, "Fräulein Anna O.," 35.

eled to brothels in Eastern Europe and the Middle East, and she participated aggressively in various international congresses for suppression of the white slave trade. She went to Russia and to Rumania, where she interviewed the queen. Pappenheim hated the double standard of sex and saw brothels as a degradation of all women. Distraught that boys in their early teens were frequenting brothels, she declared, "This is how they, the future lawmakers, get to know the female sex—as it appears despicable to them."[29]

Pappenheim's struggle for social reforms focused on the liberation of women, in particular Jewish women, whom she saw as "beasts of burden" to men.[30] A regular reader of the journal *The Women*, Pappenheim admired its editor, Helene Lange, the main theoretician of the German women's movement of the 1890s. German feminist demands for educational and career opportunities for women appealed to Pappenheim, who remained resentful throughout her life that she had not been allowed to continue formal education beyond high school, which she left at the age of sixteen. She translated Mary Wollstonecraft's *A Vindication of the Rights of Woman*, an argument for equal educational opportunity, and she contributed to the call for women's political rights. In 1899 she wrote a play titled *Women's Rights*, dramatizing women's powerlessness and exploitation by men.

Inspired by German feminists and by the tradition of Jewish women's charity work, Pappenheim started an organization in Frankfurt called Care by Women, and in 1904 she cofounded the Jüdischer Frauenbund, the League of Jewish Women, over which she presided for many years with remarkable determination. As a social worker and feminist, Pappenheim attracted many followers. She delivered speeches in England, Canada, and the United States.

As Jewish women's consciousness developed, many resented the idea of male-led women's charities. A Frauenbund member recalled her former association with one such group: "The women sat quietly, while the male chairman read the annual report. Then they were allowed to nod their approval." The Frauenbund gave its members a sense of independence and purpose. Whereas it was traditional for only men to speak up in the Jewish community, Bertha Pappenheim taught through practical examples that "women had as much right to be heard as men."[31]

29. Kaplan, *Jewish Feminist Movement*, 114.
30. Israël, *L'Hystérique*, 203.
31. Kaplan, *Jewish Feminist Movement*, 68.

Throughout her life Pappenheim lived according to an international feminist ethic. "Her vision transcended all borders."[32] Her facility with languages and her willingness to embody her ideas served her well in her role as world traveler and speechmaker in the service of redressing international crimes against women and children. In anticipation of her posthumous fame, Pappenheim composed five mordant obituaries for herself. For the *Israelite*, an Orthodox Jewish publication, she wrote, "She was by descent and training an Orthodox woman, she believed herself separated from her roots—obviously under revolutionary feminist influence—she was often hostile—but she did not defy her origins. With her descent she should have done more for Orthodoxy—let us remember that her father was a cofounder of the Schiffschul at Vienna. What a pity!" All five obituaries end with the line "What a pity!"[33] These obituaries indicate with irony how orthodox Jewish partiarchal values continued to haunt Pappenheim and how she was determined to have the last word. While visiting a mosque in Constantinople, Pappenheim meditated on what her parents might think of her: "Now instead of being married as our old *Sedergast* [Passover feast guest] always hoped, their daughter, traveling, is occupied with ideas which had no place in the world of her parents. This often disturbs me, but they would not have been able to foresee my development."[34]

In linking the two phases of her career, Lucien Israël classifies Pappenheim as one of a number of celebrated hysterics who later led altruistic public lives, substituting themselves for a male mentor who failed them.[35] Israël analyzes such women as "successful hysterics," whom he sees as founding their vocations on a fantasy of universal love and a sense of rivalry with men. The Pappenheim case, claims Israël, demonstrates very clearly that the universal love embodied in her career as rescuer of women and children was originally directed at a specific person chosen as mentor. But the mentor, or more precisely "master" (*maître*), Breuer, failing to reciprocate her love, be-

---

32. Holy Land Philatelist, Israel's Stamps, June 1955. Quoted in Jensen, "Anna O.," 270.

33. Edinger, *Bertha Pappenheim*, 99.

34. Bertha Pappenheim, *Sisyphus-Arbeit* (Leipzig, 1924), quoted in Jensen, "Anna O.," 275.

35. Israël, *L'Hystérique*, 204–5. Israël cites Mary Baker and several of Pierre Janet's patients as other examples. He states that a public career as a savior is one possible evolution of hysteria.

came an object of identification who was replaced by Pappenheim herself. Having discovered that the doctor is not all the patient had hoped, "successful hysterics" decide to incarnate his role as therapist, savior, "helper of humanity."

Israël's analysis overlooks the fact that charity work was a tradition among Pappenheim's maternal relatives. That she identified herself with the role of savior is consistent with my view of her as an Eriksonian leader who forged her charisma out of her postadolescent identity crisis. Pappenheim chose to make Breuer the gift of her symptoms and their treatment because of what he stood for as a doctor. She chose him for a significant encounter involving issues that were bigger than both of them. Ideological leaders feel that their lives must be made to count in the great historical movements of their day. The two great historical movements of Pappenheim's day were the discovery of the unconscious and the liberation of women. She made herself heard in both of them. The range of her career as a reformer indicates that Bertha Pappenheim was "in love with activity on a large scale," a phrase Erikson adopts from Woodrow Wilson to describe the qualities of which charismatic leaders are made.[36]

Although it may be true that Pappenheim's performances for Breuer were inspired by a book she had read on catharsis, one must speculate about what currents may have been at work among her hysterical counterparts in Germany and France throughout the nineteenth century, and slightly later in Switzerland, when psychoanalysis was introduced into the Burghölzli clinic. One must wonder what inspired "Elizabeth von R." to suggest the free-association method.

The nature of Pappenheim's symptoms and their treatment connect her with several other remarkable women. As Henri Ellenberger observes, aspects of Pappenheim's hysteria have never been satisfactorily explained. First of all, between December 1881 and June 1882 Pappenheim's two personalities were sharply distinct, and Breuer was able to effect a shift from one to the other by holding up an orange, the food she had chiefly lived on during the previous year. While one part of Bertha existed in the present, another part relived the previous year precisely, day by day. Thanks to a diary Mrs. Pappenheim had kept, Breuer was able to verify that the events Bertha hallucinated had occurred, day by day, exactly one year earlier. Second, certain of Bertha's symptoms supposedly occurred without an incubation pe-

36. Erikson, "Youth," 24.

riod and could be made to disappear simply by recall of the circumstances in which they had appeared the first time. Bertha had to recall all instances when the symptom had appeared, whatever the number, in exact chronological order, a unique feature of her treatment. These remarkable exercises in memory and the idea of the patient dictating appropriate therapeutic procedures to the physician, although extraordinary in the 1880s in Vienna, were not unheard of in the history of medicine. Ellenberger links Pappenheim's case with the great exemplars of "magnetic illness" who achieved fame during the early part of the nineteenth century. Katharina Emmerick (1774–1824), a poor peasant and former nun from Dülmen, Westphalia, had dreams every night that followed one another in a regular sequence according to the cycle of the liturgical year, a mnemonic feat comparable to Pappenheim's recall of each day of the previous year in exact sequence. Another subject, Friedericke Hauffe (1801–29), "the Seeress of Prevorst," spoke frequently in an unknown language, and although uneducated and the daughter of a gamekeeper, she delivered recitatives in the purest High German instead of the Swabian dialect commonly spoken by the people around her. In her "magnetic" trances the "Seeress" often prescribed treatments that unfailingly cured her exactly when predicted, just as Anna predicted the date of her recovery to Breuer. Estelle L'Hardy (1825–62), who fell ill upon her father's death, was cured of a dual personality through the dictations of a comforting angel who appeared to her during "magnetic" sleep. Her doctor managed a gradual fusion of her normal and "magnetic" states by establishing an emotional rapport that challenged Estelle's dependency on her mother. Like Anna, Estelle relied on a special relationship with her physician for her cure. Ellenberger sees Pappenheim as a kind of *revenant* of the "magnetic" patients who performed miraculous feats of memory, spoke in tongues, controlled the forms of their treatment, and predicted the dates of their "cures."[37]

Another analogue to Bertha Pappenheim is her Parisian contemporary Blanche Wittmann, known as "the queen of the hysterics" because of the impressive sculptural forms of her poses and the longevity of her engagement at the Salpêtrière Hospital. Wittmann figures in André Brouillet's painting of Drs. Jean-Martin Charcot and Joseph Babinski demonstrating hypnosis (Fig. 1) as well as in several photographs that appear in the Salpêtrière journals of the 1890s. Witt-

---

37. Ellenberger, *Discovery of the Unconscious*, 484.

Figure 1. A Clinical Lecture at the Salpêtrière, 1887. André Brouillet's painting shows Jean-Martin Charcot and Blanche Wittman demonstrating hysteria to a select audience of physicians and writers, probably at one of the famous *leçons du Mardi.* Behind Charcot is his disciple Joseph Babinski. Two nurses stand ready to sustain Wittmann when she falls on the stretcher, where she will display her full-fledged crisis. Wittman's eyes are closed and the top of her dress is down around her waist. Henri Ellenberger thinks that the painter has involuntarily shown Charcot's "fatal error": Charcot's verbal explanations and the picture on the wall suggest to the patient the pose she is beginning to enact. This painting, reproduced from Ellenberger's *Discovery of the Unconscious* (New York: Basic Books, 1970), is at L'Hôpital Pierre Wertheimer in Bron, a suburb of Lyon, France. Freud kept a print of it in his consulting room.

mann's hysteria and Charcot's role as therapist belong to a powerful iconographic tradition. Charcot worked under the aegis of Robert Fleury's painting of Dr. Philippe Pinel liberating the madwomen from their chains (Fig. 2); and Blanche Wittmann's pose in A Clinical Lecture at the Salpêtrière is apparently an allusion to Henry Fuseli's Nightmare (Fig. 3). As Freud's metaphor of hysteria as a "museum of monuments" to "hyperaesthetic memories" indicates, hysteria and art history are connected. Pappenheim became a literary artist and sponsor to other artists. The Salpêtrière hysterics were inspirations to the surrealists, who in 1928 published reproductions from the rich archives of Salpêtrière photographs. Louis Aragon and André Breton held the study of hysteria to be the greatest poetic discovery of the end of the nineteenth century.[38] The experiments with traumatic paralysis and their reproduction under hypnosis which Freud witnessed at the Salpêtrière are today regarded with scientific skepticism. Ellenberger concludes that Pappenheim's treatment was a clever trick. Yet her story and Charcot's séances were major inspirations to Freud.

During her hysteria Anna O. had taken up writing in a curious fashion. Her right hand being paralyzed, she wrote with her left hand in printed roman letters copied from her edition of Shakespeare. Such incorporation of foreign signifiers may have been linked to her desire for psychic integration. Anna's foray into scholarly language prefigures Bertha Pappenheim's later role as a translator. Pappenheim resurrected and translated the memoirs of her ancestor Glückel of Hameln (1646–1724), who was a "born writer and storyteller." Wishing to transmit Jewish culture to a world ignorant of Yiddish, Pappenheim translated into German sagas and legends from the Talmud and Midrash, together with folk tales and The Women's Bible.[39] I accord special significance to the sundry languages Pappenheim spoke in her hysteria and in later life. Her use of translation as a verbal strategy reverberates in psychoanalytic preoccupation with the term and the process. Jacques Lacan calls psychotherapy the "repatriation of alienated signifiers."

Freud refers to the Anna O. case more than forty times in his collected works and frequently in his letters. The intensity of interest these references indicate suggests that she emblematized something essential for him. At the time he was working out his theory of hysteria,

38. Louis Aragon and André Breton, "Le Cinquantenaire de l'hystérie," La Révolution surrealiste, 11 (1928).
39. Jensen, "Anna O," 288.

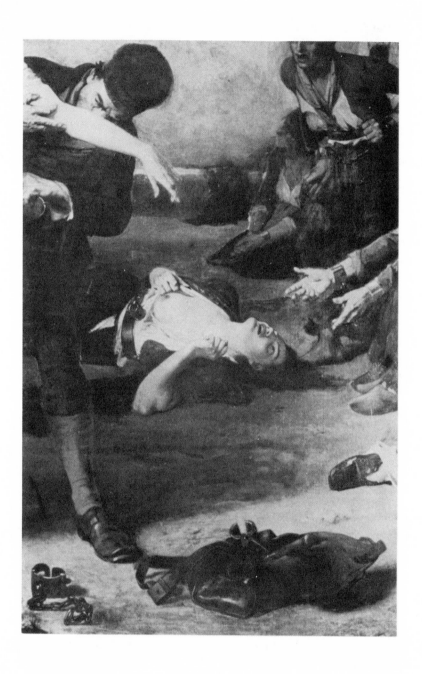

Freud was translating Bernheim and Charcot from French into German; his and Breuer's "Preliminary Communication" on the subject was immediately translated into Spanish, French, and English. Freud compared the symptomatology of hysteria to a "pictographic script which has become intelligible after the discovery of a few bilingual inscriptions." Freud uses the word "translation" to discuss the work of psychoanalysis and the work of the unconscious. In the "dream-work," the latent wish is "translated" into the imagery of the manifest content of the dream. Freud writes: "The dream-thoughts and the dream-content are presented to us like two versions of the same subject-matter in two different languages. Or, more properly, the dream-content seems like a transcript of the dream-thoughts into another mode of expression, whose characters and syntactic laws it is our business to discover by comparing the original and the translation."[40] In hysteria, psychic messages are "translated" into somatic expression. Analytic interventions are considered "translations" of the unconscious into the conscious. The "talking cure" is the "translation of affects into words." Repression for Freud is a "failure of translation." The forms in which Anna O. communicated her distress and her shifts between languages to express levels of consciousness metaphorize what developed into a psychoanalytic concept of translation.[41]

D. W. Winnicott has said that he never had a patient who could

40. Freud, *The Interpretation of Dreams*, in *Standard Edition*, IV, 277.

41. In "Freud's Psychoanalytical Concept of Translation," a paper delivered at the Congress of the International Association for Semiotic Studies, Vienna, July 1979, Patrick J. Mahony discussed the recurrence in psychoanalysis of the idea of translation. See Mahony's "Toward the Understanding of Translation in Psychoanalysis," *Journal of the American Psychoanalytic Association*, 28 (1980), 461–75.

Figure 2. Detail from Robert Fleury's *Pinel Delivering the Madwomen of the Salpêtrière*, 1878. This is the highlight of a large tableau mounted at the entrance to the Bibliothèque Charcot at L'Hôpital Salpêtrière in Paris. The centrally placed figure has just been freed of handcuffs; a locked belt is still around her waist. A chain and cuff, just removed, and a bag of tools for unfastening them lie on the ground near the foot of the attendant on the left, who supports a patient while freeing her waist of a metal belt. The left side of the tableau surrounding this detail shows Pinel dressed as an Enlightenment gentleman and worshiped as a liberator of madwomen. One patient is on her knees kissing his hand. The right side of the picture shows several women still in chains. Philippe Pinel (1745–1862) was chief physician of the Salpêtrière, where, just after the French Revolution, he took the unprecedented step of freeing the patients from their chains. In his obituary of Charcot, Freud compared him to Pinel. This reproduction was photographed from Georges Didi-Huberman's *Invention de l'hystérie* (Paris: Macula, 1982).

give back an interpretation that "wasn't a translation." We translate intrapsychically and interpersonally. Many of us read Freud in translation. Jacques Lacan is frequently read in translation. Freud conducted several analyses in translation. Particularly since its expulsion from Germany, psychoanalysis has been a multilingual movement.

Lucien Israël says that the question of whether or not hysteria is an illness has received no answer. His analysis of Bertha Pappenheim is close to the idea that feminism is transformed hysteria, or more precisely that hysteria is feminism lacking a social network in the outer world. The fact that in popular culture the word "hysterical" is often used in attempts to discredit feminist expression seems to derive from the idea that both hysterics and feminists are "out of control": neither hysterics nor feminists cooperate dutifully with patriarchal conventions. I think the attempted discrediting of feminists as "hysterical" comes from a repressive impulse similar to the defense that creates hysterical symptoms in the first place—repudiation of socially untoward feelings such as anger and resentment. Hysteria can be consid-

---

Figure 3. Henry Fuseli, *The Nightmare*, third version, 1790–91. This icon, which was widely reproduced throughout the Romantic era, suggests how male psychological concerns manifest themselves in images of women. According to H. W. Janson, Fuseli's representation of the nightmare is a projection of the painter's unfulfilled passion for Anna Landolt, whose portrait appears on the reverse side of the first version of the painting (H. W. Janson, "Fuseli's *Nightmare*," *Arts and Sciences*, 2 (1963), 23–28). Landolt was the niece of Fuseli's close friend Johann Lavater, the Swiss physiognomist. Lavater and Landolt were involved with spiritualist and mesmerist groups in Zurich, where Fuseli met and fell in love with her. When he learned that she had married a merchant, Fuseli wrote to Lavater from London that he dreamed recurrently of lying in her bed and fusing "her body and her soul" together with his own. Fuseli's frustration and jealousy found expression in this demonic transformation of the idea of the union of Psyche and Eros, soul and body, which in Greek myth is figured in the nighttime visitation of the bridegroom, the love god Eros, to Psyche, his bride. Fuseli imagines that *his* love for Anna Landolt haunts *her* at night in the form of unpleasant dreams. The sleeping woman whose arms and breasts lean back over the bed is visited by the incubus crouching on her breast. The "nightmare" on which the incubus travels sticks its head through the bed curtains as a ghostly spectator. See Bert Schiff and Werner Hoffman, *Henry Fuseli, 1741–1825*; and Peter Tomoroy, *The Life and Work of Henry Fuseli* (New York: Praeger, 1972). Freud owned a print of *The Nightmare*, which hung in his study in Vienna. The similarities in pose between Fleury's highlighted madwoman, Brouillet's representation of Wittmann in hypnotic trance, and Fuseli's projection of Anna Landolt as sleeping Psyche suggest to me that hysteria as a system of gestures is based on and perpetuates a mythic and iconic tradition. As a visible mode of expression, hysteria seems to invite spectacular treatment. Courtesy of the Goethemuseum, Frankfurt am Main, Federal Republic of Germany.

ered as a self-repudiating form of feminine discourse in which the body signifies what social conditions make it impossible to state linguistically. Aragon and Breton's celebration of nineteenth-century hysterics as fellow artists indicates that the surrealists recognized hysteria as an expressive discourse; and, we may add, it was a discourse of femininity addressed to patriarchal thought.

By seeing hysteria as a way of making the unconscious conscious, we can then think of Bertha Pappenheim as a forebear of psychoanalytic feminism. When the phrase "psychoanalytic feminism" is used, one may wonder whether feminism has appropriated psychoanalysis or psychoanalysis has appropriated feminism. Psychoanalysis entered the history of consciousness in dialogue with the subjectivity of women. Freud's discovery of the unconscious was a response to the body language of nineteenth-century hysterics. Psychoanalysis can be seen as a translation into theory of the language of hysteria. Although hysteria is associated mainly with women, Freud and Charcot demonstrated that male hysteria exists; notably, it is a function of the repressed femininity of men. At one point Freud analyzed himself as a hysteric.

Hysteria expresses in the language of the body what psychoanalysis says in words. Both psychoanalysis and hysteria subvert the reigning cultural order by exploding its linguistic conventions and decomposing its facade of orderly conduct. Both the psychoanalytic and the feminist movements are in my view intrinsically international and interlingual. I believe that the psychoanalysis of hysteria in France and Austria in the nineteenth century has contributed to the multilingualism, internationalism, and communication in translation of much contemporary feminist writing.[42] In *The Dream of a Common Language* Adrienne Rich writes, "We are translations into different dialects / of a text still

42. Anna O.'s attempt to change her world through manipulation of language on the level of the signifiers, as if language were omnipotent, prefigures some of the strategies of Mary Daly and certain contemporary French writers. See the Index of New Words in Daly's *Gyn/Ecology: The Metaethics of Radical Feminism* (Boston: Beacon, 1978); and the issue of *Les Cahiers du grif* titled "parlez-vous française?" (vol. 12, June 1976, published at Paris and Brussels). This volume, which includes articles by Françoise Collin, Luce Irigaray, and Jacqueline Aubenas, among others, proposes various spoken and written languages of the female body and some ways of feminizing the French language. Viviane Forrester's novel *Vestiges* (Paris: Seuil, 1978) is written in French and English. Hélène Cixous's *vivre l'orange* (Paris: des femmes, 1979), written in French and English, incorporates Portuguese, Italian, and German. I think Pappenheim's polylingualism prefigures the explosion of the conventions of language in contemporary feminist writing.

being written / in the original."[43] As a speaker in tongues, Anna O. represents a significant event in this unfolding. Bertha Pappenheim's psychodrama with Josef Breuer in the 1880s personifies the relationship between the body language of hysteria and psychoanalytic entrance into the history of consciousness. The hysteric's seduction of her doctor is at the heart of the introduction of the body into theory which is the psychoanalytic contribution to consciousness raising, beginning with Anna O.

43. Adrienne Rich, "Sibling Mysteries," in *The Dream of a Common Language* (New York: Norton, 1978), 51.

PART II

Rereading Patriarchal Texts

5

"This Is and Is Not Cressid": The Characterization of Cressida

JANET ADELMAN

When Troilus responds to the sight of Diomed's Cressida with the words that I have taken for the title of this essay, we feel, as so often in this play of divisions, a divided duty. On the one hand, we are bound to respond responsibly to Troilus' attempt to preserve his illusions at any cost as mad, a near-psychotic denial of an obvious reality. On the other hand, Troilus' words trouble us partly because they respond to something that *we* have found troubling about Cressida; and insofar as they echo our dim sense that this is not Cressida, we find ourselves caught up in his psychosis.[1] I shall argue that we are

1. See, for example, Henri Fluchère in response to Troilus' words: "Tortured love here presents a problem of identity which the play fails to solve" (*Shakespeare*, trans. Guy Hamilton [London: Longmans, 1953], 216). Other critics are also troubled by Cressida's failure to achieve a stable identity. Derek Traversi argues that not only Cressida but others in the play fail to have "consistent status as persons" because all are subject to time, that is, are ultimately victims not only of a world in which all constancy and value is destroyed by time but also of Shakespeare's uncertainty about how to generate meaningful characters in such a world (*An Approach to Shakespeare* [Garden City, N.Y.: Doubleday, 1956], 328–29). Traversi's view is extended in John Bayley's brilliant essay "Time and the Trojans" (*Essays in Criticism*, 25 [1975], 55–73). Bayley sees Troilus' horror at the two Cressidas as "a recognition not so much of falsity as of the fact that she is not a single coherent person" in a play in which Shakespeare dissolves the "assurances of selfhood" (70). But at the same time he is always uneasily aware of her potential as a full or novelistic character (63, 67); he

at this moment divided against ourselves because, at the deepest level, *Troilus and Cressida* enacts Troilus' fantasies, hence ensnaring us in them even as it encourages our distance from him: as Cressida becomes Diomed's, in an important sense she ceases to be her own creature; as she becomes Diomed's, she becomes oddly the creature of Troilus' needs. In fact, the shift in her status that Troilus articulates here is earlier registered in a change not so much in her character as in the means by which she is characterized and hence in the relationship that we as well as Troilus have toward her. For Cressida's inconstancy is accompanied by a radical inconsistency of characterization; and both occur at once because both are reflections of the same fantasy.

Critics frequently dismiss Cressida as "the wanton of tradition,"[2]

---

locates this potential in such moments as our discomfort with Ulysses' characterization of her as simply a "daughter of the game" (67). This uneasiness is, I think, characteristic of the best critical commentary on Cressida. See, for example, L. C. Knights's comments both on Cressida's position as a stereotypical wanton and on the note of sincerity we sometimes hear in her exchanges with Troilus ("The Theme of Appearance and Reality in *Troilus and Cressida*," in *Some Shakespearean Themes* [Stanford: Stanford University Press, 1959], 69) and Arnold Stein's analysis of Cressida both as a full character who believes that "what is precious is what the masculine 'particular will,' unsatisfied, imagines" and as a character whose dramatized reserve "prevents her from ever saying or doing what might register the feeling of her full presence" ("*Troilus and Cressida*: The Disjunctive Imagination," *ELH*, 36 [1969], 157–58). Gayle Greene's excellent account of Cressida acknowledges that her "sudden and complete violation of declared intentions damages her coherence in 'realistic' terms" ("Shakespeare's Cressida: 'A Kind of Self,'" in *The Woman's Part: Feminist Criticism of Shakespeare*, ed. Carolyn Ruth Swift Lenz, Gayle Greene, and Carol Thomas Neely [Urbana: University of Illinois Press, 1980], 135). But Greene ultimately derives this violation from Cressida's character understood realistically rather than from Shakespeare's characterization of her: she has only "a kind of self"—not an authentic self—because she is so much the creature of the values others set on her. William W. Main eliminates the problem pyrrhically by claiming that Cressida is not properly speaking a character at all but rather an unconvincing amalgam of four character types usually represented separately ("Character Amalgams in Shakespeare's *Troilus and Cressida*," *Studies in Philology*, 58 [1961], 172–73).

2. The phrase is L. C. Knights's (*Some Shakespearean Themes*, 69), yet he himself notes the inadequacy of this characterization and comments tantalizingly that "she exists mainly in the imagination of Troilus." See Carolyn Asp, "In Defense of Cressida," *Studies in Philology*, 74 (1977), 406–17; Grant I. Voth and Oliver H. Evans, "Cressida and the World of the Play," *Shakespeare Studies*, 8 (1975), 231–39; and Gayle Greene, "Shakespeare's Cressida," for partial accounts of Cressida's critical history. These critics all attempt to rehabilitate Cressida after the injuries done her by her former (mainly male) commentators; they stress her subjection to Troilus' idealism (Voth and Evans) or to a society in which there is no intrinsic value (Asp and Greene). See also R. A.

but when we first meet her, we feel her presence not as a stereotype but as a whole character. Throughout 1.2 we are encouraged to speculate about her motives; and by the end of the scene we seem to have established a privileged relationship with her. After our discomfort with Troilus' self-indulgent romanticizing and poeticizing (1.1.57–61, 102–8) we are likely to find Cressida's literalizing and deflating wit refreshing; she at least is not wallowing in imaginary lily beds.[3] And in the process of engaging us by her wit, Cressida calls attention to its psychic function and hence to her status as a whole character whose psychic processes may legitimately concern us: she relies, she tells Pandarus, on her wit to defend her wiles (1.2.273). In taking up Pandarus' metaphor of defense, she suggests the defensive function of her wit as a means of warding off serious emotion with all its threats, perhaps especially the threat of sexual vulnerability implicit in her image of pregnancy (1.2.270–82). On the other hand, we may notice that she seems to regard sexuality itself as a defense when she tells us that she will lie on her back to defend her belly; given our knowledge of the story, we may even begin to speculate that her view of sexuality as a defense will play a role in her defection to Diomed. Even while she keeps Pandarus at bay, that is, she teases us to question her. And just as we are speculating about her motives, she suddenly reveals herself, and to us alone. Her soliloquy confirms our sense that her chief concern is with her vulnerability and her means of defense against it: her entire strategy is directed toward gaining control over Troilus, her entire assumption that he will no longer love her once he has possessed her. In a declaration of passion filled with calculation, a statement of love from which Troilus himself is notably absent, replaced by abstract dicta about the typical behavior of men, in couplets so constricted that they suggest a fundamental niggardliness of the self, Cressida reveals the way in which her awareness of the crippling malaise of this world, the gap between expectation and performance,

---

Yoder's argument that Cressida is helplessly subject to the war machine (" 'Sons and Daughters of the Game': An Essay on Shakespeare's *Troilus and Cressida*," *Shakespeare Survey*, 25 [1972], 11–25). These efforts at rehabilitation have taught us to see Cressida as the victim of her world, but, valuable as they are, they all seem to me to founder because at the crucial moment of betrayal the text does not give us sufficient grounds for understanding Cressida fully in their terms.

3. References throughout are to the Signet edition of *Troilus and Cressida*, ed. Daniel Seltzer (New York, 1963).

colors her own expectations about Troilus and hence her behavior:[4] she is coy because "men prize the thing ungained more than it is" (1.2.301). It is an understatement to say that she has no sense of her own intrinsic worth. She seems to have internalized the principle of valuation that rules this society, the principle implied by Troilus' question "What's aught but as 'tis valued?" (2.2.52). Echoing the commercial language that so infects human relationships throughout the play, she identifies herself as a thing, in fact seems to identify herself with her "thing," and tells us that this thing gains its value not through any intrinsic merit but through its market value, determined by its scarcity. Beneath the deflating tendencies of her wit, then, the soliloquy reveals her vulnerability, her dependence on the love of men to establish her value even for herself, and her sense that her best defense lies in holding off, concealing her own desires.[5] And whatever we may feel about the self thus revealed, we feel that it *is* a self: the very structure of the scene establishes in us a keen sense both of Cressida's inwardness and of our own privileged position as the recipient of her revelations.

By the end of this scene, then, we have established not only some sense of Cressida but also the expectation that we will be allowed to know her as a full character, that she will maintain her relationship with us. And the scenes in Troy do not, for the most part, disappoint us. Although they contain no private revelations like that which concluded 1.2, they continually focus our attention on Cressida's inwardness by making us question her motives, even by making Cressida herself question her motives. When next we see her in 3.2 she am-

4. The gap between expectation and performance becomes definitive of sexual experience when Troilus defines the "monstruosity in love" (3.2.82) and of war when Agamemnon speaks to his demoralized commanders of the "protractive trials of great Jove" (1.3.20); it governs our aesthetic experience as the play refuses to meet our expectations, to present its heroes as heroic or to behave as a proper play with a coherent plot in which, for example, combat advertised as important will be important and endings will be conclusive.

5. These are generally the terms in which critics sympathetic to Cressida see her; insofar as I see Cressida as a realistic character, my arguments are frequently close to theirs. See, for example, Asp, "In Defense of Cressida," 409–10, 412–13. Robert Ornstein comments forcefully on the masculine ego that makes Cressida what she is: "She is a daughter of the game which men would have her play and for which they despise her" (*The Moral Vision of Jacobean Tragedy* [Madison: University of Wisconsin Press, 1960], 245). Gayle Greene persuasively associates Cressida's valuation of herself both with capitalism and with woman's tendency to see herself as an object ("Shakespeare's Cressida," 135–39, 142).

plifies our sense that fear, especially fear of betrayal, defines her relationship not only to Troilus but to herself (ll. 68–74); throughout 3.2 she seems terribly divided between impulses toward a self-protective and manipulative coyness and impulses toward a self-revelation that she feels as dangerous, even as self-betrayal. Given her vision of a world in which "things won are done" (1.2.299), in which her coy refusal seems the necessary basis for Troilus' faith (and indeed for Troilus' vision of himself as suffering lover), she cannot simply make herself known. She can be true to herself only by hiding herself; in revealing herself, she fears that she has committed a self-betrayal that will be the model for Troilus' betrayal of her: "Why have I blabbed? Who shall be true to us / When we are so unsecret to ourselves?" (3.2.126–27). But even as she chides herself for her apparent loss of self-control, she ends with a plea ("Stop my mouth") that both Troilus and Pandarus seem to take as the coquette's coy request for a kiss. As though in response to Troilus' suspicion, her reply to his kiss stresses the authenticity of her loss of control: "'Twas not my purpose thus to beg a kiss. / I am ashamed. O heavens, what have I done? / For this time will I take my leave, my lord" (3.2.139–41). In her fear of self-betrayal, Cressida tries to leave Troilus in order to leave her unreliable, "unkind" self, the self that has betrayed her to become Troilus' fool:

> *Troilus.*   What offends you, lady?
> *Cressida.* Sir, mine own company.
> *Troilus.* You cannot shun yourself.
> *Cressida.* Let me go and try.
>   I have a kind of self resides with you;
>   But an unkind self, that itself will leave
>   To be another's fool. I would be gone.
>   Where is my wit? I know not what I speak.
>
>   [3.2.145–52]

She can see love only as foolish self-abandonment; and the loss of her defensive wit seems to leave her utterly vulnerable.[6] Troilus' reply to

6. Gayle Greene comments on Cressida's "uncustomary loss of self-control"; she sees Cressida throughout 3.2 as "struggling both to maintain and to relinquish the defenses she has so carefully constructed" ("Shakespeare's Cressida," 140). Voth and Evans argue that the failure of Cressida's realistic and defensive wit leaves her ruinously subject to Troilus' idealism ("Cressida and the World of the Play," 234); their account seems to me to ignore the effects both of Cressida's own "idealistic" impulse to believe

this extraordinary revelation of her fear is devastating: "Well know they what they speak that speak so wisely" (l. 153). He cannot believe in—almost cannot hear—Cressida's perilous revelation of self. And in the face of his continued assumption that she is in control, that her self-revelation, like her request that her mouth be stopped, is part of the coquette's craft, she herself is brought to challenge the authenticity of her loss of control, hence of her unkind, loving self: "Perchance, my lord, I show more craft than love, / And fell so roundly to a large confession / To angle for your thoughts" (ll. 154–56). For Cressida at this moment, as for Troilus, there are only two choices: she is either a loving fool or a crafty coquette. And in the context created both by her own fears and by Troilus' expectations, there is no true choice. She reestablishes her dignity both for herself and for Troilus by retreating from self-revelation and from love: regaining her wit, she suggests that even her loss of self may be self-controlled, simultaneously fulfilling Troilus' expectation that she will be a stereotypical coquette and defending herself against her own fears of self-betrayal. Her retreat from her unkind self here may strike us as oddly prophetic of her later defection from Troilus; in the vow at the end of the scene, Cressida strikingly imagines herself as stereotypically false rather than true. Cressida's unkind self does not emerge again in 3.2.[7] In fact, the whole scene moves toward the increasing distance and contrivance reflected in the final vows, in which each of the triad threatens to become no more than his or her name: threatens, that is, to lose depth of character, to become merely stereotypical. That is, if we see Cressida as a stereotypical coquette in 3.2, we also see her taking on this role in response to specific psychological pressures; we are never allowed to see her merely as an uncomplicated type character.

Whether or not we feel that we understand Cressida in 3.2, and whatever the terms of our understanding, the scene clearly focuses on her inner state. Our most intense engagement is with her: through-

---

in love and of Troilus' "realistic" expectation that she will be a coquette. Emil Roy comments more broadly on Cressida's defensive use of language to acquire phallic power and to deny her vulnerable situation ("War and Manliness in Shakespeare's *Troilus and Cressida," Comparative Drama*, 7 [1973], 112).

7. Both Asp ("In Defense of Cressida," 411) and Voth and Evans ("Cressida and the World of the Play," 234) see Cressida as accepting Troilus' idealized view of herself at the end of the scene, despite her fears of vulnerability. If she does, the terms of her acceptance are very uneasy: although she ends by vowing fidelity, she does so only by imagining herself as the emblem of infidelity.

out the scene, Troilus does indeed seem "simpler than the infancy of truth" (l. 171) compared to her. Her next appearance, in 4.2, continues this intense engagement. In abandoning the caution of her 1.2 soliloquy, Cressida has shown more love than craft; and with the consummation of their union, she feels herself defenseless, as though her betrayal of herself threatens to turn at any moment into Troilus' betrayal of her. As Troilus attempts to leave her to preserve the secrecy of their union, she asks poignantly, "Are you aweary of me?" (4.2.7). Then, as though she wishes magically to prolong their sexual relationship by undoing it, she adds, "O foolish Cressid! I might have still held off, / And then you would have tarried" (ll. 17–18). This scene is in the normal pattern of Shakespearean morning-after scenes, in which the woman typically wishes to hold the man with her while the man asserts the necessities of the outside world. But both Romeo and Antony seem to have more pressing reasons for leaving than Troilus; and neither Juliet nor Cleopatra responds to the parting with the sense of betrayal, and of the reasons for betrayal, that Cressida expresses here.[8] Immediately after the consummation, that is, the lovers seem already separate. And the rest of the scene—indeed, the rest of the plot—in some sense constitutes an objective correlative to that separateness.[9] The entrance of Pandarus underscores the separation. Cressida knows that her "naughty mocking uncle" (l. 25) will mock

8. In the course of a discussion of the inadequacy of all love objects in *Troilus and Cressida* (and out of it), Stephen A. Reid comments that Troilus "does not regret that the day has come" ("A Psychoanalytic Reading of *Troilus and Cressida* and *Measure for Measure*," *Psychoanalytic Review*, 57 [1970], 267).

9. Derek Traversi's wonderful intuition that sexuality seeks union but always entails a sense of separateness seems to me very near the center of the play; he, too, sees the plot as in effect a rationalization for this inevitable movement (*Approach to Shakespeare*, 325–27). See also L. C. Knights: "The actual separation of the lovers . . . only emphasizes what is in fact intrinsic to their relationship" ("Theme of Appearance and Reality," 67). For Traversi, Troilus' sensuality dooms his passion insofar as he seeks "to extract from the refinement of the sensual a substitute for spiritual experience" (331); for Knights, it is Troilus' "subjectivism" that commits him to time and appearance, hence to separation (67). I will argue below for the close association of sexuality with separation in psychoanalytic terms. In any case, Shakespeare manipulates the plot to make us feel the separateness inherent in sexuality: 3.3, the scene in which the lovers' separation is arranged, substitutes in our imaginations for the moment of consummation, placed as it is between the scene in which the lovers move toward the bedchamber under the guidance of Pandarus (3.2) and the morning-after scene (4.2). See Norman Rabkin, who notes that arrangements for the separation are being made while

her. But by the end of their exchange, she feels Troilus' smile as mockery too: "You smile and mock me, as if I meant naughtily" (l. 37). The repetition of "mock" and "naughty" suggests a fusion of the two men in her mind; and Troilus' laugh (l. 38) may imply that the fusion is not simply in Cressida's mind. As the lovers leave the stage, Troilus indeed seems more allied with Pandarus than with Cressida.[10] And at this point the plot makes the separation between them literal. Aeneas brings the news of the political trade-off that will shape their final separation, and that separation is reflected immediately in dramatic terms: the lovers respond to this news not as a united pair but separately; we do not see them together again in this scene. Moreover, as each of the lovers responds to the news of separation, the tensions of the opening of the scene are clarified. Troilus responds rather easily to the news of the exchange. He accepts it as a fait accompli ("Is it so concluded?" [l. 66]), philosophizes upon it as though Cressida were merely one of his "achievements" ("How my achievements mock me!" [l. 69]), and makes arrangements to meet this new necessity and preserve his honor (ll. 70–71), all without any show of overwhelming emotion.[11] In the context of Troilus' ready acceptance of the news, Cressida's response to it is doubly impressive: the extremity of her grief, her assertion that nothing but Troilus matters to her, and her refusal to accept the separation ("I will not go from Troy" [l. 111]) make her response not only the most powerful assertion of her love

---

the lovers are enjoying their night together (*Shakespeare and the Common Understanding* [New York: Free Press, 1967], 50). But in fact this simultaneity is an illusion that Shakespeare achieves at some cost to ordinary temporal continuity. The second scenes of acts 3 and 4 clearly represent the beginning and end of one night; 4.2 takes place in the early morning (l. 46) of the day of the battle between Hector and Ajax. But 3.3 seems to be an outdoor daytime scene, and throughout it, the day of the battle is clearly "tomorrow" (ll. 34, 130, 247, 296). That is, 3.3 must take place before 3.2, not in the interval between 3.2 and 4.1; the simultaneity of sexual consummation and separation occurs only in our imaginations, not in the linear plot.

10. Several critics blame Pandarus for the failure of Troilus' love without noting the implicit alliance between them here and elsewhere; see, for example, Richard D. Fly (" 'I Cannot Come to Cressid but by Pandar': Mediation in the Theme and Structure of *Troilus and Cressida*," *English Literary Renaissance*, 3 [1973], 153–56) and R. J. Kaufmann ("Ceremonies for Chaos: The Status of *Troilus and Cressida*," *ELH* 32 [1965], 149).

11. Yoder comments shrewdly on Troilus' relatively easy acceptance of the separation: he is "calmed, even relieved in returning to his public role—he belongs to 'the general state of Troy' " ("Sons and Daughters of the Game," 21).

for Troilus but also one of the most emotionally charged moments in the play.

When the lovers are reunited after this brief separation, the tone of passionate expostulation has passed from Cressida to Troilus: he makes the speeches, while she replies with a numb repeated questioning of the necessity of separation (4.4.28, 30, 31, 32, 54), concluding finally by asking, "When shall we see again?" (l. 57). During the opening movement of the scene, that is, she seems painfully resistant to the bare fact of separation, while he embellishes it rhetorically, acquiescing. The emotional focus of the scene then moves from the acknowledgment of separation to Troilus' fears about Cressida's fidelity and her pained and puzzled responses to those fears. She responds first with surprise and indignation (ll. 59, 74), then with the fear that he does not love her (l. 82), and finally with a question that reflects not only her shaken faith in Troilus but also her shaken faith in herself: "Do you think I will?" (l. 92). The last words that we hear her speak to Troilus recall her own fear of being betrayed: "My lord, will you be true?" (l. 101). And these two questions—"Do you think I will?"; "My lord, will you be true?"—are the last we hear from Troilus' Cressida. We have been engaged throughout with Cressida's fears and her defenses against them; but suddenly, at the moment she is about to part from Troilus, she recedes from us. As Troilus and Diomed quarrel over her, she stands silent, as though she has become merely the object of their desire (and their competition), as though she has no voice of her own.

This sudden move into opacity remains constant for the rest of the play. In the next scene (4.5), when she kisses the Greek camp generally, she speaks her first words only after she has been kissed by Agamemnon, Nestor, Achilles, and Patroclus; her banter then seems both a response to Greek expectations about her and a return to the earlier mode of 1.2, that is, to a sexual wit that serves an essentially defensive function. But we are given no reassuring soliloquy to enable us to support this understanding; she simply exits, distressingly, with Diomed. She seems suddenly to have passed beyond us as she has passed from Troilus to Diomed. Ulysses' assessment of her as merely a daughter of the game (4.5.63) is disquieting partly because it offers us an explanation for her behavior just when we are feeling the need for one, in the absence of one by Cressida herself. Ulysses' commentary asks us to see someone that we have seen as a whole character, someone whose inwardness we alone have been privy to, as a mere character type, a person with no conflict or inwardness at all; and Shakespeare does nothing to qualify Ulysses' appraisal. The Cressida with whom we have been engaged simply does not allow us to understand her, here or later in the play. We may speculate that she leaves Troilus because his suspicion of her and his relatively easy acquiescence in the separation make her feel unknown and unloved. We may speculate that she leaves him because she fears that he will leave her, in order to ensure that she will be actively in control of her fate rather than the passive victim of his will. We may note her entire vulnerability in this society and her reliance on the opinion of men to determine her value even for herself and hence speculate that she adopts Troilus' view of her capacity for fidelity to prove his expectations right. We may locate the basis for her actions in her own pleasure in the excitement of the chase, her use of sexuality as a defense, even her genetic predisposition to treason, inherited from her father—and probably an actress will have to attempt some such construction in order to play the part at all. But after 4.4, the play gives us no place to ground our speculation: at exactly the moment at which we most need to understand what Cressida is doing, we not only are given no enlightenment but are forced to acknowledge our distance from Cressida by the structure of the scene itself. In 5.3 we are allowed to see Cressida only through the intervening commentary of Troilus, Ulysses, and Thersites. Instead of being especially privy to her thoughts, we become merely one more spectator to her new status as devalued object; indeed, we take our places as the furthest removed of the spectators as we watch Thersites watching Ulysses watching Troilus watching Cressida. That is, Cressida seems to betray *us* at the same time that she betrays Troilus; our relationship with her is broken off as sharply as hers with Troilus.

This abrupt shift in the mode of characterization, and hence in the distance between character and audience, seems to me to override any argument about Cressida's consistency or inconsistency as her allegiance shifts from Troilus to Diomedes: we know so little about her at this moment that we can no longer judge her as a whole character. But the timing of the shift may give us a way of understanding it, even if we can't understand her. The play seems to enact the fantasy that Cressida becomes radically unknowable, irreducibly other, at the moment of her separation from Troilus. And since Troilus can make no sense of the Cressida he sees in the Greek camp except by assuming that she is somehow split in two, the shift in the mode of characterization forces us to participate in his fantasy about her; even Cressida seems to participate in this fantasy when she offers as her only explanation for her actions her own helpless sense that she is split ("Troilus, farewell. One eye yet looks on thee, / But with my heart the other eye doth see" [5.2.104–5]). In order to begin to understand the change in the characterization of Cressida, then, I think we have to explore the bases for Troilus' fantasy of her as split.

Troilus is forced to imagine the existence of two Cressidas, his and Diomed's, in order to maintain his sense of Cressida's identity and hence to preserve his union with her:

> This she? No, this is Diomed's Cressida.
> If beauty have a soul, this is not she;
> If souls guide vows, if vows be sanctimonies,
> If sanctimony be the gods' delight,
> If there be rule in unity itself,
> This was not she.
>
> [5.2.134–39]

The movement of this speech makes it clear that wholeness of every kind depends for Troilus on the maintenance of his union with Cressida. So essential is that union that he will sacrifice even the "rule in unity"—the rule that guarantees that a thing must be itself and not something else—to it: to preserve his union with Cressida, he divides "a thing inseparate . . . more wider than the sky and earth" (5.2.145–46), splitting Cressida in two, separating his own Cressida from Diomed's. As reason revolts against itself to proclaim her not herself (5.2.141), Troilus' language becomes dense in its struggle to affirm and deny separation simultaneously:

> This is, and is not, Cressid.
> Within my soul there doth conduce a fight
> Of this strange nature that a thing inseparate
> Divides more wider than the sky and earth;
> And yet the spacious breadth of this division
> Admits no orifex for a point as subtle
> As Ariachne's broken woof to enter.
>
> [5.2.143–49]

There is division in a thing inseparate, but it is a division that is no division, in which there is no orifex. Both Cressida herself and his union with her are this separated thing inseparable. The assertion and denial of separation are fused here because Troilus asserts one separation to deny another: only by insisting on the division of Cressida in two can he preserve the wholeness of her identity for him and hence preserve their union.

For Troilus, the idea of union must override any sense of Cressida as a person separate from himself; Cressida becomes simply that with whom one is united and hence ceases to be herself at the moment the union dissolves.[12] We can begin to understand the force of this union for Troilus and hence the pressures behind his act of splitting as we watch his initial response to Cressida's betrayal:

Troilus.	Was Cressid here?
Ulysses.	I cannot conjure, Troyan.
Troilus.	She was not, sure.
Ulysses.	Most sure she was.
Troilus.	Why, my negation hath no taste of madness.
Ulysses.	Nor mine, my lord. Cressid was here but now.
Troilus.	Let it not be believed for womanhood!
	Think we had mothers; do not give advantage
	To stubborn critics, apt, without a theme,
	For depravation, to square the general sex
	By Cressid's rule. Rather think this not Cressid.
Ulysses.	What hath she done, prince, that can soil our mothers?
Troilus.	Nothing at all, unless that this were she.

[5.2.122–32]

The preservation of the union with Cressida is bound up with the preservation of Troilus' ideal image of his mother; like Posthumus (Cymbeline, 2.5), Troilus associates the infidelity of his beloved with the infidelity of his mother. Ulysses' puzzled question emphasizes this association and clarifies the fantasy that shapes it: for Troilus, Cressida has the power to soil a mother figure so universal that she becomes "the general sex," all "our mothers." For from the first, Troilus' desire for Cressida is invested with the power of a nostalgic longing for union with an overpoweringly maternal figure; from the first, he associates his love with his own infantilization. When we first meet Troilus, he seems to be luxuriating in the sense of his own weakness, a weakness

---

12. Terence Eagleton says, more charitably: "Cressida to him is the Cressida of their relationship; she has no meaning or existence for him outside this context," because reality and identity are social, shared creations (Shakespeare and Society [London: Chatto & Windus, 1967], 17).

described in terms that suggest the loss of his adult masculinity through love:

> ... I am weaker than a woman's tear,
> Tamer than sleep, fonder than ignorance,
> Less valiant than the virgin in the night,
> And skilless as unpracticed infancy.
>
> [1.1.9–12]

For Troilus, love is associated with the powerlessness and the inno-cent—or ignorant—trust of the infant; even in the act of telling Cres-sida that he does not believe that women can be constant, he claims that he is naive, "as true as truth's simplicity, / And simpler than the infancy of truth" (3.2.170–71).[13] And his imagination of the sexual act is given shape by images that suggest a return to the blissful and dangerous fusion of infancy. The sexual act is imagined as feeding on an exquisitely purified nectar; its consummation simultaneously prom-ises and threatens a delicious death in which distinction itself—both the capacity to distinguish and the separate identity distinguished—will be lost, and boundaries will dissolve:

> I am giddy; expectation whirls me round.
> Th'imaginary relish is so sweet
> That it enchants my sense. What will it be
> When that the wat'ry palates taste indeed
> Love's thrice-repurèd nectar? Death, I fear me,
> Sounding destruction, or some joy too fine,
> Too subtle, potent, tuned too sharp in sweetness
> For the capacity of my ruder powers.
> I fear it much; and I do fear besides
> That I shall lose distinction in my joys,
> As doth a battle, when they charge on heaps
> The enemy flying.
>
> [3.2.17–28]

Troilus' speech suggests both the desire for and the fear of a fusion in which individual identity will be lost with an intensity unequaled in Shakespeare's works: here love *is* death, a joy too sharp in sweetness,

---

13. That Troilus imagines himself an infant as he imagines the possibility of betrayal suggests not only the extent to which that possibility makes him feel utterly vulnerable but also the extent to which his image of himself as an overtrusting infant requires the confirmation of the mother's betrayal.

131

a battle, a swooning destruction in which one's powers are lost. That this fusion is imagined as the consequence of tasting love's nectar suggests the extent to which it is desired as a recapturing of the infant's first union with a nurturing maternal figure, the union out of which the adult self must be painfully differentiated, distinguished.[14]

Insofar as his union with Cressida is an attempt to recapture the infantile fusion with a maternal figure, the rupture of the union threatens to soil the idea of the mother herself. And insofar as the mother is the source both of wholeness and of nourishment, her soilure threatens to dissolve a universe felt as coherent into fragmented bits of spoiled food.

> Instance, O instance, strong as Pluto's gates;
> Cressid is mine, tied with the bonds of heaven.
> Instance, O instance, strong as heaven itself;
> The bonds of heaven are slipped, dissolved, and loosed,
> And with another knot, five-finger-tied,
> The fractions of her faith, orts of her love,
> The fragments, scraps, the bits, and greasy relics
> Of her o'ereaten faith, are given to Diomed.
>
> [5.2.150–57]

"Fractions," "orts," "fragments," "scraps," and "bits": all diagnostically proclaim the breaking of wholeness into pieces as they proclaim the spoiling of food. That is, the failure of Cressida to live out Troilus' fantasy of union with an ideally nurturing figure simultaneously turns her to a greasy relic and shatters the sense of wholeness for Troilus because the sense of wholeness itself derives from fantasies of union

14. Joel Fineman writes powerfully about the consequences of the loss of distinction, or Difference, in *Troilus and Cressida*, expanding on René Girard's brief commentary on Ulysses' speech (Fineman, "Fratricide and Cuckoldry: Shakespeare's Doubles," in *Representing Shakespeare*, ed. Murray M. Schwartz and Coppélia Kahn [Baltimore: Johns Hopkins University Press, 1980], 94–100; Girard, *Violence and the Sacred* [Baltimore: Johns Hopkins University Press, 1977], 50–51). In locating the terror at the loss of Difference in the possibility of self-obliterating fusion with the mother, Fineman moves beyond the Girardian myth by denying its explanatory force; he does not, however, discuss this possibility specifically in relation to *Troilus and Cressida* (102–4).

with such an ideally nurturing figure.[15] These are the transformations
that the splitting of Cressida is designed to undo; by its means, Troilus
will attempt to "repure" the nectar and regain the shattered unity,
denying that the betraying Cressida and the Cressida with whom he
is united are one.[16]

Ulysses asks what Cressida has done that can soil our mothers. We
might answer that she has betrayed the fantasies that were the basis

---

15. In his desire for wholeness and fear of fragmentation, Troilus is the repository
for fears and desires felt intensely throughout the play. For the whole of *Troilus and
Cressida* is invested with a nostalgia for order, wholeness, what Ulysses calls "the
unity and married calm of states" (1.3.100). This unity is everywhere subject to fracture,
figured most dramatically in Hector's myriad wounds and in Achilles' substitution of
his myrmidons for his own single heroic action. Hence, for example, the predominance
in character descriptions of disconnected lists of qualities, mere "attributes" (3.1.37)
without a center (see, for example, the descriptions of Troilus as "minced man" [1.2.263–
67] or of Ajax as "gouty Briareus" [1.2.19–30]). And hence the force of Achilles' insult
to Thersites: "fragment" (5.1.8). As in Troilus' response to Cressida's betrayal, to be
a piece rather than a whole here is to be a piece of spoiled food; in a world lacking
wholeness, everything becomes a fragment (as the predominance of lists of nouns in
Ulysses' speech and elsewhere suggests) subject to appetite, the universal wolf (1.3.121),
subject finally to utter negation as appetite, like lechery (5.4.36), eats up itself. See
J. Hillis Miller's discussion of stylistic fragmentation in "Ariachne's Broken Woof,"
Georgia Review, 31 (1977), 54. For Charles Lyons, the play concerns the gap "between
the pure and constant identity of desire and the despoiled and complex fragmentation
of identity in reality" ("Cressida, Achilles, and the Finite Deed," *Etudes anglaises*, 20
[1967], 233). R. J. Kaufmann identifies "self-consumption" as the deep theme of *Troilus
and Cressida* and notes the presence of eating and cookery images, "subversive of
ideals of wholeness and permanence," in connection with this theme ("Ceremonies
for Chaos," 142, 155).

16. Emil Roy similarly suggests that strategies of splitting in the play derive from
failed attempts to regain the nurturing mother, whose loss threatens the "loss of
separate, fixed identities. To preserve their individual autonomies, the Trojans adopt
strategies of splitting and projection . . . isolating Cressida's loving from her betraying
selves" ("War and Manliness," 118–19). Roy does not elaborate fully on this comment
and treats Troilus and Cressida only sporadically in his maddeningly chaotic and won-
derfully suggestive essay on the framing of oedipal issues in preoedipal terms in the
play. The extent to which the mother is initially idealized is implicit not only in the
concern with keeping her pure and unsoiled but also in the association of her with
nectar, the food of the gods. Many critics, following G. Wilson Knight, see Troilus'
love as in some sense idealizing, an attempt to achieve the infinite and spiritual by
finite sensual means (*The Wheel of Fire* [New York: Meridian, 1957], 63–65; see also
Traversi, *Approach to Shakespeare*, 331, 335). Troilus' passion is, I think, doubly
idealized, shaped by desire not only for an ideal maternal object but also for a total
fusion, infinite insofar as it removes the boundaries of the self, spiritual perhaps insofar
as it is appropriate only to Milton's angels ("If Spirits embrace, / Total they mix"
[*Paradise Lost*, 8.626–27]): ideal, that is, in both object and aim. Such idealization

of Troilus' desire for union with her. Her betrayal becomes in effect
the assertion of her status as a separate person, not simply the creature
of Troilus' fantasy.[17] But we might also answer that Cressida has done
nothing—that the agent of soilure is in fact Troilus himself. For ultimately, I think, it is not the rupture of the union but the consummation of the union that soils the idea of the mother for Troilus. Troilus
begins to reveal the ways in which he finds sexuality itself soiling as
he argues that the Trojans must keep Helen to maintain their honor:

> I take today a wife, and my election
> Is led on in the conduct of my will—
> My will enkindled by mine eyes and ears,
> Two traded pilots 'twixt the dangerous shores
> Of will and judgment. How may I avoid,
> Although my will distaste what it elected,
> The wife I chose? There can be no evasion
> To blench from this and to stand firm by honor.
> We turn not back the silks upon the merchant
> When we have soiled them, nor the remainder viands

produces a corresponding debasement when, inevitably, the object loses its ideality
by participating in sexuality and the aim turns out to be unattainable. Traversi hints
at the connection between Troilus' "sense of soilure" and his "abstract idealism" (*Approach to Shakespeare*, 337) without exploring it. Greene comments persuasively on
the idealization and debasement inherent in Troilus' passion from the start: "Exalting
woman as a goddess, reducing her to object, what he omits is the person" ("Shakespeare's Cressida," 138). Freud traces this bifold impulse, familiar now to feminist
critics, to the desire to protect one's original incestuous object from the current of
one's sexual feeling ("On the Universal Tendency to Debasement in the Sphere of
Love," in *Standard Edition*, XI, 179–90).

17. Her sexual betrayal is of course the ultimate sign of her status as opaque *other*:
when she gives herself to Diomed, she demonstrates to Troilus that she is both unknowable and unpossessable. But even before the lovers have parted, Troilus suggests
a magical connection between Cressida's infidelity and their separation: "Be thou true,
/ And I will see thee" (4.4.66–67), he says, as though her fidelity could magically ward
off separation. At issue here is, I suspect, a primitive fantasy in which separation *is*
infidelity: for the infant, the mother's separateness constitutes the first betrayal; insofar
as she is not merely his, she is promiscuously other. I suspect that this sense of otherness
itself as promiscuous betrayal antedates the more specific oedipal jealousies and is
retrospectively sexualized by them. The whole process is condensed in the play's
demonstration, in the character of Cressida, that separation, opaque otherness, and
sexual betrayal are one.

> We do not throw in unrespective sieve
> Because we are now full.
>
> [2.2.61–72]

This is an extraordinary analogy, not least because Troilus himself seems unaware of its relevance to his approaching union with Cressida.[18] On the verge of that union, he imagines a marriage from which he will wish to "blench" or retreat; he expects to "distaste" his choice. In this fantasy, sexual satiety leads to indifference or even disgust very much as Cressida has predicted; and the terms of the disgust are precisely those in which Troilus will later respond to Cressida's betrayal of him: the distasted wife is associated with soiled silks and leftover food no longer desirable *because we are now full*. The imagery here insists that it is not Cressida's betrayal but Troilus' own appetite— his feeding on Cressida—that has made her into "remainder viands": she is the leftovers from his great feast.

At the same time as this analogy reveals the extent to which Troilus himself is the soiling agent, it also expresses the same fear of sexuality that we have seen as Troilus waits outside Cressida's bedroom for their first encounter. Given the insistence on the possibility of male impotence throughout the play,[19] Troilus' concern that he cannot stand firm by honor if he blenches from his wife reiterates the language of impotence; the imagined wife herself becomes suggestively associated not now with India (1.1.104) but with the "dangerous shores / Of will and judgment."[20] For ultimately Troilus himself is the fearful virgin

18. In teaching this play, I have often found myself "correcting" students who assume that Troilus is announcing his impending union with Cressida; see Daniel Seltzer's footnote to this passage for a similar correction (Signet ed., 85). We all know that Troilus is simply inventing an analogy. But I think that the naive students are, as so often happens, at least partly right: they can teach us to notice Troilus' breathtaking capacity to compartmentalize, so that he can use this analogy apparently without feeling its relevance. Critical responses to this passage suggest that Troilus' capacity is catching.

19. See, for example, Pandarus' threat that Cressida will "bereave" Troilus of deeds as well as words (3.2.57), Cressida's comments on the inadequacy of male performance (3.2.86–91), Troilus' own fears that the act is a slave to limit (3.2.84–5), and Pandarus' final song about the bee's loss of its sting when it is "subdued in armèd tail" (5.10.42–45).

20. The deep fantasy associates intercourse with the boat trapped between menacing shores, but the language here is characteristically double: on the one hand, he cannot stand firm if he retreats from these dangerous shores; on the other, it is not the retreat but the wife felt as dangerous that poses the threat to standing firm.

in the night (1.1.11);[21] the union with Cressida which he so desires is simultaneously felt as fearfully dangerous to him. Both the fear with which he anticipates the union and his ready acceptance of the separation point toward the deep ambivalence of his desires. Throughout, his portrayal of himself as true in love insists on the dangerously infantile vulnerability of both truth ("the infancy of truth" [3.2.171]) and love ("skilless as unpracticed infancy" [1.1.12]). For in Troilus' fantasy of sexuality as union with a maternal figure, the fear of impotence or castration becomes the fear of maternal engulfment. If union with Cressida as the all-powerful mother promises new wholeness, it also threatens to dissolve the self; if it promises to be a tasting of repured nectar, it also threatens a feast in which one will be eaten, not eater. Immediately after their night of love together, Troilus imagines night as a witch (4.2.12), the dark side of the maternal figure with whom he desires union; and the busy day of their aubade awakens ribald crows (4.2.9), sexualized devourers.[22] And in the face of his own infantile vulnerability, Troilus seems to want to rob Cressida of her frightening power; in extraordinarily ambivalent lines, he wishes his own vulnerability on her:[23]

> Sleep kill those pretty eyes,
> And give as soft attachment to thy senses
> As infants' empty of all thought!
>
> [4.2.4–6]

Insofar as these lines suggest Troilus' desire to transfer his own felt weakness from himself to Cressida, they are prophetic of the structure

21. Troilus' "expectation" in approaching Cressida—"what will it be / When that the wat'ry palates taste indeed / Love's thrice-repurèd nectar?" (3.2.17, 19–21)—suggests his lack of sexual experience. Like *Othello*, *Troilus and Cressida* thus becomes an exploration of the consequences of the man's first sexual experience. It is part of the play's implicit identification with Troilus' fantasy that the extent of Cressida's experience never becomes clear. In Troilus' imagination, at least in 1.1, she is an unapproachable virgin; and Shakespeare allows us to participate at least partly in this fantasy insofar as his Cressida—unlike Chaucer's—is not a widow. The aphorisms of her soliloquy in 1.2 may reveal that she is "already an experienced coquette" (Fluchère, *Shakespeare*, 214) or they may be merely secondhand schoolgirl wisdom. Her morning-after response to Troilus—"You men will never tarry" (4.2.16)—is, however, chilling in its implication that Troilus is only one of many. These moments serve, I think, to make us uncomfortable with our lack of knowledge.

22. The *Oxford English Dictionary* tells us that "crow" is "in England commonly applied to the Carrion Crow (*Corvus Corone*), 'a large black bird that feeds upon the carcasses of beasts' (Johnson)."

23. Troilus' wish to infantilize Cressida is curiously echoed in Pandarus' teasing her after the consummation by using babytalk ("Hast not slept tonight? Would he not, a naughty man, let it sleep? A bugbear take him!" [4.2.32–37].

of the play as a whole. For ultimately the necessities of Troilus' character, rather than of Cressida's, require her betrayal of him. Cressida's betrayal in effect allows Troilus to blench and still stand firm by honor; it serves to free him from a union ambivalently desired while allowing him to continue to think of himself as the embodiment of truth. Moreover, if Troilus' splitting of Cressida is designed to preserve his fantasy of union with an ideal maternal figure in the face of her betrayal, her betrayal itself seems ultimately to serve the same end—to be shaped, that is, by the same underlying fantasy. For the fantasized mother threatens her infant-lover with oral engulfment in the consummation partly because the very fact of her sexuality makes her into the witch mother rather than the ideal mother with whom Troilus had sought to unite, transforming her into a soiled whore, a type of Helen.[24] That is, insofar as sexuality itself is soiling, it is incompatible with the union Troilus desires; Troilus' own sexuality transforms Cressida into a betraying whore. Cressida's betrayal then becomes in effect a rationalization, allowing Troilus to perform the act of splitting that is essential to the preservation of his union with an idealized maternal figure, a union no longer possible with Cressida herself once she has been contaminated by sexuality: by locating Cressida's sexual self in the contaminated relationship with Diomed, Troilus is free to retain an idealized, nonsexual union with the Cressida of his desires, nurtured by absence. The very sexuality that promises union with the mother is thus in fact the agent of separation; as Troilus half-knows even before the consummation, the sexual act achieves not boundlessness but a

24. In the course of the play, Cressida merges with Helen, not only insofar as she becomes sexually soiled but insofar as she becomes the foreign woman, a center of sexual desire. Both Troilus and Cressida's first meeting (3.2) and their morning-after scene (4.2) are symbolically mediated by Helen, literally present in 3.1 and figuratively present in Diomed's description of her "soilure" in 4.1; variants of "soil" are insistently used in reference to Helen (2.2.148, 2.2.70, 4.1.56) in preparation for Ulysses' use of the word to question Troilus' response to Cressida's betrayal (5.2.131). We might expect Helen to be at the center of the play, insofar as she is the cause of the war; curiously she appears only near its literal center, in 3.1, and then only vacuously, as though Shakespeare wanted to suggest an absence at the center. Emil Roy sees both Helen and Cressida as contested mother figures ("War and Manliness," 109, 110). Given the longing for maternal presence manifest in the play, the relative absence of the great mother Hecuba is particularly striking. One might speculate that the missing Hecuba is replaced by Helen and that the substitution of whore for idealized mother initiates the disease that is the play, here as in *Hamlet*. In a war seen as an extended sexual disease (2.3.18–21), Helen herself is the hollow center of disease, almost anatomically the "putrefied core, so fair without" (5.8.1), that "disarm[s] great Hector" (3.1.153).

sense of limit: "This is the monstruosity in love, lady, that the will is infinite and the execution confined; that the desire is boundless and the act a slave to limit" (3.2.82–85).[25]

Through the sexual act, then, the pure—or repured—mother with whom Troilus wished to unite is soiled and becomes a whore; and Cressida is made to enact this transformation. That Cressida acts in response to Troilus' need to separate her sexual from her ideal maternal self accounts, I think, for the opacity of her motives as she leaves Troilus: she acts less from the necessities of her own character than from the necessities of his. Moreover, in enacting Troilus' fantasies, she protects Troilus from responsibility for them. Troilus' response to Cressida's infidelity in 5.2 is strikingly close to his fantasy about marriage in 2.2, but with the onus shifted from him to her: the soil is the result of her action, not of his fantasy; she is distasted, felt as leftover food, not because he is now full but because she has betrayed her faith. Because she obligingly enacts his fantasy, he can rest assured that it is her infidelity, not his sexuality, that soils our mothers. But the play does not in fact invite us to speculate about Troilus' character in noting the transfer of guilt from Troilus to Cressida, for the transfer is of course enshrined in the plot: not only Troilus but the play itself insists on Cressida's guilt. After the moment that Cressida leaves Troy, the play everywhere exonerates Troilus at the expense of Cressida: she becomes a whore to keep him pure. Ulysses' parallel speeches on

25. This line seems to me to locate precisely the source of the psychic equivalence of sexuality and separation that shapes the love plot (see nn. 9 and 17). Sexuality entails separation not only because it soils the pure mother of desire but also because the act itself can never achieve the total union desired. The "monstruosity" is the necessary discrepancy not only between boundless desire and limited performance but also between the desire for boundlessness and the act that serves finally to remind us of our limits, our boundaries; insofar as we invest the sexual act with the promise of boundlessness, it will serve as the emblem of our separateness. Underlying the love plot is, I think, a dreamlike necessity: in place of merger, sexuality reveals the absolute otherness of the other, reveals what I have earlier called Cressida's promiscuous betrayal of the fantasy of merger; and that promiscuous betrayal itself becomes sexualized when Cressida becomes a whore. Sexuality thus entails the separation in the plot, and that separation entails sexual betrayal. Stephen Reid notes Troilus' worry that the sexual act will be disappointing as a result of "the gap between the sense of boundlessness in his desire and the limitation of the sexual act" ("Psychoanalytic Reading," 264). Although his essay locates the source of sexual dissatisfaction where Freud does, in the deflection of desire from its original incestuous objects and in the repression of pregenital components of sexuality, he curiously attributes this gap to the temporal limitations of the sexual act, noting neither Troilus' desire for oral fusion nor his association of Cressida with his mother.

Cressida and Troilus at that moment suggest some such exchange: as he directs us to see Cressida as no more than a daughter of the game (4.5.55–63), he directs us to see Troilus as a matchless hero in praise that nearly exceeds Pandarus' puffery and does not tally with our experience of Troilus (4.5.96–112); as Cressida is debased, Troilus is idealized.

The transfer of guilt from Troilus to Cressida is enshrined in the plot, but not without some traces of anxiety. Cressida's insistent worry that Troilus will betray her—in a story everyone knows is about her betrayal of him—may be one such trace: in a very real sense, she is right to be worried. For Cressida herself is an odd fusion of betrayer and betrayed. The fusion that composes her character may be recorded in Troilus' amalgam of Ariadne and Arachne in the "Ariachne" of his response to Cressida's betrayal (5.2.149): the poisonous woman-as-spider, associated with infidelity in *The Winter's Tale*,[26] is fused with the archetypal woman betrayed, as though the two betrayals were at bottom one.[27] We may thus begin to understand a habitual oddity in critical responses to the play. When Cressida tells us that "things won are done, joy's soul lies in the doing," many of us respond as though she is speaking for the world of the play in general and for Troilus in

26. *The Winter's Tale*, 2.1.45. See Murray M. Schwartz's discussion of the maternal significance of the spider ("Leontes' Jealousy in *The Winter's Tale*," *American Imago*, 30 [1973], 270–72); his suggestion that the spider signifies the sexually threatening mother and the fear of maternal engulfment is very germane to *Troilus and Cressida*. My general indebtedness to Murray Schwartz, Richard Wheeler, and especially C. L. Barber will, I hope, be evident to everyone familiar with their work. A more private debt is owed to Jann Gurvich, who shocked me years ago in a class by suggesting that Troilus wanted Cressida to be his mother. This paper is dedicated to C. L. Barber, whose living presence continues to inspire us all.

27. J. Hillis Miller prefers to see "Ariachne" as a symptom of the general challenge to Western civilization posed by the play, or at least by the deconstructionist critic's reading of the play, insofar as it asks us to hold two incongruent myths in our head at once, an impossibility in Western logocentric monological metaphysics ("Ariachne's Broken Woof," 47). As I have labored to suggest, I don't think that the myths are at the deepest level incongruent. Furthermore, I find his implicit endorsement of Troilus' response to Cressida curious. The extremity of Troilus' response surely tells us not that the story of cosmic order, "as it is told by the reasonable discourse of Western metaphysics, is itself a lie" (48) but that Troilus has impossibly located that order in the idea of his union with Cressida. As Ornstein says, Troilus "projects his inner confusion into a law of universal chaos and would have us believe that because *his* vanity is stricken the bonds of heaven are slipped" (*Moral Vision of Jacobean Tragedy*, 249). Miller's argument has a powerful—and characteristically unassuming—anteced-ent in Knights's discussion of the same passage (*Some Shakespearean Themes*, p. 71).

particular.[28] And yet the manifest love plot seems to prove her wrong: Troilus seems more than ever her devoted servant after the consummation of their union;[29] it is Cressida for whom things won are done. We respond, despite the evidence of the plot, as though Cressida is somehow obscurely right because the plot in some respects runs counter to the fantasy that shapes the play; in fact the plot serves precisely to defend against acknowledgment of the fantasy. For the effort to keep Troilus pure seems to me finally evidence of Shakespeare's failure to dissociate himself from the fantasies explored in the creation of Troilus; and insofar as the play consequently embodies Troilus' fantasies, Cressida as a whole character must be sacrificed. But Shakespeare does not rest with *Troilus and Cressida*; and when he reworks this material in *Othello*, where Desdemona is subject to very similar fantasies, he dissociates himself from these fantasies by localizing them in the minds of Iago and Othello. As a result, Desdemona remains a vigorous and independent character, larger than Othello's fantasies of her, while Cressida fades from us.

I have argued elsewhere for the need to respond to Shakespeare's characters as whole psychological entities.[30] But characters may not always permit us to respond to them in this way, or the presentation of character may shift in a way that disengages us from concern with their inwardness. At such moments the characters may be shaped by psychological pressures not their own. The psychological fantasies embedded in the creation of another character or in the play as a whole may require the sacrifice of the internal psychological consistency of any single character. I suspect that female characters are particularly prone to being so sacrificed, partly because of their status as *others*,

28. See, for example, Stein, *"Troilus and Cressida,"* 158; Kaufmann, "Ceremonies for Chaos," 155; and Rabkin, *Shakespeare and the Common Understanding*, 44.

29. This fact presents problems for Charles Lyons, who argues persuasively that the self-consuming sexual act, in which "the very consummation which appetite demands destroys the appetite and so disintegrates the source of value," is the model for all action and all valuation in the play ("Cressida, Achilles, and the Finite Deed," 233). His argument founders only when he turns to Troilus specifically, as his uneasiness about the point at which Troilus revalues Cressida indicates: "he conceives of her as a sexual object, uses her, and—when he suffers knowledge of her common behavior— he discards her" (241). My entire argument might be read as an attempt to untangle this uneasiness.

30. See Introduction to *Twentieth-Century Interpretations of "King Lear"* (Englewood Cliffs, N.J.: Prentice-Hall, 1978), 1–21.

partly because of the (related) intensity of the fantasies that are attached to the idea of the mother. To speak of character as shaped in this way is by no means to speak of artistic failure: characters so shaped may become the embodiments of our dearest shared fantasies and hence carry enormous force. Cordelia, for example, seems to me to suffer the same fate as Cressida, but the sacrifice of her character points in the opposite direction, toward idealization rather than debasement: during the play we witness her separation from the sexual self that she had defended so proudly in Act 1 at the same time as we lose touch with her inwardness; and yet she is the guarantor of many of our best dreams. But in *King Lear*, splitting is embodied not only in the change in the characterization of Cordelia but in the creation of complementary characters as well: even as the play begins, Cordelia has already been partially split from her sexual self, now located in Goneril and Regan. Troilus' splitting of Cressida from herself thus allows us to see, reproduced in the mind of a single character, the process of one of Shakespeare's major modes of generating his dramatic characters; hence our vertigo as we watch Troilus creating two characters out of one: "This is and is not Cressid."

6

Difference and Silence: John Milton and the Question of Gender

JIM SWAN

> Such was that happy Garden-state,
> While Man there walk'd without a Mate:
> After a Place so pure, and sweet,
> What other Help could yet be meet!
> But 'twas beyond a Mortal's share
> To wander solitary there:
> Two Paradises 'twere in one
> To live in Paradise alone.
>
> Andrew Marvell, "The Garden"

According to an old story, a student once wrote of John Milton that "this author got married and wrote *Paradise Lost.* Then his wife died, and he wrote *Paradise Regained.*"[1] Mistaken, or inspired, the student gave voice to something that we have often at least suspected about Milton. For generations, as readers and critics, we have singled out passages from his work in order to assert or deny their intention as

A portion of this essay, in an earlier form, was presented to a session on psychoanalysis and gender at the 1980 convention of the Modern Language Association in Houston, Texas.

1. Cited in Edward LeComte, *Milton and Sex* (London: Macmillan, 1978), 3.

142

misogyny. No one soon forgets the pain of Adam's outcry after the fall:

> O why did God,
> Creator wise, that peopl'd highest Heav'n
> With Spirits Masculine, create at last
> This novelty on Earth, this fair defect
> Of Nature, and not fill the World at once
> With Men as Angels without Feminine,
> Or find some other way to generate
> Mankind?
>
> [*PL*, 10.888–95][2]

Nor do we forget the imposing image of Sin, besides Eve the only other woman in an otherwise entirely male world and closely related to Eve symbolically: "Woman to the waist, and fair, / But ended foul in many a scaly fold / Voluminous and vast, a Serpent arm'd / With mortal sting" (*PL*, 2.650–53). There are hell-hounds, she says, about her middle:

> yelling Monsters . . . hourly conceiv'd
> And hourly born, with sorrow infinite
> To me, for when they list into the womb
> That bred them they return, and howl and gnaw
> My Bowels, thir repast; then bursting forth
> Afresh with conscious terrors vex me round.
>
> [*PL*, 2.795–801]

Sin's experience of conception "with sorrow infinite" prefigures the curse pronounced on Eve that she will, "in sorrow," bring forth children (*PL*, 10.195). But more important, I think, is the doubleness of Sin, particularly her experience of those ambivalent and orally sadistic hounds constantly violating the boundary between inside and outside. It is a catastrophic vision of birth infinitely repeating itself, a separation never to be completed and arousing a consciousness that vexes and terrifies without end. The connection, for Sin, between consciousness and a double or divided nature and the experience of sexuality is a crucial one, I think, and I want to explore it further. But first I want to introduce another moment from Milton's poetry for consideration.

Samson is probably Milton's most notorious woman hater. For him

---

2. John Milton, *Complete Poems and Major Prose*, ed. Merritt Y. Hughes (New York: Odyssey, 1957), 427. All further quotations of Milton's works are from this edition.

Dalila is a traitress, a fatally seductive Circe, "a manifest Serpent by her sting / Discover'd in the end" (*Samson Agonistes*, ll. 997–98). But Samson is more concerned with himself than he is with his hatred for Dalila. The Chorus, in a characteristic gesture, looks for the cause of her treachery in deficiencies attributed to women generally, their supposed weakness of mind, or their supposed overabundance of what Milton, here and elsewhere, rather quaintly calls "outward ornament" (l. 1025).[3] Samson, however, turns the blame on himself, complaining repeatedly of having given up his "fort of silence" (l. 235) and "divulg'd the secret gift of God / To a deceitful Woman" (ll. 201–2). Moreover, it was not just with Dalila that he violated the "sacred trust of silence" (l. 428); there was also the woman of Timna, his first wife, who persuaded him to tell her an earlier secret and promptly revealed it to his enemies. Self-betrayal, it seems, is an obsession with Samson, and it is this repeated betrayal of a silence, which is also a secret—or rather *the* secret—of the self, that intrigues me. For it implies that the encounter with sexual difference is somehow connected with the transformation of silence into speech; just as, for Sin in *Paradise Lost*, the experience of sexuality implies a vexing consciousness of her own divided doubleness of being. Like every major character in the epic, Sin realizes her doubleness as speech, as the narrative of her beginning. More than a character in her own right, Sin functions as a projection of an ambivalence located in some other subjectivity (Satan's, Milton's, God's, ours; it does not matter which), an ambivalence about one's own nature, fair and foul.

I want to pause here, though, in order to dispel an impression that I may be conveying: that the issue of woman-hating and male identity is particularly Milton's, that he is the poet who, above all, bestowed on us a vision of solitary male creativity that dominated English literary culture for centuries. There are important ways in which this is true,[4]

---

3. An excellent historical analysis of the commonplaces about woman is Ian Maclean, *The Renaissance Notion of Woman: A Study in the Fortunes of Scholasticism and Medical Science in European Intellectual Life* (Cambridge: Cambridge University Press, 1980).

4. An excellent reading of Milton's sexual politics is Jackie DiSalvo, "Blake Encountering Milton: Politics and the Family in *Paradise Lost* and the *Four Zoas*," in *Milton and the Line of Vision*, ed. Joseph Anthony Wittreich, Jr. (Madison: University of Wisconsin Press, 1975), 143–84. In addition, a lively debate on Milton's view of woman has appeared in the pages of *Milton Studies*: Marcia Landy, "Kinship and the Role of Women in *Paradise Lost*, *MS*, 4 (1972), 3–18, and "'A Free and Open Encounter': Milton and the Modern Reader," *MS*, 9 (1977), 3–36; Barbara K. Lewalski, "Milton on Women—Yet Once More," *MS*, 6 (1974), 3–20; Joan Mallory Webber, "The Politics of Poetry: Feminism and *Paradise Lost*," *MS*, 14 (1980), 3–24.

but expressions of revulsion or fear of genital and particularly female sexuality pervade Renaissance poetry, and surely these expressions are too well known for us to believe that Milton is unique in this respect. The truth is probably that Milton did what everyone else was doing; only he did it a whole lot better, or worse, depending on your point of view.

Take, for example, the portrayal of women generally in Book I of Spenser's *Faerie Queene*. Opposed to Una in her perfected oneness comes an ample number of duplicitous and misshapen figures—such as Error, the model for Milton's Sin, who "Halfe like a serpent horribly displaide, / But th' other halfe did womans shape retaine" (I.i.14). Fair above and foul below, the double image of woman is repeated throughout Book I: as Duessa, beautiful on the surface, but beneath it foul and ugly. Or as Lucifera, the sovereign of the House of Pride, enthroned above a "dreadfull Dragon with an hideous trayne" (I.iv.10). Or, again, as Duessa, now in the role of the Whore of Babylon, mounted on the dragon of the Apocalypse (I.vii.16–18). Repeatedly the figure of a woman, beautiful in appearance, is either joined significantly with a dragon or split into a double figure, fair above and dragon-like below. The true woman is named Una, and her false double, replicated in numerous other figures, is named Duessa. Two and one. The point, however, is not so much the doubleness of the fatally seductive object as the doubleness—the split, the ambivalence—of the troubled subject, such as Spenser's Red Crosse Knight.[5]

Shakespeare, too, has contributed generously to this gallery of troubled and troubling figures. Chief among them must be King Lear, with his cry of outrage at woman and her sexuality: "But to the girdle do the gods inherit, / Beneath is all the fiends': there's hell, there's darkness, / There is the sulphurous pit" (*Lear*, 4.6.126–28). And in Sonnet 134 the poet is dismayed that he has had to forfeit his beloved young man to the sexual appetite of his mistress, as if in the—punning—default of a mortgage: "Him have I lost, thou hast both him and me, / He pays the *whole*, and yet am I not free" (ll. 13–14; my emphasis). Shakespeare's sonnets develop an ideal of sublimated homoerotic friendship posed against the alternatives of woman and sexuality. This ideal turns up everywhere in the poetry of the English

---

5. See Mark Rose, *Spenser's Art: A Companion to Book One of "The Faerie Queene"* (Cambridge: Harvard University Press, 1975), 26. Quotations of Spenser are from *The Poetical Works of Edmund Spenser*, ed. J. C. Smith and Ernest de Selincourt (London: Oxford University Press, 1912).

Renaissance, and it appears to be fundamental to a shared poetic vision of culture and civilization, be it Shakespeare's or Milton's or that of any other contemporary poet. Certainly, one of the most eloquent and direct evocations of the ideal is Ben Jonson's fine ode celebrating the friendship between Lucius Cary and Henry Morison.[6]

The major tension in Jonson's ode is between sexuality and civilization. First, there is the "Brave Infant of *Saguntum*" (1), whose birth comes simultaneously and therefore symbolically merged with the "deeds of death, and night" that occur when Hannibal destroys the town. He is a "wise" child, says Jonson, because at birth he takes one look at the world and—according to the legend that Jonson follows—returns to make his mother's womb his tomb.[7] Opposing this awful vision, and triumphing over the horror of death and sexuality, is the friendship of Cary and Morison. In spite of Morison's death, they are like the two stars in the constellation of the twins, Castor and Pollux, though Lucius on earth is separated now, "the one halfe from his *Harry*" in heaven (l. 94). As friends, they form between themselves, like mutually reflecting mirrors, a perfect model of the reproduction of civilization, not by sexuality but by the "simple love of greatnesse, and of good; / That knits brave minds, and manners, more than blood" (ll. 105–6). Attracted originally by the virtue that each perceived in the other, they drew closer together, "Till either grew a portion of the other" (l. 110). Each man by his accomplishment came to be called "the Copie of his friend" (1. 112). And thereafter, in a typically Jonsonian turn, they "liv'd to be the great surnames, / And titles, by which all made claimes / Unto the Vertue. Nothing perfect done, / But as a *Cary*, or a *Morison*" (ll. 113–16). As mirrors, as twins, as portions or copies of one another, Cary and Morison become a model, prior to language, of "*Friendship*, in deed, . . . not in words" (l. 123); between them they give asexual birth to the virtue of friendship and bestow their names upon it.

For a long time I have been puzzled by Jonson's use, at the begin-

---

6. Quotations of Shakespeare are from *The Riverside Shakespeare*, ed. G. Blakemore Evans (Boston: Houghton Mifflin, 1974). Quotations of Jonson's ode "To the Immortall Memorie, and Friendship of That Noble Paire, Sir Lucius Cary, and Sir H. Morison" (*Under-wood*, no. 72) are from *The Complete Poetry of Ben Jonson*, ed. William B. Hunter, Jr. (New York: Norton, 1968), 223–27.

7. Pliny writes of the child that returned to its mother's womb in *The Historie of the World: Commonly Called, The Natural Historie of C. Plinius Secundus*, trans. Philemon Holland (London, 1601), I, 158.

ning of his ode, of the strange story out of Pliny about a suicidal infant.
Throughout the rest of the poem Jonson does not refer back to the
story or do anything to resolve the lingering dissonance of its violent
drama. But I think now that the meaning of the infant grows with the
poem as it elaborates its vision of a mode of reproduction belonging
to civilization, tradition, and art, not to woman, sexuality, and the
body. "For life," says Jonson,

> doth her great actions spell,
> By what was done and wrought
> In season, and so brought
> To light: her measures are, how well
> Each syllab'e answer'd, and was form'd, how faire;
> These make the lines of life, and that's her ayre.
> ["Immortall Memorie," ll. 59–64]

Jonson pays his highest compliment to this pair of friends: that between
them they create, indeed, give birth to a great *poem*.

I have dwelled on this reading of Jonson's ode because I believe it
provides us with a means for understanding some of the motives behind the gestures of fear and hatred toward women and sexuality that
we encounter very frequently in Renaissance poetry—which is, with
few exceptions, the work of male, not female, poets. I am concerned
especially with the link, implied by Jonson's ode, between the fantasy
of a mirroring of self and the act of naming. For I believe that the
mirror fantasy describes—and I can find no better word—the psychological *matrix* in which poetic composition or any form of creativity
takes place, and must take place if it is to occur at all.[8] Ultimately, I
want to bring this discussion back to the poetry of Milton, but the
way back there lies through the poetry of Andrew Marvell.

After all, it is Marvell who says, in lines that appear as the epigraph
to this essay, that Adam was happiest at the moment before Eve's
arrival in Eden. His tone characteristically light and ironic, Marvell
plays with ideas of number and in doing so points to a fundamental
question about gender identity that this poetry is concerned with—
not just Marvell's poetry, but Milton's and Shakespeare's, Spenser's

---

8. The concept of a mirror relationship comes from D. W. Winnicott's theory of
"transitional" experience, which takes place at the boundary between union and separation. Most of his writings on this subject are collected in *Playing and Reality* (New
York: Basic Books, 1971).

147

and Jonson's as well. "*Two* Paradises 'twere in *one* / To live in Paradise alone" (ll. 63–64). Two in one. But not sexual, not a marriage, not a coupling of opposite genders. If for Jonson two-in-one means a homo-erotic mirror relationship, as between twins, each one "a portion of the other," then what does it mean for Marvell? I think we can best answer this question by considering another of his poems, "The Mower's Song."

The Mower tells us in his song that at some original moment, now lost, he dwelled in a landscape that mirrored his desire, just as his mind at the same time mirrored the landscape: "My Mind was once the true survey / Of all these Medows fresh and gay; / And in the greenness of the Grass / Did see its Hopes as in a Glass" (ll. 1–4). The poem begins thus in an apparently conventional manner as a pastoral lament; and as it concerns a woman, we have good reason to expect that the Mower has been jilted by some shepherdess or other. But this is not at all the case. It is not Juliana's absence that disturbs the Mower—it is her presence: "For *Juliana* comes," he says, "and She / What I do to the Grass, does to my Thoughts and Me" (ll. 23–24). What Juliana does is break the mirror relationship between "Mind" and "Medows"; more, she acts like the Mower's own scythe and slices "my Thoughts" from "Me," cutting a gap in the original continuity between mind and self. There are two sets of two-in-one that Juliana cuts apart with her arrival: mind-and-landscape and mind-and-self. *Mind* is the middle term here, and it is helpful to recall how in "The Garden" the pivotal sixth stanza celebrates this middle term: the cre-ating, annihilating mind. The Mower, however, cannot endure the separation, the discontinuity and division, which the experience of *mind* necessarily implies, and which Juliana's arrival, and her differ-ence, demand of him. Instead, he threatens to commit suicide in order to restore the lost union of two-in-one. He seeks to become, literally and physically, at one with the landscape.[9]

In another of the Mower poems, Marvell's hapless speaker com-plains that Juliana so "displac'd" his mind that he will never again find his way "home."[10] Dis-*place*-ment, I think, is a crucial concept for Marvell. The mirror relationship is experienced as a place, a ground,

9. See Jim Swan, "History, Pastoral and Desire: Andrew Marvell's Mower Poems," *International Review of Psycho-Analysis*, 3 (1976), 193–202.

10. Andrew Marvell, "The Mower to the Glo-Worms," in *The Poems and Letters of Andrew Marvell*, ed. H. M. Margoliouth, 2d ed. (Oxford: Clarendon Press, 1952), I, 44–45, ll. 15–16. All further quotations of Marvell's poetry are from this edition.

from which all the creative and re-creative activity of the mind arises and to which it returns. This appears to be the lesson of "The Garden." There, in the meditative retirement of the "Garden-state," from which all purposeful, aggressive striving and all genital sexuality have been banished, the recreative mind maintains its relationship to the place of its origin of being. This place is not something that can be named or located, it has no boundaries, there is no map of it, no deed or title to convey possession of it. It exists only in the silent mirroring of self and other which makes them one, prior to speech, prior to difference, prior to all the vast fabric of discourse and exchange that is the sign of our being human.[11]

The Mower, then, the mask or voice through which Marvell plays out fantasies of origin and identity, provides an exemplary drama with which we can now return to read the drama of Milton's Samson. For the similarities between the two are not so slight as they may first appear. Of course, the Mower shares none of Samson's concern with a *prophetic* identity, his troubled attachment to the role of chosen hero in a struggle to determine the fate of a nation and the status of that nation's god.[12] If anything, the Mower's concerns are exactly the opposite. In his complaint to the "Glo-worms," he calls them "Country Comets," which, because they are of the country and not the city, of the meadow and not the court, "portend / No War, nor Princes funeral, / Shining unto no higher end / Then to presage the Grasses fall" (ll. 5–8). And yet, when it is articulated in this manner, the Mower's country innocence turns out to be dialectical in nature: its meaning arises from its being a condition of "not-politics," a condition that gauges its virtue and its pleasure by the distance it keeps from the city and the court. From this perspective, it can be seen that Samson and the Mower do in fact have in common something of considerable significance. They are both enmeshed in the dialectic between what was traditionally understood as the *vita activa* and the *vita contemplativa*, the two opposing ideals of heroic action and contemplative retirement.[13] Samson feels the tension of this dialectic virtually without

11. See Jim Swan, "At Play in the Garden of Ambivalence: Andrew Marvell and the Green World," *Criticism*, 17 (1975), 295–307.

12. For a fine reading of Samson as a prophetic actor, see William W. Kerrigan, *The Prophetic Milton* (Charlottesville: University Press of Virginia, 1974), 201–18.

13. A good, short discussion of the distinction between the *vita activa* and the *vita contemplativa* may be found in Hannah Arendt, *The Human Condition* (Chicago: University of Chicago Press, 1958), 12–17.

letup from the beginning of Milton's drama to the end: temptation presses him to disengage from the prophetically appointed conflict and to accept a life of untroubled ease, as it is offered by Manoa, his father, or by Dalila—an alternative that Manoa, even when he offers it, recognizes as "idle" and "inglorious" (ll. 579–80). For the Mower, on the other hand, there is the same tension, or its mirror opposite, in the way he remains always aware of the life he is *not* leading, the life of the city and the court, of power and wealth. In addition, Marvell has added a subtle but important change by making his speaker a laborer instead of the traditionally idle shepherd. In the Mower, the medieval ideal of contemplative retirement has been modulated to embrace the Reformation virtue of honest labor.[14] This factor leads directly in the Mower poems to the complex irony of the way in which the Mower becomes the agent of his own undoing, enacting his own displacement from the original unity of mind-and-landscape, a displacement arising from the fact that the Mower's labor inevitably distances and alienates him from the landscape he labors in.

Samson and the Mower, then, dwell at opposite ends of the spectrum connecting action and retirement. This connection they share, and they also share something else perhaps more important. For each of them is troubled by his relationship with a woman. An interesting feature of the dialectic between the active and contemplative ideals is that they are closely similar in the *solitary* quality of the life that each of them defines. Neither the active life nor the retired life, ideally speaking, is a shared life. Retirement, by definition, means withdrawal from worldly concerns and relationships, and even in contemplative communities, such as monasteries, the shared desire that brings and holds them together is the desire of each individual member to be alone with his meditations.[15] Similarly, a fundamental motive of the

14. It was a Renaissance commonplace that God favored Abel, a shepherd, over Cain, an agricultural laborer, because Abel (as Bacon tells it), "by reason of his leisure, rest in a place, and living in the view of heaven, is a lively image of a contemplative life" (Sir Francis Bacon, *Of the Proficience and Advancement of Learning* [1605], in *Works*, ed. J. Spedding, R. L. Ellis, and D. D. Heath, 14 vols. [London, 1858–74], III, 297; quoted in Hallet Smith, *Elizabethan Poetry: A Study in Conventions, Meaning, and Expression* [Cambridge: Harvard University Press, 1952], 3).

15. St. Ignatius Loyola emphasizes the proper degree of withdrawal for performance of the *Spiritual Exercises*:

> Ordinarily, the progress made in the Exercises will be greater, the more the exercitant withdraws from all friends and acquaintances, and from all worldly cares. . . . There are many advantages resulting from this separation, but the following three are the most important:

active hero is to assert his supreme singularity, to be, as Milton's Chorus says at last of Samson, the one who knows "no second" (l. 1701). Solitude is a quality that links figures as diverse as Achilles and Saint Jerome, or Oliver Cromwell and the shepherd in *Lycidas*.[16] It is also the condition that marks both Samson and the Mower. Their solitude, however, is vulnerable.

Both Samson and the Mower experience solitude as the condition

---

First, if in order to serve and praise God our Lord one withdraws from numerous friends and acquaintances and from many occupations not undertaken with a pure intention, he gains no little merit before the Divine Majesty.

Secondly, in this seclusion the mind is not engaged in many things, but can give its whole attention to one single interest, that is, to the service of its Creator and its spiritual progress. Thus it is more free to use its natural powers to seek diligently what it so much desires.

Thirdly, the more the soul is in solitude and seclusion, the more fit it renders itself to approach and be united with its Creator and Lord; and the more closely it is united with Him, the more it disposes itself to receive graces and gifts from the infinite goodness of its God.   [*The Spiritual Exercises of St. Ignatius*, trans. Louis J. Puhl, S. J. (Chicago: Loyola University Press, 1951), 9–10]

As can be seen in just this short passage, a fundamental concern of the Ignatian discipline is number: "*numerous* friends" and "*many* occupations" as against "*one* single interest." Clearly, this is a discipline for the obsessive focusing of identity, for emptying the field of consciousness, clearing it of the many, so that it can embrace the one and be "united with [the] Creator and Lord," an action that secures the wholeness and unity of the self against any potential for disintegration.

And yet, what does this private, meditative discipline, performed in solitude, have in common with the struggle of the active hero on the stage of the public world? Look at the argument with which Ulysses attempts, in Shakespeare's *Troilus and Cressida*, to stir in Achilles a desire to maintain his honor:

> Take the instant way,
> For honor travels in a strait so narrow,
> Where one but goes abreast. Keep then the path,
> For emulation hath a thousand sons
> That one by one pursue. If you give way,
> Or hedge aside from the direct forthright,
> Like to an enter'd tide, they all rush by
> And leave you hindmost.
>   [3.3.153–60]

It is the same obsession with the one against the many, the same determination to be *one*—although here it takes the form of a will to subdue and dominate the many rather than to erase them from consciousness.

16. Milton, in his official portrait of Cromwell, describes how he first disciplined himself in virtuous retirement before taking on the active life (*Second Defense of the English People*, in *Complete Poems and Major Prose*, 832). Marvell repeats this view in the "Horatian Ode," where he describes Cromwell as keeping to "his private Gardens, where / He liv'd reserved and austere" (ll. 29–30) before he joined the political struggle.

of their being who they are, and they both perceive their solitude as threatened and finally violated by a woman. For the Mower, solitude is already lost, a remembered condition of being at one with the landscape, a condition Juliana has already disrupted by her presence. Samson, too, has already lost his solitude. It was, at first, what secured his secret, the "silence" that he betrays—not once, but twice—to both his wives, the woman of Timna as well as Dalila, as if he were obsessively compelled to name it over and over again and thus to betray it repeatedly.

Repetition, in fact, fills Milton's drama with references to phenomena that are double or that happen twice. It seems to elaborate a conflict between the twoness that threatens and the oneness that affirms an identity, a conflict very much in the tradition of the one between Spenser's Una and Duessa. Not only does Samson marry twice and betray his silence twice, but he keeps remembering repeatedly that the angel twice descended to foretell his birth and destiny. He remembers that there were two cords binding him when, in a rage, he broke loose to slaughter a thousand of his enemies. And at the end there are the "two massy pillars" to which Samson applies his powerful arms with devastating effect. With a rage akin to the Mower's in "The Mower's Song," Samson, "with horrible convulsion to and fro" (l. 1649), smashes all that is contrary, collapsing it violently into one, achieving a triumphant vengeance that is also his own death. Afterward the Chorus celebrates the revival of Samson's "fiery virtue," comparing him to the legendary phoenix, "that self-begott'n bird / In the *Arabian* woods embost, / That no second knows, nor third" (ll. 1699–1701). Like the Phoenix, Samson is seen now as a genus of one, absolute in his singularity.[17] Thus Manoa, searching for an appropriate

---

17. Lactantius, in his *Carmen de ave Phoenice*, exhibits the paradoxical nature of the phoenix:

> Ipsa sibi proles, suus pater et suus heres,
> Nutrix ipsa sui, semper alumna sibi.

"He is son to himself, is his own father and his own heir, / He is his own nurse, and is ever a foster-child to himself" (trans. Ernst H. Kantorowicz, in *The King's Two Bodies: A Study in Medieval Political Theology* [Princeton: Princeton University Press, 1957], 390). Kantorowicz also quotes Baldus de Ubaldis (c. 1327–1400): "The Phoenix is a unique and most singular bird, in which the whole kind (*genus*) is conserved in the individual" (389).

simile to describe his son's achievement, chooses the inevitable tautology: "*Samson* hath quit himself / Like *Samson*" (ll. 1709–10).[18]

This resolution of *Samson Agonistes* is altogether appropriate and deeply ironic at the same time. The drama ends with an ample sense of completion. Samson has overcome his terrible experience of isolation and defeat to return triumphantly at last to being himself, "like Samson." But he achieves this state of completed identity only at the moment of death, an irony that implies something very problematic about the identity he has thus recovered. For it seems so absolute that it cannot be lived in a world of ordinary—or fallen—human dis-

18. Samson's ironic triumph is like the final, apocalyptic moment predicted for the "two-handed engine" in *Lycidas* ("ready to smite once, and smite no more" [ll. 130–31]), in that it closes up the ironies of time in one ultimate act. Milton's focus on time distinguishes his poetic from Spenser's. In *The Faerie Queene*, Error is an emblem of falsehood and deception, a figure to be read at once and recognized or not, while in *Paradise Lost*, Sin, Milton's most Spenserian figure, represents the experience of time as catastrophic repetition, arrested at the moment of origin ("hourly conceiv'd / And hourly born"). The obsessive drive of repetition drives Samson's experience in the form of dramatic irony, what Samson feels most acutely as the difference between "what once I was, and what am now" (l. 22), the fair above and foul below of Spenser's Error reconfigured as Samson's knowledge *through time* of triumph past and present pain. Thus, at one moment when close to despair, he questions why God's gifts, "desirable, to tempt / Our earnest Prayers, then, giv'n with solemn hand / As Graces, draw a Scorpion's tail behind" (ll. 358–60). In a similar manner, Dalila is finally understood to be "a manifest Serpent by her sting / Discover'd in the end, till now conceal'd" (ll. 997–98). And even Dalila herself offers as one of her several excuses for betraying Samson that "the fact more evil drew / In the perverse event than I foresaw" (ll. 736–37). That this and related forms of irony pervade *Samson Agonistes* has been well understood. In particular, Anthony Low analyzes what he calls the "irony of alternatives" by which either/or turns out finally to be both/and, as in Samson's prediction "This day will be remarkable in my life / By some great act, or of my days the last" (ll. 1388–89). In my argument below, however, I suggest that Samson's either/or points to a deeper level: not both/and but *neither/nor* (see n. 29). See Anthony Low, *The Blaze of Noon: A Reading of "Samson Agonistes"* (New York: Columbia University Press, 1974), 77–89. See also Joseph H. Summers, "The Movements of the Drama," in *The Lyric and Dramatic Milton*, ed. Summers (New York: Columbia University Press, 1965), 158–59.

There is also a different, very illuminating study of the importance of silence for Samson: Marcia Landy, "Language and the Seal of Silence in *Samson Agonistes*," *Milton Studies*, 2 (1970), 175–94. Landy sees Samson's task as a recovery of his true self, first through and then beyond the medium of language, a recovery of his "unique relationship with God," which he lost when he broke the silence that symbolized it (183). Landy focuses primarily on Samson's relation to language and its rhetorical slipperiness.

course, although at the same time it seems impossible to live without it. Accordingly, Samson, in anguish over the loss of his identity, looks toward death as a "privilege" (l. 104) and must be warned by Manoa against offending God with his despair (ll. 502–15). That Samson's desired identity transcends ordinary, fallen discourse is suggested by the silence that preserves it before he betrays it into speech. There are numerous opportunities in the drama to observe that transcendence, the best being perhaps those moments early on, when Samson seems most anxious and defeated, when he questions most sharply the causes of his humiliation.

So pained is he by his defeat that he begins to think of his own singularity as the source of his troubles. Why was he chosen from birth to be "a person separate to God, / Destin'd for great exploits" (ll. 31–32)? Why upon him alone did God entrust the awful burden of Israel's fate, especially now that he has failed so shamefully, "Made of [his] Enemies the scorn and gaze" (l. 34)? Convinced of his own complete isolation, Samson begins to feel that he is also plagued inwardly, in the separate functions of mind and body, by the same affliction. Why, for instance, was his great strength localized, symbolically, in just one place on his body, where it could easily be stolen from him? And, most painful of all, why was the faculty of sight confined to the eye alone, where it could easily be put out? As he puzzles over this question, Samson invokes the theory that the soul is always entirely present everywhere in the body.[19] The soul, in this view, is a model of identity opposed to difference and singularity. It represents instead a diffusion of identity, a dissolving of boundaries and differences, a merger of self and other in one limitless body. Significantly, the soul that Samson imagines is feminine, "she" who is "all in every part" (l. 93), just as sight is feminine when Samson pictures it diffused

---

19. Hughes, in a footnote, documents Augustine's doctrine that "the soul is *tota in qualibet parte*" (Milton, *Complete Poems and Major Prose*, 553). See John Paul Russo, "'Diffus'd' Spirits: Scientific Metaphor in *Samson Agonistes*," *Papers on Language and Literature*, 5 (1969), 85–90. Twice in *Paradise Lost* Milton evokes the undivided, unalienated perfection of the angelic body. When Satan suffers the first wound, a "discontinuous" wound (6.329), he soon heals because he is one of the "Spirits that live throughout / Vital in every part, not as frail man / In Entrails, Heart or Head, Liver or Reins" (6.344–46). Then Raphael, in answer to Adam's question about angelic lovemaking, assures him that it is an act that angels enjoy "in eminence, and obstacle find none / Of membrane, joint, or limb, exclusive bars: / Easier than Air with Air, if Spirits embrace, / Total they mix, Union of Pure with Pure / Desiring" (8.624–28). In Heaven, evidently, there are no knees or elbows.

like feeling throughout the body, "That she might look at will through every pore" (l. 96). It is as if Samson were imagining the recovery of a primal unity prior to individuation, prior to being singled out. If, indeed, sight were diffused throughout the body, then Samson would not now be "exil'd from light" (l. 96). He would be able to control his access to what he experiences as the source of his being. He would be able to commune with God's light "at will."

In meditating on his blindness, Samson imagines still another feminine figure, the silent moon:

> The Sun to me is dark
> And silent as the Moon,
> When she deserts the night,
> Hid in her vacant interlunar cave.
>
> [SA, ll. 86–89]

The silence of this moon has been often noted and praised, primarily for its synaesthetic effect.[20] A powerful metaphor, it acts not just to blend auditory and visual experience. It also serves to define the nature of Samson's spiritual isolation. Samson prefaces his comment on the moon's silence with an apostrophe to light in lines that depend for their force on the traditional play of ambiguity between physical sunlight and the spiritual light of Heaven:

> O dark, dark, dark, amid the blaze of noon,
> Irrecoverably dark, total Eclipse
> Without all hope of day!
> O first created Beam, and thou great Word,
> "Let there be light, and light was over all";
> Why am I thus bereav'd thy prime decree?
>
> [SA, ll. 80–85]

In effect, this lament equates light with the Word. Not only is the sun "dark" to Samson, but in his spiritual blindness it is also "silent" like the hidden moon. The silence that afflicts him is a spiritual silence, an absence not of words but of the unmediated Word. After all, he has already had more than enough of mere words. They are the in-

20. T. S. Eliot, "A Note on the Verse of Milton," *Essays and Studies*, 21 (1936); rpt. in T. S. Eliot, *Milton: Two Studies* (London: Faber & Faber, 1968), 13–14; E. M. W. Tillyard, *The Miltonic Setting: Past & Present* (1938; rpt. New York: Barnes & Noble, 1966), 100–102.

struments of his betrayal: Dalila's "tongue batteries" (l. 404) and "peal of words" (l. 235) as well as his own "shameful garrulity" (l. 491). The Word, itself inexpressible, is for Milton the ground of all expression; it authorizes human discourse and guarantees its status as a sign of the real. In *Paradise Lost*, Raphael describes the relationship between the Word and mere words when he explains the Creation to Adam:

> So spake th' Almighty, and to what he spake
> His Word, the Filial Godhead, gave effect.
> Immediate are the Acts of God, more swift
> Than time or motion, but to human ears
> Cannot without process of speech be told,
> So told as earthly notion can receive.
>
> [*PL*, 7.174–79]

By the "process of speech," and "by lik'ning spiritual to corporal forms, / As may express them best" (5.573–74), Raphael is able to tell of matters that, without the angel's mediation, would exceed Adam's capacity for understanding. For these matters are divine secrets and, as Raphael says, "not lawful to reveal" (5.569–70), except that God intends for Adam to learn what concerns his existence. The prohibition against revealing or prying into divine secrets is, of course, central to the conflict in *Paradise Lost*, not only for the major characters but for the poet as well. The question causes him considerable anxiety, as when he invokes God's "holy Light" and asks if he may so express it "unblam'd" (3.3); or when, in his poetic flight, he implores protection from the fate of Bellerophon, who did not just accidentally fall from Pegasus but was thrown when a gadfly sent by Jove stung the winged horse.[21] That the very act of composing such a poem as *Paradise Lost* implies a profoundly dangerous risk was recognized by Andrew Marvell in commendatory verses that often preface Milton's poem in modern editions:

> When I beheld the Poet blind, yet bold,
> In slender Book his vast Design unfold,
> *Messiah* Crown'd, *Gods* Reconcil'd Decree,
> Rebelling *Angels*, The Forbidden Tree,
> Heav'n, Hell, Earth, Chaos, All; the Argument
> Held me a while misdoubting his Intent,

21. See Hughes's footnote in Milton, *Complete Poems and Major Prose*, 346.

That he would ruine (for I saw him strong)
The sacred Truths to Fable and old Song,
(So *Sampson* groap'd the Temples Posts in spite)
The World o'rewhelming to revenge his Sight.
["On Mr. Milton's *Paradise Lost*," ll. 1–10]

Marvell's suggestion that it is spite that motivates both Milton and Samson is far wide of the mark, but he does pinpoint Milton's basic risk. And it is Samson's risk, too.

In effect, Samson at his low point represents the fantasy of divine retribution that the poet of *Paradise Lost* fears will happen to him for revealing sacred truths. What sacred truth, though, has Samson revealed? The secret location of the great strength in his hair does not, in itself, amount to anything at all profound. Perhaps, as Samson himself says, God meant to show how "slight" (l. 59) the gift of strength was by placing it there. Perhaps, too, the apparent triviality of his hair, simply as a material object, agrees with the triviality of the fruit that Adam and Eve eat in the Garden. Unimportant in itself, it signifies the profoundest of truths. Or, more to the point, its importance is precisely the disjunction, the gap, between its own triviality and the secret it is thought to represent. In *Samson Agonistes* Milton extends the meditation he pursues in *Paradise Lost* on the relationship between signs and what they signify. In order to cut Samson's hair, or to pluck the fruit and eat it, one must first reify the object as a sign of sacred truth, of divine knowledge and power. Once reified, however, the sign itself suffers a fall: cut off forever from its truth, henceforth it can represent that truth only from afar, looking across the irrecoverable distance of its fall. Once Samson tells the secret of his strength, once he puts it into *words*, he has, in effect, cut his own hair. Along with his secret, Samson suffers a fall into language, or, in Marvell's words, a "ruine" of sacred truth into narrative.

The manner of Samson's fall into language explains, I think, why Milton omits from his poem any wording from the riddle that is the subject of Samson's betrayal by the woman of Timna. In this drama about the betrayal of secrets, the riddle is the secret that Milton *keeps.* Only, like Samson's, it turns out to be no secret at all: it lies open to anyone who can read. Samson's betrayal by the woman of Timna is the first of the two betrayals that he suffers, but in light of his apparent compulsion to repeat himself, it seems appropriate to read the two betrayals as the same betrayal, the two secrets as the same secret.

157

"Out of the eater came forth meat," the riddle says, "and out of the strong came forth sweetness" (*Judges* 14:14). The riddle utters the paradox that contraries are one, while Samson's drive to *be* one means an exclusion and defeat of what is contrary, expressed repeatedly as a rage to destroy the other—which, in the end, is also a rage to destroy the self. In the well-known words of *Areopagitica*, Milton declares that what purifies us in our fallenness is *trial*, "and trial is by what is contrary." But in the same text he also declares that knowledge of the two primal contraries, good and evil, "from out of the rind of one apple tasted, . . . as two twins cleaving together, leaped forth into the world."[22] Trial is thus a perplexing experience, a struggle to distinguish and choose between alternatives that seem indistinguishable. Milton's Samson cannot utter the riddle spoken by the biblical Samson because he is struggling to distinguish between contraries that are like "twins cleaving together." He is struggling to distinguish *himself*, to reassert his identity as the one man singled out by God for heroic action—action *against* what is contrary. In that way he asserts his identity.

Of course, the modern concept of identity does not concern Milton's Samson, and it is a fair question whether it concerns Milton himself. The word "identity" seems not to be part of the Renaissance English vocabulary, certainly not in its modern, psychological meaning. It is absent altogether from Milton's poetry, and from Shakespeare's too.[23] Is it inappropriate, then, an anachronism, to speak of Samson as having and losing an *identity*? Normally, I would ignore this question as trivial. But in this case I think it must be taken seriously as a way of defining an important issue. For I believe that Milton, as poet and revolutionary, was himself a major actor in the drama that transformed what it means, in the Western tradition, to have an identity. Just a brief glance at the history of pertinent words in the *Oxford English Dictionary* (*OED*) will show how Milton's career, as well as those of Spenser, Shakespeare, Jonson, and Marvell, coincides with the moment of a crucial change in the language. "Identity," for instance, is first recorded by the *OED* in 1570, while 1638 marks its first use in the now familiar sense of "individuality" or "personality." Moreover, the *OED*'s use of the word "individuality" as a modern synonym for

---

22. Milton, *Areopagitica*, in *Complete Poems and Major Prose*, 728.

23. William Ingram and Kathleen Swaim, eds., *A Concordance to Milton's English Poetry* (Oxford: Clarendon, 1972); Marvin Spevack, *The Harvard Concordance to Shakespeare* (Cambridge: Harvard University Press, 1973).

"identity" is an especially fine coincidence, because that word, too, particularly as the familiar cognate "individual," was undergoing a change in this period which introduced a new meaning basic to the modern idea of identity. "Individuality," in fact, did not make its first recorded appearance until the early seventeenth century, apparently in response to the new development in the meaning of "individual." The history of this latter word is remarkable; it underwent almost a complete reversal of meaning. For "individual" as an adjective, two related meanings, first recorded in Middle English, became obsolete during the last half of the seventeenth century: (1) "One in substance or essence; indivisible;" (2) "Inseparable." Then two modern meanings were introduced during the seventeenth century: (3) "Existing as a separate indivisible entity; numerically one, single; particular, special;" (4) "Distinguished from others by attributes of its own." The change from the second to the third and fourth meanings, from being inseparable to being separate and distinct, is a radical one. It describes the transition to the modern experience of identity.

In his poetry, Milton uses the word "individual" only three times, always as an adjective, and each time he means the quality of undivided unity between one being and another. Thus Eve remembers that Adam at their first meeting pleaded with her to stay at his side, "Henceforth an *individual* solace dear" (*PL*, 4.486; my emphasis).[24] And God, when he names the Son as his viceregent, commands all the angels to abide under his reign, "United as one *individual* Soul / For ever happy" (5.610–11; my emphasis).[25] Appropriately, God the Father and his Son enjoy a perfect relationship of "individual" union, while at the same time the Son is always the perfect "image" in whom "all his Father shone / Substantially express'd" (3.139–40), as if the Son were a sign—or rather *the* sign—in an unimaginable, unfallen

24. The *OED* quotes this line (*PL*, 4.486) as the last recorded use of "individual" with the meaning of "inseparable."

25. In his command establishing the rule of the Son, God invokes the traditional metaphor of the body politic, which implies a contradiction at the heart of political and ecclesiastical orders. The body politic is both a mystical body and a power structure. Everyone is united "as one individual soul," but ranked "under" the rule of one who is their "head." Whoever disobeys the "head" breaks the mystical "union" (*PL*, 5.606–12). Thus the identity of each person is dependent on and subsumed under the identity of the one who is their head. In part, the English Revolution can be read as a violent undoing of this contradictory metaphor. See Sheldon Wolin, *Politics and Vision: Continuity and Innovation in Western Political Thought* (Boston: Little, Brown, 1960), 131–40.

discourse, in which there is no gap between the sign and what it signifies, and the one is wholly present in the other. Adam and Eve, however, are never without conflict over the same issue.

The contrast between these two relationships in *Paradise Lost* — the perfect union of Father and Son and the troubled union of Adam and Eve—suggests that the poem draws much of its energy from the inevitable paradox of the origins of human identity. If an infant could answer the question "Who are you?" it might answer, "I cannot speak yet of 'I' because I am still the other, the one from whom I have come just now, but with whom I am still at one." This answer—however, improbable or impossible—would speak for the transitional, ambivalent quality of the infant's experience: neither separate from nor united with the other.[26] A special problem arises with this concept, however, because the original relationship is not the same for both genders, male and female. That is, in maturity, women look back to an origin of identity with one who is the same, while men look back to an identity with one who is different. (This analysis necessarily assumes a woman in the role of mother.) There is thus no symmetry between men and women in their original experience of identity. Consequently, they experience identity itself in different ways. For men, the experience of a primal difference at the origin of identity makes it likely that they, more than women, will feel compelled to assert an identity separate and distinct from others.[27] At the originating core of his sense of who he is, a man finds himself identified with a woman. What, then, does he do with this identity if he believes that his role is to be and act like a man?

Traditional Judeo-Christian thought, especially in its later Protestant development, has held out the promise of a solution to this paradox. In the person of God the Father men encounter a primal figure adequate to their desire for an origin of identity with one who is the same, an origin free of the disturbance of difference. Father and Son, in

26. See Winnicott, *Playing and Reality*.

27. Cf. Nancy Chodorow, "Feminism and Difference: Gender, Relation, and Difference in Psychoanalytic Perspective," *Socialist Review*, no. 46 (1979), 63: "Maleness is more conflictual and more problematic [than femaleness]. Underlying, or built into, core male gender identity is an early, nonverbal, unconscious, almost somatic sense of femaleness that continually, usually unnoticeably, but sometimes insistently, challenges and undermines the sense of maleness." See also Chodorow, *The Reproduction of Mothering: Psychoanalysis and the Sociology of Gender* (Berkeley: University of California Press, 1978), 104–8, 164–70.

Paradise Lost, reflect this desire by men for a primary relationship between two who are one and the same. Such a relationship is also what Samson, in the depth of his spiritual isolation, mourns as lost. Remembering his original relationship with God, he complains, "I was his nursling once and choice delight" (l. 633). Samson's metaphor, which assigns feminine attributes to a male God, portraying him as a father who nurses his son, arises directly from the primacy of the relationship imagined. All the erotic power of the bond between mother and infant is here transferred to the bond between father and son. Thus in Samson's painful image of his isolation, the silent moon, he expresses his sense of being abandoned by the paternal Word in terms that suggest abandonment by the mother, she who, in her silence, "deserts" the night and remains hidden from view (ll. 88–89).[28] Clearly, for Samson, the paternal bond does not provide a secure and stable solution to the paradox of primary male identity. Samson himself betrays the secret of the bond, not once but twice. That he betrays the secret each time to a woman is crucial: the traditional solution lacks stability precisely because it asserts its desire for sameness against the fact that at the origin of a man's identity is inevitably one who is different, other, a woman.

The paradox of primary male identity has large consequences, particularly, I believe, for poetry. As a poet, a man may well find it valuable to accept his original identity with a woman. I would say that, in fact, as a poet he *must* accept it if he is to maintain his creativity. But as a man in a world of masculine dominance, he may find this original identity troubling and even intolerable. He may experience a difficult conflict between his roles as man and poet, between asserting a dominate masculine identity and accepting a diffuse creative identity. The conflict is not easily resolved, although I cannot say if resolution is even desirable. What does seem clear is that the poetry very often provides an occasion for realizing the conflict and working or playing it out. Milton's speaker in *Paradise Lost*, for instance, first announces

28. The line about the silent moon being "Hid in her vacant interlunar cave" (l. 89) is surely a puzzle. T. S. Eliot thought "interlunar" to be a "stroke of genius" but did not elaborate (*Milton: Two Studies*, 14). If the moon is hid in her cave, how can the cave be "vacant"? My guess is that the line condenses Samson's deeply overdetermined sense of being abandoned. "Interlunar" implies the moon's absence, and even her cave where she might be found during the interlunar period is "vacant." In effect, the line states the absolute disappearance of the moon, not just hidden, but completely vanished, nowhere, and in her *silence* is the secret that Samson mourns.

his ambition to create a poem so distinct and original that it will be like nothing ever attempted before, but then he later takes pains to deny that the poem is his own, declaring instead that it is "Hers who brings it nightly to my Ear" (*PL*, 9.47). Moreover, at the beginning of the poem he also invokes a spirit who manifests its power when, "dove-like," it sits "brooding on the vast Abyss" and makes it "pregnant" (1.21–22). The implied analogy leaves it uncertain whether the speaker imagines that, once inspired, he will make the abyss pregnant with his poem or whether he believes that inspiration will make *him* pregnant. The ambiguity of the speaker's role—both passive and aggressive, potent and pregnant—provides a good paradigm for Milton's poetic identity.

But the problematic of a poetic identity runs deeper still. As described so far, it remains grounded in relation to attributes securely recognizable by the subject as either "masculine" or "feminine," even though such attributes are determined culturally as well as dialectically in relation to each other—that is, they are arbitrary, a set of markers to assert a difference. The reason that this problematic is represented as a conflict between genders is that the either/or of gender difference *can* be represented, while the primal experience of undifferentiated, narcissistic wholeness, the neither/nor that in *Paradise Lost* is worded as an apocalyptic "All in All," *cannot* be represented, only pointed to, evoked, remembered as an absence.[29] It is a blank, nothing, a silence. It is the unspeakable Word that authorizes speech. It is Samson's secret. And the problem that Samson has with Dalila, as with the woman of Timna, is that her presence intrudes a difference that disrupts his communion with the neither/nor of undifferentiated wholeness, propelling him into a conflict that threatens to become an endless oscillation between contraries unless stopped arbitrarily by the assertion of dominance. "Therefore God's universal law," says Samson's

29. One problem with Chodorow's view of the dynamics of gender identity (n. 27, above) is that she does not depict separation as a sufficiently radical moment. The child's discovery comes late that the other is a woman, and it is not the other as woman who is ambivalently desired and repudiated as the other/self, but the undifferentiated narcissistic object, which the mother stands in for. At the primitive, originative core of identity is not femaleness or maleness but an undifferentiated wholeness that is neither. Most discussions of this issue that are based entirely on object relations theory tend to view the beginning of gender as both/and, both masculine *and* feminine. But that comes later as a reading of difference back upon a moment that is *neither/nor*.

Juliet Mitchell, in a recent talk to the Group for Applied Psychoanalysis at SUNY/ Buffalo, argued for a more radical view of gender identity in terms similar to these.

Chorus, "Gave to the man despotic power / Over his female in due awe . . . So shall he least confusion draw / On his whole life" (ll. 1053–59). Confusion comes with marriage:

> Seeming at first all heavenly under virgin veil,
> Soft, modest, meek, demure,
> Once join'd, the contrary she proves, a thorn
> Intestine, far within defensive arms
> A cleaving mischief, in his way to virtue
> Adverse and turbulent, or by her charms
> Draws him awry enslav'd
> With dotage, and his sense deprav'd
> To folly and shameful deeds which ruin ends.
> What Pilot so expert but needs must wreck
> Embark'd with such a Steers-mate at the Helm?
>
> [SA, ll. 1035–45]

This is the "female usurpation" (l. 1060) that dominance is meant to suppress. The embrace is contrary: she, not he, bears a thorn and, cleaving to him, she cleaves him mischievously in two. It is also castration, imagined as the fate of an Odysseus who allows his ship to be steered by the Siren herself, a "Steers-mate" who is also a "Steer's mate." Castration anxiety, as Freud came to understand it in his later thinking, is modeled on the moment of separation or differentiation.[30] In the sexual embrace that Samson imagines with Dalila, he falls into her snare, "swoll'n with pride":

> At length to lay my head and hallow'd pledge
> Of all my strength in the lascivious lap
> Of a deceitful Concubine who shore me
> Like a tame Wether, all my precious fleece,
> Then turn'd me out ridiculous, despoil'd,
> Shav'n, and disarm'd among my enemies.
>
> [SA, ll. 532, 535–40]

Imagined as versions of the phallus, the head and the head of hair, Samson's "capital secret" (l. 394), are like the words of a fallen language. Reified to present the undifferentiated secret, they suffer a fall. They are cut off. Incapable of presenting the secret as presence,

---

30. Sigmund Freud, *Inhibitions, Symptoms, and Anxiety* (1926), in *Standard Edition* XX, 127–29.

they can only represent it as absence, as silence. To defend against castration, Samson must assert his dominance, but he is always already in Dalila's snare, "enslav'd / With dotage" (ll. 1041–42). The defense is an illusion, mounted against a loss already suffered, and marriage, instituted as male dominance, is the illusory weapon. This perhaps is the reason for Samson's seemingly odd and unexplained strategy for the liberation of Israel: to defeat the Philistines he twice marries a Philistine woman: "I took to Wife . . . *Dalila*, / That specious Monster, my accomplisht snare . . . still watching to oppress / *Israel's* oppressors" (ll. 227–33). In the double retrospective of his narrative, Samson tells how he married a woman who was both accomplished (expert) in deceit and had accomplished (achieved) her deceit already. Moreover, for Samson it is specifically language that deceives: "I myself / Who vanquisht with a peal [also, "appeal"] of words (o weakness!) / Gave up my fort of silence to a Woman" (ll. 234–36). Like intercourse, speech is the sign of weakness, silence the sign of power.

Milton, however, is not Samson. As a poet, he is necessarily committed to speech, although at the same time he is committed to making manifest, like a prophet, the power and beauty of the unspeakable Word. In doing so, he engages in the same problematic and exposes himself to the same risks as Samson, with the result that his poetry often dwells upon a sense of indeterminacy, deferral, incompletion.

Milton, perhaps more than any other poet except Keats, is a poet of thresholds. In poem after poem he seems to stand poised at the edge of double alternatives, reluctant to make a definitive choice although aware of the necessity to do so. For instance, readers have often attempted to define the relationship between "L'Allegro" and "Il Penseroso" as a progression from a lower to a higher form of art and moral character. But that interpretation, I think, misses the profoundly dialectical quality of the relationship between the two poems, which speak together as complementary readings of experience: the first a quiet, passive delight in the surfaces of perception, the other an aggressive drive to interpret, to command the language of secrets below the surface. If it were humanly possible, if the nature of language permitted it, I believe Milton would have written the two poems as one. But the two motives are mutually exclusive: if you wish to dwell entirely on the surface, you forfeit the power to interpret, while, conversely, in your drive to interpret you inevitably violate the surface. And yet the two motives, like the two poems, are dialectically and

164

paradoxically tied together, like the sweetness and strength of Samson's unspoken riddle.

A general survey of Milton's work might reveal this powerful ambivalence at work throughout. It would show how this poet, who repeatedly urges the act of choice on his readers as the highest of moral actions, is the same poet for whom choice is a difficult and ultimately tragic act. For this essay, though, I want to offer a reading of one short poem as a model of Milton's attempt to work out his identity as a poet: the sonnet beginning "How soon hath Time." In a special way, it crystalizes many of the concerns we have encountered so far:

> How soon hath Time, the subtle thief of youth,
>   Stol'n on his wing my three and twentieth year!
>   My hasting days fly on with full career,
>   But my late spring no bud or blossom show'th.
> Perhaps my semblance might deceive the truth,
>   That I to manhood am arriv'd so near,
>   And inward ripeness doth much less appear,
>   That some more timely-happy spirits endu'th.
> Yet be it less or more, or soon or slow,
>   It shall be still in strictest measure ev'n
>   To that same lot, however mean or high,
>   Toward which Time leads me, and the will of Heav'n;
> All is, if I have the grace to use it so,
>   As ever in my great task-Master's eye.

The same kind of ambivalence that guides the form of "L'Allegro" and "Il Penseroso" guides this poem too. The speaker is in an indeterminate position, no longer a youth but not yet mature, showing neither bud nor blossom. He experiences himself anxiously as a creature of time, as if his very substance were time itself. And yet it is Time, personified as a thief, that is stealing his time away from him, his years and days. Time, in this view, is the opposite of *grace*, which is a divine gift transcending time. But the idea of grace does not occur to the speaker right away. For now, he not only feels himself being depleted of his time, but finds that as a consequence of being "timely," of existing in the irreversible process of time's passage, he is adrift and inhabits no one form of identity or another. He is now, and perhaps will be continually, in a state of nonidentity, no longer one, not yet the other. His youth has been stolen away, but he has not yet arrived at manhood: "so near," but not solidly *there*.

165

Once the speaker reaches this degree of self-doubt, he makes the predictable gesture of investing in others, projecting onto them, the possession of a "ripeness," a more fortunate relationship to time than he has. This is a dangerous moment. It can lead to deeper, more radical self-doubt and despair; or it can lead to envy, rage, and a wish to attack those others who appear to have the magical substance of being felt to be lacking in oneself. Milton, however, creates a solution that transcends both of these alternatives. The last six lines open with a gesture of grand indifference: it no longer matters whether it be "less or more," whether it come "soon or slow." Suddenly, the speaker enjoys a confidence that, whatever comes, "It shall be still" exactly what Time and Heaven eventually bring him to. Heaven is the new element here, but I am intrigued by the word "still" with its dual meaning, not only as it is usually read, as meaning "always," but also suggesting the *stillness* the speaker misses in himself as his "hasting days fly on with full career." Even Time itself is transformed into a partner with the will of Heaven in determining the outcome.

The last two lines have occasioned a good deal of puzzlement and discussion.[31] Without reviewing or responding to the variety of readings offered over the years, I want to propose one that satisfies my sense of the need to resolve an anxiety that comes with the experience of no longer having one identity but not yet having another, of having the potential of being any one of many identities but in fact being no *one*. And what particularly satisfies me about this reading is that it depends for its effect on the "timely" quality of poetry and language itself, the fact that we put words down on a page or read them, necessarily, one after the other, just as we necessarily read "L'Allegro" and "Il Penseroso" one after the other. The main clause of the final sentence is interrupted in the next-to-last line, so that initially the first two words stand as a completed statement: "All is." In this compact but sweeping gesture, Milton suddenly brushes aside the anxiety of being divided between alternatives. Gone is the division between youth and manhood, and in its place comes an indifference grounded in two words asserting the eternal presence of all things, all potentials and alternatives. "All is . . . as ever in my great task-Master's eye." The eye of eternity invoked here is also the "I," the ego of eternity

31. Several alternative readings of the last two lines are summarized by John Carey in his note to the poem, in *The Poems of John Milton*, ed. John Carey and Alastair Fowler (1968; rpt. New York: Norton, 1972), 147.

which, like the speaker himself, is neither one identity nor another, but poised forever between being *no one* and being *all*. To be "in" the great task-Master's eye/I is to participate as both an object of divine concern and a subject of divine consciousness, standing at a threshold where one may potentially become any and all identities, but refraining, even refusing actually to *be* any one identity. The speaker of the poem, in a double gesture of submission and assertion, thus realizes an identity that is exemplified in its perfection by the Son in *Paradise Lost*, who is "Mightiest in [his] Father's might" (*PL*, 6.710).[32] In this context, it should come as no surprise that this sonnet was probably written on the eve of Milton's refusal in 1632 to subscribe to the oath of allegiance and take orders in the English church, preferring instead to offer, as he calls it, a "blameless silence," and to retire to his father's estate and continue his reading.[33]

In spite of the sonnet's final indifference about time, there is still an anxious side to the refusal, and we hear it repeatedly throughout Milton's writing. There is, of course, the troubled questioning about identity in "Lycidas," and there is Milton's apology to his readers in the autobiographical section of *The Reason of Church Government* for his failure to accomplish what he promised. Then there is the anxiety of the later sonnet over his failure to make use of the talent bestowed on him—an anxiety resolved, again, in a way that justifies the desire to keep an unformed identity: "They also serve who only stand and wait." Later comes the fear implied at the outset of Book 9 of *Paradise Lost* that, "long choosing, and beginning late" (*PL*, 9.26), he may have waited too long after all. And, finally, there is the furious drive of Samson, even against himself, to be absolutely and entirely *one*.

At its most powerful the desire to keep one's identity unformed, at the threshold of an infinite potential, is what drives the creative pro-

---

32. Cf. Janet Adelman, "Creation and the Place of the Poet in *Paradise Lost*," in *The Author in His Work: Essays on a Problem in Criticism*, ed. Louis L. Martz and Aubrey Williams (New Haven: Yale University Press, 1978), 57, 59:

> The radical combination of self-assertion and self-denial in the invocation to book 9 is in fact characteristic of Milton's stance throughout the poem. . . . The "I" can emerge triumphant only when it is protected by a firm sense of its own instrumentality, as Abdiel can assert his power safely only with the simultaneous assertion that his power comes from God (6.119–20). Only thus can the "I" escape the egoism of Satan's "I therefore, I alone" (4.935); only thus can the poet be sure that his creation is not in imitation of Satan.

33. *The Reason of Church Government*, in *Complete Poems and Major Prose*, 671.

cess. For Milton, writing is a complex, elaborate process of choice that wins the poem from out of "the void and formless infinite" (*PL*, 3.12). Final achievement of the poem, however, is not altogether desirable: the temptation is to allow whatever a poem is before it becomes a poem to remain unformed, so that one may go on oneself enjoying a primal, polymorphous communion with infinitude, "brooding on the vast Abyss" (*PL*, 1.21). This is perhaps the reason why readers have been struck by the paradox of how a poem so powerfully and intricately *formed* as *Paradise Lost* also appears at all times to be dissolving its form, annihilating and creating it at the same time.[34]

For the poet and for his surrogate within the poetry, this communion with the "void and formless infinite" is the necessary matrix of creativity, but it is also a vulnerable process, easily broken off. As we have seen in the work of Milton and several other poets, what breaks it off is often the arrival of a woman whose sexual presence demands of a man that he assume a single, distinct identity, a gender identity.[35] Andrew Marvell's Mower experiences such a demand as intolerable, and when he attempts to undo its effect, he brings about a catastrophe, as if deliberately undoing himself. In a similar manner, Spenser's Red Crosse Knight acquires an anxious self-division as soon as he imagines Una as a sexual woman. So I would say that the male fear and rage expressed in Renaissance poetry against woman and her sexuality is, at a deep level, not about woman at all, not the double and divided object, beautiful and dangerous, fair above and foul below. It is about the double and divided *subject*, who suffers a fall into language but then through language seeks to recall to representation the silence that is at once a strength and a sweetness, the place without boundaries or a name, where the one who eats and the one who is eaten are the same.

34. Cf. Linda Gregson, "The Limbs of Truth: Milton's Use of Simile in *Paradise Lost*," *Milton Studies*, 14 (1980), 138: "The figures in the poem are markedly anachronistic, oxymoronic, and this is to bring us to a verge. As we get in place the sands shift. Only in movement can we be oriented toward God, who is with us but is not assimilable."

35. A useful psychoanalytic reading of the issues is Harold F. Searles, "Sexual Processes in Schizophrenia" (1961), in *Collected Papers on Schizophrenia and Related Subjects* (New York: International Universities Press, 1965), 429–42.

7

The Mother Tongue: *Christabel* and the Language of Love

MARGERY DURHAM

At the time of its publication a reviewer declared *Christabel* "the most obscene Poem in the English language." Coleridge replied, "I saw an old book in Coleorton in which the Paradise Lost was described as an 'obscene poem,' so I am in good company."[1] In its portrayal of innocence mixed with depravity, *Christabel* draws readers into its gothic atmosphere, and there it leaves them, intrigued and bewildered. Like most readers, I am puzzled by the way in which Coleridge clouds the innocence of his central female figure. The ambivalence he suggests can be understood, I think, by reading the poem in the light of certain passages in the poet's notebooks, where his entries around the time he composed *Christabel* define topics in which he was deeply, even passionately interested. Most relevant to the poem are his speculations about associative thought, as it might function in the origin of both speech and moral choice. In the notebooks Coleridge speculates that language may develop from the physical contact between infant and mother. For Coleridge, culture begins at the breast, and language is indeed the mother tongue.

A considerable body of psychoanalytic theory recognizes the infant's

---

1. Humphry House, *Coleridge* (London: Rupert Hart-Davis, 1953), 126, and *The Unpublished Letters of Samuel Taylor Coleridge*, ed. Earl Leslie Griggs, 2 vols. (London: Constable, 1932), II, 247.

relationship with the mother as the source of symbol formation and therefore of language and culture, and since Coleridge himself is credited with coining the word "psycho-analytical," it seems all the more reasonable to inquire whether any of the current theories can yield insights into his poem.[2] Since the time of Freud and his earliest associates, Melanie Klein and those who have developed the implications of her work have further advanced our understanding of the individual's relationship to culture, and the tensions they describe in this relationship are, I believe, analogous to the ambivalence one finds in *Christabel*. Klein's definition of the alternative ways, which she terms "manic" and "depressive," by which these tensions are resolved also helps us to interpret Coleridge's work. I will therefore compare the poem with both Coleridge's notebook speculations and Klein's more systematically developed theory. Relevant to this comparison is the poem's thematic resemblance, in its consideration of a fall from innocence, to *Paradise Lost*, and this parallel provides a mythic resolution of the dilemmas, logical and psychological, which Coleridge depicts.

We must avoid, however, ascribing to Coleridge any intention of assigning women a significant role in high culture. His idea of women was the conventional one of his time, expressed, for example, in his praise of an acquaintance "married to the woman of his choice, of whose mind his own had been the mould & model."[3] It seems likely that *Christabel*'s analysis of mental processes is primarily a self-examination. Coleridge's notes on his own nightmares describe aspects of the poem, and the confused feelings of both victimization and guilt which these "bad most shocking Dreams" left with him is recorded in his admittedly confessional poem "The Pains of Sleep," first published with *Christabel*:

2. See *The Notebooks of Samuel Taylor Coleridge*, ed. Kathleen Coburn, 3 vols. to date (New York: Pantheon, 1957–   , item 2670 (September 15, 1805), and Coburn, *Experience into Thought* (Toronto: University of Toronto Press, 1979), 4.

3. *Collected Letters of Samuel Taylor Coleridge*, ed. Earl Leslie Griggs, 6 vols. (Oxford: Clarendon, 1956–71), III, 70; see also 92. This work is cited below as *Collected Letters*. Coleridge protested his unhappy marriage (see *Collected Letters*, III, 60–66). His view of love can be described as platonic in, for example, the Shakespeare lectures (*Coleridge on Shakespeare*, ed. R. A. Foakes [Washington, D.C.: Folger, 1978], lectures 7 and 8, pp. 75–97). For a discussion of this aspect of Coleridge's thought, see Anthony John Harding, *Coleridge and the Idea of Love* ([London]: Cambridge University Press, 1975).

Deeds to be hid which were not hid,
Which all confused I could not know
Whether I suffered, or I did:
For all seemed guilt, remorse or woe,
My own or others still the same
Life-stifling fear, soul-stifling shame.

. . .

But wherefore, wherefore fall on me?
To be beloved is all I need,
And whom I love, I love indeed.[4]

In connecting his personal fear and guilt with the general human condition he chose a female persona, perhaps to emphasize the passivity which he indeed felt, but which in a male hero could have been unacceptable to his readers.

---

4. *The Complete Poetical Works*, ed. Ernest Hartley Coleridge, 2 vols. (Oxford: Clarendon, 1912), I, 390–91, ll. 27–32, 50–end. This poem was originally written in a letter to Robert Southey, September 11, 1803. See *Collected Letters*, II, 982–84. For the remark about the dreams, see *Notebooks*, item 2398 (January 11, 1805). Critics from Roy K. Basler in 1948 to Barbara A. Schapiro in 1983 have discussed the ambivalence in *Christabel*. All these psychoanalytic readings, however, use the poem as an index to the poet's personality; although Basler does so much less than the others, he relates the suggestions of sexuality in the poem only to Coleridge's concern about his moral reputation. I find it interesting to relate *Christabel* to his psychological speculations, as they foreshadow and impinge upon his aesthetic theory. These earlier readings also view the ambivalence in the poem as abnormal, while I consider it appropriate to and permanent within the human situation as Coleridge, Freud, and others saw it. Furthermore, I believe that Coleridge shows ambivalence as the necessary condition for artistic creation, and it is here that Klein's theory is relevant. A partial list of psychoanalytic interpretations includes Basler, *Sex, Symbolism, and Psychology in Literature* ([1948] rpt. New York: Octagon Books, 1967); Arthur Wormhoudt, *The Demon Lover* (New York: Exposition Press, 1949); Edward Bostetter, *The Romantic Ventriloquists* (Seattle: University of Washington Press, 1963); Gerald E. Enscoe, *Eros and the Romantics* (The Hague: Mouton, 1967); Geoffrey Yarlott, *Coleridge and the Abyssinian Maid* ([London]: Methuen, 1967); Norman Fruman, *Coleridge, the Damaged Archangel* (New York: G. Braziller, 1971); and Schapiro, *The Romantic Mother* (Baltimore: Johns Hopkins University Press, 1983). Jonas Spatz argues that the ambivalence which Coleridge's portrayal suggests can be wholly overcome by a mature adjustment, and that the author assumed such an outcome. See "The Mystery of Eros: Sexual Initiation in Coleridge's 'Christabel,' " *PMLA*, 90 (1975), 107–16. One sensitive and well-balanced essay is "Coleridge's Anxiety," by Thomas McFarland, in *Coleridge's Variety*, ed. John Beer (Pittsburgh: University of Pittsburgh Press, 1975), 134–65.

The Problem: Symbolization and Its Discontents

Klein began her work with the common psychoanalytic assumption that all formation of symbols (all fantasy, all conceptualization, and therefore all mental relationship to the outside world) is a projection of the infant's sense of the mother's body. Ernest Jones had pointed out that nonmaternal experience can provide a pleasure similar in quality to that received from the mother. Then, when access to the original pleasure is blocked, the infant can redirect its desire to the analogous experience. Cradling and suckling thus replace the womb. These pleasures can yield to the enjoyment of solid food, and in time to babbling, to speaking, even to writing poetry. From this redirection Klein reasoned not only that the outside world is "the mother's body in an extended sense," but also "that symbolism is the foundation of all sublimation and of every talent, since it is by way of symbolic equation that things, activities and interests become the subject of libidinal phantasies."[5] From the symbolization of infantile conflict and desire in children's play and in art, she developed her theory of reparation, according to which civilization actively remodels the world into a sublimated version of the infant's original pleasure.

Klein also found that the procedure could go wrong, and it is here that her theory first illuminates *Christabel*. If the original source of pleasure fails and no analogous equation has been made, then the former pleasures become equated with potentially analogous ones within a category of unfulfillment and therefore of pain. The child then withdraws from both the painfully tantalizing mother and the analogous outside world, and the result is paranoid delusion and in-

5. Sandor Ferenczi, "Stages in the Development of the Sense of Reality," *Psychoanalytic Review*, 1 (1913–14), 223–25; Klein, "The Importance of Symbol-Formation in the Development of the Ego," in *Love, Guilt, and Reparation and Other Works*, vol. 1 of *The Writings of Melanie Klein*, 4 vols., ed. R. E. Money-Kyrle, International Psycho-analytical Library (London: Hogarth Press and Institute of Psycho-analysis, 1975), I, 219–32; quotations here from 232 and 220. See also in the same volume "Early Analysis," 100–105. For the application of Klein's theory to aesthetics, see her "Infantile Anxiety-Situations Reflected in a Work of Art and in the Creative Impulse," *Writings*, I, 210–18, and Hanna Segal, "A Psycho-analytical Approach to Aesthetics," *International Journal of Psycho-analysis*, 33 (1952), 196–207. Segal's essay is reprinted in Klein et al., *New Directions in Psycho-analysis* (London: Tavistock, 1955), along with Adrian Stokes's "Form in Art." Stokes's later work is also significant. Simon Stuart's *New Phoenix Wings: Reparation in Literature* (London: Routledge, 1979) applies Klein's theory to Romantic poetry, especially to that of Blake and Wordsworth.

hibition, including as one extreme form the speech-inhibiting psychosis now termed autism. Putting the matter rather too simply: feeding problems can thus create stuttering and, at last, silence. Most important for our study of *Christabel*, Klein maintains that neurosis and sublimation are inversions of each other and, she adds, "for some time the two follow the same path" from original pleasure to possible alternatives and back—for better or worse—to the child. Emphasizing the necessity for ambivalence toward the mother, Klein wrote, "It is a question of a certain optimum balance of the factors concerned. A sufficient quantity of anxiety [that is, the mother's absence or other failure to satisfy the infant] is the necessary basis for an abundance of symbol-formation and of phantasy; an adequate capacity on the part of the ego to tolerate anxiety is essential if anxiety is to be satisfactorily worked over."[6]

At best, however, poetry, music, politics—all the civilized arts—become the means of creating, on the cultural level, a maternal equivalent. As we reshape the world to our satisfaction, Klein maintained, we try to recreate the life-giving environment that a mother can no longer provide, and our standard of comparison (outside the womb) is our recollection of the earliest moments at the breast. Aesthetic balance may suggest such analogous pleasure, and I shall argue that *Christabel* also symbolizes the conflicts within the reparative struggle.

In Coleridge's own time, David Hartley studied the process by which infantile pleasure may develop into complex, socially integrated action. Although Coleridge was at first enthusiastic, he eventually rejected Hartley's explanation of mental life by the association of ideas, because automatic association seemed to grant human nature only the impoverished innocence of the machine. On March 16, 1801, he wrote to his friend Thomas Poole:

> If I do not greatly delude myself, I have not only completely extricated the notions of Time, and Space; but have overthrown the doctrine of Association, as taught by Hartley, and with it all the irreligious metaphysics of modern Infidels—especially, the doctrine of Necessity.—This I have *done*; but I trust, that I am about to do more—namely, that

6. Klein, "Early Analysis," 105, and "Symbol-Formation," 221. Of interest is the history of Dick in "Symbol-Formation," 221–32. The concept of reparation also involves a repairing of the mother, whom, in the rage of desire and anxiety, the infant has imagined destroying. This reconstruction is the primary motive Klein ascribes to mature symbolization.

I shall be able to evolve all the five senses, that is, to deduce them from *one sense*, & to state their growth, & the causes of their difference—& in this evolvement to solve the process of Life & Consciousness. ... I shall ... take a Week's respite; & make Christabel ready for the Press.[7]

This letter has been taken to suggest that "to a certain extent" *Christabel* actually provided little if any respite from philosophical speculation, that in Coleridge's mind one task depended on the successful completion of the other, and that the poem might have been finished if a psychology alternative to Hartley's had taken shape.[8] One cannot claim that the poet resolved the problem abstractly; in that regard the triumphant assertion recorded less reality than hope. Nor did Coleridge feel that he had finished *Christabel*; even after its publication in 1816 he had plans for the poem's completion.[9] Nevertheless, it is possible to discern a way in which the poem deals successfully with complex connections among sense, feeling, and moral choice—relationships that Coleridge felt Hartley had failed to account for, and that involve both the symbol formation and the ambivalence described by Klein.

To readers of the poem, Christabel's name might well suggest Christ and his prototype Abel, the victim of Cain, while also presenting the belle as Christ. Of course both connections suggest innocence. While praying outside her father's castle one night, the heroine mysteriously meets the unfortunate Lady Geraldine, with whom she hospitably shares her bed. Here she sees Geraldine's wound, the "mark of ... shame" and "seal of ... sorrow"; and the woman's "touch of pain" produces a "vision of fear" in nightmares that disturb Christabel's sleep until they yield to better dreams. Meanwhile Geraldine casts a spell on the girl's speech.[10]

7. *Collected Letters*, II, 706–7 (Coleridge's emphasis).

8. See Edward E. Bostetter, "Christabel: The Vision of Fear," *Philological Quarterly*, 36 (1957), 186 n. 7.

9. For the poem's prepublication history, see *Poetical Works*, I, 213–14, and Arthur Nethercot, *The Road to Tryermaine* (Chicago: University of Chicago Press, 1939; rpt. Westport, Conn.: Greenwood, 1978), 3–21. The poem we have was written from 1798 to 1800. Coleridge planned to add three more sections and wrote some additional passages, which were never published. The first two parts circulated in manuscript until 1816. Even after their publication in that year, Coleridge hoped to compose more.

10. Quotations from *Christabel* are taken from *Poetical Works*, I, 213–36. Line numbers are cited in the text.

The next morning, although Christabel remembers her "bad most shocking dreams" and their ugly cause, she cannot articulate them. Her father receives Geraldine as the daughter of the estranged companion of his youth, Sir Roland. The spell takes effect; the girl's speech degenerates into a hiss, and her eyes seem to resemble those of a snake. Geraldine now seems likely to replace the girl's dead mother, and as father and "mother" recede, Christabel is left alone, virtually homeless, as Geraldine had been the night before. Part II concludes with a brief meditation on the frequent mixture of "rage and pain" in words of love. This final, apparently irrelevant musing, I believe, actually reminds us of the poem's central tragic idea: the origin of speech and of all achievement in the mother's touch, the rage at not possessing her completely, and the guilt incurred by either remaining with her (rejecting growth and life) or leaving her, which, as I hope to make clear later, is seen as a kind of destruction. Relevant also, I shall argue, is what Klein terms the "manic" evasion of that rage and guilt: despising the mother and by extension all women, and ignoring them.

Coleridge, I suggest, set out to discover poetically how the mind can work by a process of pleasurable association and yet be responsible for good and evil. The poem's solution is to show that this formulation of the problem is, at last, superficial, by placing it within the symbolic pattern of myth. Without evading the significant facts of desire, dependency, separation, anxiety, and rage, the poem places them in a perspective within which such apparently irreconcilable terms as "association" and "free will" or "responsibility" become irrelevant. By changing from the prose of his notebooks to the language of poetry, Coleridge develops his thought successfully, concentrating on the phenomenon of separation, first from the mother, then from both parents, and at last from life itself. If we read the poem and the notebooks together, we can see that he is concerned with separation at four stages: first in weaning; then in the development of speech with its awareness of separate yet related speaker and hearer; third, in sexual maturity and the assumption of responsibility for one's own and the next generation; and finally in death, the inevitable consequence of individuality. The dilemmas that this process involves are tragically resolved, I believe, by the myth into which the poem emerges, and it is thus that Coleridge discovers for himself what he later describes as the nature and function of poetry: the portrayal of paradox, which we feel emotionally as ambivalence. In doing so, he seems also to discover another function of art: the refinement of simple, instinctual drives into mentally nourishing symbols, in this case literary ones. The poet's notebooks introduce us to his speculations, which, while they help us to interpret the poem, nevertheless find their own resolution only in poetic form.

The Notebooks: Abstract Language Encounters Paradox

In the notebooks Coleridge indeed traces human mental development from "one sense." Referring to his infant son he says, "Hart[ley] seemed to learn to talk by touching his mother."[11] Elsewhere he locates the origin of mental life in one specific version of touch, the baby's nurture at the breast: "Babies touch *by taste* at first,—then about 5 months old they go from the Palate to the hand—& are fond of feeling what they . . . taste / Association of the Hand with the Taste—till the latter by itself recalls the former."[12] When we take note of these connections, the poem echoes loudly: "In the touch of this bosom there worketh a spell, / Which is lord of thy utterance, Christabel!" (ll. 267–68). The entry concerning speech is dated November 18, 1800; Coleridge had finished Part II of *Christabel* in October and wrote the letter to Poole the following March, about one week before he made the entry concerning taste. Although the spell is cast in Part I, written in 1798, we can see that these later psychological observations were on his mind at least by the time he completed Part II. In fact, there is evidence of some such connections as early as 1795.[13]

Several years after he completed what we now have of the poem, we find him still interested in the way in which ideas associated in the mind seemed to undergo a qualitative change, after the manner of elements combined chemically:

Scratching & ever after in certain affections of the Skin, milder than those which provoke Scratching a restlessness for double Touch / Dal-

11. *Notebooks*, item 838.

12. *Notebooks*, item 924 (March 24, 1801). Parentheses denote Coleridge's dating.

13. See *Notebooks*, item 21, which Coburn tentatively dates 1795 and which connects the pillow with both sorrow and a soothing and buoyant love. These associations, which seem irrelevant at this point in the argument, nevertheless resemble others that relate to the poem (see below). Hence it would seem that on some level of consciousness, even before he wrote Part I of *Christabel*, Coleridge made some of the mental associations I describe.

liance, & at its height, necessity of Fruition.—Fruition the intensest single Touch, &c &c &c; but I am bound to trace the Ministery [sic] of the Lowest to the Highest, of all things to Good.[14]

We can identify here an extension of the associations that begin orally, then supposedly develop into manual touching and further into speech.[15] Here in 1804 we see that Coleridge viewed sexuality as an intensification and complication of that sense of touch whose awakening he had described in 1800 as occurring at the breast. The development of sexuality is thus implicitly related to touch and therefore ultimately to what both the notebooks and the poem combine as the touch (and taste) of the breast, the same source as that of speech.

Unfortunately that which is reassuringly present can be lost. For Coleridge, the loss of the maternal touch causes fear, guilt, and finally death. When lost or withdrawn, the mother's influence seems actually destructive:

> Contact—the womb—the amnion liquor—warmth + touch
> / —air cold + touch + sensation & action of
> breathing—contact of the mother's knees + all
> those contacts of the Breast + taste & wet
> & sense of swallowing—Sense of diminished
> Contact explains the falling asleep— / this
> *is* Fear.

Again:

> To *fall* asleep—is not a real *event* in the
> body well represented by this phrase—is it
> in *excess*, when on first *dropping* asleep we
> *fall* down precipices, or *sink* down, all
> things *sinking* beneath us, or *drop down*.[16]

As one might expect from these notebook entries, the sleep that concludes Part I of *Christabel* is at first a "vision of fear" (l. 453). There the effect of losing the mother is portrayed not as passive suf-

---

14. *Notebooks*, item 827 [January 9, 1804]. Square brackets denote editor's dating.

15. On the relation of "double touch" to infant psychology, sublimation, and *Christabel*, see John Beer, *Coleridge's Poetic Intelligence* (London: Macmillan, 1977), 86–89.

16. *Notebooks*, items 1414 [July 16–19, 1803] and 1078 (May 10, 1803); Coleridge's emphasis.

fering, however, but as active and intentional persecution by the Lady Geraldine, like the paranoid fantasies that Klein describes. Not only is the heroine's protective mother absent, but the wrong "mother" is there (l. 301). I suggest that Geraldine represents, among other things, Mother Nature, with her implacable demand that we leave our "real" mother, mature, and die. Much more thought must be given Geraldine, but at present we can speculate that the connection between touch and pain in the poem may well be the same one Coleridge records in the notebooks: the connection between love and loss. The pain that he portrays in *Christabel* is indeed the pain of loss; it culminates in that moment when Sir Leoline turns his back on "his own sweet maid" (l. 653). Indeed, loss and absence dominate the poem from the start. Christabel goes out at first to pray for her absent lover (ll. 25–30); her father commemorates every morning his wife's (her mother's) death (ll. 332–44).

Only a slight shift in viewpoint changes the terms of this problem from those of happiness vs. fear to those of innocence vs. guilt. The origins of such complex activities as sexual love and speech in the simple sensations of taste and touch lead Coleridge to ethical questions. Christabel's sleep with Geraldine is vicious and holy by turns. Geraldine tells Christabel that their night together will control the girl's speech (ll. 267–68), and the means of this control is guilt. The guilt results from Christabel's terrible visions (ll. 292–97), shows itself in her snakelike appearance and her hissing (ll. 589–612), and seems apparent (though we feel it is not real) in her final isolation (ll. 621–55).

In the notebooks, too, touch and its mental associations bring Coleridge to the question of moral choice. There he sees moral choice as emerging from the perpetual opposition between conscious will and sensuous inclination. He sometimes argues that without conscious interference physical impulses must inevitably cause evil. And conversely, at least once he seems to identify all virtue with the deliberate frustration of desire. On the other hand, Coleridge also observes instances in which what he terms "streamy association" or "Volition" accomplishes positive ends. But such exceptions make him uneasy, and we are left at last with his perception that automatic association is in itself amoral yet must answer to moral demands. In these speculations he can do no more than define that self-contradiction, but we can be grateful that he does not flinch from his difficult position. The constantly self-contradictory argument makes the notebook entries troublesome to follow, yet a careful look at them helps us to appreciate Coleridge's poetic achievement. In one entry dated December 26, 1803, he insists that the role of conscious will is to frustrate an impulse that is harmful or base:

> I resisted the Impulse—Why? because I could not endure my after Consciousness. Hence derive the immense Importance to Virtue of increasing and *enlivening* the Consciousness & press upon your own mind & as far as in you lies, on others, the connection between Consciousness & Conscience / the mutual Dependence of Virtue & the Understanding on each other.

Two days later he writes in the same vein, applying his idea yet more widely:

> I will at least make the attempt to explain to myself the Origin of moral Evil from the *streamy* Nature of Association, which Thinking = Reason, curbs & rudders / how this comes to be so difficult / Do not the bad Passions in Dreams throw light & shew of proof upon this Hypothesis?— Explain those bad Passions: & I shall gain Light, I am sure—A Clue! A Clue!

But next he confronts an example that threatens his hoped-for conclusion: "Take in the blessedness of Innocent Children, the blessedness of sweet Sleep, &c &c &c: are these or are they not contradictions to the evil from *streamy* association?" Then the longing for a coherent philosophy leads him close to misanthropy as he adds, "I hope not."[17]

Hoping the worst of human nature is not Coleridge's ruling passion, and in this same month he uses a water metaphor to describe beneficent sleep:

> O then as I first sink on the pillow, as if Sleep had indeed a material *realm*, as if when I sank on my pillow, I was entering that region & realized Faery Land of Sleep—O then what visions have I had, what dreams—the Bark, the Sea . . . all the shapes & sounds & adventures made up of the Stuff of Sleep & Dreams, & yet my Reason at the Rudder / . . . & I sink down the waters, thro' Seas & Seas—yet warm, yet a Spirit.[18]

---

17. *Notebooks*, items 1763 and 1770 (December 26, 28, 29, 1803); Coleridge's emphasis.

18. *Notebooks*, item 1718 [December 6–13, 1803]. See also item 21 [1795?].

Kathleen Coburn points out disguised puns on the word "breast" occurring elsewhere in this entry.[19] A preoccupation with the breast in connection with sleep, one that whimsically or otherwise Coleridge disguised, takes us back to Christabel's night with Geraldine. And the connection thus noted between the breast and "Reason" refers us to that source of all mental action in the "one sense" of taste.

In the notebooks, therefore, we see two purposes that nullify each other. We have the poet's "Hope of making out a radical distinction between ... Volition & Free Will or Arbitrement, & the detection of the Sophistry of the Necessitarians / as having arisen from confounding the two." At the same time (and in the same entry) we see the opposite intention "to trace the Ministery ... of all things to Good."[20] If free will differs from common association in a "radical" way, however—that is, at its very root—then the lowest does not minister to the highest. The question is how mental association can produce both moral vision and nightmare:

> What is the height, & ideal, of mere association?—Delirium.—But how far is this state produced by Pain & Denaturalization? And what are these?—In short, as far as I can see anything in this Total Mist, Vice is imperfect yet existing Volition, giving diseased Currents of association, because it yields on all sides & *yet* is—So think of Madness.[21]

When Coleridge translates this problem into artistic expression, poetic language and form (by their very nature, he later believed) resolve this dilemma. The contradiction he observes in human nature becomes the stuff of tragedy, that condition in which impulses good in themselves unfold naturally yet lead inevitably to disaster. The first impulse he considers in *Christabel* is that of dependence on the breast, that is, on the mother. This initial dependency proves to be the psychological origin of poetry and myth. As Coleridge develops his symbol of the lost paradise, the breast becomes a metaphor for the entire nourishing environment, some loss of which occurs at each stage of individual growth, with a resultant increase in one's sense of vulnerability and isolation and therefore (however irrationally) of guilt. The

---

19. *Notebooks*, note to item 1718. See Coburn's references here to psychoanalytic studies.
20. *Notebooks*, item 1827.
21. *Notebooks*, item 1770.

breast symbol and its related suggestions in the poem therefore require a yet more careful look.

The Wounded Breast: The Terrors in "Splitting"

Geraldine's curse specifies, as we have seen, the relation between breast and speech:

> "In the touch of this bosom there worketh a spell,
> Which is lord of thy utterance, Christabel!
> Thou knowest to-night, and wilt know to-morrow,
> This mark of my shame, this seal of my sorrow;
>> But vainly thou warrest,
>> For this is alone in
>> Thy power to declare,
>> That in the dim forest
>> Thou heard'st a low moaning,
> And found'st a bright lady, surpassingly fair;
> And didst bring her home with thee in love and in charity,
> To shield her and shelter her from the damp air."
>
> [ll. 267–78]

From her first appearance the poem portrays Geraldine as motherly. She appears behind "the huge, broad-breasted, old oak tree" (l. 42), and other references to motherhood occur here as in the prayer "Mary mother, save me now!" (l. 69). As they sleep, Coleridge compares the women to "a mother with her child" (l. 301). We resist the identification that he suggests because Geraldine perverts the touch of reassurance into one that creates horror and guilt. She is an evil, substitute mother—a wicked stepmother. The horrible visions that follow proceed from neither Geraldine nor Christabel alone, but from a particular, painful aspect of the mother-child relationship, the aspect of inevitable separation.

At the same time, however, an equally dismaying difficulty is perceived in the opposite impulse toward identification. In Part II the curse makes Christabel resemble Geraldine, as a child resembles its mother. But what aspect does the girl assume? Not that of the beautiful lady or of the protective mother, but of the hissing, dully malevolent snake (ll. 457–59, 583–612). Geraldine's serpentine qualities are obvious (ll. 583–87). Yet there are other ways in which to curse besides making one's victim resemble oneself. Perhaps the resemblance tells us of some latent and disturbing identification between the heroine and this aspect of the mother, which the curse merely completes and reveals. Coleridge seems to have used the spell not to create something new and antithetical to its victim's nature, but to make evident and perhaps distort or exaggerate what is already there.

The night's visions result in a new understanding on Christabel's part, sexual in nature but also recalling, at least insofar as the poem reflects Coleridge's mind, "all those contacts of the Breast + taste & wet & sense of swallowing." We are shown a state of mind in which feelings are not distinct. Genital sexuality is by no means the exclusive issue here; it is scarcely distinguished as sexuality, not because Coleridge shrank from the truth but because he evokes in this scene a mental state that reaches from adulthood back to the time in which sensations have not been clearly differentiated. The latent sexuality is mingled with equally strong impulses: toward plain animal nurture in one direction and toward that more distinctively human activity of speech in the other. In the poem these connections work against the heroine in a way that corresponds to the moral doubts that Coleridge expressed in the notebooks.

Psychoanalytic theory helps us to understand this pattern of ambivalence: of mixed love and fear, of simultaneous victimization and guilt. The night with Geraldine obviously suggests oedipal identification, which we must consider later. But the notebook entries on touch as the origin of speech lead us to Klein's research in preoedipal fantasy. She held that, whether resolved positively or negatively, those moments of frustration first create fantasies of persecution by an agent of evil, who unpredictably and terrifyingly replaces the superficially identical agent of good. The mother—more specifically, the concept of "breast"—is split into contrasting opposites. From this "splitting" into "good" breast and "bad" breast Klein derives her term for this early stage, calling it the "paranoid position."

These concepts may help explain the sharp dichotomy between good and evil found in melodrama and fairy tale, including within the latter category *Christabel*. Each of us has a wicked stepmother; she is that mother who denies us some pleasure; archaically, Klein maintained, she is the breast we could not perpetually possess. As Bruno Bettelheim remarks, "The typical fairy-tale splitting of the mother into a good (usually dead) mother and an evil stepmother serves the child well. ... The fantasy of the wicked stepmother not only preserves the good mother intact, it also prevents having to feel guilty about one's angry thoughts and wishes about her."[22] This splitting into "good mother" and "bad mother" is an extension of what Klein defined as the "paranoid-schizoid position" in which the infant fantasies a "good" available breast and a "bad" or otherwise unsatisfying one. The child's first worries "go back beyond the beginnings of his understanding of speech." Klein observed that in response to inevitable dissatisfaction, infants, lacking intellectual concepts in which to formulate questions, lacking words in which to express them, and unable to understand the words of others, generate "an extraordinary amount of hate." The infant then at least partially turns this hatred against itself, in the fantasy of a persecuting breast.[23]

Here again is that "contact—the womb—amnion liquor—warmth + touch . . . all those contacts of the Breast + taste & wet & sense of swallowing," the loss of which, even in sleep, is to Coleridge "falling" and "Fear." Christabel's need and love for her mother focus, as Klein also discovered, on the breast. The breast and the woman who provides it indeed feed our mental as well as physical life. They may become hateful because we desire them yet cannot always and wholly possess them; we can fear the mother because we need her so much. In her analysis of children Klein found that the infant fantasies devouring its mother, emptying her so as to keep her forever. Geraldine's mutilated bosom ("and half her side" [l. 252]) therefore suggest the infant's cannibalistic fantasy as well as a sexual wound; to the latter the lady's abduction before we meet her (recalled in ll. 81–99) corresponds.

Like the splitting into "good" breast and "bad" breast and the start of symbol formation which that splitting entails, the poem's sexual—or to be more precise, genital—significance concerns life's requirement that one become independent and create an identity of one's own, that one relinquish the parental touch and recreate it symbolically elsewhere. But with that separation comes pain, anger, and finally death. Coleridge's metaphor for this predicament is Christabel's adolescence. She is old enough to leave her father; in fact, she is betrothed. Therefore it is while she prays for her beloved that she meets

22. Bruno Bettelheim, *The Uses of Enchantment* (New York: Knopf, 1976), 69.
23. Klein, "Early Stages of the Oedipus Conflict," *Writings*, I, 186–98; quotation from 188.

Mother Nature, the ambiguous Lady Geraldine, who seems to represent birth and growth, maturity and death.

When one relinquishes dependency in adolescence one paradoxically "touches" one's parents even more intimately than before: one assumes their identity as potentially a parent oneself and as a mortal being. Where the old intimacy brought reassurance, this later identification brings pain. Small wonder, then, that the heroine abhors what she sees in Geraldine: the wound demonstrating the body's vulnerability and therefore bringing that mingled awareness of life and death which maturity entails (ll. 250 and following). Besides reflecting the infant's fantasy, in which the mutilated breast horrifies, Christabel's "vision of fear" thus seems to include both intimations of genital sexuality and a premonition of the ultimate separation, that of death.

Manic Evasion vs. Mythic Resolution

As in Klein's theory, then, death real or fantasied may well be the source of the poem's horror. Death is indeed the event on which Coleridge focuses his study of guilt. Here, in what Klein defined as the "depressive position," the breast's taste and touch have to do with moral choice. In Klein's view, the infant's fantasies of "good breast" and "bad breast" gradually yield to a perception of the mother herself, a person by whom the baby can be both satisfied and pained. This realization comes when the child relinquishes the conviction that either itself or anything outside itself can provide constant and total pleasure. With that disappointment comes sorrow, hence Klein's term "depressive." There also arises guilt, from the impression of having destroyed the good with the bad in those earlier dreams (which seemed to the baby real acts) of aggression against the breast. Finally comes the desire to repair that damage, whence springs the impulse to preserve and satisfy the mother and also to recreate the mother symbolically in the rest of the world. "The acceptance of psychic reality involves ... the lessening of splitting. ... It means the acceptance of the idea of separateness—the differentiation of one's own self from one's parents, with all the conflicts that it implies. It also involves, as part of reparation, allowing one's objects to be free, to love and restore one another without depending on oneself."[24]

24. Hanna Segal, *Introduction to the Work of Melanie Klein*, enl. ed. (New York: Basic Books, 1974), 102. See also Klein, "A Contribution to the Psychogenesis of Manic-Depressive States," *Writings*, I, 262–89.

Besides the certainty of death, which accompanies this independence, there comes another realization, equally dismaying. By maturing, one actually replaces one's parents and apparently consigns them to irrelevance, symbolically also, then, to death. D. W. Winnicott, who has developed Klein's theories, states the problem as follows: "If, in the fantasy of early growth, there is contained *death*, then at adolescence there is contained *murder*. ... Growing up means taking the parent's place. *It really does.* In the unconscious fantasy, growing up is inherently an aggressive act. And the child is now no longer child-size." This fantasy, he continues, may be inverted to provoke persecution, much as Christabel may be said to assist, however unconsciously, in her own rejection.[25]

Coleridge focuses our attention on death through yet another fantasy—not Christabel's this time, but her father's. Christabel tells us that her mother "died the hour that I was born" (l. 197). Some measure of guilt is implied by that statement. We feel it even though, rationally considered, Christabel is no more guilty than any other mother's child. That is, however, precisely the point: rationality has no exclusive province in the mind, any more than it has in external circumstance. In the mind, fantasy and fear impel us toward neurosis as well as toward balance, toward guilt as well as toward creative reconstruction. And as Klein describes, at times the two paths are the same.

Sir Leoline is the victim of neurosis, fixing his kingdom upon the fact—even the moment—of his wife's death. Part II of the poem begins:

> Each matin bell, the Baron saith,
> Knells us back to a world of death.
> These words Sir Leoline first said,
> When he rose and found his lady dead:
> These words Sir Leoline will say
> Many a morn to his dying day!
>
> And hence the custom and law began

---

25. D. W. Winnicott, *Playing and Reality* (New York: Basic Books, 1971), 144, 148 (Winnicott's emphasis). Beyond the scope of this paper, but so closely related to it that it should be studied at greater length, is Coleridge's later theological consideration of guilt in the origin of individual will. The terms of the argument are too abstruse to define here, but the following quotation suggests additional interesting comparisons between Coleridge's theological speculation and the issues relevant to *Christabel*: "What could follow but a world of contradictions, when the first self-constituting act is in its essence a contradiction [of God's will]?" ("Opus Maximum," Huntington MS, 39–43; quoted in J. Robert Barth, S.J., *Coleridge and Christian Doctrine* [Cambridge: Harvard University Press, 1969], 112).

That still at dawn the sacristan,
Who duly pulls the heavy bell,
Five and forty beads must tell
Between each stroke.

[ll. 332–42]

With the perception of radical ambivalence characteristic of this poem, Coleridge uses the identification between mother and daughter to condense into one moment events usually separated by a lifetime, and thus to posit nature's paradox: that the joy in a new life implies, because it must someday confront, the sorrow of death. By his decree the Baron then attempts to create a world in which death is the only reality. Yet to do so requires the banishment of birth and growth. In such a world no one fully lives, but no one grieves because there is no joy to lose. This is very like the unproductive "manic evasion" of death and grief which Klein described. In its poverty the Baron's artificial kingdom is enviably if perversely under control. It is a civilization whose discontents are accepted, even worshiped, in which life and living women are out of place. Here mourning is really what Freud elsewhere described as melancholia. In Klein's terminology, it is the persistence of splitting and the identification of culture literally with the harsh, depriving alternative to satisfaction, the absence of woman and of that pleasure of which she is both source and symbol.

Klein held that this archaic splitting, though never wholly given up, does not dominate the healthy personality. As we have seen, she believed that in order even to enter the ødipal stage, one must see the parents as persons separate from oneself, capable of actions good, bad, and indifferent to oneself, yet also trusted and indeed loved. When she thus claimed that guilt for the fantasied destruction of the mother precedes and actually mitigates the aggression of the Oedipus complex, she was repudiated by Freud. Defended to some extent by Ernest Jones, she upheld the principles by which she had challenged psychoanalytic orthodoxy, and thereby prepared the way for such later theorists as Winnicott to claim that civilization is not wholly sadistic, but mediates between the archaic fantasies of absolute good and absolute evil. The symbolic re-creation of the mother becomes a means of union with her, accepted sorrowfully for what it is—and for what she is—loved but impermanent, intimate with us but free from our absolute control.[26]

26. See Klein, "Mourning and Its Relation to Manic-Depressive States," *Writings*, I, 344–69; and Freud, "Mourning and Melancholia," in *Standard Edition*, XIV, 243–

The blending of good and evil is presented as confusion in *Christabel*. To understand it we do best to heed what may be the poem's one authoritative voice, that of Bracy the Bard. Bracy mocks the Baron's morbid religiosity, as does another strange company. "Three sinful sextons' ghosts" send back their own knell to meet the sacristan's tune, and they are often followed by "a merry peal" from the "devil" himself. Furthermore, hearing the devil's laughter, Geraldine "rises lightly from the bed" (ll. 345–63).

Bracy has had his own vision of fear in a dream of

> That gentle bird, whom thou dost love,
> And call'st by thy own daughter's name—
> Sir Leoline! I saw the same
> Fluttering, and uttering fearful moan.
>
> . . .
>
> I stooped, methought, the dove to take
> When lo! I saw a bright green snake
> Coiled around its wings and neck.
> Green as the herbs on which it couched,
> Close by the dove's its head it crouched;
> And with the dove it heaves and stirs,
> Swelling its neck as she swelled hers!
>
> [ll. 532–54]

"Christabel with Geraldine!" one wants to say, and the poem indeed involves Christabel intimately with the witch, as the dove is involved with the snake. Yet although at first glance Christabel's identity seems restricted to the dove, that attribution is made by her father, the Baron, who may not have interpretive authority. It may be that, more precisely, the dove and serpent together form one image for the mixed qualities of guilt and innocence in the suffering and contagion that afflict both women. If so, we can understand the exact form of the witch's curse, which takes effect a few lines after Bracy reports his dream (ll. 583–606). Here we learn that Christabel "passively did imitate" Geraldine's serpent-like qualities (l. 605), that is, the horrifying or "fallen" aspect of nature; both this event and Bracy's dream thus recall and interpret Christabel's sleep with Geraldine.

Two conflicting interpretations of Bracy's dream point up this im-

---

58, whose implications Klein developed. The relevance of Freud's *Civilization and Its Discontents* is, I hope, apparent.

plication of the one woman with the other. Bracy himself plans to cure the evil by oral magic, "with music strong and saintly song" (l. 561). The Baron, however (like any ordinary person, perhaps), thinks Bracy is quixotic. Sir Leoline uses only common practical sense: "With arms more strong than harp or song, / Thy sire and I will crush the snake!" he assures Geraldine (ll. 570–71). His interpretation of the dream is univocal and straightforward. But I believe that Coleridge here rejects the terms of chivalric romance, in which good defeats evil when the knight beheads the dragon. He works with the knowledge that physical force cannot eradicate evil from the world because evil never really appears in a melodramatic distillation. It may be illuminating to assume that the fallible Baron, whose rejection of Christabel later we perceive as a mistake, reads Bracy's dream mistakenly, too. He cannot, after all, "crush the snake" without also killing the dove. Only "song"— that is, art—can comprehend the problem as a paradox, and in so doing constructively contain its conflict.

It seems that Bracy's dream, like the poem itself, resumes Coleridge's inquiry at the point where it is left in "Total Mist" in the notebooks. If the dream presents one ambiguous symbol and not two simple opponents, then the dove and serpent finally represent the tangle of impulses in human minds and hearts. Univocal, abstract language misrepresents this confusion for the sake of logical order, and we must always effect a compromise between the confusion encountered in life and the logical constructs by which we try to manipulate the world. On the other hand, iconic, equivocal language in dreams, poetry, and myth faithfully represents human ambivalence and paradox, but therefore requires logical interpretation through the media of analysis and criticism. As both poet and literary theorist Coleridge came to understand this relationship—indeed, it was he who explained it to us. When the poem is read with these ideas in mind, *Christabel* implicitly emphasizes the inadequacy of abstract language and connects an overconfidence in logic (the Baron's clear-cut dualism) with the failure to perceive the fact that identifying real people with absolutes of good and evil is a projection of archaic splitting.

Like Bracy's account of his dream and like the words described in the poem's Conclusion, the dialogue between the tolling bell and its mocking echo is an example of expression whose meaning is not obvious or straightforward. In this manner the poem dramatically presents the confusion between good and evil which we have traced in the notebooks.

This blending illustrates one step by which the mind attunes itself
to reality. It is what Geraldine requires of Christabel, even to the
extent of alienating the girl from her father and from her illusion of
immortality. Through the deliberate confusion of good with evil Coleridge prepares to consider the nature of art, using the ambiguous
figure of Geraldine to save the Baron from his paralyzing resignation.
The wounded lady, evidently tolerated and perhaps approved by heavenly powers (ll. 226–32), shows us that we need not be paralyzed,
only, like her, badly scarred, or like "Clubfoot" (Oedipus), crippled.

Yet one must resist the opinion that whatever is, is right. In the
poem, the concept of corruption contains both its moral and its physical
meanings. Helpless victim though she may be, Geraldine perpetuates
misery, imparts (perhaps unwillingly) the curse. As Mother Nature
she is fallen, deadly, in league with the Devil, even while she bears
her sad disfigurement. In secular terms she is both the victim of death
(since nature is what dies) and its cause. Even if we admit that Christabel, being natural, is corruptible by herself, Geraldine precipitates
and epitomizes that condition. She is everyone's tragic flaw, as Christabel is our image of innocence (and at last, beyond the scope of our
present study, of redemption).

Christabel resists identification with the lady. "This woman send
away!" she cries out (l. 617). By speaking against "this woman" (which
is really "this womanhood"), she tries to preserve her father's kingdom
as she has known it. Ironically, just at this time her father breaks his
own law, takes Geraldine to himself, and rejects his daughter, who
has now offended against two laws that are mutually exclusive, contradictory, and hence the cause of inevitable guilt. One is that of her
father, who would erect a civilization resistant to time, growth, and
change. Within the perspective of the Baron's fears all nature, Christabel included, is guilty because it leads to death. Since death is indeed
implicit in growth and change, even in birth itself, the Baron is half
right. But the poem does not approve his answer. Nature's own law
opposes his arrangements, requiring Christabel to mature and eventually to die. Sharing her father's view, Christabel protests against
nature and against "this woman" whom she has come to resemble,
through whom she participates in nature's fallen state. To refuse natural growth, however, is precisely her father's error, and so, with
cruel irony, Coleridge has the Baron change his mind. As Sir Leoline
departs with Geraldine, he refuses to accept the implications of his
own regime. He leaves Christabel to bear the hopelessly contradictory

imperatives of nature and civilization, of maturing and yet of resisting the fate of all natural beings. At the point at which Christabel stands, ready to assume maturity and so to marry, she is damned if she does and damned if she does not.

Unable to possess the perfect mother and with her eternal joy and life, Christabel emerges into her own "world of death." One might say, with other readers, that she must also fail morally.[27] In our present context her moral corruption would then function as both a symbol of and a justification for her eventual death. Her father's paralyzing melancholy rightly yields to life; why not also her innocence? In the manner we have considered, it does: she cannot escape natural aging and death, yet she tries to stop that progression, or perhaps at least to block it from consciousness, to render it unspeakable, "a sight to dream of, not to tell" (l. 253). If language here represents civilized form, then Christabel's realization of death's inevitability eludes, in the dilemma in which the poem represents it, logical formulation. Yet civilization insists on overcoming the formless, the silent, on verbalizing that which nevertheless surpasses complete conceptualization.

If we apply here only the terms and methods of rational argument, the deadlock of paradox is the only possible result. We are indeed with Coleridge in "total mist," unable to resolve the contradiction between unconscious drives and conscious choice, between guilt and innocence, between natural flux and civilized form. Each logically negates the other. An alternative approach is needed, and it seems that Coleridge finds it in the moral neutrality of art.

As psychoanalysis, with its commitment both to scientific fact and to healing, looks on moral tempests and is never shaken, so also art, in this case the genre of tragedy, contemplates with equanimity what the poem portrays. Both disciplines find their model in Sophocles, and both take us beyond the realization that Christabel's guilt, however real it may be, is also irrational. Since her conscious will remains innocent and therefore, morally, so does she, it seems useful to distinguish between innocence and immunity: in relation to consciousness and moral choice, her innocence remains; what yields is her unawareness of the human dilemma and her wholly fictional immunity

27. See Enscoe, *Eros and the Romantics*; Yarlott, *Coleridge and the Abyssinian Maid.*

to anxiety.[28] Both her insouciance and her father's simplistic solution of the contradictions in human life must give way to a more complex realization. In Bracy's projected song, that realization introduces the alternative of forgiveness, much as growth into a new phase of unconscious fantasy enables the act that Klein terms "reparation."

At the start of the oedipal phase, Klein maintained, fallen as we are, separate, vulnerable to death, we begin our restorative work, remaking reality into the image of what we have lost, aware now, however, that the world cannot conform to a merely private version of perfection. Here the Oedipus myth, Genesis, and *Paradise Lost*, all seem traceable to the same psychological roots. Tasting the forbidden fruit (so like the breast in appearance and in function) brings the knowledge of good lost and evil got, but also of good to be restored—on the symbolic, therefore communal or cultural level now and, Klein would argue, through the work of the human imagination.

Civilization and Its Contents: Ambivalence and the Language of Love

Coleridge's use of iconic language to reconcile the conflict that he saw between sensuous stimulation and moral choice leads us to consider further the function of art in this pattern of guilt and reparation. Authorship repaired, for Coleridge, much of the painful conflict within himself. As he saw it, "affection and bodily feeling" direct that treacherous "streamy association," as the creative process shapes an other-

28. This distinction permits us to avoid two critical difficulties. On the one hand we can accept the poem's presentation of sexuality as tragically flawed. In that case we need not adopt what seems to me a naive view, equating sexual activity wholly with freedom and joy, and we thus avoid the sentimentality I find in Enscoe and Yarlott, and even in the view of mature love described by Spatz. Nor need we allow the view that at first seems the logically necessary opposite: that Christabel is in some way actually corrupted (see Harding, *Coleridge and the Idea of Love*, 74, although earlier [72] he argues that she is not. See also Carl Woodring, "Christabel of Cumberland," *Review of English Literature* 7 [1966], 46–51). John Beer distinguishes carefully between her innocence and her role as victim: "She is to accept [evil], subsume it, and finally transfigure it. The demonic must nevertheless enter her so deeply that she takes on, temporarily, its actual appearance to unenlightened eyes" (*Coleridge the Visionary* [London: Macmillan, 1959; rpt. New York: Collier, 1962], 202). Of course I would argue that "the demonic" is more than appearance, and that it is not all externally caused. But Christabel's moral innocence remains.

wise chaotic mental flux into moral and intelligent structures.[29] This shaping, not any arbitrary or even wholly conscious power, is what he calls "Will . . . strictly synonimous [sic] with the individualizing Principle, the 'I' of every rational Being." His recollections center around physical pleasure or pain and around affection: joy in union and sorrow in loss. The artifact then produced results from a power whose exertion is both the effect and the cause of psychic healing, much as physical exercise both tests a set of muscles and improves their performance in the future.[30]

In poetry, therefore, Coleridge mastered the dilemma that he recorded in the notebooks. He did so perhaps inadvertently, anticipating in practice the theory that he developed later. Psychoanalytic theory also maintains that the evil he saw in the mind, the dangerous impulses and even madness, indeed exist inextricably with good. In *Christabel* this observation becomes more than a disturbing aspect of associative thought; it provides the irrational dilemma behind a rather startling analogy. Starting with the personal sense of love and loss, Coleridge leads us to consider universal guilt and reparation. Nor are consciousness, free will, and "arbitrement" negated in the poem, but they become much less important than they are in the notebooks because the poetic vision reveals the truth that such terms as "sense" and "matter," "will" and "spirit" could not make clear: that good and evil spring from a level that includes but goes beyond consciousness and logical opposites; that being good requires, as it does for the Ancient Mariner, that one bless life, unaware.

In this case only the poetic symbol could express Coleridge's complex perception of good and evil. As we see in the notebooks, without that symbol he was left either to condemn human nature, or to accept the shallow materialism that he abhorred, or to struggle incoherently with both these contradictory positions. The solution was the one that Klein and Winnicott seek to integrate with psychoanalytic theory: the sublimation of instinctual conflict into symbolic action, whereby literal expression that would be merely guilty and isolating (like murder or incest) finds its archetypal analogue. In this way individual pain opens out into sympathy and compassion. Instead of murdering one's father or mother, one fears and pities the sins of Adam and Cain, or the crime of Oedipus, or the horrified fascination of Christabel.

29. Quoted in House, *Coleridge*, 148.
30. House, *Coleridge*, 155–56.

In telling his myth of the Fall, therefore, Coleridge may be said to have enacted the reparation whose psychic sources *Christabel* mysteriously presents. He analyzed the creative process while he practiced it. His poem stands as evidence of his individual effort toward psychic recovery, a recovery gained not by evading but by describing and recreating our tragic situation. We are left with further questions, especially about the possible links or parallels between the reparative state of mind and Coleridge's later ideas of justification or redemption. We would be mistaken if, while admiring his understanding of psychology, we were to lose sight of the puzzling relationship in the poem among Christabel, Geraldine, and "all . . . who live in the upper sky" (l. 227). Meanwhile, the way in which *Christabel* connects the psychological dynamics of love and loss with a radical sense of guilt lends additional credibility to Klein's views on symbol formation, including that which is involved in the production of language and literature. As Coleridge reflects on linguistic ambiguity at the poem's close, Klein's theory helps us to understand why he does so. Both the process by which the poem is made and the experience we have in reading it show that, provided it accepts ambivalence and moral ambiguity, culture can nourish and, perhaps only approximately, heal. This puts one in mind of Bracy's song. When freed from the manic denial of the mother (and of all women, since they become the mother's symbolic equivalent), when women are perceived not as agents of male satisfaction or of its opposite but as the center of their own tragedy (exiles from the Garden like everyone else), then civilization is not deadly but redemptive. In creating Christabel to represent his own tragic situation, Coleridge inadvertently reveals this fact.

Nevertheless, the comparatively barbaric impulse to simplify life into fantasies of absolute good and evil never dies, and in its persistence, the poem suggests, the image of woman, so long as she is mother, is inextricably involved. Women must therefore come to terms not only with their own vulnerability as separate, mortal beings, but also with the anger of those, male and female, who cannot outgrow their infantile rage or cannot deal with their "depressive" guilt. One task of civilization, however, is to relieve this double jeopardy, directly and especially indirectly, through the symbolic reconstruction of community within the shared immortality that a cultural heritage provides. Coleridge's poem, as both an achieved work of art and a portrayal of the condition it seeks to rectify, is an insightful contribution to the communal effort at reparation.

8

Mrs. Hawthorne's Headache:
Reading *The Scarlet Letter*

DAVID LEVERENZ

When Hawthorne read the end of *The Scarlet Letter* to his wife, it "broke her heart and sent her to bed with a grievous headache—which I look upon as a triumphant success!" His Chillingworth-like tone belies his own feelings. Ostensibly his "triumphant" sense of professional satisfaction depends on breaking a woman's heart and mind, much as his narrative pacifies the heart and mind of its heroine. But Hawthorne's "success" also depends on evoking great sympathy for female suffering. Several years later he vividly recalled "my emotions when I read the last scene of the Scarlet Letter to my wife, just after writing it—tried to read it, rather, for my voice swelled and heaved, as if I were tossed up and down on an ocean, as it subsides after a storm." As Randall Stewart notes, "Hawthorne was not in the habit of breaking down." This scene, and the shaking sobs that overcame him at his dying mother's bedside, "are the only recorded instances of uncontrolled emotion" in Hawthorne's career.[1]

Mrs. Hawthorne's headache is a rare moment in the history of

1. Randall Stewart, *Nathaniel Hawthorne: A Biography* (New Haven: Yale University Press, 1948), 95, cites both the first quotation, which is from a letter to Horatio Bridge, February 4, 1850, rpt. in *Hawthorne: The Critical Heritage*, ed. J. Donald

American reader responses. It reveals not only a spouse's ambiguously painful reaction but also the author's incompatible accounts of his own first reading. Both responses seem deeply divided: one with a splitting headache, the other with a split self-presentation. If we accept at face value the goal announced by Hawthorne's narrator in the first paragraph of "The Custom-House," to seek a self-completing communion with his readers, his quest to discover "the divided segment of the writer's own nature" ends in frustration. Both Hawthorne and his most intimate sympathizer experience inward turmoil and self-controlled withdrawal. As several first readers commented in print, Hawthorne's romance left them with similarly intense and unresolved feelings—of sadness, pain, annoyance, and almost hypnotic fascination.

The Scarlet Letter's strange power over its contemporary readers derives from its unresolved tensions. What starts as a feminist revolt against punitive patriarchal authority ends in a muddle of sympathetic pity for ambiguous victims. Throughout, a gentlemanly moralist frames the story so curiously as to ally his empathies with his inquisitions. Ostensibly he voices Hawthorne's controlling moral surface, where oscillations of concern both induce and evade interpretive judgments. Yet his characterizations of Hester and Chillingworth bring out Hawthorne's profoundly contradictory affinities with a rebellious, autonomous female psyche and an intrusive male accuser. The narrative's increasing preoccupation with Dimmesdale's guilt both blankets and discovers that fearful inward intercourse. D. H. Lawrence's directive to trust the tale, not the teller, rightly challenges the narrator's inauthentic moral stance.[2] But that becomes a complicating insight, not a simplifying dismissal. In learning to see beyond Hawthorne's narrator, readers can see what lies beneath the author's distrust of any coercive authority, especially his own. Though the narrator sometimes seems quite self-consciously fictionalized, he functions less as a character than as a screen for the play of textual energies.

The plot establishes incompatible centers of psychological power: Hester's fierce private passion, at once radically independent and voluptuously loving, and Chillingworth's equally private rage to ex-

Crowley (New York: Barnes & Noble, 1970), 151, and the second quotation, which is from Hawthorne's English Note-Books, September 14, 1855.

2. D. H. Lawrence, *Studies in Classic American Literature* (Garden City, N. Y.: Doubleday, 1951), 13; see also his discussion of *The Scarlet Letter* as a "colossal satire" full of "inner diabolism" (92–110).

pose, control, and accuse. These centers have surfaced in modern criticism as feminist or psychoanalytic responses to the text. The narrator's voice acts as a safety valve, releasing and containing feelings in socially acceptable ways. His very self-conscious relation to his readers, whom he frequently appeals to and fictionalizes, both abets, displaces, and conceals his story's unresolved tensions.

The narrator also mirrors the limits of his contemporary American reader's toleration for strong subjectivity, especially anger. As Trollope noted, "there is never a page written by Hawthorne not tinged by satire." The narrator of *The Scarlet Letter* skillfully intermingles earnest appeals for sympathy with mocking exposure of rage distanced as cruelty.[3] His tolerance for human frailty, his addiction to multiple interpretations, and his veiled hints at self-disgust deflect his fear that anger destroys a lovable self. In claiming that art should veil self-exposure, he invites both sympathy and self-accusation. He is a Dimmesdale who doesn't quite know he is a Chillingworth.

Several nineteenth-century readers sensed Chillingworth's ascendance in the narrator as well as his narrative. Trollope and Henry James both noted with some surprise that the romance was oddly a hate story, and James speaks of Hawthorne's constant struggle between "his evasive and his inquisitive tendencies."[4] Anne Abbott felt "cheated into a false regard and interest" by Hester's seeming suffering and Dimmesdale's seeming faith, because Hester's pride destroys her Christian character, while Dimmesdale's suffering becomes "aimless and without effect for purification or blessing to the soul." "A most obstinate and unhuman passion, or a most unwearying conscience it must be," she continues, " . . . but such a prolonged application of

---

3. "The Genius of *The Scarlet Letter*," in *The Scarlet Letter: An Annotated Text, Backgrounds and Sources, Essays in Criticism*, ed. Sculley Bradley, Richmond Croom Beatty, and E. Hudson Long (New York: Norton, 1962), 242; see also "He is always laughing at something with his weird, mocking spirit" (244). The article in the Norton edition is a partial reprint of Anthony Trollope, "The Genius of Nathaniel Hawthorne," *North American Review*, September 1879, 203–22.

4. Trollope, "Genius of *The Scarlet Letter*," 243; Henry James, *Hawthorne*, introd. Tony Tanner (London: Macmillan, 1967), 109–10. Taylor Stoehr, *Hawthorne's Mad Scientists: Pseudoscience and Social Science in Nineteenth-Century Life and Letters* (Hamden, Conn.: Archon, 1978), 116, stresses Chillingworth's function as "an evil chorus figure whose perspective has much in common with that of the reader and the author." An angry Salem Whig found nothing but Chillingworth in Hawthorne; see Benjamin Lease, "Salem vs. Hawthorne: An Early Review of *The Scarlet Letter*," *New England Quarterly*, 44 (1971), 110–17.

the scourge." Finally, the man whom Hawthorne considered his most astute critic, E. P. Whipple, concluded that the narrator's tendency to "put his victims on the rack" establishes an uncomfortably compelling despotism. Though the morbid suffering appalls sensible readers, he said, they yield despite themselves to "the guidance of an author who is personally good-natured, but intellectually and morally relentless."[5]

The narrator is protected by his duplicitous stance from full exposure, as he half admits. The rhetorical strategies that can give his reader a headache preserve his good name. Yet under his interpretive equivocations, unresolved conflicts about anger, authority, and female autonomy continuously impel the contradictions in his voice as well as his story. A close reading of *The Scarlet Letter* along these lines, as I try to offer here, raises the possibility of using formalist methods to explore the text's intimate, ambivalent relationship to the author's own life and his contemporary interpretive community.[6]

I

A surprisingly aggressive feminist interpretation seems self-consciously mandated as the storytelling begins. The narrator's first sentence deflates church and state to "steeple-crowned hats," while the

5. Anne W. Abbott, review of *The Scarlet Letter*, in *North American Review*, July 1850, rpt. in *Critical Heritage*, 164–67; see 166. E. P. Whipple, "Nathaniel Hawthorne," *Atlantic Monthly*, May 1860, rpt. in *Critical Heritage*, 340–50; see 344, 346. Whipple's 1850 review of *The Scarlet Letter* is also reprinted in *Critical Heritage*, 160–62.

6. In arguing that close reading opens out to questions of social history, I am opposing the antiformalist stance taken by Jane Tompkins in her December 1981 MLA talk on how critics have preserved Hawthorne's reputation at the expense of, say, Susan Warner's. I agree with Tompkins' larger contention that textual meanings are established by readers at any historical moment. But if I am right to say that *The Scarlet Letter* induces, replicates, and undermines the interpretive expectations of its contemporary readers, a more ambivalent relation is posited between text and community than the theory of interpretive community so far allows. Various writings by Tompkins, Stanley Fish, and Walter Benn Michaels have been developing the theory; Steven Mailloux usefully summarizes them and others in *Interpretive Conventions: The Reader in the Study of American Fiction* (Ithaca: Cornell University Press, 1982). Mailloux uses Hawthorne to orient the theory toward a view of texts as complex ethical judgments.

first paragraph associates those hats with the iron spikes on the prison door. As the next paragraph explains, the colony's patriarchs have appropriated "the virgin soil" for graves and a prison, while stifling their utopian hopes with a grave distrust of human nature. Hats and "sad-colored garments" blend with the "beetle-browed and gloomy front" of the prison in a shared exterior gloom.[7] Inwardness has been shut up and spiked, along with youthful hopes and the virgin land.

The narrator's implicit symbolic advocacy becomes overt with his presentation of the "wild rose-bush," growing beside "the black flower of civilized society." If the prison is massive, forbidding, even "ugly," the rosebush brings out feminine delicacy and "fragile beauty." It also promises to awaken the body to imaginative life. It "might be imagined" to offer fragrance to a prisoner, "in token that the deep heart of Nature could pity and be kind to him." Perhaps, the narrator muses, this rosebush "survived out of the stern old wilderness, so long after the fall of the gigantic pines and oaks that originally overshadowed it" (39–40). Without pinning himself down, he allegorically intimates that patriarchs will die while tender flowers endure.

Or perhaps, he continues, the rosebush sprang up under the footsteps of "the sainted Ann Hutchinson"—the adjective lets loose his anti-Puritan, even Papist bias—as she walked through the prison door. In either case, his interpretive alternatives evoke a woman's triumphant survival beyond her towering, glowering elders, or at least her stubborn public opposition. As new elders die the natural death of Isaac Johnson, the first dead Puritan patriarch, they will retreat to "the congregated sepulchres" that define their eternity as interchangeably as their gravity defines their lives, while the rose and true womanhood may persevere toward a more naturally blossoming future.

Taking a final swerve from patriarchal authority by abdicating his own, the narrator refuses to "determine" which alternative should hold. Instead he presents the rose to his reader, since it grows "so directly on the threshold of our narrative, which is now about to issue from that inauspicious portal" (40). With a lushly symbolic self-consciousness the narrator has established a broad array of sympathies joining feminism, nature, youth, the body, and imaginative life. This

7. *The Scarlet Letter: An Authoritative Text, Backgrounds and Sources, Criticism,* ed. Sculley Bradley, Richmond Croom Beatty, E. Hudson Long, and Seymour Gross, 2d ed. (New York: Norton, 1978), 39; further page references in the text are to this edition.

associational array opposes patriarchal oppression, which doubly oppresses itself. The narrator's rhetorical strategies awaken reader expectations as well as sympathies. When Hester walks through the prison door, she will "issue" as the narrative itself, with all the hopes embodied in what is now the reader's wild red rose.

Yet Hester also walks forth into narrative hopelessness. With a hand even heavier than his heart the narrator suddenly imposes his gloomy end on her brave beginning. He tells us that the rose may "relieve the darkening close of a tale of human frailty and sorrow." That portentous phrase shuts the door on her wild possibilities as massively as the prison door dwarfs the rose. His plot will undercut the hopes his voice has just raised. His other alternative, that the rosebush may symbolize "some sweet moral blossom," seems deliberately anemic beside the contending passions his introduction promises. The narrator's sudden deflection from the rose's prospects suggests his fatalistic alliance with the prison's "darkening close." His narrative will be both, inextricably. He opens and shuts the door.

What seems here to be only a slight discomfort with the rose's radical implications eventually becomes an ambivalent inquisition into the dangers of Hester's lawless passion. The narrative issues forth as Chillingworth as well as Hester. Chillingworth's probing brings out the reader's powers of psychological detection while Hester's character encourages feminist responses. At once rebel and inquisitor, the narrator falsely joins these poles in a mystifying voice-over. He implies that the law can be transcended through Dimmesdale's growth toward spiritual purity or softened through Hester's growth toward maternal sympathy. To the degree that we can also perceive his own voice as an "issue," we can locate the unresolved tensions under his still more mystified "sweet moral blossom" of being true to oneself.

Hester Prynne's first gesture, to repel the beadle's authority, refocuses narrative sympathies. Her radical feminism goes further than Hyatt Waggoner's sense of her as a champion of the oppressed, and beyond Nina Baym's various arguments that she champions the private imagination.[8] In Chapter 13 she goes so far as to imagine the "hopeless

---

8. Hyatt H. Waggoner, *Hawthorne: A Critical Study*, rev. ed. (Cambridge: Harvard University Press, 1963), 145; Nina Baym, *The Shape of Hawthorne's Career* (Ithaca: Cornell University Press, 1976), 124–35. Judith Fryer makes a more dubious argument for Hester's potential "androgyny" in *The Faces of Eve: Women in the Nineteenth-Century American Novel* (New York: Oxford University Press, 1976), 74–84. See also Baym, "The Significance of Plot in Hawthorne's Romances," in *Ruined*

task" of building the whole social system anew, changing sex roles so completely that both womanhood and manhood will become unrecognizable to themselves (120). It seems an extraordinary instance of negative capability that Hawthorne, who forbade his daughter to write because it was unfeminine, could imagine the most radical woman in nineteenth-century New England, even retrospectively.[9] Though his narrator several times interjects that Hester's mind has gone so astray only because her heart "had lost its regular and healthy throb" (120), his abstracted, fitful cavils seem to heighten our sense of her sustained independence.

Hester's private question about the "race" of women can still leap off the page for modern readers: "Was existence worth accepting, even to the happiest among them?" (120). She has long since "decided in the negative" this question for herself. Later, from her radical freedom of fresh perception, she sees all social institutions "with hardly more reverence than the Indian would feel for the clerical band, the judicial robe, the pillory, the gallows, the fireside, or the church" (143). Not even Melville, with his more impulsive extremes of negation, offers such a laconic, liberating list. For Hester the comforts of fireside and church grow from the punitive powers of the clergy and judiciary, as interlocked and equivalent institutions.

Yet Hester's rebellious autonomy shields two very different kinds of loving. Why is it, the narrator asks in Chapter 5, that Hester does not leave Salem? She could go to Europe, where she could "hide her character and identity under a new exterior," or she could enter the forest, "where the wildness of her nature might assimilate itself with a people whose customs and life were alien from the law that had condemned her." In rejecting both these ways of abandoning herself, whether to a civilized mask or to diffused natural passion, Hester consciously chooses to define her "roots" as her "chain." Her identity is the sin so "galling to her inmost soul." But the clear separation of outer sin from inner soul shows how unrepentant her desire remains. She becomes the jailer of a fearful secret: her dream of "a union, that, unrecognized on earth, would bring them together before the bar of

---

Eden of the Present: Hawthorne, Melville, and Poe: Critical Essays in Honor of Darrel Abel, ed. G. R. Thompson and Virgil L. Lokke (West Lafayette, Ind.: Purdue University Press, 1981), 49–70.

9. Edward Wagenknecht, *Nathaniel Hawthorne: Man and Writer* (New York: Oxford University Press, 1961), 17–18 and 150–53, remarks on Hawthorne's ambivalence concerning strong women.

final judgment, and make that their marriage-altar, for a joint futurity of endless retribution." I don't think any commentator has noticed the sacrilegious force of the hope that really impels her heart: to be united with Dimmesdale forever, in hell. A Dantesque fantasy of condemned love lurks in her depths "like a serpent" (61).[10] It terrifies her more consciously self-reliant conceptions of herself.

Hester's dream of a love forever framed by patriarchal punishment allows the narrator to present her as more victim than rebel. She is a woman more sinned against than sinning. Moreover, she is a mother as well as a woman in love. Her daughter's existence providentially prevents her from becoming a radical prophetess like Ann Hutchinson. The narrator observes that mothering, like knitting, fortunately "soothes" Hester's tendency toward conflict. In the task of educating Pearl, "the mother's enthusiasm of thought had something to wreak itself upon" (120).[11] To reduce her ideas to an "enthusiasm" ready to be "wreaked" shows the narrator's bias. As a solitary, victimized woman Hester can rethink all social relations. But as a mother she has to nurture conventional womanhood, in herself as well as her daughter. As Dimmesdale says to John Wilson in Chapter 8, the child "was meant, above all things else, to keep the mother's soul alive" (85). The narrator recurrently echoes the minister's sense of this "softening" charge: "Providence, in the person of this little girl, had assigned to Hester's charge the germ and blossom of womanhood, to be cherished and developed amid a host of difficulties" (120). The narrator veils his ambivalence about Hester's intellectual independence and her passionate desire by reinforcing what Nancy Chodorow has called "the institution of mothering" as the cure for all her ills.[12]

A less ambivalent narrator would see himself as part of his heroine's problem. Hester is far from liberated, even inwardly, despite her extraordinary perceptiveness about social repression. She avoids any struggle for public power except to preserve her conventional role as

10. Every Hawthorne commentator I have read has missed Hester's secret dream of reunion in hell. They assume she hopes for heavenly reconciliation. See, for example, Richard H. Brodhead, *Hawthorne, Melville, and the Novel* (Chicago: University of Chicago Press, 1976), 66; and Michael Davitt Bell, *The Development of American Romance: The Sacrifice of Relation* (Chicago: University of Chicago Press, 1980), 178.

11. I am indebted here and throughout this essay to Richard Brodhead's incisive commentary on an earlier draft, as well as to helpful responses from Walter Herbert and *Nineteenth-Century Fiction*'s two readers.

12. Nancy Chodorow, *The Reproduction of Mothering: Psychoanalysis and the Sociology of Gender* (Berkeley: University of California Press, 1978).

mother. She realizes that her winning advice to Dimmesdale—"Preach! Write! Act! Do anything, save to lie down and die!" (142)—can apply only to men, not to herself. Yet she does not realize how grossly inadequate a man Dimmesdale will turn out to be, as lover, parent, and friend. While the narrator seeks to shift Hester's ground from radical thought and sexual intimacy to more acceptable maternal love, Hester's tenacious affirmation of her continuously punished union holds fast despite increasingly glaring flaws in her man as well as the man who tells her story.

One scene in particular becomes a graphic paradigm of the forces converging to bring her strength within the sphere of Dimmesdale's weakness. In "The Child at the Brook-Side" Pearl stands across the brook from the two lovers, deliberately disregarding Hester's anxious pleas to come to them. When Hester tries to coax her across by saying that Pearl will have twice as much love as before with Dimmesdale beside her, the child fixes her eyes on her mother and the minister "as if to detect and explain to herself the relation which they bore to one another." Then, "assuming a singular air of authority, Pearl stretche[s] out her hand, with the small forefinger extended." She stamps her foot and "burst[s] into a fit of passion," with "piercing shrieks," her finger seeming to point at Hester's bosom, which now lacks the scarlet letter. Dimmesdale, never one to relish strong feelings, erupts with the immemorial plea of a father bent on adult matters: "Pacify her, if thou lovest me!" (149, 150).

As with any key scene, the incident focuses larger issues. To demand that Hester pacify Pearl if she loves him implies, most immediately, that Dimmesdale will continue to avoid the role of parent himself. Hester has to accept his abdication as part of loving him. More subtly, Dimmesdale's "if" is both a bargain and a threat. He can measure Hester's love for him by her success or failure in disciplining Pearl. Dimmesdale's habit of mind here reflects town values of authority and accounting, what the narrator satirizes in "The Custom-House," rather than wilderness intimacy. It is one of the narrator's more sympathetic cues, here and elsewhere, that we know Hester by her first name and Dimmesdale by his last. Using her first name encourages intimacy with her freedom from her husband, and from other imposed self-definitions, while the near-impossibility of calling him "Arthur" indicates his anxious conformity to inherited social codes.[13]

13. This view of first name as implying intimacy and last name as social code should be qualified by the fact that in American culture one way of patronizing a woman has been to call her by her first name, whereas use of the last name implies respect.

Yet the scene prefigures Hester's own accommodation to those codes. The narrator already has taken some care to assert that Pearl is Hester's hidden nature. She is a classic female double, in terms that Sandra Gilbert and Susan Gubar have made familiar. She embodies the lawless passion and impetuous rages constrained in her mother. But as Hester senses from the first, her disturbingly alien "imp" also embodies society's punishing judgment, as well as the letter's own imperiousness.[14] To pacify these contending elements in Pearl, Hester reassumes the scarlet letter. That acceptance of Pearl's pointing finger means accepting love defined in Dimmesdale's terms, as a self-pacification.[15]

As the story continues, Dimmesdale becomes the primary agent for Hester's change from perceptive radical to sad-eyed sympathizer. In their forest colloquy, for instance, Hester seems not to notice that the minister prefaces her heretical claim to their wilderness "consecration" by comparing their "sin" to Chillingworth's "blacker" sin (140). His mind still hovers anxiously in a patriarchal hierarchy of sin, guilt, and violation. Equally symptomatic, his first response to her urgent assertion of mutual sanctity is "Hush, Hester!" For him to rise and say he has not forgotten, as he then does, avoids confronting the impasse between his sense of violation and her sense of holiness. His association of intimacy with violation also connects him to the narrator. The very first paragraph of "The Custom-House" both solicits and denies the possibility of "perfect sympathy" between writer and reader by associating knowledge of "the inmost Me" with veils and violation.

A comprehensive fear of public anger, suffusing the entire narrative, generates Dimmesdale's self-accusations. His obsessive guilt for a moment of consummated desire masks a deeper reluctance to expose aspects of himself that might displease authority. His pain becomes a

---

14. Brodhead, *Hawthorne, Melville, and the Novel*, 56–57, emphasizes Pearl's oscillation between incompatible modes, especially in this scene. Most critics simply see Pearl as Hester's double. On doubles in general see Sandra M. Gilbert and Susan Gubar, *The Madwoman in the Attic: The Woman Writer and the Nineteenth-Century Literary Imagination* (New Haven: Yale University Press, 1979), esp. 69–92.

15. My analysis of this scene opposes the more narcissistic readings offered by John Irwin, *American Hieroglyphics: The Symbol of the Egyptian Hieroglyphics in the American Renaissance* (New Haven: Yale University Press, 1980), 250–51, which stresses the interplay of mirrors with absence; and by Sharon Cameron, *The Corporeal Self: Allegories of the Body in Melville and Hawthorne* (Baltimore: Johns Hopkins University Press, 1981), 84, which stresses Pearl's connection to the letter as part of Hester's body. Both readings illuminate narrative doublings and problems of identity but avoid the interpersonal issues that generate narcissistic fears. Cameron in particular reduces feelings of anger to acts of violence.

mystified accommodation that internalizes authority as self-punishment. Overtly the narrator disengages himself from Dimmesdale's morbid self-scrutiny. He accuses the minister of selfishness, egotism, and cowardice, while presenting Dimmesdale's closet self-flagellations as bizarre. Yet the narrator frequently locates the sources of both art and truth within Dimmesdale's "anguish." When the minister speaks publicly, as he does several times "in tongues of flame," his eloquence becomes analogous to the writer's capacity for "addressing the whole human brotherhood in the heart's native language." Such eloquence must "gush" with "its own throb of pain" (104). For the narrator all art seeks ways of sharing that pain, without full self-exposure. "The only truth, that continued to give Mr. Dimmesdale a real existence on this earth," the narrator concludes in Chapter 11, "was the anguish in his inmost soul" (107). This anguish, he explains a few pages later, is not guilt but "all the dread of public exposure" (112).[16]

Twice in the narrative Dimmesdale allows flashes of anger to break through, and twice the feelings subside to a guilty sadness. In Chapter 10 the minister suddenly demands of Chillingworth, "But who art thou, that meddlest in this matter?—that dares thrust himself between the sufferer and his God?" He rushes from the room with a "frantic gesture." But after secluding himself for several hours, he makes "the amplest apologies" to "the kind old man" for the "violence" of his "unseemly outbreak of temper." As Chillingworth calculates, manipulating his anger is a "step" toward exposing "the hot passion of his heart." The physician's cool malice toys with the minister's heated wrath to show the dangers of self-exposure. "As with one passion, so with another!" Chillingworth says to himself (101).

When Hester tells Dimmesdale that Chillingworth is her husband, her lover explodes with rage. Now the frightening extremes of his anger disturb the narrator as well as Hester. Suddenly imposing a hierarchical interpretive frame, the narrator associates violence, blackness, and intermixture with the Devil's "portion."

> The minister looked at her, for an instant, with all that violence of
> passion, which—intermixed, in more shapes than one, with his higher,

16. This reading differs from Christian readings that see Dimmesdale's "tongues of flame" eloquence as the romance's central truth; see, e.g., Roy Male, "Hawthorne's Literal Figures," in *Ruined Eden of the Present*, 90. My reading also differs from those who see Dimmesdale's guilt in primarily sexual terms; see Joel Porte, *The Romance in America: Studies in Cooper, Poe, Hawthorne, Melville, and James* (Middletown, Conn.: Wesleyan University Press, 1969), 98–114.

purer, softer qualities—was, in fact, the portion of him which the Devil claimed, and through which he sought to win the rest. Never was there a blacker or a fiercer frown, than Hester now encountered. For the brief space that it lasted, it was a dark transfiguration. [139]

Dimmesdale's "lower energies" yield, but only because he has "been so much enfeebled by suffering." "Woman, woman, thou art accountable for this!" he cries, again invoking the town's habit of punitive accounting. "I cannot forgive thee!" But when Hester throws her arms around him with "sudden and desperate tenderness," he allows his forgiveness to emerge, "out of an abyss of sadness, but no anger." God, they agree, should be the punisher (139, 140). The narrator's recoil from his character's rage diminishes Dimmesdale's passion to guilt and constricts Hester's passion to tenderness.

Outwardly Hester seems to have long since accepted her "stain," a taint that at last precludes any role for her as prophetess. In some respects, as Nina Baym and others have emphasized, her compromise compels the townspeople to soften their harsh views of her. Her "power to do," when she restricts it to the "power to sympathize," makes "the world's heavy hand" ordain her a Sister of Mercy, her last Papist transfiguration (117). At the end Hester returns to Salem to live out her life as a quiet force for sympathy if not immediate change, invigorating other despondent women with the hope of some future prophetess.[17]

But her real passions remain buried except for one last try. On the scaffold with her lover, she desperately resurrects her secret dream of union in hell: "Shall we not meet again? . . . Shall we not spend our immortal life together? Surely, surely, we have ransomed one another, with all this woe!" (181). Once again she claims that their relation can be "ransoming" in its own terms, though now through the more equivocal authority of martyrdom.

Characteristically, Dimmesdale's first response again is "Hush, Hes-

17. Baym, "Significance of Plot," makes a strong argument for Hester's consistent social power. Baym also stresses Dimmesdale's moral inadequacy, though the sexism she attributes to Darrel Abel should be lodged with the narrator. I think Baym overstates Hester's consistency and underplays the narrator's ambivalence. The narrator's Catholic associations for Hester—the "sainted" Ann Hutchinson, the "madonna" that a "Papist" would have seen, and here a "Sister of Mercy" whose letter "had the effect of the cross on a nun's bosom" (118)—may be meant to evoke suspiciousness as well as approval, given the anti-Catholic feelings that ran so high in the 1850s.

ter, hush!" He has set his "bright, dying eyes" on higher spiritual possibilities for himself. As he cites God, soul, reverence, and the impossibility of "an everlasting and pure reunion," his language shows an ascendant selfishness. Hester, willing to sacrifice purity for love, finds her love sacrificed for his purity. Once again she is abandoned, as Roger Prynne had abandoned his wife for almost two years, as her lover abandoned both her and her daughter for much longer.[18] The men in her life have maintained their intellectual or spiritual self-control by rejecting intimacy. The last she hears from her lover's lips is not her name but "Praised be his name! His will be done! Farewell!" (181).

Hester's experience here finally does to Hester what Dimmesdale demands for Pearl in that scene by the brookside. It pacifies her. Her capacity to love diminishes to a tender mothering, the defeated residue of a passionate equality. Pearl's own change toward tenderness, when she kisses the minister on the scaffold, has been foreshadowed by several narrative admonitions about her dangerous lack of "heart," as Hester was found wanting. Now Pearl gains her narrator's praise for returning to femininity. Her tears, beyond anger at last, indicate her "pledge" that she will no longer "do battle with the world, but be a woman in it" (181). Similarly, Hester realizes that her future prophetess must never be stained with sin, shame, or even a lifelong burden of sorrow. Mutely accepting the conflation of town with narrative values, she must be content with conflating all the traditional female roles: nurse, seamstress, mother, helpmeet, confidante, and tender heart.

Several critics, notably Nina Baym and Michael Colacurcio, have argued that the ending shows Hester achieving at least partial self-fulfillment.[19] That may be true in terms that the town can recognize. But it seems to me that the narrative ponderously thwarts the twin sources of her rebellious strength: her tenacious desire and her fierce

18. The narrator implies twice that Chillingworth had been detained against his will by Indians for much of that time. Chillingworth is called "Master Prynne" by a townsman in chap. 3. His "Peace, Hester, peace!" concluding chap. 14 parallels Dimmesdale's later formula.

19. See Baym, "Significance of Plot," and Michael J. Colacurcio, "Footsteps of Ann Hutchinson: The Context of *The Scarlet Letter*," *ELH*, 39 (1972), 459–94, an essay that rightly connects Hester to Ann Hutchinson and Dimmesdale to John Cotton but wrongly reduces Hester's radical perceptions to her sexuality. He concludes that both the teller and the tale force Hester to abandon conclusions to which we are sympathetic.

mind. More specifically, the narrator breaks his explicit promise of reunion with Dimmesdale.

As the minister assures Pearl on the midnight scaffold, all three will stand together "At the great judgment day!" The narrator, too, sees them illuminated in "the light that is to reveal all secrets, and the daybreak that shall unite all who belong to one another" (112). But Dimmesdale's revelation leads to eternal separation, not reunion. In the procession he had seemed "unattainable in his worldly position, and still more so in that far vista of his unsympathizing thoughts, through which she now beheld him" (170). Now the narrator's final words bury Hester's hopes in a permanent gloom, nervously commented on by the most sensitive early reviewers and symbolized by her tombstone's legend of red based on black. That tombstone is all that unites the two graves, whose dust, as the narrator at last concludes, "had no right to mingle" (186). After the child who danced on Isaac Johnson's grave in Chapter 10 is reduced to tears, the narrator escorts Hester to her "darkening close" among the congregated sepulchres. Hester's life has been a motherly survival among imprisoned possibilities.

II

A narrative that begins by challenging patriarchal punishment ends by accepting punishment as a prelude to kindness. From Anthony Trollope to Frederic Carpenter and beyond, the ending has disturbed many readers who like Hester's spirited subjectivity. As one critic noted in 1954, "unlike his judicial ancestor, who consigned a witch to the gallows with an undismayed countenance, Hawthorne would have sprung the trap with a sigh. If one were the witch, one might well wonder wherein lay the vital difference."[20]

Though my reading continues that tradition, I question whether the narrator represents all of Hawthorne. While he provides a safely overarching frame of moral values to which both Hawthorne and his

20. Morton Cronin, "Hawthorne on Romantic Love and the Status of Women," *PMLA*, 69 (1954), 98. See also Frederic I. Carpenter's fine essay "Scarlet A Minus," *College English*, 5 (1944), 173–80; rpt. in both the first and second editions of the Norton Critical Edition of *The Scarlet Letter*.

audience could consciously assent, the narrator's evasive mixture of sympathy and judgment also provides a safe way of going beyond socially responsible norms to investigate dangerously attractive interior states of mind. From the first paragraph of "The Custom-House" Hawthorne presents his "intrusive author" as a solicitous, sensible, yet receptive interpreter whose movement from torpid business surroundings to a romantic sensibility opens the door for Hester's story. His first reaction to the scarlet letter, after all, is hilariously inappropriate: he measures it, and finds that "each limb proved to be precisely three inches and a quarter in length" (27). This habit of precise accounting would seem perfectly natural to the "man of business," the "main-spring" of the Custom-House, who could "make the incomprehensible as clear as daylight," and for whom a "stain on his conscience" would be no more troublesome than an error in his accounts or an inkblot in his record books (22). But the scarlet letter takes the narrator beyond his own more satirical accounts. Its meanings "streamed forth from the mystic symbol, subtly communicating itself to my sensibilities, but evading the analysis of my mind" (28).

A tension between sensibility and analysis persists through the narrative. The power of authority to take the shameful measure of vulnerable subjectivity terrifies the narrator. Yet he seems equally terrified of the heart-freezing isolation inherent in aggressive autonomy. Fleeing coercive authority, including his own, he defines himself simply as an imaginative recreator of Surveyor Pue's manuscript and imagines Hester's rebellious self-reliance with sustained flights of empathy. Fleeing self-reliance, he chastises Hester's pride and relentlessly accuses Chillingworth's self-possessed malice. For him subjectivity seems always vulnerable to alien invasion. Chillingworth's own invasion of Dimmesdale's soul manifests the devil's entry into the scholar-physician. Perpetually oscillating between subjectivity and authority, the narrator dodges being pinned down to one mode or the other. To commit himself either way might expose his fearful cruelty of heart or his equally fearful vulnerability to violation.[21]

21. Recent criticism has begun to explore these oscillations. See esp. Brodhead, *Hawthorne, Melville, and the Novel*; Kenneth Dauber, *Rediscovering Hawthorne* (Princeton: Princeton University Press, 1977), though Dauber is taken in by the narrator's claims for intimacy; and Edgar A. Dryden, *Nathaniel Hawthorne: The Poetics of Enchantment* (Ithaca: Cornell University Press, 1977), which argues for Hawthorne's alternation between postures as his way of managing "a menacing otherness at his own center" (21).

His solution, for both himself and his heroine, is the fluidity of sympathetic relationship. He strives to "stand in some true relation with his audience," fictionalizing his reader as "a kind and apprehensive, though not the closest friend." Without such a relation, he says, "thoughts are frozen and utterance benumbed" (7). The metaphor comes close to self-exposure. Seeking a nonthreatening communication that protects him from real intimacy, he indicates his fear of a solidifying self-possession. The audience has to warm the intrinsic coldness of his heart and tongue.

Similarly, the coldness of Hester's radical speculations must be warmed by her mothering heart. "A woman," he concludes, "never overcomes these problems by any exercise of thought"; she can solve them only by letting the heart "come uppermost" (120). Having established Hester's radical potential, the narrator now undercuts her force by dramatizing her transformation back to lovability, not toward public combat. The "magic touch" to bring about her "transfiguration," as he says earlier (119), sets the second half of the narrative in motion. She vows to redeem Dimmesdale from his own weakness and his malevolent tormentor. She will accomplish "the rescue of the victim" from her husband's "power" (121).

Why the sudden swerve toward selfless liberation of a man whom, even near the end, she can hardly forgive for deserting her? As the narrator says so empathetically in one of his last oscillations, "thus much of woman was there in Hester, that she could scarcely forgive him ... for being able so completely to withdraw himself from their mutual world; while she groped darkly, and stretched forth her cold hands, and found him not" (170). Yet here, nine chapters earlier, she resolves to rescue her self-absorbed lover. In part the narrator advocates a maternal sympathy that can subdue Hester for her own good. More deeply, by both investigating and identifying with the victim, the narrator encourages a Chillingworth-like interpretive mode that intensifies punitive perceptions of guilt, on all sides. In its latest form this mode has become psychoanalytic detection of the Chillingworth-Dimmesdale relation.

It seems obvious to post-Freudian readers that Chillingworth's revengeful penetration into Dimmesdale's bosom constitutes the climactic moment of physical intimacy in the story. His intrusive, sadistic rape first awakens protracted "throb[s] of pain," then culminates in the "moment of his ecstasy," when his discovery of what lies on the sleeping minister's chest sends Dimmesdale into a "shudder" and

Chillingworth into a "ghastly rapture" of riotous gestures (102). The sexualization of revenge accompanies the desexing of love. More broadly, the narrator's overt language of sympathy frequently masks his fascination with the violation of inward spheres. Various readers have noted that Chillingworth bears the same relation to Dimmesdale that Pearl often has to Hester: the unrestrained underside of socially conforming energies.[22] Dimmesdale's self-preoccupied guilt, to take this view further, licenses Chillingworth's rage for penetration, possession, and violation even as it recalls the minister's own moment of violation in the past. In the psychological allegory to which the narrator seems increasingly disposed, malicious intrusion is guilt's double.

The narrative itself becomes a further stage for contrary energies, as Richard Brodhead's fine discussion of its mixed modes indicates. After establishing initially intense sympathies with Hester's resolute integrity and defiant creativity, it moves toward framing her, in several senses. It also induces a covert fascination with violating her inwardness and humbling her strength. This drama is displaced from Hester to Dimmesdale. The sexuality of victimization and the intellectualized control of rage move Hester's subjectivity toward the margins of Hawthorne's romance.

Psychoanalytic readings tend to suppress Hester's struggle for autonomy to reflect the Chillingworth-Dimmesdale connection. Both Frederick Crews and John Irwin, the two most prominent psychoanalytic investigators, assume the role of detective on the trail of a narcissist. Crews presents the story entirely as if it were the narrator's ambiguously ironic relation to Dimmesdale's libidinal repression, while Irwin's Lacanian reading finds narcissistic mirroring doubled and redoubled throughout the text. But Dimmesdale's growth from narcissism to sublimated independence, like the narrator's ironic pursuit, is a flight from feeling. Whether seeing Freudian desire or Lacanian absence at the heart of the text, both Crews and Irwin mistake the narrator's defenses for narrative truths.[23]

22. See Leslie A. Fiedler, *Love and Death in the American Novel*, rev. ed. (New York: Stein & Day, 1966), 437; and Baym, *Shape of Hawthorne's Career*, who differs from my view in saying that at the end "the two shattered personalities become whole again and the symbolic characters disappear" (130).

23. Irwin, *American Hieroglyphics*, 239–84; Frederick C. Crews, *The Sins of the Fathers: Hawthorne's Psychological Themes* (New York: Oxford University Press, 1966), 136–53. Irwin sees Dimmesdale's guilt as the "true" self opposing his false public role and presents Hester as the double for a Dimmesdale-like narrator. Crews mocks Hester

Anxiety about anger, more fearful to him than sexual desire, generates the narrator's incompatible fascinations with Hester's independence and Chillingworth's malice. Both these frozen stances intimate anger, in opposite ways. But because Chillingworth's rage has its base in intimacy, unlike Hester's more generalized social rebellion, he is punished far more severely by the narrator, who makes the cuckolded husband his prime villain. To the narrator anger and desire are the same thing: low, base, the devil's plaything. They lead to violence and violation, not love. Yet his idea of love is finally a mystified self-projection. In affirming sympathy as the key, he defines it as the capacity to complete one's divided self without undue self-exposure, from the first paragraph of "The Custom-House" to the last pages of the story. That narcissistic definition avoids acknowledging conflict as part of intimacy. In fact it avoids otherness altogether, because for the narrator otherness brings a terror of unloving regard. For him, anger is the terror of unloving strangeness within oneself. In rigidifying Chillingworth's anger as possessive malice the narrator controls that terror as allegory, while in transforming Hester's more complicated subjectivity to maternal sympathy he diffuses that terror as romance.[24]

By the end of the story both Dimmesdale and the narrator release emotions only through an ascension of words that nobody quite understands. Dimmesdale's new power of unclear statement, in his sermon and his confession, mirrors a broader narrative mystification of pain as the source of eloquence and transfiguration. From an initial appreciation of Hester's strength and fascination with Chillingworth's power, the narrator has moved toward exalting Dimmesdale's weak-

---

for "prating" of freedom and finds that the minister's anxious egotism finally achieves "heroic independence" of Hester by sublimating desire in oratory (143, 149). Baym, *Shape of Hawthorne's Career*, 138–39, briefly suggests a Freudian perspective, that Pearl may be Hester's id and Chillingworth Dimmesdale's superego.

24. In *Rediscovering Hawthorne* Dauber astutely discusses the shift toward Dimmesdale as allegory's socialization of the forest's romance world. Brodhead, *Hawthorne, Melville, and the Novel*, associates interpretive openness with Hester's symbolic mode, while Chillingworth embodies tendencies toward allegorical rigidity and the punitive realism of a hierarchic male society. Bell, *Development of America Romance*, 176–77, similarly argues that Hester's rebellion is "the central 'story'" but that she, as well as society, represses herself to become a "victim of allegory." Both Poe and Henry James vehemently opposed Hawthorne's allegorizing as artistically destructive, a perspective sometimes adopted by Hawthorne himself.

suffering. Through insistent narrative framing, his masochism becomes the scaffold for self-magnifying transcendence, culminating in the narrator's advocacy of spiritualized male narcissism as the way to complete one's divided self.

Dimmesdale's feminized pain first brings some traditional male rewards. Though he forsakes his own fatherhood from the moment of conception, he ascends to meet his heavenly father after receiving a weepy kiss from his daughter, whom he barely has time to acknowledge before his death. Pearl's childhood is an extreme instance of the absent father and the overpresent mother so basic to American middle-class society, and experienced by Hawthorne in his own life.[25] Consider her father as an American success story, made possible by his flight from woman and child. He has no distractions from his work, and he can exercise to the full his intellectual powers. He makes an extraordinary social impact, gains respect as a public and private adviser, and after a satisfactory dark night of the soul gains his final reward of celestial approval. Meanwhile Hester, like a good mistress, remains bonded to her child, her duties, her isolation, her marginal status, and her hopeless dreams of union.

The narrator's astonishing corollary to Hester's decline into sympathy unites Chillingworth, Dimmesdale, and himself in a loving ascension. After Dimmesdale spurns Hester to gain an uncontaminated integration for his purified maleness, we are asked to imagine him united in heaven not just with God but with Chillingworth as well. In the middle of the story the narrator oddly interpolates that "hatred, by a gradual and quiet process, will even be transformed to love," if new irritations of hostility do not impede the process (116). At several other points he implies that rage and desire fuse as violent passion. Now the narrator inverts the devil's work. He takes the ability to transform hate into love as his final test of the reader's tender capacities.

Asking his readers to be merciful to Chillingworth, he wonders "whether hatred and love be not the same thing at bottom." Each supposes "intimacy and heart-knowledge." Each needs dependence. Each dies if the object withdraws.

> Philosophically considered, therefore, the two passions seem essentially the same, except that one happens to be seen in a celestial radiance,

25. See Chodorow, *Reproduction of Mothering*; also see the last chapter of David Leverenz, *The Language of Puritan Feeling: An Exploration in Literature, Psychology, and Social History* (New Brunswick, N. J.: Rutgers University Press, 1980), 258–71.

and the other in a dusky and lurid glow. In the spiritual world, the old physician and the minister—mutual victims as they have been—may, unawares, have found their earthly stock of hatred and antipathy transmuted into golden love. [183–84]

The passage still seems to me the strangest in all of Hawthorne. Transforming devilish rage into divine love, it takes Dimmesdale's hierarchy of high and low to its highest extreme. If the narrator hesitates to assert their fanciful union as spiritual fact, he has no qualms about describing them as "mutual victims." Anne Abbott cited this passage as a prime example of Hawthorne's "mistborn ideas" and asked "if there be any firm ground at all" here. Yet she also jmused, in some perplexity, that Hawthorne seems to share that "doubt."[26] Her reaction is quite right, because the passage substitutes loving victims for strong selves in conflict. Its several levels of meaning bring the reader's contrary responses to their final suspended inversion.

The possibility of spiritual union in heaven joins the two whose intercourse on earth comes to center the story: revengeful father and violated/violating son. The cuckold and the lover rise together to an all-male paradise, while Hester mutely returns to Salem. The narrator's fantasized embrace of father and son gives a more openly oedipal dimension to the classic American fantasy, first described by Leslie Fiedler, of two men in flight from strong women. Moreover, the transmutation suggests an integration of the male self as well, if only in coupling two sides of a self-falsification. Intrusive sadism and guilty vulnerability come together at last, released from any pressure to come to terms with anger, love, or fear.

Most significantly, the union occurs not in the plot but in the narrator's relation to his audience. He sets his readers a last challenge: can you take your sympathy that far? In asking readers to sympathize with Dimmesdale and Chillingworth as "mutual victims" and to imagine hate transmuted into golden love, the narrator brings himself into that embrace, with his reader as witness. All three male voices, iron-

26. Abbott, review of *The Scarlet Letter*, in *Critical Heritage*, 165. Bell, *Development of American Romance*, 178, suggests that even God "becomes a kind of allegorical double" for Dimmesdale's "guilty self-justification." Leslie Fiedler, *Love and Death*, 235, describes this passage as "an equivocation which undercuts, at the last moment, the whole suggested meaning of his book."

ically at odds on earth, escape together, free from the body's sexuality and the mind's conflicts, and free from genuine intimacy.[27]

Yet this narrative flight, like all his extremes, is momentary. Returning to earth, he sympathetically concludes with Hester's solitude, not Dimmesdale's transcendence. Part of the narrator's strategy for reconciling conflicts is to condemn fixity of any kind, physical or spiritual. If rigidity seems fearfully demonic, associated with anger and the lower parts of the soul or body, flexible sympathy becomes the narrator's vague placebo. This tactic allows him momentary participations in his contradictory extremes. But it also establishes multiple authorial interpretations as a shifting medium for the plot. His self-dramatizing ceaselessly pacifies and resurrects his plot's tensions, while deflecting attention from his punitive plotting to the sympathetic puppeteer.

Pearl represents what most needs pacification: her rebellious impulses toward creative autonomy and her aggressive impulses to detect and accuse. Dimmesdale, far from being the "true self" of the romance, unites two weak contemporary defenses against Pearl's strong impulses. He enacts a male accommodation to public role and a female sense of self as vulnerable victim. If Pearl joins contradictory strengths, Dimmesdale joins fragile defenses. As the narrative awakens contrary energies of rebellion and intrusion, the narrator's voice quells these polarized versions of anger and authority through his rhetoric of sympathy and his intimacy with what he often calls Dimmesdale's "tremulous" voice. His feminized hero, a dimmed valley even in his name, becomes both the narrator and the object of his inquisition.

In the narrator's increasingly oedipal allegory, a regressive, inquisitorial family triangle of cruel impersonal father, kind despairing mother, and tortured triumphant son all but drives out early expectations for Hester's adult subjectivity against public patriarchy. A sadomasochistic symbiosis of father and son becomes a vision of transcendent, victimized love. Yet the narrative insistently returns to its latent subversion of male inauthenticity. Hester's integrity mutely survives. If Pearl ceases to do battle with the world, she finds a wider world unimaginable to Salem, or for that matter to the narrator himself, whose Puritan

27. See Hélène Cixous, "sorties," in *New French Feminisms: An Anthology*, ed. Elaine Marks and Isabelle de Courtivron (Amherst: University of Massachusetts Press, 1980), 91–92, on the reduction of woman to the maternal implied in the ascension of man to the father.

roots "have intertwined themselves" with his own nature (12). This is as close as he comes to directly acknowledging his Chillingworth side. At the same time, however, his presentation of himself gives access to strong subjectivities beyond his conscious accommodations.

A psychoanalytic focus on anger and dependence might illuminate Hawthorne's biography here, especially if complemented by a feminist analysis of the polarized sex-role expectations so basic to his time. Hawthorne's remarkable empathy with a solitary woman and his fear of an unloving other insinuated into his own psyche probably have their contradictory sources in his ties to his mother, whose death helped to impel Hester's creation. The intensities of that bond go deeper than the more obvious oedipal guilt for having possessed a woman whose husband strangely disappeared.[28] Yet the complexities of narrative dissociation in *The Scarlet Letter* have as much to do with Hawthorne's canny relation to his audience as with his uncanny relation to himself.

In conforming to his audience's expectations for a morally comfortable narrator, Hawthorne fictionalizes himself so as partially to undermine his own characterization. His fragmenting empathies outstrip the narrator's growing alliances with Dimmesdale's self-centering scrutiny and Chillingworth's intrusive detection. He seems fully aware that his readers will accept Hester only while she suffers for her sin; as no fewer than three reviewers remarked, the narrator avoids the dangers of "the French school" by making his heroine satisfactorily miserable.[29] Yet while silencing Hester with values he and his audience hold dear, he makes his readers uncomfortable with those values.

28. As John Franzosa has established for "The Custom-House," anger and dependence are issues more basic than guilt and sexuality. See "'The Custom-House,' *The Scarlet Letter*, and Hawthorne's Separation from Salem," *ESQ*, 24 (1978), 57–71. Franzosa argues that a guilty identity balances impulses toward hostile intrusion and isolated self-possession, and allows inauthentic identity within the narrator's community. Franzosa explores Hawthorne's "negotiations" with his readers more fully in "A Psychoanalysis of Hawthorne's Style," *Genre*, 14 (1981), 383–409. Baym defends Hawthorne's mother from Hawthorne in "Nathaniel Hawthorne and His Mother: A Biographical Speculation," *American Literature*, 54 (1982), 1–27. While suggesting that Hawthorne's various presentations of her mask her "oppressive" presence in his psyche, Baym sees *The Scarlet Letter* as a creative reversal that temporarily frees Hawthorne from dependency on maternal power.

29. The phrase is Whipple's (*Critical Heritage*, 161–62). Henry F. Chorley, in a review in the *Athenaeum*, June 15, 1850, praised *The Scarlet Letter* for being "so clear of fever and of prurient excitement" because "the misery of the woman" is always present (rpt. in *Critical Heritage*; see 163), while E. A. Duyckinck, in a review in

When he at last offers his "sweet moral blossom," it turns out to be a version of Dimmesdale's anguish over self-display: "Be true! Be true! Be true! Show freely to the world, if not your worst, yet some trait whereby the worst may be inferred!" (183). This is the hesitant exhibitionism of a disembodied Salem Flasher, who encourages his readers to imagine his worst while showing their own. He assumes that his readers share with him not only a self worth hating but also the ambivalent desire to detect, to be detected, and to stay respectably hidden. A mutual revelation of guilty subjectivity constitutes his idea of true sympathy, true community, and true interpretation. As he quietly observes, just after Dimmesdale has seen his A flash across the sky, "another's guilt might have seen another symbol in it" (113). At such moments, while interpretive authority disintegrates, writing and reading converge. They become equivalent, equivocal acts of shared self-exposure and accusation. Uneasy lies the tale that wears that crown.

Finally, however, *The Scarlet Letter* takes readers beyond its narrator and his imagined audience. Dimmesdale's guilt, like the narrator's, conceals a fear of losing approval. But Hawthorne's romance evokes strong subjectivity in opposition to dependence of any kind. Throughout, like an anxious referee, the interpreter's voice strives to rise above the fray. Trying to sympathize, judge, and reconcile, he imposes the masks he wants to lift. Yet while the storyteller oscillates between guilt and decorum, his story brings out a much more risky inwardness, whose unresolved tensions sent Mrs. Hawthorne to bed and Hester to a deeper solitude. Hester's epitaph suitably blazons forth her red strength against her black background. By contrast, the narrator's epitaph could be the remark he addresses to "the minister in a maze": "No man, for any considerable period, can wear one face to himself, and another to the multitude, without finally getting bewildered as to which may be the true" (154). In accommodating his voice to the contradictions of public authority, the narrator joins Salem's congregated sepulchres, while Hester's life continues to speak with embattled vitality.

Literary World, March 30, 1850, was happy to see a "writer who has lived so much among the new school" handle "this delicate subject without an infusion of George Sand" (rpt. in *Critical Heritage*; see 156–57). On the other hand, both Abbott's review and the review by Orestes Brownson in *Brownson's Quarterly Review*, October 1850, condemn the romance because Hester is not sufficiently repentant, as does the infamous review by Arthur Cleveland Coxe in the *Church Review*, January 1851 (rpt. in *Critical Heritage*; see 165–66, 177–78, 183).

9

Eugénie Grandet:
Mirrors and Melancholia

NAOMI SCHOR

If, at this early stage, one can discern anything like a consensus among critics of French literature working in Lacan's wake, it would be that modern texts—the classical *Bildungsroman* as well as modern autobiographies[1]—rehearse a recurrent developmental saga: the successful or failed but in any event necessary passage from the Imaginary into the Symbolic, from the dangerous seductions of the mirror stage into the sobering realities of the law of the father.[2] What remains unexplored are the specificities—if any—of the feminocentric examples of these genres. What, one may ask, are the literary consequences

1. I am referring here in turn to Fredric Jameson, "Imaginary and Symbolic in *La Rabouilleuse*," *Social Sciences Information*, 16 (1977), 59–81, and Jeffrey Mehlman, *A Structural Study of Autobiography* (Ithaca: Cornell University Press, 1974).

2. Although, as Jean Laplanche and J.-B. Pontalis—authors of the remarkable *Language of Psychoanalysis*—remind us, it is "contrary to the spirit of Lacan's thought" to provide "strict definitions" of his key conceptual terms, because Lacan's thought "refrains from establishing a fixed relationship between signifier and signified" ("Symbolic," trans. Peter Kussel and Jeffrey Mehlman, *Yale French Studies*, 48 [1972], 201–2), given the relative unfamiliarity of these terms and the extensive use I make of them throughout this article, a brief gloss is in order here. When I speak of the Imaginary I shall be referring to that psychic register which is synonymous with the exclusive, dual infant-mother relationship, what Freud calls the pre-Oedipus. As Lacan's choice

of the anatomical differences between the sexes at the point of articulation of the Imaginary and the Symbolic? And this question implies
another: What is the incidence of sexual difference on each of these
psychic registers?

To raise these questions is not merely to perform the "ritual" of
feminist hermeneutics: the subjection of all paradigms to the test of
sexual discrimination in the name of the search for a sometimes elusive
feminine specificity. What is at issue in what follows—and I am anticipating a good deal—is the ongoing recuperation of Lacan's developmental schema which attempts to suppress the Imaginary and its
discourse. It is perhaps not a coincidence that it should be a female
Lacanian, Shoshana Felman, who would write: "It has been under-

---

of the word Imaginary indicates, however, his emphasis is on the prevalence of the
image in the pre-Oedipus, on the manner in which the human subject's ego is constituted through a process of identification with images: the images of the other as self
(mother) and of the self as other (mirror image). Because all inter- and intrasubjective
relationships are rooted in narcissism and illusionism, the subject is prey to the lure
of identification as well as to deathly struggles for prestige. The Symbolic register,
equivalent to Freud's Oedipus, is presided over by the father and the cultural order
he represents: the subject enters into the Symbolic order at the very moment when
she is inscribed in the kinship system and is, as it were, reinscribed when she acquires
language and, through the mediation of the father, takes her place in society. Whereas
the Imaginary implies identity as well as identification, the Symbolic relies on difference, sexual (castration) as well as linguistic. The analogies I have drawn between
Freud's pre-Oedipus/Oedipus and Lacan's Imaginary/Symbolic should not obscure a
crucial distinction: Lacan's registers are not in any orthodox Freudian sense stages of
development. Nevertheless—as the prevailing tendency to temporalize Lacan's registers indicates—there is enough ambiguity in Lacan to make possible and perhaps
even inevitable a slippage in the direction of the developmental, a slippage against
which what follows struggles but to which it does occasionally succumb. The basic
texts in which Lacan elaborates these notions are *Écrits* (Paris: Seuil, 1966); *Séminaire
I: Les Écrits techniques de Freud* (Paris: Seuil, 1975), and *Séminaire II: Le Moi dans
la théorie de Freud et dans la technique de la psychanalyse* (Paris: Seuil, 1978). In
addition to the standard works on Lacan's thought by Anika Rifflet-Lemaire, *Jacques
Lacan* (Brussels: Dessart, 1970); Anthony Wilden, *The Languages of the Self* (Baltimore: Johns Hopkins University Press, 1968); and Jean Laplanche and J. B. Pontalis,
The Language of Psychoanalysis, trans. Donald Nicholson-Smith (New York: Norton,
1973), among recent writings on Lacan I have found the following articles particularly
useful: Fredric Jameson, "Imaginary and Symbolic in Lacan: Marxism, Psychoanalytic
Criticism, and the Problem of the Subject," *Yale French Studies*, 55/56 (1977), 338–
95; Gregory Ulmer, "The Discourse of the Imaginary," *Diacritics*, 10 (Spring 1980),
61–75; Malcolm Bowie, "Jacques Lacan," in *Structuralism and Since: From Lévi-
Strauss to Derrida*, ed. John Sturrock (Oxford: Oxford University Press, 1979), 116–
53; and Jane Gallop, "Lacan's 'Mirror Stage': Where to Begin," *SubStance*, 37/38 (1982),
118–28.

stood in France and elsewhere, on the basis of Lacan's theory, that the 'specular' is to be eliminated, that the term 'imaginary' is above all a *pejorative* term, subordinated to the positive that is constituted here by the antithesis of the 'real' or of the 'symbolic.' But this is not the case."[3] What follows attempts to restore the Imaginary to its rightful pride of place, to view it not as a stage to be outgrown but as an ineradicable constituent of the human psyche and, more important, as the essential, indeed the only matrix of fantasy and fiction. To do so does not, however, signify an uncritical endorsement of the Imaginary: for if as the maternal register the Imaginary has been negatively valorized by certain male critics, as the empire of the specular it has, as we shall see, come under attack by one feminist psychoanalyst and not the least, Luce Irigaray.

I have chosen *Eugénie Grandet* as my text at least in part because, as is becoming increasingly evident, Balzac's fiction dwells with particular insistence on precisely the junction of the Imaginary and the Symbolic. And within the Balzac canon few works body forth so nakedly as does *Eugénie Grandet* the imbrication of the maternal and paternal spheres of influence. In a great literary tradition—the French psychological novel—characterized by the conspicuous absence of either mothers (as in *Manon Lescaut* and *Madame Bovary*) or fathers (as in *La Princesse de Clèves* and *L'Education sentimentale*), *Eugénie Grandet* stands out as a novel where the oedipal configuration is writ large, as a unique nuclear family romance.

From the outset, Eugénie's relationship with her mother is described as both unusually close and closed, confined as they both are to the womblike locus of the Grandets' livingroom:

> In the window nearest the door stood a straw-bottomed chair, raised on blocks of wood so that Madame Grandet as she sat could look out at passers-by in the street. A work-table of bleached cherry-wood filled

---

3. Shoshana Felman, *The Literary Speech Act: Don Juan with J. L. Austin, or Seduction in Two Languages*, trans. Catherine Porter (Ithaca: Cornell University Press, 1983), 138. Cf. these remarks by Michèle Montrelay regarding the treatment by certain analysts of the "female imaginary" as a "poor relative": "Can we not ask ourselves instead whether the imaginary by giving 'consistency,' as Lacan puts it, to the symbolic which is a gap, is not just as operative, just as determining of the structure as are the real and the symbolic. To give consistency, to give body to the symbolic fractioning: that operation precedes any possible grasp of the subject in its image and that of the other. There exists a primary *imaginaire* which is not unrelated to feminine jouissance" (*L'Ombre et le nom: Sur la féminité* (Paris: Minuit, 1977), 155–56).

the other window recess, and Eugénie Grandet's little armchair was set close by. Day after day, from April to November, for the last fifteen years, time had passed peacefully for mother and daughter here, in constant work.

Dans la croisée la plus rapprochée de la porte, se trouvait une chaise de paille dont les pieds étaient montés sur des patins, afin d'élever madame Grandet à une hauteur qui lui permît de voir les passants. Une travailleuse en bois de merisier déteint remplissait l'embrasure, et le petit fauteuil d'Eugénie Grandet était placé tout auprès. Depuis quinze ans, toutes les journées de la mère et de la fille s'étaient paisiblement écoulées à cette place, dans un travail constant, à compter du mois d'avril jusqu'au mois de novembre.[4]

Not only the living room but the whole of "Monsieur Grandet's house" (37) images a mother-daughter relationship that is quite literally monstrous: "Indeed, the lives of the famous Hungarian sisters, attached to one another by one of nature's errors, could scarcely have been more closely joined in sympathetic feeling than those of Eugénie and her mother, living as they did always together in the recess of the window, together in church, breathing the same air even while they slept" (" . . . la vie des célèbres soeurs hongroises, attachées l'une à l'autre par une erreur de la nature, n'avait pas été plus intime que ne l'était celle d'Eugénie et de sa mère, toujours ensemble dans cette embrasure de croisée, ensemble à l'église, et dormant ensemble dans le même air" [105/71]). This final notation—the conclusive hyperbole—draws our attention to a bizarre and telling architectural feature of the house's second-story sleeping quarters: "Madame Grandet had a bedroom beside Eugénie's with a glass door between. Her husband's room was separated from hers by a partition . . . " ("Madame Grandet avait une chambre contiguë à celle d'Eugénie, chez qui l'on entrait par une porte vitrée. La chambre du maître était séparée de celle de sa femme par une cloison . . . " [88/58]).

Balzac has here taken the mother-daughter relationship far beyond the paradigmatic bounds set forth in Madame de La Fayette's *Princesse de Clèves*, where, however strong the filial bond, the generational differences that structure society are in no danger of collapsing. In *Eugénie Grandet*, on the other hand, the necessary distance between

4. Honoré de Balzac, *Eugénie Grandet*, trans. Marion Ayton Crawford (Harmondsworth: Penguin, 1955), 51, and *Eugénie Grandet* (Paris: Garnier-Flammarion, 1964), 30. All subsequent references to these editions will be included in the text.

mother and daughter has been reduced to catastrophically narrow proportions—only the most fragile of barriers, a glass pane, prevents their total fusion—catastrophic because in the end fatal to both members of the dyad: to the mother, who dies of what we might call "terminal identification," and to the daughter, who survives but never transcends her homosexual bond with her mother.[5]

What I am suggesting is that the extreme, even pathological nature of Eugénie's love for her cousin Charles bears the unmistakable stamp of its matrix: Eugénie's intense and persistent attachment to her mother. It is "this desperate paradise of the dual relationship" that Charles's sudden arrival on the scene serves both to reveal and to reinforce.[6] This observation brings us to what is surely the most characteristic manifestation of the Imaginary in everyday life, romantic love, in this instance Eugénie's narcissistic passion for her cousin. As Freud remarks in his essay "On Narcissism: An Introduction" (1914), "overvaluation" is a distinctive "narcissistic stigma in the case of objectchoice,"[7] and Eugénie's overestimation verges on idolatry; at first sight she falls in love not so much with a man as with a graven image:

> It seemed to Eugénie, who had never in her life seen such a paragon of beauty, so wonderfully dressed, that her cousin was a seraph come from heaven . . . In fact, if such a comparison can convey the emotions of an ignorant girl who spent all her time darning stockings and patching her father's clothes, who had passed her life by that window under the dirty wainscoting, looking in the silent street outside to see scarcely one passer-by in an hour, the sight of this exquisite youth gave Eugénie the sensations of aesthetic delight that a young man finds in looking at the fanciful portraits of women drawn by Westall for English *Keepsakes*, and engraved by the Findens with a burin so skillful that you hesitate to breathe on the vellum for fear the celestial vision should disappear.[73]

> Eugénie, à qui le type d'une perfection semblable, soit dans la mise, soit dans la personne, était entièrement inconnu, crut voir en son cousin une créature descendue de quelque région séraphique . . . Enfin, si toutefois cette image peut résumer les impressions que le jeune élégant produisit sur une ignorante fille sans cesse occupée à rapetasser des

---

5. One might describe the mother-daughter relationship in *Eugénie Grandet* in the terms provided by Nancy Chodorow in *The Reproduction of Mothering: Psychoanalysis and the Sociology of Gender* (Berkeley: University of California Press, 1978): " . . . prolonged symbiosis and *narcissistic overidentification* are particularly characteristic of early relationships between mothers and daughters" (104; emphasis added).

6. Mehlman, *Structural Study*, 25.

7. Freud, "On Narcissism: An Introduction," in *Standard Edition*, IV, 91.

bas, à ravauder la garderobe de son père, et dont la vie s'était écoulée sous ces crasseux lambris sans voir dans la rue silencieuse plus d'un passant par heure, la vue de son cousin fit sourdre en son coeur les émotions de fine volupté que causent à un jeune homme les fantastiques figures de femme dessinées par Westall dans les Keepsake anglais, et gravées par les Finden d'un burin si habile, qu'on a peur, en soufflant sur le velin, de faire envoler ces apparitions célestes.[47]

The reference to Freud is, however, problematic, for, it will be recalled, in the essay on narcissism, Freud clearly distinguishes between male and female types of narcissistic object choice, and, according to this typology—which, Freud remarks, is "of course not universal"—the telltale overestimation is a male prerogative. As for "the purest and truest" feminine type of women: "Strictly speaking, it is only themselves that such women love with an intensity comparable to that of man's love for them. Nor does their need lie in the direction of loving, but of being loved."[8] Eugénie—who loves according to the masculine model—would then be a "case of female narcissism running counter to the psychoanalytic theory," a theory amply corroborated by Balzac in other novels. The myth of female narcissism is indeed alive and well in Balzac's fictional universe: one has only to think of the "woman without a heart," the courtesan Foedora in *La Peau de chagrin*, a woman who lives in a state of autarchic splendor that drives her would-be lovers to distraction. What, under these circumstances, are we to make of Eugénie's "unfeminine" object choice? We might begin by simply rejecting Freud's distinction—a step many other critics have taken before us[9]—and seek to divorce gender from narcissism. This is, of course, precisely the strategic move Lacan effectuates in his return to and departure from Freud's writings on narcissism: the mirror stage during which the narcissistic foundation of the ego is laid is presented as unisexual, before sexual difference.

Now, in as much as it has been said, accurately I think, that narcissism is "the keystone of the Lacanian system"[10] (and is also to my

8. *Standard Edition*, XIV, 89.

9. I am thinking in particular of René Girard's commentary on this aspect of Freud's essay in *Des Choses cachées depuis la fondation du monde* (Paris: Grasset, 1978), 391–405. For a feminist critique of Girard's reading of Freud on female narcissism, see Sarah Kofman, "The Narcissistic Woman: Freud and Girard," *Diacritics*, 10 (Fall 1980), 36–45.

10. André Green, "Un, Autre Neutre: Valeurs narcissiques du Même," in *Narcisses: Nouvelle Revue de Psychanalyse*, 13 (1976), 43.

mind the key to our understanding of *Eugénie Grandet*), the question raised by a Lacanian reading of feminocentric literature is the question raised by Juliet Mitchell with reference to preoedipal infantile development: "Is there any [gender-bound] differentiation . . . within this level of the Imaginary relationship epitomized (though not completely) by narcissism?"[11] In other words, is the difference between the sexes operative during the formative mirror stage? Does the female infant perceive her imago differently from the male infant, does she perceive herself as different (inferior to) the ideal (male) model? Is there a specifically female entry point into the Imaginary? Mitchell hedges her answer: "Everything Freud writes confirms that there is no important psychological differentiation in this pre-Oedipal situation. But this situation is not a stage, not an amount of time, but a level. At another level, the culturally determined implication of the sexual difference is then always in waiting."[12] According to this Lacano-Derridean formulation of the question, sexual difference is inscribed from the outset, but its revelation is deferred: Mitchell seems to subscribe to the notion of something we might call sexual differ*a*nce.

Had Mitchell had the benefit of reading Luce Irigaray's feminist post-Lacanian deconstruction of Freud's two essays on femininity, as well as of Lacan's *Encore*, her answer would have been, I am quite certain, less contorted and more audacious. One cannot come away from a reading of either *Speculum* or *Ce Sexe qui n'en est pas un* still believing in the myth of a sort of prelapsarian pre-Oedipus, indeed in the innocence of the very notion of the mirror stage. Lacan's mirror, as Irigaray shows, is but the most recent avatar of a philosophical topos, the plane mirror that has been, at least since Plato, in the service of a philosophical tradition dedicated to valorizing sameness, symmetry, and most important of all, visibility. The Phallus as unique sexual standard. According to Irigaray, the mirror stage is not in any sense of the word neutral; the figure in the mirror is implicitly male:

And, *as far as the organism is concerned, what happens when the mirror reveals nothing?* No sex, for example. As is the case for the little girl. To say that "the sex (of the congener) matters little" in the constituent effects of the mirror image, and further that "the specular image seems to be the threshold of the visible world," does not that amount to

11. Juliet Mitchell, *Psychoanalysis and Feminism* (New York: Vintage, 1974), 42–43.
12. Mitchell, *Psychoanalysis and Feminism*, 52.

stressing that the female sex will be excluded from it? And that it is a male or an asexual body that will determine the features of the *Gestalt*, that irreducible matrix of the introduction of the subject into the social order? Hence its functioning according to laws so foreign to the feminine?[13]

Far from being the ecstatic experience that it is for the male infant, the mirror stage, still according to Irigaray, deals the little girl the first of her "narcissistic wounds."[14] Under the sway of the prevailing scopic economy, the female Imaginary—for that is what I have been describing here—can but be marked by an alienation far more radical than that affecting the male ego, a sort of secondary alienation grafted onto the primary alienation constitutive of the ego in the Lacanian scheme. Consequently, contemplating her image in the mirror, a woman in love can but experience a devastating sense of inadequacy, a dysphoria far in excess of the loss of "self-regard" which is the corollary of the idealization of the love object.[15] When, the morning after Charles's unexpected arrival from Paris, Eugénie looks at herself in the mirror, her narcissism is definitely of the negative sort: "She rose restlessly to her feet again and again, to go to her mirror and look at her face, in just the spirit of a conscientious writer reading his work through, criticizing it and saying hard things about it to himself: 'I am not good looking enough for him!' " ("Elle se leva fréquemment, se mit devant son miroir, et s'y regarda comme un auteur de bonne foi contemple son oeuvre pour se critiquer, et se dire des injures à lui-même. —Je ne suis pas assez belle pour lui" [94/62]). Balzac's analogy is eloquent: first, because it attests to Eugénie's status as an artifact, an object of communication and exchange, and second, because it reveals the always implicit presence of a male observer in all scenes of female autocontemplation. As John Berger so aptly notes in

13. Luce Irigaray, "La 'Méchanique' des fluides," in *Ce Sexe qui n'en est pas un* (Paris: Minuit, 1977), 115.

14. Irigaray, *Speculum de l'autre femme* (Paris: Minuit, 1974), 71. Irigaray is, of course, quoting from Freud, "Some Psychical Consequences of the Anatomical Distinction between the Sexes," in *Standard Edition*, XIX, 253.

15. On this point there is a striking convergence of Balzac's and Freud's formulations: "This was Eugénie's humble thought . . . . The poor child was unjust to herself; but humility, or rather the fear of being unworthy, is one of the first awakened attributes of love" (94); " . . . it is easy to observe that libidinal object-cathexis does not raise self-regard. The effect of dependence upon the loved object is to lower that feeling: a person in love is humble. A person who loves has, so to speak, forfeited a part of his narcissism" (*Standard Edition*, XIV, 98). Cf. Green, "Un, Autre Neutre," 63.

his *Ways of Seeing*: "The surveyor of woman in herself is male: the surveyed female."[16]

Balzac, however, does not content himself with revealing the hidden mainspring of female narcissism—male mediation; he also exposes the prime mediator, which, under patriarchy, can only be the father, "the sole possible agent of her [the little girl's] narcissization."[17] There is then a second mirror scene, which takes place after Grandet has locked Eugénie up in her room for refusing to tell him what she has done with her gold:

> Next day Grandet went to take a few turns round his little garden, as he had formed the habit of doing ever since Eugénie had been locked up. He chose for his walk a time when Eugénie was accustomed to brush her hair, by the window. When the cooper had walked to the big walnut tree and beyond it, he used to stand there hidden by its trunk for several minutes, watching his daughter brushing out her long chestnut locks . . .
>
> He often sat for some time on the crumbling wooden seat where Charles and Eugénie had sworn that they would love each other for ever, while Eugénie in her turn stole stealthy glances at her father or watched him in her mirror. [204]

> Le lendemain, suivant une habitude prise par Grandet depuis la réclusion d'Eugénie, il vint faire un certain nombre de tours dans son petit jardin. Il avait pris pour cette promenade le moment où Eugénie se peignait. Quand le bonhomme arrivait au gros noyer, il se cachait derrière le tronc de l'arbre, restait pendant quelques instants à contempler les longs cheveux de sa fille. . . . Souvent il demeurait assis sur le petit banc de bois pourri où Charles et Eugénie s'étaient juré un éternel amour, pendant qu'elle regardait aussi son père à la dérobée ou dans son miroir. [146]

What is remarkable about this scene is less its frankly erotic overtones—in this otherwise chaste novel no man shall ever desire Eugénie with the perverse intensity of her fetishistic father—than its exemplary allegorization of the interpenetration of the Imaginary and the Symbolic, for, it should be emphasized, the separation of these two registers may be a useful heuristic device or a sought-after therapeutic ideal, but it is hardly an existential reality. If, on the one hand, the capture of Grandet's image in his daughter's looking-glass attests to

16. John Berger, *Ways of Seeing* (Harmondsworth: Penguin, 1972), 47.
17. Irigaray, *Speculum*, 106.

the persistent pull of the imaginary field, on the other, Eugénie's very imprisonment testifies to the overriding force of the father's law. The Imaginary is, as it were, contained or recontained within the Symbolic. Far from being the matrifocal romance we have made it out to be, *Eugénie Grandet* is one of Balzac's major patriarchal manifestoes. Neither pathetic (like Old Goriot, the "Christ of paternity") nor a mad scientist (like Balthazar Claes in *La Recherche de l'absolu*) nor a prisoner of sex (like Baron Hulot in *La Cousine Bette*), to name a few unworthy Balzacian bearers of the phallic standard, Grandet—as his surname indicates—is a uniquely strong father figure. To reduce him to the reassuringly familiar figure of the Miser is to miss his salient function as a fount of law: " . . . his most trivial acts had the weight of judicial decisions" ("Sa parole, son vêtement, ses gestes, le clignement de ses yeux faisaient loi dans le pays" [42/23]). The "bourgeois tragedy" ("tragédie bourgeoise" [185/131]) enacted in the very classical twenty-four-hour time frame encompassing Charles's arrival in the provincial town of Saumur, Eugénie's enamoration, and Grandet's "sovereign decree" ("l'arrêt paternel et souverain" [100/67]) forbidding their union is the tragedy of the Symbolic as it shapes a female destiny; *Eugénie Grandet* is Iphigenia transposed into an era when more "than in any previous era money is the force behind the law, politically and socially" ("plus qu'en aucun autre temps, l'argent domine les lois, la politique et les moeurs" [126/87]), and Mammon, it turns out, is as pitiless a deity as Artemis.

The particular crisis day Balzac has chosen to focus on is, let us recall, Eugénie's twenty-third birthday and the morning after, an occasion whose inaugural significance is repeatedly underscored, first by constant references to Eugénie as a child, second by the reiteration of the formula "for the first time," as in "After dinner, when the question of Eugénie's marriage had been raised for the first time" ("Après ce dîner, où, pour la première fois, il fut question du mariage d'Eugénie" [59/36]); "Nanon burst out laughing at this joke, the first she had ever heard her young mistress make" ("Nanon laissa échapper un gros rire en entendant la première plaisanterie que sa jeune maîtresse eût jamais faite" [76/49]); "For the first time in her life she wished to look her best" (" . . . souhaitant, pour la première fois de sa vie, de paraître à son avantage" [92/61]). Eugénie's birthday is in fact a rebirthday, the occasion on which, emerging from a prolonged childhood, she becomes aware in a cascading series of revelations both of the workings of and her place in two of the homologous, interlocking exchange systems that constitute patriarchal culture: marriage and finance.[18] What Eugénie begins to understand is that even as she enjoyed the shelter of the symbiotic mother-daughter relationship, even then she lived under the sway of the Symbolic, the order in which she was inscribed before her birth: "For the first time in her life the sight of her father struck terror into Eugénie's heart. She realized that he was master of her fate" ("Pour la permière fois, elle eut dans le coeur de la terreur à l'aspect de son père, vit en lui le maître de son sort" [96/65]).

The question then becomes: How does Eugénie negotiate the passage from the Imaginary into the Symbolic, or rather, how does she reconcile their conflicting imperatives? The answer to these questions is deferred nine years, during which time first Eugénie's mother dies, then her father, leaving her an immensely wealthy heiress, free to marry the love to whom she has remained true, while he was off in India making his fortune. After nine long years of silence, he finally writes her, only to announce his engagement to someone else. Devastated by this cruel blow, Eugénie is ready to retire to a convent, but is dissuaded by her local pastor, who tells her: "If you wish to work out your salvation, there are only two courses open to you to follow, either you must leave the world or you must live in it and obey its laws, you must follow either your earthly destiny or your heavenly vocation" ("Si vous voulez faire votre salut, vous n'avez que deux voies à suivre, ou quitter le monde ou en suivre les lois. Obéir à votre destinée terrestre ou à votre destinée céleste" [237/170]).

It is at this juncture in the novel that Eugénie ceases to be a type and reveals herself to be what she has in fact been all along: a case. In a remarkable display of neurotic ingenuity, Eugénie charts a third course, one inconceivable in the binary (masculine) logic of the pastor, but closely patterned on the princess of Clèves's controversial and often misunderstood choice. However, whereas the princess reconciles the imperiousness of desire with the imperatives of society by electing to live alternately "in the convent" and "in the world," Eugénie selects conjunction over disjunction, a polysyndeton is the figure of her destiny, she shall be *both married and a virgin*: "Such is the

---

18. In a recent article titled " 'Sleeping Beauty' as Ironic Model for *Eugénie Grandet*," *Nineteenth-Century French Studies*, 10 (Fall–Winter 1981–82), 28–36, John Gale likens Eugénie's pre-Charles state to that of Perrault's sleeping princess and observes that for Eugénie Charles's arrival "turns into a true rebirth" (29).

story of this woman, who is in the world but not of the world" ("Telle est l'histoire de cette femme qui n'est pas du monde au milieu du monde" [200/179]).[19] Eugénie shall marry her faithful suitor, M. de Bonfons, but on one condition, namely, that the marriage remain unconsummated, for, as she informs him: "I must tell you frankly that I cherish memories which time will never efface. All I have to offer my husband is friendship" ("Je ne dois pas vous tromper, monsieur. J'ai dans le coeur un sentiment inextinguible. L'amitié sera le seul sentiment que je puisse accorder à mon mari" [241/174]). In short, Eugénie submits to the laws of exchange but without relinquishing her most autistic fantasy; against all expectations grounded in masculine developmental models, she enters into the Symbolic while remaining fixated in the Imaginary.

What are we to make of this bizarre final solution, of this extraordinary blank upon which the novel closes? We might begin by naming it, borrowing again from Irigaray, "the 'melancholic' solution."[20] This borrowing must be qualified, however, for it raises questions regarding the divergences between what we might call Balzac's "theory of femininity" and Irigaray's and, ultimately, the nature of Eugénie's narcissism. Having shown the devastating analogy between Freud's description of the little girl's reaction to the discovery of castration (in "Femininity") and the symptomatology of melancholia (as analyzed in "Mourning and Melancholia"), Irigaray goes on to conclude:

> In fact it is not melancholia that the little girl shall choose as her privileged mode of retreat. Possibly she has too few narcissistic reserves
> .... The economy of female narcissism, the fragility of the little girl's, of the woman's "ego" render almost impossible the constitution—at least in any prevailing and stable form—of this syndrome. Which is not

19. The novel is, let us note, placed under the sign of Mariolatry; the name of the woman to whom it is dedicated—Maria—serves as a matrix, a master signifier of the fiction. On several occasions Eugénie is compared to Mary (see in particular 94 and 183). There are then (at least) two Christian narrative programs operative in Balzac: the Christic model (e.g., *Père Goriot*) and the Marial model (e.g., *Eugénie Grandet*), in other words, the masculine and feminine Christian novels.

20. *Speculum*, 78. Irigaray introduces this notion in her discussion of the little girl's response to the discovery of woman's castration. Irigaray suggests that the little girl might opt for melancholia, all the more as Freud's description of her reaction to this unwelcome discovery bears a striking, almost point-by-point similarity to the symptomatology of melancholia. Implicit in this analogy is the fact that the penis belongs to that class of objects whose loss cannot be overcome through mourning work (78–84).

to say that the sexuality of the "dark continent" does not exhibit many of its symptoms. But they will be dissociated rather than organized in any permanent and coherent fashion. . . . [21]

Precisely because what is involved here is not the suffocating application of a clinical grid to a literary text, rather, to use Shoshana Felman's suggestive term, a recognition of their mutual implication, the lack of congruence between Balzac's theory and Irigaray's should not be taken to signify a flaw in Balzac's pre-Freudian intuitions. [22] What it does signify is that in fiction the "melancholic solution" is made possible and plausible by the facts of literary history. *Eugénie Grandet* is a case study of that dread romantic disease melancholy. But there is more: Eugénie's adoption of the melancholic solution points up a hitherto hidden aspect of her narcissism: its evolution. Negative at the outset, Eugénie's narcissism ripens in the course of the novel until in the end she has become in the most ordinary, positive, not to say Freudian sense of the term a narcissist:

This chorus of praise was something quite new to Eugénie, and embarrassed her at first, but little by little her ear attuned itself to hearing her beauty acclaimed, however gross the flattery might be, so that if some newcomer had considered her plain, the criticism would have touched her more nearly than it would have done eight years before. In the end she came to love this homage, which she secretly laid at her idol's feet. So, by degrees, she became accustomed to allowing herself to be treated as a queen, and to seeing her court full every evening. [223]

Ce concert d'éloges, nouveaux pour Eugénie, la fit d'abord rougir; mais insensiblement, et quelques grossiers que fussent les compliments, son oreille s'accoutuma si bien à entendre vanter sa beauté, que si quelque nouveau venu l'eût trouvée laide, ce reproche lui aurait été beaucoup plus sensible alors que huit ans auparavant. Puis elle finit par aimer

---

21. Irigaray, *Speculum*, 84–85.

22. Felman, "To Open the Question," *Yale French Studies*, 55/56 (1977), 8–9. In outlining the *new* psychoanalytic mode of reading she is proposing to present and practice, Felman writes:

The notion of *application* would be replaced by the radically different notion of *implication*: bringing analytical questions to bear upon literary questions, *involving* psychoanalysis in the scene of literary analysis, the interpreter's role would here be, not to *apply* to the text an acquired science, a preconceived knowledge, but to act as a go-between, to *generate implications* between literature and psychoanalysis—to explore, bring to light and articulate the various (indirect) ways in which the two domains do indeed *implicate each other*, each one finding itself enlightened, informed, but also affected, displaced, by the other.

des douceurs qu'elle mettait secrètement aux pieds de son idole. Elle
s'habitua donc par degrès à se laisser traiter en souveraine et à voir sa
cour pleine tous les soirs. [160]

Eugénie's melancholy is then firmly rooted in her strong reserves of
narcissism, reserves drawn from her seduction of/identification with
her father.

Melancholy pervades the novel; from the first page to the last, there
is a perfect, characteristically Balzacian adequation between the con-
tainer (house) and the contained (Eugénie): "In some country towns
there exist houses whose appearance weighs as heavily upon the spirits
as the gloomiest cloister, the most dismal ruin, or the dreariest stretch
of barren land" ("Il se trouve dans certaines villes de province des
maisons dont la vue inspire une mélancolie égale à celle que provo-
quent les cloîtres les plus sombres, les landes les plus ternes ou les
ruines les plus tristes" [33/17]); "the house at Saumur, cold, sunless,
always overshadowed by the ramparts and gloomy, is like her life"
("La maison de Saumur, maison sans soleil, sans chaleur, sans cesse
ombragée, mélancolique, est l'image de sa vie" [247/178–79]). This
observation should not be taken to mean that Eugénie's character is
in any sort of mechanical, naturalistic way determined by her environment; rather it is meant to stress the fact that melancholy serves
as a unifying principle of the novel. Indeed, if Eugénie's melancholy
is determined by any single factor, it is by her identification with her
mother. Their complicity is sealed by what I would term a stoical
pact;[23] Madame Grandet's dying words—"there is happiness only in
heaven" ("il n'y a de bonheur que dans le ciel" [213/153])—become
Eugénie's guiding maxim, indeed constitute the maxim that ensures
the verisimilitude of this self-styled implausible narrative.[24] Thus, when

23. In their fine full-length study of *Eugénie Grandet* (*Balzac: Sémiotique du per-
sonnage romanesque: L'Exemple d'"Eugénie Grandet"* [Montreal: Presses de l'Univ-
ersité de Montréal, Didier Erudition, 1980], 254), which appeared after this article
was written, Roland Le Huenen and Paul Perron also use the word "pact" to describe
the mother-daughter generic bonding.

24. Balzac is indeed at great pains to stress the implausibility of his fiction:

Quite often the things that human beings do appear literally incredible [*littér-
airement parlant invraisemblables*] although in fact they have done them. We
might be less incredulous, perhaps, if we did not nearly always omit to throw a
sort of psychological light on impulsive decisions, by examining the mysterious
birth of the reasons that made them inevitable. Perhaps Eugénie's passion should
be traced to the source from which its most delicate fibers sprang, its roots in

all hopes of happiness here on earth are dashed by Charles's cynical letter, Eugénie is destroyed but not surprised:

> She raised her eyes towards heaven, remembering the last words of her mother ... then, thinking of her mother's death and the life which had preceded it, which seemed to foretell what her own would be, she looked at her destiny face to face, and read it at a glance. There was nothing left for her to do but to develop her wings, aspire towards heaven, and live a life of prayer until the day of her deliverance. "My mother was right," she said weeping. "One can only suffer and die." [236]

> Elle jeta ses regards au ciel, en pensant aux dernières paroles de sa mère ... puis, Eugénie, se souvenant de cette mort et de cette vie prophétique, mesura d'un regard toute sa destinée. Elle n'avait plus qu'à déployer ses ailes, tendre au ciel, et vivre en prières jusqu'au jour de sa délivrance.—Ma mère avait raison, dit-elle en pleurant. Souffrir et mourir. [170]

The axis of sexual difference, for Balzac, runs parallel with the axis of algomania. On one level, the most explicit (not to say superficial), *Eugénie Grandet* is a novel whose central thesis is "doloristic," in keeping with a deep Romantic fascination with pain as a fundamental ontological experience. Through her identification with her mother, Eugénie assumes her femininity, for her mother's last words are in fact nothing but a brief quotation from the complete "text" of women's lives:

> In every situation women are bound to suffer more than men, and feel their troubles more acutely. Men have physical robustness, and exercise some control over their circumstances. They are active and busy, can think of other matters in the present, look forward to the future and find consolation in it. That was what Charles was doing. But women stay at home, alone with their grief, and there is nothing to distract them from it. They plumb the depths of the abyss of sorrow ... and

---

the depths of her nature, and analyzed there, for it became, as would be sneeringly said in the future, a disease, and influenced her whole existence. [127–28]

Gérard Genett has demonstrated in his classical essay "Vraisemblance et motivation," in *Figures II* (Paris: Seuil, 1969), that in Balzac the creation of an "artificial verisimilitude" masks the "arbitrariness of the narrative." For a ground-breaking feminist reading of Genette's text, see Nancy Miller, "Emphasis Added: Plots and Plausibilities in Women's Fiction," *PMLA*, 96 (January 1981), 36–48.

fill it with the sound of their prayers and tears. And that was Eugénie's fate. She was taking the first steps along her destined path. In love and sorrow, feeling and self-sacrifice, will always lie the theme of women's lives, and Eugénie was to be in everything a woman, save in what should have been her consolation. [182]

En toute situation, les femmes ont plus de causes de douleur que n'en a l'homme, et souffrent plus que lui. L'homme a sa force, et l'exercice de sa puissance: il agit, il va, il s'occupe, il pense, il embrasse l'avenir et y trouve des consolations. Ainsi faisait Charles. Mais la femme demeure, elle reste face à face avec le chagrin dont rien ne la distrait, elle descend jusqu'au fond de l'abîme qu'il a ouvert, le mesure et souvent le comble de ses voeux et de ses larmes. Ainsi faisait Eugénie. Elle s'initiait à sa destinée. Sentir, aimer, souffrir, se dévouer, sera toujours le texte de la vie des femmes. Eugénie devait être toute la femme, moins ce qui la console. [129]

Eugénie Grandet (daughter of Felix!) is then the paradigmatic Romantic heroine (indeed, the paradigmatic Romantic hero is a heroine), and her suffering must be excessive. It is, however, the very hyperbolic nature of Eugénie's erotomonomania that transforms the Romantic lie into a certain kind of fictional and even theoretical truth.

It is time now to return to the question of narcissism, which we have not in fact ever really departed from, for, according to Freud, melancholia is intimately bound up with narcissism, melancholia often taking the form of a regression from a narcissistic object choice to narcissism. But, as Freud remarks: "The conclusion which our theory would require—namely, that the disposition to fall ill to melancholia (or some part of that disposition) lies in the predominance of the narcissistic type of object-choice—has unfortunately not yet been confirmed by observation."[25] *Eugénie Grandet* offers us, I suggest, precious literary confirmation of Freud's hypothetical conclusion, for, viewed in this optic, Eugénie's undying passion for Charles appears to be motivated by a more insidious form of narcissism than the one we had diagnosed at the outset: if, as we have noted, Eugénie is initially bedazzled by Charles's ornithological perfections—he is compared to both a peacock and a phoenix—ultimately she falls in love with his extreme sorrow. Grief-stricken by the news of his father's suicide,

25. *Standard Edition*, XIV, 250.

Charles appears to Eugénie as her *idealized melancholic double*.[26] Her love is a love for a *fallen dandy*:

> His grief was unaffected, sincere, and deeply felt, and the tense, drawn look of suffering gave him the pathetic charm women find so attractive. Eugénie found it so, and was more in love than ever. Perhaps, too, his misfortunes had brought him closer to her. Charles was not now the wealthy and handsome young man living in a sphere out of her reach that he had been when she first saw him; he was a relative in deep and terrible distress, and grief levels all distinctions. [135–36]

> Il ne jouait pas la douleur, il souffrait véritablement, et le voile étendu sur ses traits par la peine lui donnait cet air intéressant qui plaît tant aux femmes. Eugénie l'en aima bien davantage. Peut-être aussi le malheur l'avait-il rapproché d'elle. Charles n'était plus ce riche et beau jeune homme placé dans une sphère inabordable pour elle; mais un parent plongé dans une effroyable misère. La misère enfante l'égalité. [94]

In a very real sense the narcissistic object Eugénie chooses to love—and it is of the essence that she does choose: "There and then she vowed to herself that she would love him always" ("elle se jura d'abord à elle-même de l'aimer toujours" [158/111])—is melancholy itself: "Theirs was a first passion with all its childish ways, all the more tender and dear to their hearts because their hearts were surrounded by shadows. The mourning crêpe in which their love had been wrapped at its birth only brought it into closer harmony with their surroundings in the tumbledown old country house" ("Ce fut la passion première avec tous ses enfantillages, d'autant plus caressants pour leurs coeurs, qu'ils étaient enveloppés de mélancolie. En se débattant à sa naissance sous les crêpes du deuil, cet amour n'en était d'ailleurs que mieux en harmonie avec la simplicité provinciale de cette maison en ruines" [169/119–20]). Small wonder, given the nature and depth of her identification with both her mother and her cousin—and in the kinship system depicted in nineteenth-century French novels, "a cousin is

26. Cf. Le Huenen and Perron's Jungian analysis of the Eugénie-Charles relationship (*Balzac*, 193–99). Despite our different psychoanalytic approaches—for Le Huenen and Perron, Eugénie and Charles's is a romance of *anima* and *animus*—I concur in viewing Eugénie's attraction to Charles as rooted in an imaginary identification. According to Le Huenen and Perron, Eugénie is initially fascinated by Charles's femininity; what they exchange in the course of their relationship is nothing other than their sexual identities: Charles becomes a man, while Eugénie is feminized. Transcoded and generalized: love in the mirror stage is always homosexual.

better than a brother, he can marry you" ("un cousin est mieux qu'un frère, il peut t'épouser" [174/124])—small wonder that Eugénie responds to Charles's desertion by withdrawing from life and regressing into narcissism: she has always been in mourning.

Indeed, the entire novel can be read as a variant of the folk theme analyzed by Freud in his essay "The Theme of the Three Caskets" (1913), a particularly interesting variant because in contradistinction to the several examples cited by Freud, which all center on *"a man's choice between three women,"*[27] *Eugénie Grandet* features a situation in which a female protagonist chooses among three suitors (the number three is particularly insistent in this novel: there are the three women, Madame Grandet, Nanon, and Eugénie, the three Cruchot and the three des Grassins). Furthermore, two of these suitors offer Eugénie caskets. There is first the silver workbox Adolphe des Grassins gives Eugénie on her birthday: "He kissed Eugénie on both cheeks and offered her a workbox with fittings of silver gilt. It was a trumpery enough piece of goods, in spite of the little shield bearing the initials E.G. carefully engraved in Gothic characters, a detail which made the whole thing appear more imposing and better finished than it in fact was" "([Il] l'embrassa sur les deux joues, et lui offrit une boîte à ouvrage dont tous les ustensiles étaient en vermeil, véritable marchandise de pacotille, malgré l'écusson sur lequel un E.G. gothique assez bien gravé pouvait faire croire à une façon très soignée" [63/39]). Then there is the gold dressing case Charles gives Eugénie in exchange for the gold purse she offers him: "He took up the box, drew it from its leather cover, opened it and sadly showed his wondering cousin a dressing-case shining with gold, in which the fine workmanship of the fittings greatly enhanced the value of the precious metal" "(Il alla prendre la boîte, la sortit du fourreau, l'ouvrit et montra tristement à sa cousine émerveillée un nécessaire où le travail donnait à l'or un prix bien supérieur à celui de son poids" [162–63/115]). Now in a seemingly radical departure from the male model of this "ancient theme," Eugénie, the miser's daughter, chooses the solid-gold casket. But this deviation does not in effect call into question the main thrust of Freud's analysis, for in *Eugénie Grandet* the gold casket stands for death, just as surely as the lead one does in *The Merchant of Venice*: the dressing case is in fact a reliquary, containing the portraits of Charles's dead parents.

27. *Standard Edition*, XII, 292.

A potentially more disruptive disparity between the male and female versions of the theme would appear to be the absence of the third casket. While it is worth recalling here one of the basic principles of the structural analysis of myth, that all the constituent units or my-themes of a myth are not present or necessarily present in a particular version of the myth,[28] I think we need not invoke this principle here: a reading attentive to detail will show that the missing element is not missing, simply concealed and displaced. The third casket is mani-fested in the novel, but it does not participate in the system of ex-change; it is, as it were, out of circulation. It takes the form of an awkward and enigmatic analogy that protrudes from the surface of the text in the course of the description of the Grandets' garden: "At the far end of the courtyard the eight dilapidated steps leading to the garden gate were half-buried under high-growing plants, and looked like the tombstone of some medieval knight, put there by his widow at the time of the Crusades, and neglected ever since" ("Enfin les huits marches qui régnaient au fond de la cour et menaient à la porte du jardin, étaient disjointes et ensevelies sous de hautes plantes comme le tombeau d'un chevalier enterré par sa veuve au temps des croisades" [92/61–62]). Atropos the inexorable is, then, present in the novel, in the appropriate textual form of a figure of speech that cannot be turned away from. On one level we might "recuperate" this extended simile, this hypertrophied detail, by reading it as a commentary on, or *mise en abîme* of, the main plot: when Charles goes off to the Far East like some sort of latter-day Crusader, Eugénie erects an empty crypt, a cenotaph in his memory, conflating mourning and melancholia. "The object has not perhaps actually died, but has become lost as an object of love (e.g., the deserted bride)."[29] But this reading, while perfectly plausible, fails to take into account the most arresting feature of this mininarrative, its form, its very incongruity. To right this misappro-priation would entail reading this detail not as a symbol but rather as an allegory of the workings of the Symbolic order, which, according to Lacan, is always under the aegis of a dead man, the primal father of Freud's *Totem and Taboo*. This is surely not the place to attempt to read "The Theme of the Three Caskets" in conjunction with *Totem*

---

28. Claude Lévi-Strauss, "The Structural Study of Myth," in *Structural Anthro-pology*, trans. Claire Jacobson and Brooke Grundfest Schoepf (Garden City, N.Y.: Anchor, 1967), 207.

29. *Standard Edition*, XIV, 245.

and Taboo (both texts appeared in 1913), but on the basis of what we have seen so far, it would appear that Eugénie's love of death is the wages of the subject's entry into the Symbolic.

The question then becomes: Why does the daughter pay a higher price? Or rather: Why does the son successfully perform the work of mourning while the daughter remains mired in melancholia? These are the questions raised by the deliberately parallel but antithetical destinies of Eugénie and Charles Grandet. Indeed, as Charles's cynical letter to Eugénie makes clear, Eugénie's male counterpart has no trouble making a smooth and easy transition from one psychic register to the other: "The death of our parents is in the natural order of things, and we must follow them in our turn. I hope that you are consoled by this time. Time cures every pain, as I have found by experience. Yes, my dear cousin, I'm sorry to say boyhood's illusions are over for me. . . . I am a man now, where I was a child when I went away" ("La mort de nos parents est dans la nature, et nous devons leur succéder. J'espère que vous êtes aujourd'hui consolée. Rien ne résiste au temps, je l'éprouve. Oui, ma chère cousine, malheureusement pour moi, le moment des illusions est passé. . . D'enfant que j'étais au départ, je suis devenu homme au retour" [233/167]). I suggest that a tentative answer to these questions might be teased out of Freud's essay on narcissism. However questionable, not to say mystified, Freud's remarks on female narcissism, one observation in that famous or infamous passage bears rereading. Speculating on why it should be that "the purest and truest" type of female should upon reaching adolescence enter into an autarchic state of self-love, Freud writes: "Women, especially if they grow up with good looks, develop a certain self-contentment which compensates them for the social restrictions that are imposed upon them in their choice of object."[30] Seen in this light, the female protagonist's melancholic retreat into narcissism may in fact be the only form of autonomy available to her in a society where woman's assigned function in the Symbolic is to guarantee the transmission of the phallus. Eugénie's sentimental education—she receives no other— culminates, like that of the princess of Clèves's before her, in what I would call a lucid romanticism, which is perhaps the female form of fetishism.

Like Eugénie, I find myself poised between two equally compelling contradictory impulses—the revalorization of a psychic register often

30. Standard Edition, XIV, 88–89.

connoted as feminine and associated with asocial behavior, and the denunciation of a social order that both condemns women to deviancy and defines its terms. I refuse to opt for one of two readings, Eugénie as heroine of the Imaginary, Eugénie as victim of the Symbolic. My double reading inhabits the paradoxical space allotted woman under patriarchy, a space neither inside nor outside, where what appears as lack in one order shows up as excess in another. Eugénie's halfhearted entry into the Symbolic (the unconsummated marriage) may thus be viewed as subversive at the same time as her retreat into the Imaginary (the undying love for Charles) appears as a measure of woman's limited options under patriarchy. This much can be affirmed, however. When one compares Eugénie's destiny not to Charles's, but to that of Lucien de Rubempré, the protagonist of *Illusions perdues* and *Splendeurs et misères des courtisanes* and Eugénie's true melancholic double, the benefits to be derived from fetishistic undecidability are made manifest: for, whereas Lucien cannot survive the loss of his illusions, Eugénie can and does survive the loss of hers.[31] Now the advantages of death-in-life over suicide may not be overwhelming in everyday life, but in fiction, survival is everything, particularly for a female protagonist. To the extent that as Leo Bersani has written, "The realistic novel is the 'mirror stage' of literature,"[32] any nineteenth-century novel that imagines for its protagonist a life beyond adolescence represents something of a generic triumph. However bittersweet, Eugénie's survival into the present of the narrator's enunciation— "Such is the story of this woman, who *is* in the world, but not of the world" (248; emphasis added)—suggests that as long as the Imaginary persists unbound below the baseline of the Symbolic, the classical text and with it the (female) protagonist's options will remain open.

31. In my "Female Fetishism: The Case of George Sand" (*Poetics Today*, forthcoming), following Sarah Kofman, *L'Enigme de la femme* (Paris: Galilée, 1980), and Elizabeth Berg, "The Third Woman," *Diacritics*, 12 (Summer 1982), 11–20, I take woman's deliberate indecision as symptomatic of female fetishism: ultimately woman's indecision is always grounded in the refusal to decide the question of sexual difference.

32. Leo Bersani, "The Subject of Power," *Diacritics*, 7 (Fall 1977), 16.

PART III

Women Rewriting Woman

10

A Map for Rereading; or, Gender and the Interpretation of Literary Texts

ANNETTE KOLODNY

Appealing particularly to a generation still in the process of divorcing itself from the New Critics' habit of "bracketing off" any text as an entity in itself, as though "it could be read, understood, and criticized entirely in its own terms,"[1] Harold Bloom has proposed a dialectical theory of influence between poets and poets, as well as between poems and poems, which in essence does away with the static notion of a fixed or knowable text. As he argued in *A Map of Misreading*, in 1975, "a poem is a response to a poem, as a poet is a response to a poet, or a person to his parent." Thus, for Bloom, "poems ... are neither about 'subjects' nor about 'themselves.' They are necessarily about *other poems.*"[2]

To read or to know a poem, according to Bloom, engages the reader in an attempt to map the psychodynamic relations by which the poet at hand has willfully misunderstood the work of some precursor (either single or composite) in order to correct, rewrite, or appropriate the prior poetic vision as his own. As first introduced in *The Anxiety of*

Reprinted from *New Literary History*, 11 (1979–80), 451–67, by permission of The Johns Hopkins University Press.

1. Albert William Levi, "*De Interpretatione*: Cognition and Context in the History of Ideas," *Critical Inquiry*, 3 (Autumn 1976), 164.

2. Harold Bloom, *A Map of Misreading* (New York: Oxford University Press, 1975), 18.

Influence in 1973, the resultant "wholly different practical criticism
... give[s] up the failed enterprise of seeking to 'understand' any
single poem as an entity in itself" and "pursue[s] instead the quest of
learning to read any poem as its poet's deliberate misinterpretation,
as a poet, of a precursor poem or of poetry in general."[3] What one
deciphers in the process of reading, then, is not any discrete entity
but rather a complex relational event, "itself a synecdoche for a larger
whole including other texts."[4] "Reading a text is necessarily the reading
of a whole system of texts," Bloom explains in *Kabbalah and Criticism*,
"and meaning is always wandering around between texts."[5]

To help purchase assent for this "wholly different practical criticism," Bloom asserted an identity between critics and poets as equal
participants in the same "belated and all-but-impossible act" of reading
(which, as he hastens to explain in *A Map of Misreading*, "if strong is
always a misreading").[6] As it is a drama of epic proportions, in Bloom's
terms, when the ephebe poet attempts to appropriate and then correct
a precursor's meaning, so, too, for the critic, his own inevitable misreadings or *misprisions* are no less heroic—or any the less creative.
"Poets' misinterpretations or poems" may be "more drastic than critics'
misinterpretations or criticism," Bloom admits, but since he recognizes no such thing as "interpretations but only misinterpretations ...
all criticism" is necessarily elevated to a species of "prose poetry."[7]
The critic's performance thus takes place as one more "act of misprision
[which] displaces an earlier act of misprision"—presumably the poet's,
or perhaps that of a prior critic; and in this sense the critic participates
in that same act of "defensive warfare" before his own critical forebears,
or even before the poet himself, that the poet presumably enacted
before his poetic father/precursor.[8] Their legacy, whether as poetry
or as "prose poetry" criticism, consequently establishes the strong

3. Harold Bloom, *The Anxiety of Influence: A Theory of Poetry* (New York: Oxford
University Press, 1973), 43.
4. Harold Bloom, *Kabbalah and Criticism* (New York: Seabury, 1975), 106. This
concept is further refined in his *Poetry and Repression: Revisionism from Blake to
Stevens* (New Haven: Yale University Press, 1976), 26, where Bloom describes poems
as "defensive processes in constant change, which is to say that poems themselves are
acts of reading. A poem is ... a fierce, proleptic debate *with itself*, as well as with
precursor poems."
5. Bloom, *Kabbalah and Criticism*, 107–8.
6. Bloom, *Map of Misreading*, 3.
7. Bloom, *Anxiety of Influence*, 94–95.
8. See Bloom, *Kabbalah and Criticism*, 125, 104, 108.

survivors of these psychic battles as figures whom others, in the future, will need to overcome in their turn: "A poet is strong because poets after him must work to evade him. A critic is strong if his readings similarly provoke other readings."[9] It is unquestionably Bloom's most brilliant rhetorical stroke, persuading less by virtue of the logic of his argument than by the pleasure his (intended and mostly male) readership will take in the discovery that their own activity replicates the psychic adventures of The Poet, every critic's *figura* of heroism.[10]

What is left out of account, however, is the fact that whether we speak of poets and critics "reading" texts or writers "reading" (and thereby recording for us) the world, we are calling attention to interpretive strategies that are learned, historically determined, and thereby necessarily gender-inflected. As others have elsewhere questioned the adequacy of Bloom's paradigm of poetic influence to explain the production of poetry by women,[11] so now I propose to examine analogous limitations in his model for the reading—and hence critical—process (since both, after all, derive from his revisionist rendering of the Freudian family romance). To begin with, to locate that "meaning" which "is always wandering around between texts,"[12] Bloom assumes a community of readers (and thus critics) who know that same "whole system of texts" within which the specific poet at hand has enacted his misprision. The canonical sense of a shared and coherent

9. Bloom, *Kabbalah and Criticism*, 125. By way of example, and with a kind of Appolonian modesty, Bloom demonstrates his own propensities for misreading, placing himself amid the excellent company of those other Super Misreaders, Blake, Shelley, C. S. Lewis, Charles Williams, and T. S. Eliot (all of whom misread Milton's Satan), and regrets only "that the misreading of Blake and Shelley by Yeats is a lot stronger than the misreading of Blake and Shelley by Bloom" (125–26).

10. In *Poetry and Repression*, 18, Bloom explains that "by 'reading' I intend to mean the work both of poet and of critic, who themselves move from dialectic irony to synecdochal representation as they confront the text before them."

11. I refer here to the comments by Lillian Faderman and Louise Bernikow in *Signs*, 4 (1978), 188–91 and 191–95, respectively. They objected to the use of the Bloomian model as invoked in Joanne Feit Diehl's discussion of Emily Dickinson, Elizabeth Barrett Browning, and Christina Rosetti in her " 'Come Slowly—Eden': An Exploration of Women Poets and Their Muse," *Signs*, 3 (1978), 572–87. In her original essay, however, Feit Diehl had attempted to correct what she saw as Bloom's repeated avoidance of "the question raised by his own speculations, 'What if the poet be a woman?' " (573). More recently, Sandra M. Gilbert and Susan Gubar have also tried to address the necessary omission of women writers from Bloom's male psychodynamic in *The Madwoman in the Attic: The Woman Writer and the Nineteenth-Century Literary Imagination* (New Haven: Yale University Press, 1979).

12. Bloom, *Kabbalah and Criticism*, 107–8.

literary tradition is thus essential to the utility of Bloom's paradigm of literary influence as well as to his notions of reading (and mis-reading). "What happens if one tries to write, or to teach, or to think or even to read without the sense of a tradition?" Bloom asks in *A Map of Misreading*. "Why," as he himself well understands, "nothing at all happens, just nothing."

> You cannot write or teach or think or even read without imitation, and what you imitate is what another person has done, that person's writing or teaching or thinking or reading. Your relation to what informs that person *is* tradition, for tradition is influence that extends past one generation, a carrying-over of influence.[13]

So long as the poems and poets he chooses for scrutiny participate in the "continuity that began in the sixth century B.C. when Homer first became a schoolbook for the Greeks,"[14] Bloom has a great deal to tell us about the carrying over of literary influence; where he must remain silent is where carrying over takes place among readers and writers who in fact have been, or at least experienced themselves as, cut off and alien from that dominant tradition. Virginia Woolf made the distinction vividly, over a half century ago, in *A Room of One's Own*, when she described being barred entrance, because of her sex, to a "famous library" in which was housed, among other treasures, a Milton manuscript. Cursing the "Oxbridge" edifice, "venerable and calm, with all its treasures safe locked within its breast," she returns to her room at the inn later that night, still pondering "how unpleasant it is to be locked out; and I thought how it is worse perhaps to be locked in; and, thinking of the safety and prosperity of the one sex and of the poverty and insecurity of the other and of the effect of tradition and of the lack of tradition upon the mind of a writer."[15] And, she might have added, on the mind of a reader as well. For while my main concern here is with reading (albeit largely and perhaps imperfectly defined), I think it worth noting that there exists an intimate interaction between readers and writers in and through which each defines for the other what s/he is about. "The effect . . . of the lack of tradition upon the mind of a writer" will communicate itself, in one

13. Bloom, *Map of Misreading*, 32.
14. Bloom, *Map of Misreading*, 33–34.
15. Virginia Woolf, *A Room of One's Own* (1927; rpt. Harmondsworth: Penguin, 1972), 9–10, 25–26.

way or another, to her readers; and, indeed, may respond to her readers' sense of exclusion from high (or highbrow) culture.

An American instance provides perhaps the best example: Delimited by the lack of formal or classical education, and constrained by the social and aesthetic norms of their day to conceptualizing "authorship as a profession rather than a calling, as work and not art,"[16] the vastly popular women novelists of the so-called feminine fifties often enough, and somewhat defensively, made a virtue of their sad necessities by invoking an audience of readers for whom aspirations to "literature" were as inappropriate as they were for the writer. As Nina Baym remarks in *Woman's Fiction*, "often the women deliberately and even proudly disavowed membership in an artistic fraternity." " 'Mine is a story for the table and arm-chair under the reading lamp in the livingroom, and not for the library shelves,' " Baym quotes Marion Harland from the introduction to Harland's autobiography; and then, at greater length, Baym cites Fanny Fern's dedicatory pages to her novel *Rose Clark*:

> When the frost curtains the windows, when the wind whistles fiercely at the key-hole, when the bright fire glows, and the tea-tray is removed, and father in his slippered feet lolls in his arm-chair; and mother with her nimble needle "makes auld claes look amaist as weel as new," and grandmamma draws closer to the chimney-corner, and Tommy with his plate of chestnuts nestles contentedly at her feet; then let my unpretending story be read. For such an hour, for such an audience, was it written.
>
> Should any *dictionary on legs* rap inopportunely at the door for admittance, send him away to the groaning shelves of some musty library, where "literature" lies embalmed, with its stony eyes, fleshless joints, and ossified heart, in faultless preservation.[17]

If a bit overdone, such prefaces point up the self-consciousness with which writers like Fern and Harland perceived themselves as excluded from the dominant literary tradition and as writing for an audience of readers similarly excluded. To quote Baym again, these "women were expected to write specifically for their own sex and within the tradition of their woman's culture rather than within the Great Tradition. They

16. Nina Baym, *Woman's Fiction: A Guide to Novels by and about Women in America, 1820–1870* (Ithaca: Cornell University Press, 1978), 32.

17. See Baym, *Woman's Fiction*, 32–33.

never presented themselves as followers in the footsteps of Milton or Spenser."[18]

On the one hand, of course, increased literacy (if not substantially improved conditions of education) marked the generation of American women at mid-century, opening a vast market for a literature that would treat the contexts of their lives—the sewing circle rather than the whaling ship, the nursery instead of the lawyer's office—as functional symbols of the human condition.[19] On the other hand, while this vast new audience must certainly be credited with shaping the features of what then became popular women's fiction, it is also the case that the writers, in their turn, both responded to and helped to formulate their readers' tastes and habits. And both together, I suggest, found in women's fiction a means of accepting (or at least coping with) the barred entryway that was to distress Virginia Woolf in the next century. But these facts of our literary history also suggest that from the 1850s on, in the United States at least, the meanings "wandering around between texts" were wandering around somewhat different groups of texts where male and female readers were concerned.[20] So that, with the advent of women "who wished to be regarded as artists rather than careerists"[21] toward the end of the nineteenth century, there arose the critical problem with which we are still plagued, and which Bloom so determinedly ignores: the problem of reading any text as "a synecdoche for a larger whole including other texts" when that necessarily assumed "whole system of texts" in which it is embedded is foreign to one's reading knowledge.

The appearance of Kate Chopin's novel *The Awakening* in 1899, for example, perplexed readers familiar with her earlier (and intentionally "regional") short stories not so much because it turned away from themes and subject matter implicit in her earlier work, and even less

18. Baym, *Woman's Fiction*, 178.

19. I paraphrase rather freely here from some of Baym's acutely perceptive and highly suggestive remarks (14).

20. The problem of audience is complicated by the fact that in nineteenth-century America, distinct classes of so-called high- and lowbrow readers were emerging, cutting across sex and class lines; and, for each sex, distinctly separate "serious" and "popular" reading materials were also being marketed. Full discussion, however, is beyond the scope of this essay. In its stead, I direct the reader to Henry Nash Smith's clear and concise summation in the introductory chapter to his *Democracy and the Novel: Popular Resistance to Classic American Writers* (New York: Oxford University Press, 1978), 1–15.

21. Baym, *Woman's Fiction*, 178.

because it dealt with female sensuality and extramarital sexuality, but because her elaboration of those materials deviated radically from the accepted norms of women's fiction, out of which her audience so largely derived its expectations. The nuances and consequences of passion and individual temperament, after all, fairly define the focus of most of her preceding fictions. "That the book is strong and that Miss Chopin has a keen knowledge of certain phases of feminine character will not be denied," wrote the anonymous reviewer for the *Chicago Times-Herald*. What marked an unacceptable "new departure" for this critic was the impropriety of Chopin's focus on material previously edited out of the popular genteel novels by and about women, which, somewhat inarticulately, s/he translated into the accusation that Chopin had "enter[ed] the overworked field of sex fiction."[22]

Charlotte Perkins Gilman's initial difficulty in seeing "The Yellow Wallpaper" into print repeated the problem, albeit in a somewhat different context; for her story located itself not as any deviation from a previous tradition of women's fiction but instead as a continuation of a genre popularized by Poe. And insofar as Americans had earlier learned to follow the fictive processes of aberrant perception and mental breakdown in *his* work, they should have provided Gilman, one would imagine, with a ready-made audience for *her* protagonist's progressively debilitating fantasies of entrapment and liberation. As they had entered popular fiction by the end of the nineteenth century, however, the linguistic markers for those processes were at once heavily male-gendered and highly idiosyncratic, having more to do with individual temperament than with social or cultural situations per se. As a result, it appears that the reading strategies by which cracks in ancestral walls and suggestions of unchecked masculine willfulness were immediately noted as both symbolically and semantically relevant did not, for some reason, necessarily carry over to "the nursery at the top of the house" with its windows barred, and even less to the forced submission of the woman who must "take great pains to control [her]self before" her physician husband.[23]

22. From "Books of the Day," *Chicago Times-Herald*, June 1, 1899, 9; excerpted in Kate Chopin, *The Awakening*, ed. Margaret Culley (New York: Norton, 1976), 149.

23. Charlotte Perkins Gilman, *The Yellow Wallpaper*, with Afterword by Elaine R. Hedges (New York: Feminist Press, 1973), 12, 11. Page references to this edition will henceforth be cited parenthetically in the text, with references to Hedges' excellent Afterword preceded by her name.

A reader today seeking meaning in the way Harold Bloom outlines that process might note, of course, a fleeting resemblance between Gilman's upstairs chamber—with its bed nailed to the floor, its windows barred, and metal rings fixed to the walls—and Poe's evocation of the dungeon chambers of Toledo. In fact, a credible argument might be made for reading "The Yellow Wallpaper" as Gilman's willful and purposeful misprision of "The Pit and the Pendulum." Both stories, after all, involve a sane mind entrapped in an insanity-inducing situation. Gilman's "message" may then be that the equivalent revolution by which the speaking voice of the Poe tale is released to both sanity and freedom is unavailable to her heroine. No deus ex machina, no General Lasalle triumphantly entering the city, no "outstretched arm" to prevent Gilman's protagonist from falling into her own internal "abyss" is conceivable, given the rules of the social context in which Gilman's narrative is embedded. When gender is taken into account, then, so this interpretation would run, Gilman is saying that the nature of the trap envisioned must be understood as qualitatively different, and so too the possible escape routes.

Contemporary readers of "The Yellow Wallpaper," however, were apparently unprepared to make such connections. Those fond of Poe could not easily transfer their sense of mental derangement to the mind of a comfortable middle-class wife and mother; and those for whom the woman in the home was a familiar literary character were hard-pressed to comprehend so extreme an anatomy of the psychic price she paid. Horace Scudder, the editor of *The Atlantic Monthly* who first rejected the story, wrote only that "I could not forgive myself if I made others as miserable as I have made myself!" (Hedges, 40). And even William Dean Howells, who found the story "chilling" and admired it sufficiently to reprint it in 1920, some twenty-eight years after its first publication (in *The New England Magazine* of May 1892), like most readers, either failed to notice or neglected to report "the connection between the insanity and the sex, or sexual role, of the victim" (Hedges, 41). For readers at the turn of the century, then, that "meaning" which "is always wandering around between texts" had as yet failed to find connective pathways linking the fanciers of Poe to the devotees of popular women's fiction, or the shortcut between Gilman's short story and the myriad published feminist analyses of the ills of society (some of them written by Gilman herself). Without such connective contexts, Poe continued to be a well-traveled road, while Gilman's story, lacking the possibility of further influence, became a literary dead end.

In one sense, by hinting at an audience of male readers as ill equipped to follow the symbolic significance of the narrator's progressive breakdown as was her doctor-husband to diagnose the significance of his wife's fascination with the wallpaper's patternings, and by predicting a female readership as yet unprepared for texts that mirrored back, with symbolic exemplariness, certain patterns underlying their empirical reality, "The Yellow Wallpaper" anticipated its own reception. For, insofar as writing and reading represent linguistically based interpretive strategies—the first for the recording of a reality (that has, obviously, in a sense, already been "read") and the second for the deciphering of that recording (and thus also the further decoding of a prior imputed reality)—the wife's progressive descent into madness provides a kind of commentary on, indeed is revealed in terms of, the sexual politics inherent in the manipulation of those strategies. We are presented at the outset with a protagonist who, ostensibly for her own good, is denied both reading and writing and who, in the course of accommodating herself to that deprivation, comes more and more to experience her self as a text that can get neither read nor recorded.

In his doubly authoritative role as husband and doctor, John not only appropriates the interpretive processes of reading—diagnosing his wife's illness and thereby selecting what may be understood of her "meaning," reading to her rather than allowing her to read for herself—but also determines what may get written, and hence communicated. For her part, the protagonist avers, she does not agree with her husband's ideas: "Personally, I believe that congenial work, with excitement and change, would do me good." But given the fact of her marriage to "a physician of high standing" who "assures friends and relatives that there is really nothing the matter with one but temporary nervous depression—a slight hysterical tendency—what is one to do?" she asks. Since her husband (and, by extension, the rest of the world) will not heed what she says of herself, she attempts, instead, to communicate it to "this . . . dead paper . . . a great relief to my mind." But John's insistent opposition gradually erodes even this outlet for her, since, as she admits, "it *does* exhaust me a good deal—having to be so sly about it, or else meet with heavy opposition" (10). At the sound of his approach, following upon her first attempt to describe "those sprawling flamboyant patterns" in the wallpaper, she declares,

"There comes John, and I must put this away,—he hates to have me write a word" (13).

Successively isolated from conversational exchanges, prohibited free access to pen and paper, and thus increasingly denied what Jean Ricardou has called "the local exercise of syntax and vocabulary,"[24] the protagonist of "The Yellow Wallpaper" experiences the extreme extrapolation of those linguistic tools to the processes of perception and response. In fact, it follows directly upon a sequence in which (1) she acknowledges that John's opposition to her writing has begun to make "the effort ... greater than the relief"; (2) John refuses to let her "go and make a visit to Cousin Henry and Julia"; and (3) as a kind of punctuation mark to that denial, John carries her "upstairs and laid me on the bed, and sat by me and read to me till it tired my head"— it is after these events that the narrator first makes out the dim shape lurking "behind the outside pattern" in the wallpaper: "it is like a woman stooping down and creeping" (21–22).

From that point on, the narrator progressively gives up the attempt to *record* her reality and instead begins to *read* it, as symbolically adumbrated in her compulsion to discover a consistent and coherent design amid "the sprawling outlines" of the wallpaper's apparently "pointless pattern" (20, 19). Selectively emphasizing one section of the pattern while repressing others, reorganizing and regrouping past impressions into newer, more fully realized configurations—as one might do with any complex formal text—the speaking voice becomes obsessed with her quest for meaning, jealous even of her husband's or his sister's momentary interest in the paper. Having caught her sister-in-law "with her hand on it once," the narrator declares, "I know she was studying that pattern, and I am determined that nobody shall find it out but myself!" (27). As the pattern changes with the changing light in the room, so do her interpretations of it. And what is not quite so apparent by daylight becomes glaringly so at night: "At night in any kind of light, in twilight, candle light, lamplight, and worst of all by moonlight, it becomes bars! The outside pattern I mean, and the woman behind it is as plain as can be." "By daylight," in contrast (like the protagonist herself), "she is subdued, quiet" (26).

As she becomes wholly taken up by the exercise of these interpretive strategies, her life, she claims, "is very much more exciting now than

24. Jean Ricardou, "Composition Discomposed," trans. Erica Freiberg, *Critical Inquiry*, 3 (Autumn 1976), 90.

it used to be. You see I have something more to expect, to look forward to, to watch" (27). What she is watching, of course, is her own psyche writ large; and the closer she comes to "reading" in the wallpaper the underlying if unacknowledged patterns of her real-life experience, the less frequent becomes that delicate oscillation between surrender to or involvement in and the more distanced observation of developing meaning. Slowly but surely the narrative voice ceases to distinguish itself from the woman in the wallpaper pattern, finally asserting that "I don't want anybody to get that woman out at night but myself" (31), and concluding with a confusion of pronouns that merges into a grammatical statement of identity: "As soon as it was moonlight and that poor thing began to crawl and shake the pattern, I got up and ran to help her. *I* pulled and *she* shook, and *I* shook and *she* pulled, and before morning *we* had peeled off yards of that paper" (32; my emphasis).

She is, in a sense, now totally surrendered to what is quite literally her own text—or rather, her self as text. But in decoding its (or her) meaning, what she has succeeded in doing is discovering the symbolization of her own untenable and unacceptable reality. To escape that reality she attempts the destruction of the paper that seemingly encodes it: the pattern of bars entrapping the creeping woman. " 'I've got out at last,' said I, 'in spite of you and Jane. I've pulled off most of the paper, so you can't put me back!' " (36). Their paper pages may be torn and moldy (as is, in fact, the smelly wallpaper), but the meanings of texts are not so easily destroyed. Liberation here is liberation only into madness. For in decoding her own projections onto the paper, the protagonist had managed merely to re-encode them once more, and now more firmly than ever, within.

With the last paragraphs of the story, John faints away—presumably in shock at his wife's now totally delusional state. He has repeatedly misdiagnosed, or misread, the heavily edited behavior with which his wife has presented herself to him, and never once has he divined what his wife sees in the wallpaper. But, given his freedom to read (or, in this case, misread) books, people, and the world as he chooses, he is hardly forced to discover for himself so extreme a text. To exploit Bloom's often useful terminology once again, Gilman's story represents less an object for the recurrent misreadings, or misprisions, of readers and critics (though such misreadings, of course, continue to occur) than an exploration of the gender-inflected interpretive strategies responsible for our mutual misreadings, and even horrific misprisions, across sex lines. If neither the male nor the female reading audience was prepared to decode "The Yellow Wallpaper" properly, even less, Gilman understood, were the two audiences prepared to comprehend one another.

It is unfortunate that Gilman's story was so quickly relegated to the backwaters of our literary landscape because, coming as it did at the end of the nineteenth century, it spoke to a growing concern among American women who would be serious writers: it spoke, that is, to their strong sense of writing out of nondominant or subcultural traditions (both literary and otherwise), coupled with an acute sensitivity to the fact that since women and men learn to read different worlds, different groups of texts are available to their reading and writing strategies. Had "The Yellow Wallpaper" been able to stand as a potential precursor for the generation of subsequent corrections and revisions, then, as in Bloom's paradigm, it might have made possible a form of fiction by women capable not only of commenting on but even of overcoming that impasse. That it did not—nor did any other woman's fiction become canonical in the United States[25]—meant that, again and again, each woman who took up the pen had to confront anew her bleak premonition that, both as writers and as readers, women too easily became isolated islands of symbolic significance, available only to, and decipherable only by, one another.[26] If any Bloomian "meaning" wanders around between women's texts, therefore, it must be precisely this shared apprehension.

On the face of it, such statements should appear nothing less than common-sensical, especially to those most recent theorists of reading who combine an increased attentiveness to the meaning-making role of the reader in the deciphering of texts with a recognition of the links between our "reading" of texts and our "reading" of the world and one another. Among them, Bloom himself seems quite clearly to understand this when, in *Kabbalah and Criticism*, he declares that "that

25. The possible exception here is Harriet Beecher Stowe's *Uncle Tom's Cabin; or, Life among the Lowly* (1852).

26. If to some of the separatist advocates in our current wave of New Feminism this sounds like a wholly acceptable, even happy circumstance, we must nonetheless understand that for earlier generations of women artists, acceptance within male precincts conferred the mutually understood marks of success and, in some quarters, vitally needed access to publishing houses, serious critical attention, and even financial independence. That this was *not* the case for the writers of domestic fiction around the middle of the nineteenth century was a fortunate but anomalous circumstance. Insofar as our artist mothers were separatist, therefore, it was the result of impinging cultural contexts and not (often) of their own choosing.

which you are, that only can you read."[27] Extrapolating from his description of the processes involved in the reading of literary texts to a larger comment on our ability ot take in, or decipher, those around us, Wolfgang Iser has lately theorized that "we can only make someone else's thought into an absorbing theme for ourselves, provided the virtual background of our own personality can adapt to it."[28] Anticipating such pronouncements in almost everything they have been composing for more than a hundred years now, the women who wrote fiction, most especially, translated these observations into the structures of their stories by invoking that single feature which such critics as Iser and Bloom still manage so resolutely to ignore: the crucial importance of the *sex* of the "interpreter" in that process which Nelly Furman has called "the active attribution of significance to formal signifiers."[29] Antedating both Bloom and Iser by more than fifty years, for example, Susan Keating Glaspell's 1917 short story, "A Jury of Her Peers," explores the necessary (but generally ignored) gender marking that *must* constitute any definition of "peers" in the complex process of unraveling truth or meaning.[30]

The opening paragraph of Glaspell's story serves, essentially, to alert the reader to the significations to follow: Martha Hale, interrupted at her kitchen chores, must drop "everything right where it was" in order to hurry off with her husband and the others come to fetch her. As "her eye made a scandalized sweep of her kitchen," she noted with distress that it "was in no shape for leaving: her bread all ready for mixing, half the flour sifted and half unsifted." The point, of course, is that highly unusual circumstances demand her leaving, and "it was no ordinary thing that called her away." When she seats herself "in the big two-seated buggy" alongside her impatient farmer husband, the sheriff and his wife, and the county attorney, the story proper begins.

All five drive to a neighboring farm where a murder has been com-

27. Bloom, *Kabbalah and Criticism*, 96.

28. Wolfgang Iser, *The Implied Reader: Patterns of Communication in Prose Fiction from Bunyan to Beckett* (Baltimore: Johns Hopkins University Press, 1974), 293.

29. Nelly Furman, "The Study of Women and Language: Comment on Vol. 3, no. 3," *Signs*, 4 (1978), 184.

30. First published in *Every Week*, March 15, 1917, the story was then collected by Edward O'Brien, ed., in *Best Short Stories of 1917*. My source for the text is Mary Anne Ferguson's *Images of Women in Literature* (Boston: Houghton Mifflin, 1973), 370–85. As will be indicated below, it is elsewhere collected. Since no textual difficulties are involved, I have omitted page references to any specific reprinting.

mitted—the farmer strangled, his wife already arrested. The men intend to seek clues to the motive for the crime, while the women are, ostensibly, simply to gather together the few necessities required by the wife during her incarceration in the town jail. Immediately upon approaching the place, however, the very act of perception becomes sex-coded: the men look at the house only to talk "about what had happened," while the women note the geographical topography, which makes it, repeatedly in the narrative, "a lonesome-looking place." Once inside, the men " 'go upstairs first—then out to the barn and around there' " in their search for clues (even though the actual crime took place in the upstairs master bedroom), while the women are left to the kitchen and parlor. Convinced as they are of "the insignificance of kitchen things," the men cannot properly attend to what they might reveal, and seek elsewhere for " 'a clue to the motive,' " so necessary if the county attorney is to make his case. Indeed, it is the peculiar irony of the story that although the men never doubt Minnie Foster's guilt, they nonetheless cannot meaningfully interpret this farm wife's world—her kitchen and parlor. And, arrogantly certain that the women would not even " 'know a clue if they did come upon it,' " they thus leave the discovery of the clues, and the consequent unraveling of the motive, to those who do, in fact, command the proper interpretive strategies.

Exploiting the information sketched in the opening, Glaspell has the neighbor, Mrs. Hale, and the sheriff's wife, Mrs. Peters, note, among the supposedly insignificant kitchen things, the unusual and, on a farm, unlikely remnants of kitchen chores left "half done," denoting an interruption of some serious nature. Additionally, where the man could discern no signs of " 'anger—or sudden feeling' " to substantiate a motive, the women comprehend the implications of some "fine, even sewing" gone suddenly awry, " 'as if she didn't know what she was about!' " Finally, of course, the very drabness of the house, the miserliness of the husband to which it attests, the old and broken stove, the patchwork that has become Minnie Foster's wardrobe—all these things make the women uncomfortably aware that fully to acknowledge the meaning of what they are seeing is " 'to get her own house to turn against her!' " Discovery by discovery, they destroy the mounting evidence—evidence that the men cannot recognize as such; and, sealing the bond between them as conspirators in saving Minnie Foster, they hide from the men the canary with its neck broken, the ultimate clue to the strangling of a husband who had so systematically destroyed all life, beauty, and music in his wife's environment.

Opposing against one another male and female realms of meaning and activity—the barn and the kitchen—Glaspell's narrative not only invites a semiotic analysis but, indeed, performs that analysis for us. If the absent Minnie Foster is the "transmitter" or "sender" in this schema, then only the women are competent "receivers" or "readers" of her "message," since they alone share not only her context (the supposed insignificance of kitchen things) but, as a result, the conceptual patterns that make up her world. To those outside the shared systems of quilting and knotting, roller towels and bad stoves, with all their symbolic significations, these things may appear trivial, even irrelevant to meaning; but to those within the system, they comprise the totality of the message: in this case, a reordering of who, in fact, has been murdered and what has constituted the real crime in the story.

For while the two women who visit Minnie Foster's house slowly but surely decipher the symbolic significance of her action—causing her husband's neck to be broken because he had earlier broken her canary's neck—the narrative itself functions, for the reader, as a further decoding of what that symbolic action says about itself. The essential crime in the story, we come to realize, has been the husband's inexorable strangulation, over the years, of Minnie Foster's spirit and personality; and the culpable criminality is the complicity of the women who had permitted the isolation and the loneliness to dominate Minnie Foster's existence: " 'I wish I had come over to see Minnie Foster sometimes,' " declares her neighbor guiltily. " 'I can see now—' She did not put it into words."

> "I wish you'd seen Minnie Foster [says Mrs. Hale to the sheriff's wife] when she wore a white dress with blue ribbons, and stood up there in the choir and sang."
> The picture of that girl, the fact that she had lived neighbor to that girl for twenty years, and had let her die for lack of life, was suddenly more than she could bear.
> "Oh, I *wish* I'd come over here once in a while!" she cried. "That was a crime! That was a crime! Who's going to punish that?"

The recognition is itself, of course, a kind of punishment. With it comes another recognition, as each woman reveals an experience in her own life of analogous isolation, desperate loneliness, or brutality at the hands of a man. Finally, they conclude: " 'We all go through the same things—it's all just a different kind of the same thing! If it weren't—why do you and I *understand?* Why do we *know*—what we know this minute?' " By this point, the narrative emphasis has shifted. To understand why it is that they know what they now know is for these women to recognize the profoundly sex-linked world of meaning which they inhabit; to discover how specialized is their ability to read that world is to discover anew their own shared isolation within it.

While neither the Gilman nor the Glaspell story necessarily excludes the male as reader—indeed, both in a way are directed specifically at educating him to become a better reader—they do insist that, however inadvertently, he is a *different kind* of reader, and that, where women are concerned, he is often an inadequate reader. In the first instance, because the husband cannot properly diagnose his wife's problem or attend to her reality, the result is horrific: the wife descends into madness. In the second, because the men cannot even recognize as such the very clues for which they search, the ending is a happy one: Minnie Foster is to be set free, no motive having been discovered on which to base a case against her. In both, however, the same point is being made: lacking familiarity with the woman's imaginative universe, that universe within which their acts are signs,[31] the men in these stories can neither read nor comprehend the meanings of the women closest to them, despite the apparent sharing of a common language. The stories are, in short, fictive renderings of the dilemma of the woman writer. For while we may all agree that, in our daily conversational exchanges, men and women speak more or less meaningfully and effectively with one another, thus fostering the illusion of a wholly shared common language, it is also the case that where figurative usage is invoked—that usage which often enough marks the highly specialized language of literature—it "can be inaccessible to all but those who share information about one another's knowledge, beliefs, intentions, and attitudes."[32] Symbolic representations, in other words, depend on a fund of shared recognitions and potential inference. For their intended impact to *take hold* in the reader's imagination, the author simply must, like Minnie Foster, be able to call upon a shared

31. I here paraphrase Clifford Geertz, *The Interpretation of Cultures* (New York: Basic Books, 1973), 13, and specifically direct the reader to the parable from Wittgenstein quoted on the same page.

32. Ted Cohen, "Metaphor and the Cultivation of Intimacy," *Critical Inquiry*, 5 (Autumn 1978), 78.

context with her audience. When she cannot, or dare not, she may revert to silence, to the imitation of male forms, or, like the narrator in "The Yellow Wallpaper," to total withdrawal and isolation in madness.

It may be objected, of course, that I have somewhat stretched my argument so as to conflate (or perhaps confuse?) *all* interpretive strategies with language processes, specifically *reading*. But in each instance, it is the survival of the *woman as text*—Gilman's narrator and Glaspell's Minnie Foster—that is at stake; and the competence of her reading audience alone determines the outcome. Thus, in my view, both stories intentionally function as highly specialized language acts (called "literature") which examine the difficulty inherent in deciphering other highly specialized realms of meaning—in this case, women's conceptual and symbolic worlds. And, further, the intended emphasis in each is the inaccessibility of female meaning to male interpretation.[33] The fact that in recent years each story has increasingly found its way into readily available textbooks,[34] and hence into the Women's Studies and American Literature classroom, to be read and enjoyed by teachers and students of both sexes, happily suggests that their fictive premises are attributable less to necessity than to contingency. Men can, after all, learn to apprehend the meanings encoded in texts by and about women, just as women have learned to become sensitive readers of Shakespeare and Milton, Hemingway and Mailer.[35] Both stories function, in effect, as prods to that very

33. It is significant, I think, that the stories do not suggest any difficulty for the women in apprehending the men's meanings. On the one hand, any such difficulty is not relevant to either plot; and, on the other, since in each narrative the men clearly control the public realms of discourse, it would of course have been incumbent on the women to learn to understand them. Though masters need not learn the language of their slaves, the reverse is never the case: for survival's sake, oppressed or subdominant groups always study the nuances of meaning and gesture in those who control them.

34. For example, "The Yellow Wallpaper" may be found, in addition to the Feminist Press reprinting previously cited, in Gail Parker, ed., *The Oven Birds: American Women on Womanhood, 1820–1920* (Garden City, N.Y.: Doubleday, 1972), 317–34; and "A Jury of Her Peers" is reprinted in Lee R. Edwards and Arlyn Diamond, eds., *American Voices, American Women* (New York: Avon, 1973), 359–81.

35. That women may have paid a high psychological and emotional price for their ability to read men's texts is beyond the scope of this essay; but I enthusiastically direct the reader to Judith Fetterley's provocative study of the problem in *The Resisting Reader: A Feminist Approach to American Fiction* (Bloomington: Indiana University Press, 1978).

process by alerting the reader to the fundamental problem of "reading" correctly within cohabiting but different conceptual worlds.

To take seriously the implications of such relearned reading strategies is to acknowledge that we are embarking upon a revisionist rereading of our entire literary inheritance, and in the process demonstrating the full applicability of Bloom's second formula for canon-formation, "You are or become what you read."[36] To set ourselves the task of learning to read a wholly different set of texts will make of us different kinds of readers (and perhaps different kinds of people as well). But to set ourselves the task of doing so in a public way, on behalf of women's texts specifically, engages us—as the feminists among us have learned—in a challenge to the inevitable issue of "*authority* ... in all questions of canon-formation."[37] It places us, in a sense, in a position analogous to that of the narrator of "The Yellow Wallpaper," bound, if we are to survive, to challenge the (accepted and generally male) authority who has traditionally wielded the power to determine what may be written and how it shall be read. It challenges fundamentally not only the shape of our canon of major American authors but, indeed, that very "continuity that began in the sixth century B.C. when Homer first became a schoolbook for the Greeks."[38]

It is no mere coincidence, therefore, that "readers" as diverse as Adrienne Rich and Harold Bloom have arrived, by various routes, at the conclusion that *re-vision* constitutes the key to an ongoing literary history. Whether functioning as ephebe/poet or would-be critic, Bloom's reader, as "revisionist," "strives to *see* again, so as to esteem and *estimate* differently, so as then to *aim* 'correctly.' "[39] For Rich, "re-vision" entails "the act of looking back, of seeing with fresh eyes, of entering an old text from a new critical direction."[40] And each, as a result—though the motives differ—strives to make the "literary tradition ... the captive of the revisionary impulse."[41] What Rich and other feminist critics intend by that "re-visionism" has been the subject of this essay: not only would such revisionary rereading open new

36. Bloom, *Kabbalah and Criticism*, 96.
37. Bloom, *Kabbalah and Criticism*, 100.
38. Bloom, *Map of Misreading*, 33–34.
39. Bloom, *Map of Misreading*, 4.
40. Adrienne Rich, "When We Dead Awaken: Writing as Re-Vision," *College English*, 34 (1972), 18; rpt. in *Adrienne Rich's Poetry*, ed. Barbara Charlesworth Gelpi and Albert Gelpi (New York: Norton, 1975), 90.
41. Bloom, *Map of Misreading*, 36.

avenues for comprehending male texts but, as I have argued here, it would, as well, allow us to appreciate the variety of women's literary expression, enabling us to take it into serious account for perhaps the first time, rather than, as we do now, writing it off as caprice or exception, the irregularity in an otherwise regular design. Looked at this way, feminist appeals to revisionary rereading, as opposed to Bloom's, offer us all a potential enhancing of our capacity to read the world, our literary texts, and even one another anew.

To end where I began, then, Bloom's paradigm of poetic history, when applied to women, proves useful only in a negative sense: for, by omitting the possibility of poet/mothers from his psychodynamic of literary influence (allowing the feminine only the role of Muse—as composite whore and mother), Bloom effectively masks the fact of an *other* tradition entirely—that in which women taught one another how to read and write about and out of their own unique (and sometimes isolated) contexts. In so doing, however, he not only points up the ignorance that informs our literary history as it is currently taught, but pinpoints (however unwittingly) what must be done to change our skewed perceptions: all readers, male and female alike, must be taught first to recognize the existence of a significant body of writing by American women and they must be encouraged to learn how to read it within its own unique and informing contexts of meaning and symbol. *Re-visionary rereading*, if you will. No more must we impose on future generations of readers the inevitability of Norman Mailer's "terrible confession . . . —I have nothing to say about any of the talented women who write today. . . . I do not seem able to read them."[42] Nor should Bloom himself continue to suffer an inability to express useful "judgment upon . . . the 'literature of Women's Liberation.' "[43]

42. Norman Mailer, "Evaluations—Quick and Expensive Comments on the Talent in the Room," collected in his *Advertisements for Myself* (New York: Putnam, 1966), 434–35.
43. Bloom, *Map of Misreading*, 36. What precisely Bloom intends by the phrase is nowhere made clear; for the purposes of this essay, I have assumed that he is referring to the recently increased publication of new titles by women writers.

11

Class, Gender, and Family System: The Case of George Sand

WENDY DEUTELBAUM

AND CYNTHIA HUFF

It is as common to bemoan the lack of attention bestowed on personal and psychic relations in socialist accounts of history as it is to criticize the lack of attention in psychoanalytic theory to the social contexts of psychological processes. Yet a feminist psychoanalytic approach, by its simultaneous focus on subjectivity and culturally constructed gender, begins to articulate what one Marxist critic has called the "almost-unthinkable": that the structure of the psyche is historical and has a history.[1] The purpose of this essay is to explore that psychic structure in the case of George Sand in such a way as to appreciate how her internalized family drama made certain narrative and political formulations possible and satisfying for her. Our gesture, as psychoanalytic feminist critics, will be to examine not only how a single individual acts out her whole family's tensions, but how the family itself acts out the sexual, economic, and political conflicts patriarchal society as a whole refuses to resolve.

---

1. "That the structure of the psyche is historical, and has a history, is, however, as difficult for us to grasp as that the senses are not themselves natural organs but rather the results of a long process of differentiation even within human history" (Fredric Jameson, *The Political Unconscious: Narrative as a Socially Symbolic Act* [Ithaca: Cornell University Press, 1981], 62).

Despite the rain and the mud, enthusiastic students were already lined up at 10 *a.m.* in front of the Odeon, on February 29, 1864, hoping to get tickets to the opening of George Sand's play *Le Marquis de Villemer*.[2] *Le Marquis* had in many ways a typical Sand plot: despite their class differences, a young noble succeeds in marrying his mother's *demoiselle de compagnie*. From her youthful novels through the plays of her middle years to her old-age correspondence with the crabby Flaubert, Sand would never surrender her utopian conviction that love could transform a classist, racist, and bloody world into an Eden of mutual caring and perpetual progress.

In this highly clerical Second Empire, however, the students who stood in line for seats to *Le Marquis de Villemer* came to applaud the author of a novel published a year earlier, *Mademoiselle la Quintinie*, in which Sand had debunked the Catholic church for its backward doctrine of hell and its archaic practices of confession and asceticism. Rumors that day suggested a clerical cabal, and the students of the Latin Quarter readied themselves for a counteroffensive. Emperor Napoleon III and the empress would be in their box that evening, too, less to applaud Sand's unorthodoxies than to signal their enduring gratitude for the letter she had written Napolen some years earlier, when he was imprisoned and she still believed in his expressions of socialist faith.

Despite the rumors, there was no cabal that night: each scene was met with cheers, songs, and applause. When the play was over, two hundred people—actors, friends, and strangers—rushed to embrace Sand, and when she was finally able to make her way out of the theater, she was met with wild cries of "Vive George Sand! Vive la Quintinie!" At the same time that she was trying to find a quieter spot at the Café Voltaire, six thousand people, mostly taunting students, charged over to the Catholic Club and the Jesuit House to sing mocking songs. Two cavalry regiments were readied and the police were on the spot to break up the crowd. Arrests were made, though no one was wounded.

This, in 1864, was George Sand at sixty: feminist critic of bourgeois marriage, enemy of religious authoritarianism, articulate, impassioned socialist visionary. She was known for her novels—first scandalous,

---

2. For a full account of the opening of *Le Marquis de Villemer*, see Claude Tricotel, *Comme deux troubadours: Histoire de l'amitié Flaubert-Sand* (Paris: SEDES, 1978), 13–16.

then socialist, finally pastoral. She was recognized as the cigar-smoking authoress who had proclaimed in 1842 that she had written her first novel, *Indiana*, "with a deep and genuine feeling that the laws which still govern women's existence in wedlock, in the family and in society are unjust and barbarous."[3] And she was remembered as the muse of communism for having encouraged the popular revolt of 1848. She had published novels, plays, political pamphlets, and self-justificatory volumes. The bourgeoisie frankly detested her and a church decree of December 15, 1863, had censored her entire oeuvre.

As with other early women writers to whom we as women readers now return with a desire to find them perfect, daring, and free from contradiction, we must guard against sentimentality and idealization. However much Sand's name has come to embody the effort toward women's liberation in the mid-nineteenth century, the limits of her feminism and her socialism are nonetheless real. During the period when women took to the streets to demand their rights, her harshest critics contend, Sand seems to have used her prestige to dispute rather than support their struggle.

The declaration of a new republic following the Revolution of 1848 fired feminists with new hope for an era of justice and equality. Although women had not yet been given the right to vote, the feminist daily *La Voix des Femmes* proposed the worthy candidature of George Sand for the Constituent Assembly. "A joke," "a ridiculous pretension," Sand responded to the feminists' homage.[4] This was not the first time that Sand had expressed skepticism about the campaign for women's political rights. In an 1834 letter to Marie Talon she had written: "Women haven't yet anything to say, it seems to me. What will their revolution accomplish? When the male world will be converted, women will be too, without our need to be concerned with them."[5] By 1848 Sand was virtually the minister of propaganda of the new republican government. Though she expressed in *Les Bulletins de La République* the opinion that women suffer the heaviest load of

---

3. "Preface to the Edition of 1842," *Indiana*, trans. George B. Ives (Chicago: Academy Press, 1978). Further quotations from *Indiana* will be from this edition and will be documented as *I* in the text.

4. Cited in Maïté Albistur and Daniel Armogathe, *Histoire du féminisme français*, 2 vols. (Paris: Editions des Femmes, 1977), II, 452. Unless otherwise indicated, all translations from the French are ours.

5. Cited in Marguerite Grepon, *Une Croisade pour un meilleur amour* (Brussels: Société générale des éditions, 1967), 49.

oppression, she argued at the same time against women's political rights, a position whose ultimately classist effect was to exclude poor women from the circle of society.

The more one examines Sand's position during this period, the more her feminist demands seem limited to the revision of civil rights for married women, that is, divorce. She opposed Jeanne Deroin's attempt to become a candidate for the Legislative Assembly and she accused feminists of having held back women's liberation by twenty years of preaching "without discernment, taste, or enlightenment."[6] In 1864, some sixteen years later, she expressed her integrationist version of woman-as-political muse in the following way:

> Women who pretend that they would have time to be senators and raise their children haven't raised them themselves. ... At a given moment, woman can inspire a social and political role, but not fulfill a function that deprives her of her natural mission: love of family.[7]

This conservative ideology presents the cultural creation *woman* as if it were an aspect of Nature itself, thus confining women to their roles as reproducers and domestic laborers and effectively excluding them from any more active participation in society. In light of these actions and opinions, it is not surprising that contemporary critics should see Sand as sentimental, individualistic, and elitist.[8]

Sand is vulnerable to this critique, for she was, in a century of persistent feminist insight, surprisingly blind. Other voices competed with the romantic mythology of the eternal feminine, and other actions realized women's aspirations for civil and political equality. There was Claire Bazard, the favorite disciple of the Saint-Simonian Enfantin, who refused to occupy the empty armchair reserved for LA MERE. "In vain," she wrote,

> would you place me on a throne, above all other women, in vain would you proclaim me first among them. ... Oh, enough of these passing elevations from which we have always so painfully fallen, enough of these illusory distinctions that have never brought us closer to you and have always distanced us from our sisters ... , enough of these isolated

6. Cited in Edith Thomas, *Les Femmes de 1848* (Paris: Presses Universitaires de France, 1948), 68.

7. Cited in Jules Tixerant, "Le Féminisme à l'époque de 1848 dans l'ordre politique et dans l'ordre économique," thesis, Paris, 1908, 48.

8. *Histoire du féminisme français*, II, 404.

thrones that make of the being who occupies it a being without a place among others.[9]

There was the socialist-feminist Charles Fourier, who proclaimed, "As a general thesis, social progress and historical changes operate to further women's progress toward liberty. . . . The extension of women's rights is the general principle of all social progress."[10] There were also the feminist periodicals, such as the *Tribune des femmes*, founded on the principle of coalition among women of all classes.[11] And there was, to give one last example, Flora Tristan, who struggled equally for workers' and women's emancipation.[12]

There were, then, other voices. It was just that Sand did not, would not, or could not hear them. Though her resistance frustrates our need to find her consistently progressive and self-affirming, it at the same time opens her case up to the much more challenging and rewarding process of trying to understand the pressures that kept her from bonding with other women or even from assigning primacy to their struggle. Class conflict, psychic conflict, sexual conflict: we have a fairly clear

9. Cited in Marguerite Thibert, "Le Féminisme dans le socialisme français de 1830 à 1850," thesis, Paris, 1926, 205.

10. "Théorie des quatre mouvements," in Fourier, *Textes choisis* (Paris: Editions Sociales, 1969), 124.

11. The *Tribune des femmes* was begun in August 1832 by two young workers, Marie-Reine Guindorf, age twenty, and Désirée Veret, age twenty-two. While a more bourgeois, Christian women' magazine such as *Le Journal des femmes* was content to disapprove of stereotypical womanly behavior—frivolity in studies, feminine virtues, and servitude to the matrimonial industry—the working women of the *Tribune des femmes* had a clear sense of the relation between classism, sexism, and imperialism. They denounced the plight of blacks in the United States. They encouraged the liberation struggles of all colonized peoples. And they believed that all women must join in solidarity, regardless of their class. Working women's servitude, they argued, was more profoundly anchored in partriarchal mentality than in their inferior proletarian status. "Let us not form two clans," they asked bourgeois women in issue no. 1, "one of women of the people and another of the privileged: our interest must bind us" (cited in Evelyne Sullerot, *Histoire de la presse féminine en France, des origines à 1848* [Paris: Armand Colin, 1966], 159).

12. Some ten years before Marx, Tristan asserted that workers' liberation must be an act of the workers themselves and that women, too, must constitute themselves as a class to demand equal education and equal salary, as well as the right to divorce and be head of a family. But women's liberation would not be easy, Tristan acknowledged, for it would demand radical change in mentality and mores: "The most oppressed man can oppress another, who is his wife. She is the very proletarian's proletarian" (cited in Dominique Desanti, *Flora Tristan: Vie et oeuvre mêlées* [Paris: Union générale des editions, 1974], 7).

264

sense of how a Marxist, psychoanalytic, or feminist interpretation might begin to account for Sand's behavior; we have a less clear sense of how these separate analyses might be articulated.

We shall focus on class and sexual rivalry within the context of Sand's family politics because the point of articulation is most clearly accessible there. As the nexus of power relations, the family system acts out the sexual and economic hierarchies that fragment collective life as a whole, just as individual family members, in their turn, act out the conflicts the family refuses to resolve.[13] George Sand's case offers a particularly sharp and poignant example of the circulation among psyche, family, and history. The family is the primary place where the psyche assumes a gender and a history, and George Sand's case reminds us that none of these terms exists uncontaminated by the others, however much each has been separated out and privileged by psychoanalytic, Marxist, and feminist hermeneutics.

"The [family] system perpetuates itself over generations," R. D. Laing writes. "The young are introduced to the parts the dead once played. Hence the drama continues. The dramatic structure abides, subject to transformations whose laws we have not yet formulated and whose existence we have barely begun to fathom."[14] One tool for the investigation of repetitious family dynamics, according to Laing, is the autobiography. Though contemporary theories of autobiography are quick to point out the limited nature of this form, Laing seems to have anticipated this critique.[15] The proper role of the psychiatrist, he be-

---

13. For two excellent examples of the recent body of theories and techniques known as structural family therapy, see Salvador Minuchin, *Families and Family Therapy* (Cambridge: Harvard University Press, 1974), and Augustus Y. Napier and Carl A. Whitaker, *The Family Crucible* (New York: Harper & Row, 1978). While Freud's focus on the individual was vulnerable to the critique by family therapists that it only further victimized the "identified patient" by helping him or her adapt to a sick family system, family therapists may themselves want to ask to what extent their work merely better adjusts an "identified" family to a brutalizing, dysfunctional society.

14. R. D. Laing, *The Politics of the Family and Other Essays* (New York: Vintage, 1972), 29.

15. Despite this caution, biographies of Sand rely chiefly on *Histoire de ma vie* for information concerning her early years. See Curtis Cate, *George Sand: A Biography* (Boston: Houghton Mifflin, 1975); Francine Mallet, *George Sand* (Paris: Bernard Grasset, 1976); and Joseph Barry, *Infamous Woman: The Life of George Sand* (Garden City, N. Y.: Doubleday, 1977). Barry notes that *Histoire de ma vie* is "the most important source, together with [George] Lubin's edition of Sand's *Correspondance* for students of Sand" (385).

lieves, is to "uncover a story," to interpret "one person's way of defining the situation." In writing *Histoire de ma vie*, Sand began to process for herself this story, acutely aware of the dead hand of her ancestors: "The dead are alive within us. That is certain," she wrote to her publisher. "There is a mysterious link feeding our lives with theirs."[16]

Sands seems to have experienced earliest family life as if it were untouched by the class conflicts that actually directed it. Living in poverty with her parents in Paris, she invented endless tales "which my mother called my novels," long serialized stories with good princes, beautiful princesses, a few wicked beings, and many happy endings.[17] These visions of social justice, where "everything always came right," accorded well with her childish perceptions of familial experience. Until the age of four, she played boyish games and felt the love of parents who were "happy only in their family circle," that small sphere that Sand shared with her aristocratic father, Maurice; her proletarian mother, Sophie; and Sophie's illegitimate daughter, Caroline.

But unknown to Sand, this familial harmony was built on shaky foundations. At twenty-nine, Sand would describe her complex family background to the proletarian poet Charles Poncy in this way:

> I who was born, it appears, into the ranks of the aristocracy am of the people by blood as much as by heart. My mother was more lowly placed than yours in our bizarre, hard society. She did not belong to the hardworking, conscientious class which gives you a title of nobility among the people. She was of the degraded, vagabond race—the Bohemians of the world. She was a dancer, no, less than a dancer, a bit player in one of the lowest theaters of Paris, and rich men removed her from this degradation only to subject her to worse.[18]

In wedding Sophie, Maurice had defied the wishes of his mother, the aristocratic Aurore de Saxe, who at the turn of the century still tried to live as if the French Revolution had never taken place. After the death of her elderly husband, Aurore de Saxe had given all her love

16. George Sand, *Correspondance*, ed. George Lubin, 11 vols. (Paris: Gallimard, 1964), VIII, 264.

17. George Sand, *My Life*, trans. and adapted by Dan Hofstadter (New York: Harper & Row, 1979), 29. Further quotations from *My Life* will be from this edition and will be documented as *ML* in the text.

18. George Sand, *In Her Own Words*, ed. and trans. Joseph Barry (New York: Doubleday, 1979), p. 287.

to her only son, Maurice. Implicating the erotic overinvolvement of mothers in their sons in patriarchal culture, Sand states that her grandmother was a woman who "never had any passion but maternal love" (*ML*, 5). Indeed, when Maurice finally announced his marriage, some while after it had occurred, Aurore de Saxe accused him of loving Sophie more than he loved her and tried hard to annul their marriage.

Maurice labored with difficulty to reconcile the competing claims of a "beloved mother" and an "adored wife." It is important to note that Maurice's strategies, if they brought about a temporary peace, did so by using his daughter as barter. Maurice had first tried to win his mother's approval by persuading his mother's maid to pretend that the pretty child was her own granddaughter:

> "Just look at my pretty little granddaughter," she said. "Her nurse left her off with me today, and I can't get enough of her."
> "My, she *is* fresh as a daisy," said my grandmother, reaching for her bonbonniere.
> At that moment the good concierge—who was playing her part to perfection—sat me upon my grandmother's lap. My grandmother gave me a sweet and began to scrutinize me with a certain astonishment. All at once she held me at arm's length.
> "Liar!" she said to the concierge. "This child doesn't look a bit like you!" [*ML*, 26]

Although Aurore de Saxe was deeply troubled by the marriage, the moment she laid eyes on her young namesake she recognized and claimed her, and for a short time Aurore de Saxe and Sophie behaved civilly, curbing their rivalry, exchanging the "sweet names 'mother' and 'daughter' " (*ML*, 27). This story marks the first in a painful series of declared ownerships that would mark Sand's entire childhood. From it we can begin to assess the young Aurore's value within the complex exchange pattern of patriarchal family politics.

The untimely death of Maurice when Sand was four revived the two women's rivalry for Maurice by displacing it onto a desperate struggle for the little Aurore. The tendency to equate Sand with her father was already established among the servants at the family estate at Nohant, who considered all the women in Maurice's sphere as his extensions, referring to Sophie, for example, as "Madame Maurice." The tendency to equate Aurore and Maurice was greater still within the family circle. Maurice had initiated the confusion when he dressed up his three-year-old daughter in military uniform whenever she was to appear before his commanding officer, and Aurore came to be known jokingly as his aide-de-camp. Sophie maintained the confusion by accepting the parts of her daughter that represented Maurice and rejecting the other parts: "My mother loved Maurice in me," Sand remarks, "and hated my grandmother and Deschartes [Maurice and Aurore's tutor] in me." And so much did Aurore's habits and features remind Sand's grandmother of her dead son that she often called her by *his* name and referred to her as "my son," as if by so doing she could resurrect her past and once again become her young son's mother.

The place Sand came to occupy in her family mythology—that of the dead father—was determined largely by the psychological needs of the family members to reanimate Maurice in Aurore. As Laing writes of a young patient:

> His body was a sort of mausoleum, a haunted graveyard in which the ghosts of several generations still walked, while their physical remains rotted away. This family had buried their dead *in each other*. . . . This young man was tied in a knot; it had taken at least four, perhaps five or more, generations to tie it.[19]

However clearly motivated by the two women's sexual rivalry, the knot Sand represents is no less a rivalry of economic proportions. Had Sophie remained childless, her relationship with Maurice would have signified only a sexual mésalliance to Aurore de Saxe. But there was little Aurore, the fruit of a utopian desire that would fuel Sand's own desires. If Aurore de Saxe had for a brief moment embraced son, wife, and child, her first task after Maurice's death was to reassert old class distinctions. Sophie and her granddaughter had to be separated, for from her conservative position Aurore de Saxe perceived in personal, domestic terms the imminent threat of a real class struggle she had to win. Once Sophie's existence had threatened her mother-in-law's primacy in Maurice's affections; now her existence threatened the family property, which could pass from the precapitalist aristocratic world she shared with her son into the market-value or cash-nexus world represented by her proletarian daughter-in-law. The solution was to buy off Sophie, offer her a lifetime pension in exchange for legal possession of Aurore, and in this way draw back into her control both the child and the property she could pass on through inheritance.

19. Laing, *Politics of the Family*, 57.

An ironic but predictable aspect of Aurore de Saxe's strategy is the way it transfers from one generation to the next the exploitive sexual and class politics of her own family. Aurore de Saxe had been born the natural daughter of Maurice de Saxe, victor of the battle of Fontenoy, himself the illegitimate son of Frederick Augustus, elector of Saxony and king of Poland. Her mother, one of Maurice de Saxe's last amours, was Mlle Verrières, euphemistically known as a "dame of the Opera." Aurore's father died when she was only two, and she was adopted by her father's half sister, King Augustus' daughter and mother of Louis XVIII. "La Dauphine," as she was known at the court of Versailles, placed Aurore de Saxe in the Ecole Saint-Cyr, the finest school for young ladies in the realm; forbade her to see *her* mother, a commoner; and subjected her to the strictest aristocratic education. After an unconsummated marriage at fifteen to the comte de Horn, who died soon thereafter, she married Louis-Claude Dupin de Francueil, whose enormous wealth easily made up for his lack of noble birth. This history is significant in a number of ways: it gives us a general sense of the power and endurance of a complex family "system" that was waiting to repeat itself upon the birth of the infant Aurore, and it alerts us specifically to the way in which one member of the family, in each case the female child, is elected to play out the class conflict that disturbed the family as a whole.

Aurore de Saxe wanted possession of her granddaughter in order to recreate her own familiar and familial relationships. But why did Sophie surrender her daughter? Her abandonment of Aurore appears heartless, especially when we know how terrified Aurore was that Sophie would capitulate and renounce her for money: "Maybe we'd be poor, but we'd be together!" Aurore implored (*ML*, 14). But as Sophie watched her daughter at Nohant, the family estate, she wondered, Sand records, whether she wouldn't be happier with her grandmother and whether she would blame her later for having deprived her of education, property, and prestige. Sophie considered her own position, too, and that of her illegitimate daughter, Caroline: if Aurore de Saxe cut off Sophie's income, all three of them—mother and daughters alike—would find themselves as destitute as Sophie had been during her own adolescence. So Sophie submitted to the rules of social survival and to the perpetuating power of an intricate family structure of which she, much like Mlle Verrières a generation before, had become a part. The message was clear: the affection of "common" mothers for their "aristocratic" daughters was to be subordinated to the prior claims of patriarchal and aristocratic prestige. Sophie renounced the utopian dream of her marriage and made the best arrangement she could. The bargain was for herself and Caroline a lifetime pension, and for Aurore, property, education, and prestige.

Much of Sand's childhood bespeaks her attempt to preserve or reconstruct the wholeness that had been lost when Maurice died. In *Histoire de ma vie* Sand tells us that she never bypassed an opportunity to daydream or to read, activities that helped her regain a unified world in fantasy. But Sand also, at a very early age, began to write, and in this endeavor she was assisted by an androgynous muse she called Corambé. Corambé was used especially to reconcile the differences between her two mothers. He/she symbolized the unity of historical, religious, and literary knowledge, and something more personal as well:

> Corambé took form all on his own in my brain. He was as pure and charitable as Christ, as radiant and beautiful as Gabriel. But I supplied a needed nymph-like grace and a touch of Orpheus' poetry. Thus he was less austere than the Christian's God and his sensibility more spiritual than Homer's. And then I completed him by dressing him sometimes as a woman. . . . In short, he had no sex; he assumed all different forms.[20]

Corambé, then, stood for the child's freedom to mix, exchange, and transmute both mythologies and sexualities; essentially creative, radically plural, this kindly bisexual figure would for years whisper the stories Aurore would then record.

But even Corambé could not counterbalance the aristocratic conservatism into which Sand at five had been abandoned. Increasingly she came under the sway of her grandmother and the servants, who, instead of easing her conflict, exacerbated it. Sand names Deschartes as "the main hindrance" to any reconciliation between Sophie and Aurore de Saxe, but Julie, the personal maid of her grandmother, hampered it as well. Both had personal and economic motives for advocating Aurore's aristocratic upbringing. Deschartes, like Aurore de Saxe, had been passionately devoted to Maurice, and he too strove to recapture the aristocratic Maurice in Aurore. Julie, in order to woo her employer, made dry jokes about Sophie and upheld Aurore de Saxe's aristocratic standards.

20. Sand, *In Her Own Words*, 298.

If Deschartes and Julie represented "my grandmother's party," as Sand calls it, "Rose, Ursule, and me" represented "my mother's party." Neither Rose nor Ursule, however, supported her mother's camp as strongly as Aurore de Saxe's representatives backed hers. Originally a servant in the household of Sand's parents, Rose won Aurore's affection because "she loved my mother, she was the only one who ever mentioned her, and always with admiration and tenderness" (ML, 121). Despite a love and a strength that Sand thought recalled Sophie's, Rose would nevertheless slap Aurore for such inconsequential offenses as taking three stitches instead of two in marking her stockings. Rose rationalized her recurrent beatings as enforcing Aurore de Saxe's exacting standards.

Julie's niece Ursule, a few years older than Sand, was also a member of "my mother's party," but, like Rose, also surrendered to the aristocratic mores of Nohant. She tried to calm Aurore's distress over the two women's rivalry by describing Nohant as Aurore's "golden age," an age signified by "a big house, and a big garden to stroll in, and carriages, and dresses, and good things to eat every day" (ML, 65). Riches were what lay behind this paradise, she said, and she urged Sand to enjoy these luxuries as long as possible.

Aurore de Saxe, for her part, set the example for the servants. She groomed her granddaughter to service the feudal family by becoming a perfect young "heiress." She made Aurore wear gloves and drop curtsies, took her on tedious visits to her aristocratic friends, and instilled a sense of shame, which more than other strategies functioned to repress Sand's spontaneity and her attachment to her mother. While class rivalry between the two women goes far to explain the constant conflict in Sand's childhood between her emotions and her mother, on the one hand, and the world of society and her grandmother, on the other, the conflict also parallels quite clearly what Freud describes in *Civilization and Its Discontents* as the regimentation of the instincts by the superego, "the renunciation of instincts," through the fear of external authority.[21] And thanks to recent psychoanalytic work on preoedipal mother-daughter bonds, we can also see how Sand's conflict exemplifies the repression by patriarchal oedipal socialization of the more nurturant, less competitive relations characteristic of this earlier mother-daughter bond.[22]

21. Freud, *Civilization and Its Discontents*, in *Standard Edition*, XXI, 74.
22. See, for example. Nancy Chodorow, *The Reproduction of Mothering: Psychoanalysis and the Sociology of Gender* (Berkeley: University of California Press, 1978).

Aurore de Saxe's attempt to smother her granddaughter's spontaneity in the name of grace and duty honed both Aurore's indignation and her sense of comedy. "This so-called grace," she wrote,

> was a certificate of clumsiness and physical weakness. All those lovely ladies and fine gentlemen who were so adept at walking on carpets and bowing or curtseying couldn't take three steps on God's good earth without collapsing of fatigue. [*ML*, 106]

But her grandmother's techniques had deeper effects that were not so easily dismissed. In a chilling passage from *Histoire de ma vie*, Sand explains: "I was horribly afraid of becoming like her. I felt that she was asking me to be dead" (*ML*, 83). Sand's fear of this death made her long still more intensely for the "life that [I] would never get back again" (*ML*, 98). Perhaps Aurore de Saxe could have succeeded in weaning her granddaughter from these earlier memories had she not used such harsh measures to secure her control. One evening, for example, while Sand played on the rug and her grandmother dozed in her chair, Rose called to her. Aurore de Saxe awoke and immediately demanded to know why the maid had called to the child behind her back. When Rose blurted out that Caroline, Sand's half sister, had come to visit, Aurore de Saxe responded sharply: "My granddaughter no longer knows her; I do not know her" (*ML*, 91). Caroline's stifled sobs revived Sand's memory of her "real family," and Aurore de Saxe finally gave in to this overwhelming sentiment by allowing Sand to visit from time to time the shabby apartment her mother and half sister occupied in Paris: "I'm home, I'm home, I'm home," Sand would cry. "There I'm at my grandmama's. Here I'm home!" (*ML*, 98).

Unable by any other means to prevent Aurore from wanting to return to her "real family," Aurore de Saxe insisted on telling the thirteen-year-old Aurore her version of Sophie's sordid life. It was not until years later that Sand would fully appreciate what an ugly rendition this was, for Aurore de Saxe had ignored the exploitation of lower-class girls by aristocratic men and had put all the blame on Sophie, even to the point of conveniently neglecting to mention that her son had seduced the daughter of a local carpenter and that the fruit of their secret liaison was none other than Hippolyte, Aurore's playmate and half brother. The immediate effect of this story was devastating and dramatic. Aurore felt she was dying; each word was a dagger. "I was aware," she writes, "only of a contempt for the entire universe and of a bitterness toward life and toward whatever it might bring; in brief, I no longer loved myself. If my mother was contemptible, then so was the fruit of her womb" (*ML*, 129). Aurore de Saxe had practiced a most potent technique for forcing a family member to conform: "One does not tell him what *to be*," as Laing summarizes this method of attribution, "but tells him what he *is*."[23]

What must the psychological effect on Sand have been, to play pawn in this way in the brutal family politics of her mother and grandmother? If she conceived of herself as her mother's child, she was evil and unlovable—evil because she, like her mother, was fallen and unworthy, unlovable because her mother had abandoned her. If, on the other hand, she thought of herself as her grandmother's child, she was dead—dead because Maurice was dead and she was to occupy his place, and dead again because Aurore de Saxe's structured, sterile, aristocratic world offered only a death-in-life existence. I am dead and I am bad: these two, probably unconscious, self-images are the internal inheritance Sand would struggle to survive, *her* subjectivity the battleground of *their* rivalry, a rivalry that ultimately functioned to ensure their own continuing victimization.

Though Sand locates the interest of her autobiographical *My Convent Life* in its social commentary (it will instruct the curious as to the good and bad influences of convent education, she says), for us her volume articulates a particularly significant personal apprenticeship.[24] Sand entered the English convent in Paris at fourteen overwhelmed by self-images of being dead and evil and left it two years later, transformed, productive, and quite alive. What happened during those years she would later call the "happiest of my life"?

If the convent first seemed a "prison," cut off from the outside world by grated windows stuffed with white cloth, Aurore soon found within these cloistering walls a much needed freedom from her family. Here no one knew much about her past or cared much about her future, for the nuns were less concerned with the education of their pupils than with their own spiritual salvation. Free to live largely as she pleased within this "genial family of women," Sand soon chose to join

---

23. Laing, *Politics of the Family*, 78.
24. George Sand, *My Convent Life*, trans. Maria Ellery McKay (Chicago: Academy Press, 1978). Further quotations from *My Convent Life* will be from this edition and will be documented as *MCL* in the text.

the ranks of the *"diables,"* the troublemakers led by Mary, "the boy
... proud and outspoken, remarkable for her strength and agility and
still more phenomenal boldness" (*MCL*, 26). The *diables* scaled the
convent rooftops, pretending they were cats, and explored its unlit,
labyrinthian passages in their constant search "for the victim"; they
imagined themselves descending into "a whole world of darkness,
terror and mystery . . . as fraught with imaginary peril as the descent
into hell of Aeneas or Dante" (*MCL*, 36). In becoming a *diable* Aurore
doubtless continued the behavior that had scared Aurore de Saxe into
sending her to the convent in the first place, but she also learned self-
esteem, self-sufficiency, and courage from the *diables* strict code: never
lie, never flinch under punishment.

It was a custom in the convent for girls to select one of the nuns as
a "mother" who would direct their education. Sand first chose Mother
Alicia, the distant, intellectual, and attractive woman none of Sand's
peers would have dared to claim as their mentor. Mother Alicia's
aristocratic connections must have recalled Aurore de Saxe's, and the
harmony she represented may have reminded Sand, as well, of the
peace she had experienced before Maurice's death. "In coming into
contact with her," Sand writes, "one felt that there was no inward
struggle in her life, and that she naturally tended to all that was good
and beautiful. Everything about her was harmonious" (*MCL*, 83).

Despite Aurore's alliance with the troublemakers, Mother Alicia
accepted her plea for mothering and continued to love her with a
consistency that must have seemed quite incomprehensible to the
"bad" Aurore. But as Aurore in time tired of being a *diable*, her bond
with Mother Alicia seems to have weakened proportionately. At this
point she selected a second mother. Like Sophie, Sister Helen was a
woman of low birth. She had repudiated her family for a higher spiritual calling and practiced her faith as a form of masochistic martyrdom,
always insisting on doing the most lowly of labors. "You are right—
you are at peace with yourself," Sand says to herself as she thinks of
Helen. "I will be a nun; it will be the despair of my family and my
own too" (*MCL*, 161).

Sand's identification with Sister Helen led her from a state of spiritual awakening to one of morose dependency, a journey downward
into that death-in-life existence that had so terrified her when she felt
suffocated by her grandmother's aristocratic education. "I loved to
dream of a life that would be a sort of living death," she explains, "of
an existence intellectually torpid, indifferent to all earthly consider-

ations, absorbed in contemplation without end" (*MCL*, 175). Yet in fashioning herself a martyr, Aurore began to suffer both severe religious uncertainty and acute self-doubt. Her fanaticism soon reached such an intensity that her confessor, Abbé Prémord, who felt it necessary to intervene and to redirect Aurore's misplaced sense of mission, reminded her that God wanted only "reasonable service" from his believers.

Bad, then dead: Aurore's downward journey is reminiscent of the regressive process Laing describes as a "sort of death-rebirth sequence from which, if it is successfully negotiated, the person returns to the world feeling new-born, refreshed, and reintegrated at a higher level of functioning than before."[25] Aurore does return, liberated from her delusions of being dead and being evil, as the producer of convent theatricals: she chooses actresses, assigns parts, orders dresses, and makes the end of the classroom toward the garden her theater. "Come author! come, life and soul of the company. ... Let us have a superb performance—six acts,—two or three pieces!" her cohorts would shout (*MCL*, 200). The girls had acted pieces taken from the sentimental plays of Madame de Genlis every year on the superior's birthday, but Aurore, like her playful father, wanted something more comical and lively. Though Molière's works were prohibited in the convent, Aurore was well versed in them, and she felt sure that neither the pupils nor the nuns knew a line of his plays. By leaving out the "love passages" and the "coarseness," she managed to arrange enough scenes from *Le Malade imaginaire* and a comic chase from *M. de Pourceaugnac* for an evening entertainment. She rehearsed the actresses and gave them a general notion of the play's main ideas. The result was a huge success: "Never in the memory of nuns had they laughed so heartily" (*MCL*, 202). Aurore was overwhelmed with compliments for the wit and gaiety of her inventions. The convent's sharply drawn distinctions between "good" girls, "stupid" girls, and *diables* soon faded into a loving, egalitarian network of "rose-water *diables*": through Sand's writing the dynamics of the convent had changed. The theater continued to attract the superior and the nuns every Sunday.

The actions recorded in *My Convent Life* look back toward their familial determinations and forward to their literary transformations. It must have appeared to Aurore that only Maurice could have protected her from the unending dispute between Aurore de Saxe and

25. Laing, *Politics of the Family*, 52.

Sophie. Having introjected into an internal, psychic drama the deadening self-images inherited from her two mothers' rivalry, Aurore could surmount them only by herself becoming a mediating Maurice. When Sand was transplanted into the world of the convent, it was precisely this solution that took root and flourished: by taking on the voice of an Enlightenment male figure, Aurore/Maurice/Molière could both silence her internal despair and transform systems of female conflict into networks of female love. Felicitous as this solution may have first appeared to Sand, however, it was not without its problems. Like her mother and grandmother, it ignored the culpability of patriarchal hierarchy in creating female rivalry in the first place, and it demanded as well that Sand borrow a relatively safe narrative voice from which much of her later work, with its unquestioning romanticism, heroic posturing, and often mawkish sentimentalism, would suffer.

Sand left the convent only to be thrust back into her aristocratic milieu, where she was soon married, for her money and her property, by the roguish Casimir Dudevant. Once again Sand experienced, though never fully analyzed, the way in which personal bonds are subordinate to considerations of class, sex, and property. Sand's unhappiness with Casimir no doubt informed certain feminist elements of her early novels, stories in which, time and time again, unhappy young women yearn for more egalitarian arrangements. Yet however much the details may have changed from *My Convent Life* to *Indiana*, for example, a familiar, underlying pattern remains easily discernible.

A male narrator presents us with the frail Indiana, suffocating in a loveless marriage to Colonel Delmare, a brute who shoots Raymon, the intruder. Raymon's physical injury, unlike Indiana's psychic wounds, is merely superficial, and when he recovers, he and Delmare become allies in their mutual adherence to a coercive status quo, societal for one and military for the other. While Delmare functions as the tyrannical bourgeois husband whose misplaced use of force slowly destroys his fragile wife, Raymon plays out the role of Indiana's savior and subduer: only when she meets Raymon can her undeveloped passion emerge, allowing her escape from a death-in-life existence with Delmare. Indiana's own concept of love, though more reciprocal than Aurore's in *My Convent Life*, still contains a stereotypic dose of self-sacrifice. "You must be ready to sacrifice everything to me," she tells Raymon, "fortune, reputation, duty, business, principles, family—everything, monsieur, because I shall place the same absolute devotion in my scale, and I wish them to balance" (*I*, 113). Indiana sacrifices everything to Raymon, but the callous seducer will have none of her bargain.

From this state—dead, then evil and outcast—the plot takes a predictable turn toward the utopian. Before Indiana married Delmare, she lived in bliss with her childhood guardian, Sir Ralph. Throughout her marriage, Sir Ralph watches over and tries to protect her. Unlike Delmare and Raymon, the marginalized Ralph advocates the destruction of the status quo, and like Indiana, he comes to serve as a moral voice within the novel. Ralph proposes they escape the horrors of social bondage by committing suicide together, but in the end leads her to a remote island where mutual love and respect reign over all: here blacks and whites live in social equality; here worldly strife and patriarchal grasping are unknown; here Indiana can finally live out the utopia foreshadowed by her childhood felicity.

However different her circumstances may be, Indiana's journey shows all the signs of repeating Aurore's in *My Convent Life*: like Aurore, Indiana has to go through trials of being dead and being evil before she can enter an Eden of mutual caring. And in both stories, this paradise is brought about by union with an enlightened male figure: in *My Convent Life*, through Maurice's mediating role and the comic voice of Molière; in *Indiana*, through the custody and guidance of Sir Ralph. Indiana's solution may frustrate the reader who expects a development from *My Convent Life*, for here Sand imagines not the birth of a self-affirming woman writer but an idealized union between father and daughter in an appropriately socialist setting. It is as if Sand cannot take the plot of a young girl living in the world beyond the clichés of French Romantic literature, as if she cannot conceive that a woman's voice, alone or in consonance with other women's, might itself be capable of generating harmony and resolving conflict. This inability to affirm a self-affirming young woman may account for Sand's repeated use of male narrators throughout her work, as well as her tendency to refer back to an idealized father-daughter romance. Whatever the aesthetic and didactic limits of Sand's narratives, however, it seems clear that they were successful at least on one level: as symbolic resolutions of an obsessive family drama.

My Convent Life and *Indiana* can be best understood as attempts to express and resolve the psychic conflicts Sand inherited from her patriarchal family drama. Her later mixture of socialism and antifeminism can be understood in the same way. Both her Romantic novels and her politics imagine a utopian marriage between social (un)equals that will be brought about by an enlightened father figure. Both assert, justify, and idealize Sand's own origins and the superiority of masculine roles. What Sand neither experienced in her family nor imagined in her work was a world in which women themselves, women of all social classes, could join forces to end their own oppression.

If we now turn to George Sand as our foremother, it is not only to praise the woman who freely insulted the clerics and was cheered by six thousand students. It is also to understand the limits of her vision and the pressures that maintained them, for these limits predict some of our own. From a methodological point of view, we think Sand's case exemplifies the kinds of connections between the personal and the social which feminist psychoanalysis strives to grasp. Like our reading, the "psychocritique" practiced by Charles Mauron locates obsessive dramatic relations between characters in order to describe an author's "personal myth," an expression of his or her intrapsychic situation.[26] While attentive to these formal and psychological elements, however, most psychoanalytic readings fail to articulate their historical or collective connections. A strict feminist analysis might focus on the failures of Sand's political stance, a subject not necessarily of interest to the psychoanalytic critic, and would be able to locate the causes of this failure by pointing to the overvaluation of the phallus by women educated to take their place in the sexual hierarchy by an ideology of male superiority. But unlike Juliet Mitchell or Luce Irigaray, to mention only two of our British and French feminist colleagues, most American feminists have been reluctant to use and transform psychoanalytic methodology, finding Freud's theories more prescriptive than descriptive of patriarchal society.[27] Finally, a Marxist critic would tend to focus on class conflict, accounting for Sand's narrative and political decisions as symbolic resolutions of insurmountable social contradictions, but ignoring the parallel and equally damaging effects of sexual inequalities.[28] By exploring the family politics in which

26. See Wendy Deutelbaum, "Two Psychoanalytic Approaches to Reading Literature," in *Theories of Reading, Looking, and Listening*, ed. Harry A. Garvin (London and Toronto: Associated University Presses, 1981), 89–101.

27. Juliet Mitchell, *Psychoanalysis and Feminism* (New York: Pantheon, 1974), and Luce Irigaray, *Speculum de l'autre femme* (Paris: Minuit, 1974).

28. See, for example, Lucien Goldmann, *Pour une sociologie du roman* (Paris: Gallimard, 1964), and Fredric Jameson, *Political Unconscious*.

the unconscious assumes a gender and a history, we have tried to join these various perspectives. In a powerful and poignant way, the case of George Sand exemplifies the necessity of our making these connections.

12

Women and Men in Doris Lessing's *Golden Notebook*: Divided Selves

GAYLE GREENE

I'm convinced that there are whole areas of me made by
the kind of experience women haven't had before ...

—Doris Lessing

I

"Don't you see it's all much worse for us than it is for you?" says Milt
(or Saul Green in the blue notebook), urging Anna "to see us [men]
through.... Because you're tougher, you're kinder, you're in a position to."[1] Lessing's portrayal of men in *The Golden Notebook* affirms
that contemporary society is "worse for" men than for women, leaving
them damaged, divided, dehumanized. The male characters in this
novel illustrate what has been variously described as "the hazards of
being male," "the limits of masculinity," "dilemmas of masculinity,"

---

1. *The Golden Notebook* (New York: Ballantine, 1971), 662-63. Further references
to this edition are included in my text.

and "the confines of masculinity."[2] The men Anna encounters on her journey toward wholeness—"sexual cripples" (484) with "mother trouble" (581) whose postures of "Cool, cool, cool" (545) are defenses against feeling—illustrate the repression and rigidity that (according to Nancy Chodorow and others) originate in the infant's earliest experiences with an all-powerful female nurturer. Whereas the female "experiences herself ... as a continuation or extension of ... her mother in particular, and later of the world in general," and so tends "toward boundary confusion and a lack of separateness from the world," the male "has engaged, and been required to engage, in a more emphatic individuation and a more defensive firming of experienced ego boundaries."[3] Moreover, since men derive more of their identities than women do from participation in what Lessing calls "a dying society" (545), they identify more with their culture's ideal of gender, an ideal that leaves them maimed. No man in the novel, whatever his position or nationality, is untouched by his culture's image of masculinity. It affects the exiled and unemployed—blacklisted American writers who, like Saul, "move about the world" (658) but remain "competitive about everything" (578)—just as it does men of property and power—those who, like Richard, maintain "the forms" of success. England may be " 'full of women going mad all by themselves' " (167),

2. Herb Goldberg, *The Hazards of Being Male* (New York: New American Library, 1976); Andrew Tolson, *The Limits of Masculinity* (London: Tavistock, 1977); Mirra Komarovsky, *Dilemmas of Masculinity* (New York: Norton, 1976); "the confines of masculinity" is Warren Farrell's term in *The Liberated Man, or Beyond Masculinity: Freeing Men and Their Relationships with Women* (New York: Bantam, 1975), 29–31. For a review of the recent literature on men, see James B. Harrison, "Review Essay: Men's Roles and Men's Lives," *Signs* (Winter 1978), 324–36. Of particular interest are Janet Saltzman Chafetz, *Masculine/Feminine or Human: An Overview of the Sociology of Sex Roles* (Itasca, Ill: F. E. Peackock, 1974); Shepherd Mead, *Free the Male Man!* (New York: Simon & Schuster, 1972); Harvey Kaye, *Male Survival* (New York: Grosset & Dunlap, 1974; Betty Roszak and Theodore Roszak, *Masculine/Feminine* (New York: Harper Colophon, 1969); Joseph H. Pleck and Jack Sawyer, *Men and Masculinity* (Englewood Cliffs, N.J.: Prentice-Hall, 1974); Joe E. Dubbert, *A Man's Place: Masculinity in Transition* (Englewood Cliffs, N.J.: Prentice-Hall, 1979); Joseph H. Pleck, *The Myth of Masculinity* (Cambridge, Mass.: M.I.T. Press, 1981).

3. Nancy Chodorow, *The Reproduction of Mothering: Psychoanalysis and the Sociology of Gender* (Berkeley: University of California Press, 1979), 102, 110, 166–67; and Dorothy Dinnerstein, *The Mermaid and the Minotaur: Sexual Arrangements and Human Malaise* (New York: Harper & Row, 1976). (Further references to these works are included in my text.) See also Philip E. Slater, *The Glory of Hera: Greek Mythology and the Greek Family* (Boston: Beacon, 1968).

but it is also full of mad men who pass as sane and occupy positions from which they perpetuate collective insanity.[4]

The male characters in *The Golden Notebook* have been stereotyped as losers to whom Anna and Molly are drawn because of their inadequacies,[5] or as "fictitiously whole beings" whom Anna creates to compensate for her own fear of chaos.[6] Not much is known about the men, according to one critic, who calls the novel "too exclusively a woman's world," but what we do know suggests that they are more in control, in a better position to combat despair, than the women.[7] Another critic describes them as "healthier than women" for being "active, creative, immersed in and energised by their value-giving work."[8] Whereas *The Golden Notebook* has been acclaimed for its portrayal of "women in our time" (579),[9] typically the male characters have been either ignored or oversimplified—though there is, for that matter, little agreement about the novel's view of women. Some critics place Lessing in the tradition of "feminine sensibility" for her depiction of woman as the center and source of value in the modern world;[10] others discern in

4. Elayne Antlar Rapping's description of the *Four Gated City* applies also to *The Golden Notebook*: whereas women retreat into private worlds of madness in a process that is therapeutic, men "transform their fantasies into concrete public projects for which they are rewarded" and become perpetuators of "madness, perversion, and violence" on a collective level (" 'Unfree Women': Feminism in Doris Lessing's Novels," *Women's Studies*, 3 [1975], 38).

5. Frederick R. Karl, "Doris Lessing in the Sixties: The New Anatomy of Melancholy," *Contemporary Literature*, 13 (1972), 18–19. Elaine Showalter, *A Literature of Their Own: British Women Novelists from Brontë to Lessing* (London: Virago, 1978), also calls the man "deficient in the ability to love" (308).

6. Dagmar Barnouw, "Disorderly Company: From *The Golden Notebook* to *The Four-Gated City*," in *Doris Lessing: Critical Studies*, ed. Annis Pratt and L. S. Dembo (Madison: University of Wisconsin Press, 1974), 78.

7. Barnouw, "Disorderly Company," 77–78.

8. Alice Bradley Markos, "The Pathology of Feminine Failure in the Fiction of Doris Lessing," *Critique: Studies in Modern Fiction*, 16 (1974), 92, 89–90.

9. Ellen W. Brooks, "The Image of Women in Lessing's *The Golden Notebook*," *Critique: Studies in Modern Fiction*, 11 (1973), describes Lessing's depiction of woman as "the most thorough and accurate of any in literature" (101). Rapping calls the novel "a nearly pure expression of feminine consciousness . . . a fictional world which honestly reflects the truths of feminine experience" (" 'Unfree Women,' " 30). Lynn Sukenick, "Feeling and Reason in Doris Lessing's Fiction," in *Doris Lessing*, ed. Pratt and Dembo, calls it "an anatomy of woman's independence and the impediments to it" (107).

10. See Brooks, "Image of Women," 104, 106. Rapping describes women in *The Golden Notebook* and *The Four-Gated City* as "the receptacles of all the psychic and emotional tennsion which the male world creates but will not acknowledge or deal with" (" 'Unfree Women,' " 39).

her novels "an aversion to the feminine sensibility" for their association of woman with "masculine" strengths of rationality and control;[11] still others see her female characters as the most badly mangled victims of the contemporary world, "almost humans *manqué*."[12] Margaret Drabble hails the novel as "a document in the history of liberation."[13] whereas Elaine Showalter feels that "Lessing has not yet confronted the essential feminist implications of her own writing [and] is alienated 'from the authentic female perspective.' "[14] The question is further complicated by Lessing's qualification of her feminism—her insistence, in the Introduction to the 1971 edition, that the novel is "not a trumpet for Women's Liberation" or "a tract about the sex war" (ix–x)—and by her development, in subsequent novels, of what she calls "less personal" interests.[15]

But a work that is so fundamentally concerned with "relationship"— with, in Lessing's words, "look[ing] at things as a whole and in relation to each other" (Introduction, xiv)—impels us to view the men in relation to the women and to see both as part of the social milieu that shapes them. Lessing is concerned here, as in *The Children of Violence*, with "the individual conscience in its relations with the collective."[16] "The personal [is] general," she writes in the Introduction (xiii), and she demonstrates that men's behavior is, as surely as women's, a crippling adjustment to an intolerable world. Michael defines himself as " 'a man who is the history of Europe' " (332); Anna imagines Saul saying, " 'I am what I am because the United States is such and such politically. I am the United States' " (579); she calls him " 'a profoundly political man,' " " 'large enough to include all sorts off things, politics, literature and art' " (591, 598); and to Milt's offer to " 'go into the sociological reasons' " for his behavior, she replies that she " 'already knows them' " (661). She understands also women's tendency to privatize guilt, observing, " 'This country's full of women

---

11. Showalter, *Literature of Their Own*, 309. Sukenick "Feeling and Reason," claims that Lessing deliberately dissociates women from traditional qualities of emotion and sensibility, seeing them as a trap.

12. Markos, "Pathology of Feminine Failure," 88.

13. Quoted in Showalter, *Literature of Their Own*, 311.

14. Showalter, *Literature of Their Own* (311), agrees with Ellen Morgan and quotes her "Alienation of the Woman Writer in *The Golden Notebook*," in *Doris Lessing*, ed. Pratt and Dembo, 63.

15. Jonah Raskin, "Doris Lessing at Stony Brook: An Interview," *New American Review*, 8 (New York: New American Library, 1970), 173.

16. "The Small Personal Voice," in *Declaration*, ed. Tom Maschler (London: MacGibbon & Kee, 1957), 25.

going mad all by themselves,' " all certain that " 'there must be some-thing wrong with me' " (167). The problem faced by both sexes in Lessing's novels is less what Paul calls " 'the revolution . . . of women against men' " (213) than it is the survival of the whole, feeling person in a world where "pain is our deepest reality" (350) and "the truth for our time [is] war" (591). But Lessing's insistence on "relationship"—of the personal to the political, of the individual to the collective—makes her "feminist" in the broadest sense, in the sense defined by Adrienne Rich, as concerned with "a profound transformation of world society and of human relationships" (which Rich distinguishes from "tokenism," "includ[ing] more women in existing social structures.")[17] I would also argue that—contrary to Showalter's assertion[18]—Lessing is in what Showalter calls the "female tradition" for her portrayal of woman as "tougher, kinder." Those strengths that allow Anna to sur-vive, especially the relatedness to the world which enables her to participate in others' sufferings and to extend the limits of her own being, are qualities that are traditionally attributed to woman—and that have been recently analyzed by feminist psychoanalysts.

II

Exhausted, numbed, on the verge of "cracking up," Anna is in a state of dissociation and fragmentation that is a "normal" response to a "dying society" where people limit emotion "because at the end of every emotion are property, money, power" (545); where " 'every time you open a door, there's someone there in pieces' " (658). People's lives are fragmented in numerous ways: by the diversity of roles—personal, sexual, social, professional—required in a complex society; by class (187); by work—"Everyone works reluctantly . . . or with a divided mind" (220).[19] Anna's character, Ella, who is a split-off part

17. Adrienne Rich, "Disloyal to Civilization: Feminism, Racism, Gynephobia," in *On Lies, Secrets, and Silence: Selected Prose, 1966–1978* (New York: Norton, 1979), 279. This sense of "relationship" is a legacy of Lessing's Marxism, which may be difficult—as Pratt cautions—for critics coming from the formalism of the fifties to grasp (Introduction, *Doris Lessing*, ed. Pratt and Dembo, xviii).

18. See my notes 11 and 14.

19. According to Roberta Rubenstein, "cracking up . . . is, paradoxically, the major unifying thread of the novel" (*The Novelistic Vision of Doris Lessing* [Urbana: Uni-versity of Illinois Press, 1979], 73).

of her author, observes of the houses on Paul's block "that probably they were all . . . in fragments, not one of them a whole, reflecting a whole life, a whole human being; or, for that matter, a whole family" (222). Anna's search for coherence leads her to the Communist party, but she finds there only other sorts of contradictions (161); and when she confesses to Jack the day she leaves the party, "My mind is a mass of totally contradictory attitudes about everything" (358), she is advised to accept her condition as an inevitable response to a specialized society. Most people find refuge from such confusions by fitting themselves to the prescribed limits of conventional "forms" or institutions, which means that they "block off at this stage or that" (469). What passes for "normality" is, in R. D. Laing's terms, "adaptation . . . to a world gone mad," "repression, denial, splitting."[20] Significantly, Michael/Paul, Anna/Ella's lover, is a Laingian psychiatrist, the ' "sort of doctor who sees his patients as symptoms of a world sickness' " (212); and though the Jungian Mrs. Marks opens Anna to feeling, this process leaves her "in pieces," still faced with "the burden of recreating order out of the chaos my life had become" (619).

Anna makes various attempts to find refuge in conventional "forms," in love, work, and political activity, but is thwarted by forces that are partly internal and partly external: by her own honesty, on the one hand, and by historical circumstances that have destroyed once-viable institutions and values, on the other hand.[21] The "form" that has the strongest hold on her is the convention of romantic love—" 'my strongest need—being with one man, love, all that' " (625)—but the roles

20. Laing, *The Politics of Experience and the Bird of Paradise* (Harmondsworth: Penguin, 1970), 55, 23. "Torn, body, mind, and spirit, by inner contradictions, pulled in different directions, Man cut off from his own mind, cut off equally from his own body, a half-crazed creature in a mad world" (46–47). (Further references to this edition are included in my text.) As Marion Vlastos suggests, Lessing shows "a striking similarity to the views of R. D. Laing, not only in her emphasis on madness but also in her very articulation of its value"; both are "social analysts" and "social visionaries, prophets of contemporary culture" ("Doris Lessing and R. D. Laing: Psychopolitics and Prophecy," *PMLA*, 91 [March 1976], 246). *Politics of Experience* was published four years after *The Golden Notebook*; but since Lessing and Laing were friends, the direction of influences is unclear.

21. Mary Cohen, " 'Out of the Chaos a New Kind of Strength': Doris Lessing's *The Golden Notebook*," in *The Authority of Experience: Essays in Feminist Criticism*, ed. Arlyn Diamond and Lee R. Edwards (Amherst: University of Massachusetts Press, 1977), describes "Anna's battle against the forms and institutions which limit or falsify human response" (181). But Anna puts nearly as much effort into fitting herself to such forms as she does into resisting them.

it offers, "the woman in love," mistress, wife, no longer provide justification for a woman's life: "I don't live that kind of life, and I know
few women who do" (314). Stalinism puts an end to her hope of finding
meaning in political ideologies or institutions, and her decision to leave
the party coincides with the end of her affair with Michael, leaving
her undefined and vulnerable in two major areas of her life. She rejects
her earlier fiction, *Frontiers of War*, whose "lying nostalgia" now
strikes her as a "longing for formlessness" (63), but is also dissatisfied
with the conventional novel she is currently attempting ("The Shadow
of the Third") and with her other experiments—at journal, parody,
pastiche. Nor is she satisfied by her system of dividing her writing
into the four notebooks; as Tommy points out, such ordering is only
a surrender to the problem it is intended to deal with: ". . . you despise
people like my father, who limit themselves. But you limit yourself
too . . . you take care to divide yourself up into compartments. If
things are a chaos, then that's what they are" (274–75). Deprived,
finally, even of her definition as mother by Janet's departure, Anna
is stripped of the support of all forms and is forced, in the final episodes,
to confront formlessness.

Her struggle to overcome her "writer's block" is, therefore, no
private, idiosyncratic matter. Nor is it merely an aesthetic problem:
" 'If I saw it in terms of an artistic problem, then it'd be easy' " (41).
It is a personal, aesthetic, *and* political problem, for in order to write
"the only kind of novel which interests" her, Anna feels that she must
encompass "those areas of life [her] way of living, education, sex,
politics, class bar [her] from" and achieve "a new imaginative com-
prehension" of the Chinese peasant and Algerian soldier who seem to
enter her room as she begins to write (61)—who seem to demand,
" 'Why aren't you doing something about us?' " (639). The ideal to
which Anna aspires, which she identifies with humanism as " 'stand[ing]
for the whole person . . . striving to become as conscious and responsible as possible about everything in the universe' " (360), represents
the primary moral imperative of the individual—to achieve wholeness
and feeling in a world given over to pain and destruction. So closely
has Lessing interwoven aesthetic, psychological, social, and political
significances of this novel that "personal" and "aesthetic" problems
are inseparable from the social milieu that shapes them.

Anna's search for literary form is thus the correlative of her efforts
to shape her own life at a time when conventional forms have lost
their meaning. It is only when she can cast off conventional roles in

her life that she can take comparable chances in her fiction—risks that enable the creation of "something new" (61, 472–73, 479). Her search requires her to "break . . . [her] own form, as it were" (466) and to forge a new shape for her life and her art which is a surrender neither to conventional form nor to formlessness. It demands that she remain open to feeling though feeling is pain, that she remain undefined at the risk of chaos, wresting "out of the chaos a new kind of strength" (467).

But this route is not taken by any of the male characters. Fatally involved with a world that does not bear looking into, and indeed well trained not to look into it, men stay sane by limiting and dividing themselves. Thus though they seem to be more in control than the women, they achieve their control by sacrificing a portion of the self. Richard, the male character who is most deeply integrated into his world and who best represents its values, provides the clearest example of this male basis of selfhood; and the opening scene, which pits his values against those of the "free women" in a struggle for the loyalties of his son, makes clear its cost in human terms. Though Anna and Molly are particularly vulnerable at this point—their failures in love, work, and politics leaving them open to a contempt that Richard does not spare—Tommy takes their part against his father's, understanding that they have the advantage by being simply what "they are." Whereas Richard boasts of "preserv[ing] the forms," they pride themselves on not "giving in" (" 'To what?' " Richard asks; " 'If you don't know we can't tell you,' " they reply [253]). Though the "forms" by which Richard defines himself—money, position, power—are those his society accepts as measures of success, his conformity to them means (as Tommy realizes) that he will never be anything other than what he does (36), whereas the "free women's" refusal of the "forms" makes them stronger, open to the possibility of "something new": " 'They could change and be something different' " (36).

Tommy, however, does not have the option that the women do, merely to "be," though he would like to; and he regrets having his mother's character and his father's looks: " 'It should have been the other way around' " (33). Whereas no one worries about what Janet will do—not only because she is younger, but primarily because she is female—everyone, including Tommy, assumes it is necessary for him to find something to do.[22] (Anna's one fear for Janet's future focuses

---

22. In one of her bemused monologues to her infant daughter, Caroline, Martha Quest suggests that women, at least before marriage, are "more free than men" because

on Janet's relation to men, on how she will survive "in a country full of men who are little boys and homosexuals and half-homosexuals" [404]). Finding his "divided mind" (264) unbearable, Tommy literally kills off a part of himself, and his suicide attempt leaves him "all in one piece for the first time" (378). His resolution, though extreme, is representative of the way taken by most men in the novel; most have performed "leucotomies" on themselves which leave them diminished but unaware of their limitations—a principle that is caricatured in the American brain surgeon, Cy Maitland, who boasts of " 'cut[ting] literally hundreds of brains in half " (328). Professionally adult, sexually adolescent, emotionally infantile, Cy Maitland demonstrates the divisions Anna encounters repeatedly in men which cause her to wonder that "in their emotional life all these intelligent men use a level so much lower than anything they use for work, that they might be different creatures" (457).

The male characters take to extremes of frozenness or schizophrenic division the numbness and fragmentation that Anna fears in herself. They live either permanently blocked off from one portion of the self or shifting erratically from one side to the other. Those who are fixed in one attitude are Richard, Cy Maitland, the Americans whom Anna calls "measured, shrewd, and cool" (544); the Canadian script writer, "frozen," with a "cool and masklike attitude as a lover" (461). The more complex men—Michael/Paul, Nelson, Saul Green—fluctuate wildly between bully and child, child and adult, between the mature, feeling self and the impotent or cruel. None can "connect"; none challenges the divisions that hedge in their lives; in fact, they actively seek them, in flight from themselves. But this limitation of the whole, feeling self, this "locking of feeling . . . refusal to fit conflicting things together to make a whole . . . means one can neither change nor destroy; . . . means ultimately either death or impoverishment of the individual" (65). Anna understands the connection between repression and "cool," that "people everywhere are trying not to feel. Cool, cool, cool, that's the word. . . . In a world as terrible as this, limit emotion" (545). Since male identity is—according to Chodorow—based on sep-

"men *have* to do something, but you'll find when you grow up . . . that your will will be your limit. Anything'll be possible" (*A Proper Marriage* [New York: New American Library, 1970], 205). As Tolson suggests, so crucial is professional status to a man's identity that not working attacks his sense of self-worth in a way that affects all aspects of his being (*Limits of Masculinity*, 56); and even men who consciously decide not to work cannot escape the competition that is the concomitant of professional ambition.

aration from the female, "Men . . . suppress relational capacities and repress relational needs."[23] In order to ensure the separation from the feminine which is the basis of male identity—Chodorow explains— the male cultivates a contempt for "the feminine," a contempt that "serves to free him not only from his mother but also from the femininity within himself . . . [which] becomes entangled with the issue of masculinity and is generalized to all women" (182). Such repression also prepares men to participate in the "world of alienated work" (207): "the same repressions, denials of affect and attachment, rejection of the world of women and things feminine . . . that create a psychology of masculine superiority also condition men for participation in the capitalist work world" (186).[24]

The divisions that hedge in men's lives determine their views of and relationships with women. Divided in themselves, they are divided from others. Incapable of wholeness, they are incapable of seeing others whole, and so reduce women to stereotypes that deprive them of humanity: " 'Even the best of [men] have the old idea of good and bad women' " (458). Unwilling to risk freedom in the most basic sense, every man in the novel with the exception of Saul holds to the security of marriage from which to experiment: " 'What's the use of us being free if they aren't?' " Julia complains (458). Anna realizes that the misogyny of homosexuals, the mockery that is their defense against women, is only an extreme version of the barriers heterosexual men place between themselves and women; is "nothing more than the polite over-gallantry of a 'real' man, the 'normal' man who intends to set bounds on his relationship with a woman, consciously or not. . . . It was the same cold, evasive emotion, taken a step further" (393).

Richard's views and requirements of women are characteristic. He blames the failures of his marriages on his wives, seeing Molly and Marion as " 'both rather stupid, and their characters . . . disastrous' " (383). He remains faithful to Marion " 'just as long as most men are,

---

23. Chodorow, *Reproduction of Mothering*, 207. See also Ingrid Bengis, *Combat in the Erogenous Zone* (London: Wildwood House, 1973), 41–44, and Shulamith Firestone, *The Dialectic of Sex: The Case for Feminist Revolution* (New York: Bantam, 1972), 135–37. Goldberg discusses "cool" as an attribute of "the male hero image" (*Hazards of Being Male*, 42) and suggests that "the male . . . has been heavily socialized to repress and deny almost the total range of his emotions and human needs in order that he can perform in the acceptable 'masculine' way" (44).

24. Tolson notes that "highly developed divisions of labor" cost a man's "psychological unity" (*Limits of Masculinity*, 48). Goldberg suggests that "success in the working world is predicated on the repression of self" (*Hazards of Being Male*, 43).

that is, until ... her first baby' " (27), then embarks on a series of affairs with increasingly younger but otherwise interchangeable "nut-brown maids." Marion realizes that he never loved her, only a type; and her understanding, " 'it's got nothing to do with me' " (399) is the same as that shared by Anna and Nelson's wife—"well, it's got nothing to do with either of us, not really" (493). Richard defends his infidelities on the grounds of a " 'problem you [women] haven't got—it's a purely physical one. How to get an erection with a woman you've been married to for fifteen years' "; to which Anna retorts, " 'At least we've got more sense than to use words like physical and emotional as if they didn't connect' " (31). Whereas men's sexual pleasure seems to depend on a division of the physical from the emotional, women are unable to "have an orgasm unless [they] love [the man]" (458). Though again, what seems a disadvantage on one level turns out to be an advantage on another, since woman's inability to divide sex from love is a kind of integrity—"integrity is the orgasm" (325)—and integrity, as the root of the word suggests, is related to integration.

Dorothy Dinnerstein explains this difference between female and male abilities "to integrate or separate sensuality and sentiment" (71) as male defense against union with the female—union that threatens fusion or dissolution. Since woman has more chance of embodying the powerful mother within herself, she is less vulnerable, "less afraid of being plunged back into the atmosphere of helpless infancy, and there-fore typically better able to fuse intense emotional and intense physical intimacy" (67); but men must "keep heterosexual love superficial ... or dissociate its physical from its emotional possibilities" (66). Men protect themselves against the threat of engulfment by dividing "an-gry, predatory" impulses from "the protective, trusting side ... [they] keep tender and sensual love separate by expressing them toward different women, or toward the same women in different situations or moods" (70).[25] Very few can afford real sensuality or affection; they relate to women according to a standard of "sexual achievement" that makes themselves into "performance objects" and women into "sex objects," turning relationships into power struggles in which (as War-

25. See also Carol Gilligan, *In a Different Voice: Psychological Theory and Women's Development* (Cambridge: Harvard University Press, 1982): "Men and women may perceive danger in different social situations and construe danger in different ways—men seeing danger more often in close personal affiliation than in achievement and construing danger to arise from intimacy, women perceiving danger in impersonal achievement situations" (42).

ren Farrell suggests) "after the challenge has worn off, after the object has been conquered ... the possibility of impotence sets in."[26]

The particular kind of division that fragments a man's consciousness determines which of the available stereotypes he fits woman to. Those who are frozen into one portion of themselves are set in their attitudes toward women and fix them in categories of dominated or dominator. The worst, like Richard, Monsieur Brun, and the men who rush over to seduce Anna and Molly whenever their wives leave town, are frozen into predatory postures that reduce women to prey. Others are fixed in childish postures that make the woman the mother and turn the "typical" English marriage, such as Jimmy's or Jack's, into a sexless companionship. Those with whom Anna becomes most deeply involved—Michael, Nelson, Saul—are torn by divisions in themselves: shifting from dominated to dominator, they view women accordingly, either reducing them to objects of exploitation or clinging to them as protectors and then railing against them as "the voice of society" (630). The male characters in the final episodes demonstrate an aversion to sexuality which is increasingly compulsive: Nelson is crippled sexually; Saul cannot stay with a woman who loves him; and Milt, who is unable to sleep with a women who loves him or to love a woman with whom he has slept, logically concludes the pattern, in his separation of love from sex to the destruction of both. Though Anna assumes the existence of "real" men, if by "real" she means the qualities to which she herself aspires—"becoming as conscious and responsible as possible about everything in the universe"—no such man appears in the novel.

Women cooperate in this shirking of selfhood, consenting to relationships that diminish them. Anna and Molly admit that their real loyalties are to men and try repeatedly to fit themselves to conventional patterns rather than striking out to create new forms of relationships. Anna responds to "the rake" in Saul Green, to "the cool sardonic stare" (557); and, understanding that "'no one does anything to me. I do it to myself'" (622), she is skeptical of "the new note women strike, the note of being betrayed ... a solemn, self-pitying organ note" (596). But this very clarity is double-edged, keeping the women honest but also undermining their self-respect. Their failure to provide "models" of female strength and independence has disappointed some

26. Farrell, *Liberated Man*, 174, 54. Goldberg describes the connection between "performance fears, achievement fears, and competitive fears" and "male potency problems" (*Hazards of Being Male*, 74).

feminist critics; but Lessing's portrayal of woman is making another point, that woman's complicity in her oppression is at least partly responsible for its continuance.[27]

The role that provides Anna/Ella with the most lasting and effective opiate is that of Michael/Paul's mistress. Through her character Ella, Anna explores the role of "woman in love," a role that requires the suppression of her critical faculty and evokes what she calls her " 'negative' self" (208)—submissive and placating (484). Though Ella's initial reponses to Paul are bristling with criticism—of his guardedness, his predatory qualities—this awareness is "put to sleep" by her love; her happiness with him depends on a suppression of the "knowing, doubting, sophisticated Ella" (211) which creates a division in her corresponding to the division in him. His split is so pronounced that Ella senses two selves in Paul: "Paul with me is using his 'positive' self," but he has also a "negative" self "stand[ing] in the wings of his personality . . . waiting to return"—a "compulsive, self-hating womaniser" (208), "a self-hating rake . . . casual, heartless" (207), which she must ignore in loving him. This realization about him makes her understand her own dual potential—"that I am using with him my 'negative' self" (208).

Michael's ambivalence expresses itself in sudden withdrawals, to which Anna responds with shifts of her own:

> We are happy together most of the time, then suddenly I have feelings of hatred and resentment for him. But always for the same reasons: when he makes some crack about the fact I have written a book—he resents it, makes fun of my being "an authoress"; when he is ironical about Janet, that I put being a mother before loving him; and when he warns me he does not intend to marry me. He always makes this warning after he has said he loves me and that I am the most important thing in his life. [237]

That such attacks occur just when he has admitted his love and that they are directed at her strengths indicate that they stem from his fear of her and of closeness. Paul's response to the publication of Ella's

27. Simone de Beauvoir begins *The Second Sex* with the observation "Along with the ethical urge of each individual to affirm his subjective existence, there is also the temptation to forgo liberty and become a thing . . . [to] avoid the strain involved in undertaking an authentic existence. When man makes of woman the 'Other' he may, then, expect her to manifest deep-seated tendencies toward complicity" (trans. and ed. H. M. Parshley [New York: Random House, 1972], xii, xxiv).

novel—" 'Well, we men might just as well withdraw from life' " (213)—
is an admission of fear. Afraid to bring all of himself into one person
or to give all of himself to one person, he needs to compartmentalize—
needs "the smart, gay, sexy mistress" who is "the other side of the
sober respectable little wife" (223), keeping the one in the city, the
other in the suburbs. Similarly, his dismissal of Ella by means of the
humiliating epithet intended to get back to her through office gossip
reveals his ugly conventionality and reduces her to a series of stereotypes—the loose woman ("a pretty flighty piece"), the aging woman
("not so young . . . actually"), the desperate woman ("pestering him
to marry her" [225]).

Catapulted out of this relationship against her will, Ella, "in pieces,"
realizes that she has never been "free": "I was sheltering under him.
I was no better than that frightened woman, his wife . . . [who] kept
Paul by never asking questions" (313). She admits that her interest in
art, politics, philosophy—even her writing—was nothing compared to
her happiness with Paul. And in fact Anna has given up her writing
to keep Michael, because their relationship has cost her the active,
creative self, the "shadow" she has projected onto "the third"—"good
. . . grown-up and strong and unasking" (208)—and has evoked a "negative self," which she will need to shed in order to write again. Her
acceptance of this relationship and her response to its ending are
measures of her distance from the "freedom" that she now associates
with the name she gave up in marriage—" 'I want to walk off by
myself, Anna Freeman' " (471)—and that she recognizes as her goal.

III

Subsequent sexual experiences jolt her out of the passive, unthink-
ing stance she assumed with Michael into more active, creative ways
of relating which do not fall within the rubric of romantic love, or
indeed of any conventional form. That these relationships are her
vehicle for wholeness and health is in some sense paradoxical, since
the men become more divided and destructive. Their cruelty is a
function of testing, experimenting—a means of discovering "limits" in
a time of transition when concepts of gender are in process of redef-
inition. Anna's education does not follow the customary route of women
in fiction, self-discovery through discovery of a good man; nor does it

lead to either of the traditional conclusions, marriage or death. Rather, it takes her on a radically new and uncharted route, through the "emotional no man's land" (457) encountered in the men after Michael—Nelson, de Silva, Saul Green—which, in almost direct proportion to their destructiveness, releases the strong, positive potential in her that she had sought in a "real" man. This is the significance of the dream of the dwarf, which she names "joy in malice, joy in a destructive impulse" (477), and which evolves through various male incarnations to rest finally in her. Healed by immersing herself in their sickness, accepting it in herself, she changes from victim to active participant in her life.

Anna's descriptions of woman's sexuality as being "contained," "created" by the man's (445, 215) have been cited as evidence of Lessing's reactionary attitudes. But critics who take these statements out of context to represent Lessing's opinion have confused the author with her protagonist.[28] In fact Lessing shows Anna as needing to outgrow this cherished notion of herself, since the correlative of being Michael's "creation" is the suppression of her own creative self. Anna's sense of other possibilities begins as she learns, with Cy Maitland, that she can "do the directing" (323); with the Canadian script writer she also "gives pleasure," though she resents this new role, criticizing him on the grounds that "the man's desire creates a woman's desire, or should, so I'm right to be critical" (546). Anna does not easily relinquish the claims of the passive self: "Women's emotions are still fitted," as she says, "for a kind of society that no longer exists" (314). But against this clinging to old notions there struggles a new sense of her own powers of creation, as prefigured by the short story sketches concerning the creation of selves in response to relationships (460–61) and by the insight that a man with an "ambiguous uncreated quality" (532) may be more attractive than one who is "formed."

The task faced by Anna and her author is enormous. Having rejected

28. Diana Trilling cites them approvingly as evidence that "the culture in which [The Golden Notebook] was written was more intelligent about women than is our more recent culture. . . . A few years later in the history of sexual politics, Mrs. Lessing would have been ridden out of the Party for that passage" (Times Literary Supplement, October 1978, 1165). Showalter does rather "ride her out" of the movement, citing the discussion of "real" as opposed to clitoral orgasms (215) as evidence that Lessing has not "confronted the essential feminist implications of her own writing" (Literature of Their Own, 311). Neither critic makes any distinction between Lessing and her protagonist.

conventional forms, in life and in art, both must imagine new ways of being and creating. The discovery of new form is simultaneously a personal and an aesthetic problem that involves imagining new ways of relating and creating fictional modes to express them. The first experiments are not very satisfactory. But as Anna moves closer to a "freedom" that consists of changed attitudes toward men and herself, her role in relationships evolves from that of created to creator—to so "creative" a role that we are not always certain which portions of these final episodes are "real." The last part of the novel moves into a mode where dreams figure prominently, prefiguring, recalling, resolving "actual" incidents—a mode that symbolizes Anna's discovery and incorporation of unconscious material as she moves toward integration. The dreams and the breakdown of the notebook divisions raise questions as to what "actually" happens and what is imagined.[29]

Nelson, the blacklisted American writer, is the first human being to find his way into the dream of the dwarf and to be associated with the principle of joy in destruction (497). Anna is initially attracted to him because he seems "grown-up" and sympathetic to her position as a woman. But he turns suddenly loud and hysterical, beating his breast over his part in the party betrayals, "his hysteria . . . a defense against feeling, because it's too terrible" (483). He demonstrates the same sorts of divisions as Michael, between feeling and fear, only they are more extreme, erratic shifts between adult compassion and childish aggression. Bound by pain to a wife who torments him for his failure to write and whom he in turn blames for that failure, he is—psychologically, sexually, professionally—in pieces. In the hysterical exchange between him and his wife (overheard by Anna at their party),

29. The breakdown of notebook divisions prepares for the fusion that occurs in the final section. The political meeting where Anna meets Nelson, for example, is recorded in the blue notebook rather than the red notebook, as it would have been earlier. Both red and black notebooks are taken over by newspaper clippings that were formerly confined to the blue notebook (524–25). In the yellow notebook at about the same time, the names Ella and Anna begin to be used interchangeably. It is not clear whether the short story sketches (531–34) are Anna's or Ella's, or whether they are fictional sketches for the "real" version or for a more fully developed fictional version that is, however, recorded inappropriately in the blue notebook. Anna implies that the sketches uncannily prefigure the Saul Green episode when she says, coming across one of his journal entries, "I had already written it, out of some other knowledge" (472). Such fusion calls into question the "reality" of the entire last portion of the novel: perhaps, as Rubenstein suggests, none of the versions is "true," or all are "true," and Lessing is suggesting that "objectivity is an aesthetic and epistemological convention; there is only the subjective point of view" (*Novelistic Vision*, 74).

both of them state precise understanding of their plight: " 'You need Mom, God help me' "; " 'Yeah, you're my mom ... you make me guilty, I'm always in the wrong with you, I have to be, mom's always right' "; but he adds—sounding like Milt—" 'You've got to stand it. ... Because I need you to stand it' " (491).

Nelson's confusion of woman with mother, his professional failure and self-hate account for his "mortal terror of sex" (484). His fear of sex alternates with bullying; self-denunciation alternates with "hysterical abuse of all women ... 'a woman' ... 'the enemy' " (485). When he proposes marriage to "test his power" on Anna, the experience takes her into a realm of unreality and prompts a dream that is emblematic of male-female relationships in the novel:

> A man and a woman on a roof-top ... They wander aimlessly ... sometimes embracing, almost experimentally as if they are thinking: How does this taste?—then they separate again and aimlessly move about the roof. Then the man goes to the woman and says: I love you. And she says, in terror: What do you mean? He says: I love you. So she embraces him and he moves away, with nervous haste, and she says: Why did you say you loved me? And he says: I wanted to hear how it would sound. And she says: But I love you, I love you—and he goes to the very edge of the roof and stands there, ready to jump—he will jump if she says even once again: I love you. ... Now it was not on a roof-top but in a thin tinted mist or fog. ... She was trying to find him but when she bumped into him, or found him, he nervously moved away from her; looking back at her, then away, and away again. [494]

Their movements suggest testing, tentativeness. Man's withdrawal and willingness to risk death rather than intimacy are abetted by woman's ambivalence; avoidance alternates with attraction, to the final defeat of relationship—"then away, and away again." But Anna is more an accomplice than an unwitting victim in this relationship. She continues with Nelson out of choice, in fact, out of a desire to create—"the need to build a man up," the need women feel "to create men" as they become "fewer and fewer" (484). She senses a "kinship between us ... [in] a certain kind of self-knowledge and despair" (485), expressing this affinity by incorporating him into the dream of the dwarf.

Anna's experience with de Silva brings her to a new nadir, closer to chaos. Insisting on "just sex" (499–500), he is the most predatory of the men she encounters. He makes her feel "cold and detached. Blasted" (501) and takes her to a realm where "it didn't matter" (the phrase that keeps recurring in his conversation): "Again I felt the atmosphere of the dream of the fog—meaningless, the emptiness of emotion" (502). Yet he is also like a child who needs a mother—and the incongruity between his dependence and detachment is grotesque. His "experiment" of picking up a woman and pretending to love her but withdrawing when she responds is a stylized, deliberate version of what the other men do inadvertently. When Anna recognizes in de Silva the human incarnation of the dwarf (503), her initial impulse is to project the principle onto him: "Of course it's him, not me. For men create these things, they create us." But she qualifies this with a new insight: "Remembering how I clung, how I always cling on to this, I felt foolish. Because why should it be true?" (501).

Saul Green is also divided in ways that are familiar—between child and adult, dependent and predator. But he is the most disturbed and disturbing of all the men in the novel: "a creature at the limits of itself" (590), Saul articulates and takes to extremes potentials that are implicit in the others—the guardedness, the terror of intimacy, the shifting among roles and attitudes toward women. His most extraordinary division is between his intelligence and sexuality. Talking to Anna like a "grown-up," he suddenly subjects her to "a cold and almost hostile sexual inspection" (551), assuming a pose that—with hands linked in belt pointing toward genitals—makes him "a caricature of that young American we see in the films—sexy he-man, all balls and strenuous erection" (553). Anna can hardly believe "that this was the same man" (551): "There were two different languages being spoken to me" (553). Nor is this his only division: he seems to be "several different people at once" (574). He admits that he is "making use of" Anna (564, 574), that her professional success threatens his "sexual superiority" (604), and that he enjoys the privileges of living in a sexist society (605). Yet he is also like a child needing a mother, a need that turns to resentment and terror of women and accounts for the pattern "he is repeating . . . over and over again: courting a woman with his intelligence and sympathy, claiming her emotionally: then, when she began to claim in return, running away. And the better a woman was, the sooner he would begin to run" (587–88). Moreover, his consciousness is so fragmented that one side has no memory of the other, indicating, in Judith Kegan Gardiner's term, the function of forgetting "in the service of identity maintenance": "men maintain a coherent sense of themselves by repression."[30]

30. Gardiner, "On Female Identity and Writing by Women," *Critical Inquiry*, (1981), 358, 359.

He courts Anna, claims her, then responds to her claim by running for his "freedom." Anna confronts Saul with "what he most dreads, a woman saying I love you" (534), and he expresses determination not to be "trapped" (598), "corralled" (632), "locked up" (580), "imprisoned" (584). He insists on his right to have other women and makes sure that Anna knows about them.[31] Anna "names" Saul's "mothertrouble": "You've fixed on me for your mother. You have to outwit me all the time, it's important that I should be outwitted. It's important to lie and be believed. Then, when I get hurt, your murderous feelings for me, for the mother, frighten you, so that you have to comfort and soothe me" (581). But Saul has further reasons for his determination to stay "free": "There's no one left who speaks my kind of language. We were the world changers, now they've chucked it all for the wife and kids. So I hate the wife and kids and I'm right to hate them" (624). Like Nelson's friend F., who fears his wife not for herself but for "the obligations to society she represent[s]" (544), Saul resents "the wife and the kids" as "the jailors, the consciences, the voice of society" (630). Saul is the only male in the novel who has not "given in" (552). Blacklisted by Hollywood for his role in the party and by the party for his attitude toward Stalin (560), he has not allowed himself to be limited by conventional forms of political alliance, a regular job, or marriage. But still he is not "free." In fact, his situation represents a reversal of a positive interaction of self and society, for he has neither the support of the "forms" nor the freedom that should come from breaking them: he is trapped in the clichéd attitudes that are their concomitants. Though he has been blacklisted by Hollywood, his sexuality is a Hollywood cliché; though exiled from America, he is "competitive about everything" because "it's a competitive country" (578). Even his nostalgia for his "buddies" is banal: he tells Anna that " 'the only time in my life I've been happy' " was " 'when I was in the gang of idealistic kids on the street corner' " (625); and though Anna mocks this sentimentality—" 'Whenever I meet an American man, I wait for the moment when his face really lights up—it's when he's talking about the group of buddies' " (625)—she sympathizes with the desire

31. His behavior corresponds to the pattern described by Firestone as male defense against the threat of commitment: "balancing [women] against each other so that none of them can get much of him. . . . He may consistently exhibit unpredictable behavior . . . being indefinite . . . offering a variety of excuses . . . for he needs her anxiety as a steady reminder that he is still free" (*Dialectic of Sex*, 136).

for "freedom" that it represents (615).[32] But without the support of any "forms," his personality splinters, and he represents the disintegration Anna fears in herself.

Enacting the various potentials of man as she enacts those of woman, Saul is "the position of men"—"a classic . . . story of our time" (560)— just as Anna is "the position of women in our time" (579). Consulting a psychologist about his sickness, she is assured that "it's all due to the times we live in" (574). But as their relationship brings her closer to chaos, it opens her, paradoxically, to new potentials in herself. "At the limits of" himself, he pushes her to the limits of herself: "Both at the end of their tether. Both cracking up because of a deliberate attempt to transcend their own limits" (467). Anna, who has never been good at playing roles, learns, by responding to his shifts of identity and mood, to play roles and to enter experiences beyond her own consciousness: "We played against each other every man-woman role imaginable. . . . It was like living a hundred lives" (603–04). Anna becomes "part of him" (587), takes on his self, in a process ironically reminiscent of the merging of identities associated with romantic love. Entering other selves and allowing other selves to enter her, she draws on her capacity for relatedness, for "oneness with everything" (561), which she has developed playing "the game"—so that her very "boundary confusion" becomes her salvation.[33]

"Breaking down" into each other, Anna and Saul "break through" in the sort of destructive-creative process described by Laing, a process that requires that the participants be "equals" and be equally involved with one another (unlike the hierarchical relationship of traditional therapy), and that accomplishes "the dissolution of the normal ego, that false self complacently adjusted to our alienated social reality" (119). But it is Saul's sickness rather than his strength that Anna partakes of, and, by recognizing it in herself, realizes the complicity of both of them in "the logic of war" (559). Anna's recognition of the

---

32. See Farrell, *Liberated Man*, 90–91; and Goldberg, "The Lost Art of Buddyship," in *Hazards of Being Male*, 126–40.

33. As Rubenstein suggests, Anna's experience resembles that "characterized by William James, Evelyn Underhill, and other commentators as mystical—a mode of awareness in which the perceiver knows himself as identical with what he perceives . . . merging with the All." But this "loss of boundaries of the ego . . . characterizes both mystical vision and insanity. . . . While the positive form . . . approaches the state of transcendental union, the negative form resembles the schizophrenic condition experienced as terrifying dissociation" (*Novelistic Vision*, 95).

destructive principle within unleashes her creative energy and allows her to "dream the dream positively":

> This time there was no disguise anywhere. I was the malicious male-female dwarf figure, the principle of joy in destruction; and Saul was my counterpart, male-female, my brother and my sister, and we were dancing. . . . But in the dream, he and I, or she and I, were friendly, we were not hostile. . . . We came together and kissed . . . it was the caress of two half-human creatures, celebrating destruction. There was a terrible joy in the dream. [594–95]

The destruction that has so terrified her enables the creation of "something new" (472–73, 479, 481), releasing a third "friendly" figure who is whole. In fact, Saul may be a kind of symbolic guide created by Anna from the men she has known and from herself—in Jungian terms, her animus, or male potential, whose release represents integration and the attainment of a "transcendent" whole.[34] Whereas the red and black notebooks broke off into fragments or newspaper clippings of war and destruction, the blue notebook ends with a reintegrative resolution, as she resolves to "put all of [her]self into one notebook" (607).

In the golden notebook, two dream sequences further Anna's movement toward integration and provide perspective on Saul as a potential of her. The first is dreamed as a film controlled by a "projectionist" identified as Saul, who insists that Anna go back and look at scenes from her past presented as a film. In these scenes, Michael and Paul merge to create a composite figure who rephrases Paul's hopeless pronouncement "we are the failures" (219)—for being "boulder pushers"—to "we are not the failures we think we are" (618), thus affirming the value of preserving the humanist values of the past. Though Anna attributes this statement to Michael/Paul and "projects" control to the "projectionist," these dream figures are expressions of herself. The

---

34. Saul's "independent existence as a 'character,' " Rubenstein notes, is "problematic": "he participates in that blurring of the distinctions between 'reality' and 'fiction,' one of the consistent subversions of narrative convention upon which the novel depends" (*Novelistic Vision*, 104–5). Rubenstein (81–82) cites Jung on the release of a "transcendent" self by discovery of the animus or anima: "The recognition of anima or animus gives rise, in a man, to a triad, one third of which is transcendent: the masculine subject, the opposing feminine subject, and the transcendent anima. With a woman the situation is reversed" (Carl Jung, *Aion*, trans. R. F. C. Hull, *The Collected Works*, Bollingen Series XX [New York: Pantheon, 1959], IX, 22).

extent to which Anna and Saul are potentials of one another is seen in the way Saul's novel resolves Anna's worst terror, a terror expressed by her nightmare of the firing squad. In this dream, a dream that "cancelled all creative emotion" (345), two men who are divided by party lines exchange cynical glances and trade places before the firing squad. In the novel Saul writes, of which Anna provides the first line, two men overcome their party alliances by talking to one another, though they are shot for it. That Saul's novel "cancels" Anna's nightmare of negation suggests that he is her creation, and that the person who prevents the disintegration of Anna is Anna, who has learned to use her dreams creatively and her writing therapeutically.

The second sequence is prompted by a confrontation with form-lessness which leads to a new understanding of form:

> But once having been there [in the place ... where words, patterns, order dissolve] there's a terrible irony, a terrible shrug of the shoulders, and it's not a question of fighting it, or disowning it, or of right or wrong, but simply knowing it is there, always. It's a question of bowing to it, so to speak, with a kind of courtesy, as to an ancient enemy. All right, I know you are there, but we have to preserve the forms, don't we? And perhaps the condition of your existing at all is precisely that we preserve the forms, create the patterns. [634]

On this basis, Anna dreams, again, of her life as a film, a film that releases her from her own form and integrates images that were previously separate: "... the film was now beyond my experience, beyond Ella's, beyond the notebooks, because there was a fusion; and instead of seeing separate scenes, people, faces, movements, glances, they were all together" (635).

The Golden Notebook is concerned with Anna's transcending her own form and creating a new form capable of encompassing the experience of the Algerian soldier and Chinese peasant—figures that recur in these dream sequences (596, 600, 635, 639) to symbolize the collective life she feared her art was debarred from. But it also concerns her acceptance of form, the forms that enable one to endure—getting a job, moving into a smaller flat, pulling oneself together for the sake of a child, "the small painful sort of courage" that she comes to realize is "bigger than anything" (635–36). That Anna should derive strength from the "forms" may seem strange when we recall Richard's comic complacency about "preserving the forms" and Anna's own repudiation of them. But the novel has gone a long way about, in its exploration of form, to broaden and redefine the notion: form is accepted within full ironic recognition of the limits of form. It is irony, with its acknowledgment of other perspectives and the incompleteness of each, that makes the difference between those forms that limit and those that allow for the depth and complexity they cannot themselves contain. Irony, not "terrible" but "courteous," emerges as an ideal, a quality "we need very badly in this time," which Anna associates with Tom Mathlong, "the man who performed actions, played roles, that he believed to be necessary for the good of others, even while he preserved an ironic doubt about the results of his actions" (597). Such form is related, finally, to growing up; and, interestingly, Anna ends the destructive cycle with Saul by telling him no, assigning him limits "as [she] would have done to a child" (606), refusing to give him the golden notebook—though she later, when it no longer matters, capitulates.

IV

Neither men nor women are particularly privileged in this world, but whereas we participate in Anna's new strength and wholeness, Saul leaves, still in pieces, in flight from her love, unsure of his way, "not mature yet" (642). Though both pride themselves on not "giving in" (642), it is her achievement we live through, with no sense that he accomplishes anything comparable. "Cracking up," Anna has created "something new": by relinquishing her identity, risking the dissolution that initially terrified her, she has been "changed by the experience of being other people" (602). Anna has "expand[ed] her limits beyond what has been possible" (619) precisely because her "ego boundaries" are not fixed. In a sense she becomes "that mythical woman" (588) she had wished to become, "grown-up ... strong ... unasking" (208), "able to walk off by myself, Anna Freeman" (471): "I realized I was ... creating 'the third'—the woman altogether better than I was. ... I was thinking that quite possibly these marvellous, generous things we walk side by side with in our imaginations could come in existence, simply because we need them, because we imagine them" (637). As Anna lets go of relationships and men that would diminish her, she reclaims parts of herself sacrificed to conventional roles, and her changed sense of herself and of men makes her capable of writing—or of acknowledging the writing she has done all along. However, her nearest male counterpart, Saul, remains locked into "I," "the naked ego" (629), an "I" that sounds through his speech like a gun—and though he too writes a novel that overcomes divisions, it begins with this image of a gun. Besides, Saul's "Free Women" version Milt is in even greater "extremity" (657): "inhabitant of a country of desperation still uncharted by Europe" (654), " 'a feeder on women' " (659), unable to sleep alone or to make love to a woman he cares for. His claim rings true—" 'It's all much worse for us than it is for you' " (662–63)—and his challenge to a self-pitying Anna, " 'How'd you like it, being me?' " (661), is unanswerable.

Anna does not get the "all" that contemporary female protagonists declare is their right. In a sense her failure may be seen as an inability to resolve woman's traditionally irreconcilable conflict between love and her "creative self." But "love" in our culture does not work to the advantage of either men or women: women cling and suppress their intellects; men flee from intimacy and repress their emotions.[35] The situation corroborates Laing's observation that in a world governed by violence, "most personal action must be destructive both of one's own experience and of that of the Other" (29). The state of male-female relationships in this world is summed up in a short despairing exchange between Milt and Anna toward the end: " 'I love my wife . . . that's why I'm divorcing her'; 'Well, a man loved me once. . . . And so he ditched me'; 'Understandable. Love is too difficult. . . . It's the times we live in' " (656–57). Anna and Saul do forge a new kind of relationship, as of brother and sister—" 'We're a team, we're the ones who haven't given in, who'll go on fighting' " (642)—though it is not a relationship that can give definition to their lives. Nevertheless, Anna ends with the strength to go forward alone, "a completely new type of woman" (4) "living the kind of life women never lived before" (472).

The novel Anna writes, named for the notebook into which she puts all of herself, emerges from her integration and furthers that integration. As Anna forges new forms for her life, she finds new forms for her fiction and can allow the golden notebook to become part of the

35. This criticism is consistent with Lessing's sense of "romantic" love elsewhere; cf. Martha Quest's sense of romantic love as "illusory," "a mirage" (*A Proper Marriage*, 26), and her refusal to allow the "woman in love" to be reborn in her (*The Four-Gated City* [New York: Bantam, 1970], 301).

complex that is *The Golden Notebook*, a whole—"crude, unfinished, raw, tentative" (236)—with the qualities she admires. The novel includes conventional forms, but, in Lessing's words, "breaks . . . and goes beyond them":[36] each notebook is partial and incomplete in itself, but each gains significance by its relationship with the others. By juxtaposing these forms, Lessing reveals the limits of conventional form and creates a whole that is more than the sum of its parts and extends the boundaries of form. This form is adequate to express a complex, multidimensional reality, even while it suggests the difficulties of such expression and acknowledges all that cannot be expressed. Moreover, the novel involves the reader in an integrative process by requiring her/him to perceive the relationships among the parts, and so makes the reading of the novel an exercise in seeing things whole which is, according to Lessing, the primary moral imperative.

Although it is Anna's distinctively "female" qualities that make her capable of becoming "something new," ultimately Lessing's breadth of vision causes her to lose interest in feminism. In the 1971 introduction to *The Golden Notebook*, she distances herself from the women's movement, "not because there is anything wrong with [its] aims, but because it is already clear that the whole world is being shaken into a new pattern by the cataclysms we are living through [which make] the aims of Women's Liberation. . . look very small and quaint" (xviii–ix). Her novels since *The Golden Notebook* have become, in her own term, "less personal." Her vision has widened to encompass the "global" in *The Four-Gated City* and *The Summer Before the Dark*, and the "cosmic" in *Memoirs of a Survivor* and *Canopus in Argos*— from which perspective "Women's Liberation" looks "small and quaint" indeed. We can see the beginnings of this change in *The Golden Notebook*; but in this one novel Lessing addresses "the position of women in our time" (579) and allows a woman to counter the crippling dependence that is her past and tradition. Though Anna began with the passivity of Lessing's earlier protagonists, who drifted, like Mary Turner and Martha Quest, into destructive relationships, staying in them longer than they should, she becomes, by the end of the novel, "intelligent enough to let [men] go" (" 'You could do worse,' " Milt quips; " 'you could keep them' " [568]). Anna cannot reverse the death

36. Dust jacket of British edition, quote in John L. Carey, "Art and Reality in *The Golden Notebook*," in *Doris Lessing*, ed. Pratt and Dembo, 20.

drift of her society or provide the future with "a different shape" (473), but her affirmations—being a "boulder pusher," "keeping the dream alive" (276)—are more than "personal."[37] But the real affirmation of the novel is the existence of the novel itself—a work that gives shape and coherence to a nightmarish reality and provides "a new way of looking at life" (61). Given the network of forces—psychological, social, political, economic, historic—that enmesh men and women in this world, this accomplishment is considerable.

37. "How can anyone be sane when everyone else is going crazy? . . . Lessing poses this question in *The Golden Notebook* but does not answer it" (Ann Singleton, *The City and the Veld* [Lewisburg, Pa: Bucknell University Press, 1977], 129). According to Rubenstein, Anna's "psychic integration implies a personal synthesis achieved within a fragmented and still chaotic outer reality" (*Novelistic Vision*, 109).

13

Writing As Difference in Violette Leduc's Autobiography *La Bâtarde*

MARTHA NOEL EVANS

Violette Leduc was born in Arras, France, in 1907. The beginning of her life reads like a novel. Her mother, a servant in a great house, was seduced by the master's son and was sent away as soon as her pregnancy became known. Leduc's father gave some financial support to her and her mother, but rarely saw them. Later Leduc's mother made a good marriage and her daughter was educated at a boarding school.

Leduc then moved to Paris, where, during the war, she attempted suicide. Encouraged by a friend, the writer Maurice Sachs, she published her first book, *L'Asphyxie*, in 1946. It was a slim autobiographical work in which she described one short period of her life. In 1948 and in 1955, Leduc published two more books, *L'Affamée* and *Ravages*, in which she again wrote about discrete episodes in her life.

It was not until 1964, with the publication of *La Bâtarde*,[1] that

Reprinted from "La Mythologie de l'écriture dans *La Bâtarde* de Violette Leduc," *Littérature*, no. 46 (May 1982), 82–92, by permission of the publishers, Larousse (Paris).

1. Paris: Gallimard. Published in English under the same title, trans. Derek Coltman (New York: Farrar, Straus & Giroux, 1965). In spite of its popular success, *La Bâtarde* has attracted very little critical comment over the years. One could almost say that it has been ignored. The best and most comprehensive study of Violette Leduc's work is in Jacob Stockinger's unpublished dissertation, "Violette Leduc: The Legitimations of la Bâtarde," University of Wisconsin–Madison, 1979.

Violette Leduc, at age fifty-seven, produced her first autobiographical work that purported to give a complete chronological account of her life. Or almost complete, for *La Bâtarde* ends with the end of the war, on the eve of the publication of her first book, *L'Asphyxie*. This ending with the author's coming to writing recursively structures the book as a kind of artist's novel. Not only is the author of *La Bâtarde* a bastard child, but the book itself is a bastard of another kind: a mongrel genre, a cross between an autobiography and a *Kunstlerroman*. This crossing of genres in *La Bâtarde* highlights one of the main issues presented both in the book and by the book: the relationship of life and writing.

Autobiography provides a kind of limit case for the study of this relationship, because this writing presents itself as a repetition or a reproduction of the author's own life. She lived it once as a living being, now she is "living" it again in writing as an author. The difference between living and writing is thus ideally reduced to the smallest possible interval. The life and the autobiography become a minimal pair. And the difference between living and writing, thus reduced to its minimal aspect, becomes paradoxically glaring; its radicalness emerges.

For unless autobiography is an entirely gratuitous enterprise, which is possible, it seems to be adding something to the author's life that that life would otherwise have lacked: an affirmation, a shape, a meaning. Writing comes after living, then, as its supplement, its supplement of meaning. From this point of view, the difference between living and writing appears to be the difference between presence and absence—presence of life or its absence, presence of meaning or its absence. But it can also be envisioned as an interval of deferring, an interval that, Derrida says, implies some impurity in the original.[2] The interval of deferring between living and writing involves, according to Derrida, both a postponement—of meaning, of shape—and a yielding to the priority of writing.

For Violette Leduc, this interval of difference, as minimal as it may be, at first imposes the sense of radical incompatibilities between her life and her autobiography. The writing seems to cancel out the very validity of the life whose meaning it is to complete. In a significant analogical shift, she expresses this sense of incompatibility and devaluation as a difference in gender. Not surprisingly, she associates

2. Jacques Derrida, *L'Écriture et la différence* (Paris: Seuil, 1967), 366.

biological birth and life with her female gender, while writing becomes a masculine enterprise. Autobiography appears, then, to be a male affair: a paternal supplement to the maternal process of giving birth. The very act of writing by which Leduc asserts her claim to identity simultaneously invalidates an autonomous female mode of definition. Her wish to authorize herself by her writing entails for Leduc the paradoxical and painful necessity of self-repudiation.

Leduc's attempt to come to terms with her autobiographical project carries with it a simultaneous confrontation with sexual difference. She envisions this difference at first as a mythic struggle between warring gods and goddesses. But the coherent identity of both male and female, the "purity" of both genders, is finally revealed as spurious. The difference between male and female, living and writing, is not the contrast between opposite genders, incompatible essences. Nor is it the deference of one to the other. She sees it rather as the infinitesimal interval between repetitions of apparently identical agencies which opens wide the possibility of play, of freedom, of indifference to legitimacy. As Leduc puzzles over the relationship of her life and her writing, she deconstructs the mythology of gender and autobiography, and discovers in a different principle of difference the source of meaning and identity.

The Father

From the very beginninng of her autobiography, Leduc emphasizes the puzzle of identity, which she represents as a conflict of mutually exclusive and gender-oriented explanations: "Here I am, born in a city-hall register at the point of a city employee's pen. No dirtiness, no placenta: writing, a certificate. Who is Violette Leduc?" (19).[3] Does her identity proceed from her birth—the "dirty affair of women"— or is it created by her civil status—the male domain of writing?

Leduc goes on to emphasize the illegitimacy of the female subject and to express a longing for purity, a purity that she associates with Art: "I would have liked to be born a statue; I am a slug buried under my own dung" (19). At the very moment she is claiming to be a repulsive creature, Leduc is nevertheless beginning to mold that slug

---

3. Page references are to the French edition. Translations are my own.

into a statue by writing. She begins to reshape her messy and unjus-
tified female existence in the pure lines of a life history.

Her existence as a female is rendered doubly illegitimate by her
father's refusal to recognize her. While she first experiences this lack
of recognition as a humiliation, she turns that paternal denial to her
advantage. If she can succeed in occupying the empty place of her
procreator, she will simultaneously annul the anguish of her abandonment and become herself the guarantor of her own legitimacy.
Her flaunting of her bastard birth thus becomes a way of reversing
her abandonment and of disinheriting her father in turn. By proclaim-
ing the absence of her father, she preempts his powers of creation.

In order to occupy the father's place, Leduc invents a complex and
ambiguous game in which the sexuality of both men and women is at
once inverted and denied. She plays *"le petit bonhomme,"* the little
man, for Gabriel, the soft and feminine man she eventually marries.
She says: "I did not desire Gabriel, and I didn't want him to desire
me" (125). Her relationship with the writer Maurice Sachs is inscribed
in the same register of muted and blurred sexuality where male heterosexual desire is effaced so that the difference between the sexes
will not be manifest. She describes her feelings for Sachs in a deper-
sonalized mode: "She could not imagine him any other than homosexual. His erect sex would have been for her a masquerade" (383).

By denying the masculinity of men and declaring it a "masquerade,"
she disarms her adversaries, castrates them in order to take their place.
By erasing difference, she becomes free to wield male generative
power. Leduc applies this strategy of denial and castration to her
literary fathers as well. The opening sentence of the book, "My case
is not unique" (19), brashly reverses the prologue of the *Confessions*
of Leduc's autobiographical predecessor, Jean-Jacques Rousseau, for
whom, let it be noted, paternity was such a troublesome problem and
who produced, according to his own claim, not one but five bastard
children.[4]

Literary creation becomes then for Leduc a strategy analogous to
her shoplifting (cf. 178–81). Just as she steals merchandise, she
usurps and steals the creative power of men. But, like her shoplifting—which she describes as a capricious adventure—her theft of
male power, of writing, is in the end not motivated by a desire for

---

4. Jean-Jacques Rousseau, *Les Confessions*, in *Oeuvres complètes*, 3 vols. (Paris:
Gallimard, 1959), I, 5, and 344–46.

gain but serves as the expression of a gratuitous impulse. As Leduc begins to write, she describes herself as a god creating a new world. Imbued with a sense of olympian power and independence, she emphasizes nevertheless the arbitrariness of her will to create: "I wanted a tree, I got a tree. I wanted a house, I got a house. I wanted night, . . . I could have anything. All I had to do was imagine it" (314).

As the vindication of the primacy of the imaginary over the real, this world engendered by the sole will to create is thus purified of any contamination by the contingency of need. By virtue of its very gratuitousness, writing attains that purity which was symbolized at the beginning of the book by the birth certificate registered by an indifferent scribe: "Light with the lightness of Maurice, my pen was weightless. I continued with the insouciance and the easiness of a boat pushed by the wind. Innocence of a beginning" (399). As she undertakes her autobiography (not *La Bâtarde* but *L'Asphyxie*, published in 1946), Leduc plays the role of the creator who created her. But this time, conception will be free of the betrayal and humiliation that accompanied her "real" conception. By taking the place of the male—God, the father, Maurice—she redeems her birth by re-creating it in the form of an activity she performs as an indifferent instrument: she is pushed by the "wind." This writing that is at once *of* and *for* the father obliterates all difference by effacing need. As the author of her autobiography, Leduc deifies herself in a mythology of pure creation: her identity is synonymous with the presence of the Word, which is actualized without desire and thus without deferral or difference.

But Leduc writes with a borrowed pen, and the myth of the full word ends up emptying writing of its own efficacy. Writing is erased by its own tautology; it becomes "superfluous": "the pleasure of forseeing that my grandmother was going to be reborn, that I would give birth to her . . . Writing—that seemed superfluous when I remembered my gentleness with her, her gentleness with me" (400).

The Mother

Writing is made superfluous by Leduc's pleasure in remembering the reciprocity of love between her and her grandmother, the "angel Fidéline," as she habitually calls her. The "wind" pushing Leduc's pen is here seen not as a gratuitous will to create but rather as the pleasure of giving birth. The troubled and complex relationship between Leduc and her mother yields to the memory of the dazzling symbiosis of adoration which enclosed her and her grandmother. Not responsible for the shameful birth of the bastard child, her grandmother, Fidéline, represents a return to a pure maternal origin that founds the pleasure of writing: "You will become my child . . . I carry you in my head. Yes, for you, my loins are a volcano of warmth" (20). The birth of the mythic mother in and by writing recalls the birth of Athena, who emerged pure and intact from Zeus's head; but here, paternal birth is transmuted by the volcanic warmth of love into the maternal loins of the text. Leduc becomes both the mother of her grandmother and the mother of the child she herself was in the past. Putting off the shirt and tie she wore to be Gabriel's "little man," she dons the sky-blue apron of the angel Fidéline to give birth to herself in a life untainted by bastardy.

Leduc seeks this maternal relationship with her readers as well: "Reader, my reader. June 15, 1961. The sun is sweltering, my children. Summer is in a good mood" (300). This gentle voice that speaks to us and calls us her children emanates from a place outside the autobiographical narration. It introduces into the chronological history of the past the geometry of another time and another space that are supposed to exist in the present: "8 o'clock in the morning of June 24, 1962. I've switched places, I am writing in the woods because of the heat" (20). The coordinates of time and date which always accompany the interventions of the author's maternal voice project at their intersection a second being and a second world that are presented as more immediate, more "real" than the beings and the world evoked in the autobiograhical narration.

In this second world, chronology follows the cycles of love, generations are interchangeable, and birth is reproduced as a gift of writing oblivious of itself: "August 22, 1963. The month of August is today, reader, a rosette of heat. I offer it to you, I give it to you" (462). By separating herself from her text and by making herself our mother in the present of her writing and the present of our reading, Leduc creates a maternal writing more authentic than the voice of her history. This authentic maternal writing where author and reader are to meet thus becomes the arena of love, a space where difference—between moments, between generations, between author and reader, between life and writing—does not exist.

The Mask

This extratextual space is, however, part of the texture of the text, and the "reality" of the dates and hours depends finally on the connivance of literary convention. The purity of this mythically real world and the love it gives voice to can be maintained only by its removal from the play of convention. Leduc must therefore subvert the authenticity of her own writing in order to establish it as a game she plays at will. Like a magician who slows down his hands to reveal the secrets of his tricks, Leduc makes the trickery of her writing an object of observation: "It took me two and a half hours to write that, two and a half pages in my cross-ruled notebook ... May 15, 1961, 9:20 in the morning in a village of Vaucluse. I haven't changed; I yield to my desire to juggle vocabulary in order to be noticed. A new combination, that's my number" (315).

For the maternal author who wishes to protect her integrity and to possess her reader-children outside of the text, the enterprise of writing her life becomes a pretext, a "number." The strategy she must use to preserve the purity of her textual birth paradoxically results in a fictionalizing of her writing; it becomes fixed in the false purity of a mask. The illusion of the contingency of the writing object makes composition an artifice where the logic of the lure performs its ambiguous acrobatics:

> Drum rolls that I need when I write ... with you it's the right tone. I too play; I tap dark cream on my Nordic face ... a few taps on the left cheek, a few taps on the right cheek since you're supposed to dab it on before spreading it out, that's the secret of natural makeup, of a perfect makeup. [201]

Instead of being a field of transparency and union, writing hardens into a barrier, a disguise hidden, however, by the naturalness of a "perfect makeup." As a result, the author's truth risks going unnoticed: "I go by unnoticed. It's horrible, it's unacceptable. I am not the center of the world" (203). Caught in the trompe l'oeil of her writing, Leduc is obliged to wish to fool us; she is obliged to imitate the truth in a futile effort to make herself recognized, or misrecognized, as the wearer of a mask. Her autobiography therefore becomes a disguise by means of which she hopes to be identified behind the multiple masks of the past.

Snared in the existential and teleological paradox of her project of writing, Leduc hurls her autobiography at us like a challenge that registers the feigned contrariness of her enterprise. The gesture of the narrator as narrating and narrated becomes a sadomasochistic endeavor in which her will to fool the other so as to be seen is expressed by an emphasis on her own dark baseness—"I tap dark cream on my Nordic face." As a part of her perverse device of travesty, Leduc exhibits, like a terrifying mask, her own ugliness, her frailties, her cruelty, even her crimes. Describing herself as an "ugly young lady without faith, without principles" (72), as a shoplifter and the successful organizer of a black-market operation, she is placed outside the law by her acts as well as by her birth.

This sullied woman of the past is the lure by which Leduc hopes to undo the deceptive historicity of her autobiography. She fixes her identity—but a false one—by fixing the look of the other; by disguising herself, she remains intact—but invisible—behind her mask.

Caught in the anguishing aporia of mask and mimicry, Leduc tries to emerge from this dilemma, to master it through an allegory of costume. Attempting to insert herself in an unequivocal semiotic system, she makes her styles of dress into a kind of sartorial writing where she hopes her identity for herself and for others will coincide. During her liaison with Hermine, Leduc immerses herself in the world of female fashion. Determined to make herself over, she visits the famous hairdresser Antoine and emerges transformed, or perhaps one should say unrecognizable.

The Waltz

In the episode following her visit to Antoine's, the mythology of writing as the gratuitous emanation of a unified self-present male or female deity is dramatically put into question. The godlike prototypes of the writing human subject are reversed in a catastrophic confrontation: their very fullness and self-sufficiency reveal them to be nightmarish figures of death. Their function as givers of life is shown to be nothing more than a myth, that is, an illusion.

Leduc makes a special appeal to the reader to accompany her in this initiatory pilgrimage through the trials of despair and death. In an unusual gesture of supplication, she pleads with the reader to share her descent into the primordial domain of silence: "Reader, follow me. Reader, I fall at your feet so that you will follow me . . . Reader, we will say: we stepped onto the sidewalk, we jumped, our feet together, into silence. A long, long scarf of raw silk grasped between thumb and forefinger" (216).

The scene, which takes place on the Pont de la Concorde, begins with the infliction of a symbolic wound, an insult shouted at Leduc by an unknown passer-by. The immediate effect of this insult is metaphorically to cut through Leduc's newly acquired costume, to unveil her, to divest her of her protective mask: "My Schiaparelli suit leaves me. My stockings fall down over my heels" (217). But the unveiling proves to be even more profound: the metaphor of verbal abuse is literalized; Leduc feels a blow to her body as well. This painful and hyperbolic wounding reveals to Leduc her body's former function as a protective envelope and mask. In a nightmarish experience of helplessness and mutilation, she feels her body flowing out of itself, becoming exterior to her, taking on a life of its own: "My wounds wounded the sidewalk. I walked inch after inch on the soft flesh of a butchery" (217). The arbitrary autonomy of her body is represented by a sensation of uncontrollable growth: her nose—which she detests and which has become the symbol of her ugliness—seems to grow until it becomes a huge appendage, a trunk sweeping over the sidewalk of the bridge.

The sensation of no longer being one with her body, of no longer controlling it, is repeated on the level of language as well. Leduc's sense of linguistic helplessness is expressed by the metaphor of infancy. Her protective mask of language deserts her and, unable to speak, to pronounce words, she finds herself gurgling primitive sounds: " 'You open your mouth, but nothing comes out,' said Hermine. 'A E I O U,' I mumbled" (219).

Stripped of the defensive disguises that defined her as a consistent self, Leduc seeks psychological refuge in the mythological paternal and maternal figures with which she identified as writer. But the paternal god-head now takes shape in a bizarre vision: "Calf's head, color of livid flannel, languidly lying on the greenery at the tripeseller's, calf's head, give me your peace, give me the ecstasy of your slashed mouth" (218). As a way of parrying the word-wound of the language of the other, this vision of the animal's head represents, like a primitive and macabre god, the fusion of face and mask in death. The truth underlying the masculine mask of writing is revealed to be violence: as the symbol of the recuperation of self-presence in authentic language, this textual god-head inscribes its smiling wound, that imitation of a mouth, as a writing that dissolves into the silent ecstasy of self-destruction.

The figure of the mythological mother appears next: a voice speaks sweetly and seductively from the *gorge* (throat or breast) of the river. This soothing maternal voice promises to enfold Leduc in love and admiration just as she was wrapped in her grandmother's apron: "I am available and free, enter, come into the water, this throat said to me. I will enter, I will effortlessly make my way down a row of men and women, lovers kneeling in a sign of approval" (220).

The mouth-wound of the god-head here becomes the throat-breast-womb of the angel mother who promises the easy achievement of wholeness, of centrality, by the nourishment of adoration. The river-book reproduces this phantasized apotheosis of the maternal author who, like a new Isis, will bathe in the reflection of the worshiping looks of her readers. But this vision of plenitude is dissolved by its very fullness; the ecstatic fusion of adoring and adored becomes a smothering tyranny that drowns both words and life.

The narrative changes here from the mode of vision and hallucination to a mode of lyric description. The symbolic shifter between these two modes is Leduc's nose; this inescapably ugly object obtrudes, by its irreducible grotesqueness, into the world of the imaginary. The impossibility of integrating this piece of flesh into a mythology of the godlike autonomous subject has the effect of drawing Leduc back into the world of the real.

The narrator turns to Hermine and finds her sprawled on the riverbank weeping, although she does not understand the cause of her companion's misery. Leduc's desperation expressed in and through her lover's tears turns this despair into an act of generosity. The self-reflexive gift of life and love that Leduc sought to generate and embody in her writing comes to her unexpectedly from the outside—like the insult—at the moment she has become empty and thus able to receive it. An abundance of wretchedness unites the two women; their despair becomes a dance:

> We cried entwined together, we turned in place, we turned on the deserted riverbank, Hermine's snot flowed down my cheek, my snot flowed down hers. Cried also with us the wind, the sky, the night. Charity of sex. Our ovaries and clitorises melted. She licked my snot, I licked hers. "*Mon petit, ma petite.*" We turned, we cried, she called me, I called her "*mon petit, ma petite,*" to infinity. Tell me what that woman said to you. That woman said, If I had a mug like that, I'd kill myself. Let's waltz, my love. Let's waltz, *ma chérie.*" [221]

The word-wound of the other has opened Leduc to the presence of a world outside her that she has not created and that dances with her. Blasting the myth of self as plenitude and as origin of speech, the gratuitous insult strikes Leduc like a redemptive coup de grace. The project of legitimizing and possessing herself in a self-defined language and a self-defined gender is revealed finally as illusory.

As we see in the passage just quoted, language no longer functions as a mask or as an instrument of dominance: words are exchanged, like the snot and the tears, as a gift and as an appeal to the other across the indeterminate space that separates two embracing bodies. The different genders—"*mon petit, ma petite*"—are named and exchanged without neutralizing each other. Paradoxically coexisting in the same bodies, gender's dance of difference turns and twirls into infinity.

Placed at the center of the text, this episode becomes a dynamic focus of force which draws the entire structure of the book into its whirling waltz. For the revelations of this episode never determine a linear evolution of recognition and development, and my chronology of presentation has introduced an analytic structure that is not present in *La Bâtarde*. Leduc's recognition of the illusory nature of the mythology of gender and engenderment, while it represents a dialectical endpoint, is at the same time both a logical and emotional beginning, an opening. *La Bâtarde* is not a recursive structure: unlike so many memoirs and autobiographical works, it does not at the end return to its beginning. On the contrary, Leduc ends with the beginning of another book *L'Asphyxie*, while the composition of *La Bâtarde* is at a sixteen-year remove from its own conclusion.

The structure of *La Bâtarde* reproduces, then, the logical spiral of its own thematics. It is a three-step dance put into motion by the tension of its own paradoxical aspirations. First, the aspiration toward purity and legitimacy embodied in the myth of the undivided male subject who creates a life history justified by its very gratuitousness, a history that is the certification in writing of a birth. Another aspiration toward the realization of an unending and unlimited love of herself as female embodied in the myth of the pure and generous mother-author whose movement of parthenogenesis is inscribed in a text at once necessary and superfluous.

In both of these projects, Leduc's life and the text of her autobiography blend. The mystery of birth and the mystery of meaning blur, as they traditionally have, producing a mythological figure who is the autonomous origin of both Life and the Word. In writing her autobiography,

316

in recreating these myths, Leduc attempts to be the source of sources, the origin of origins.

These projects of self-reflexiveness, of plenitude and self-justification, are persistently transected, however, by the shadow of an unassimilable reality—represented variously in the text by her nose, by her aborted child, by the word of the other—which prevents Leduc from ever co-inciding with herself as narrator and narrated. It is her recognition of difference—between herself and her own body, between herself and her own language, between herself and her own gender—that opens the space of the textual dance, that creates the field of fiction where this mythical drama can be played out. In this space Leduc can recreate in a dazzling fabric of words, as her lover Isabelle does with her hands, a self that is at once her and beyond her: "She molded the charity we had around our shoulders. Her careful hand traced lines on my lines, curves on my curves. Under my eyelids, I saw the halo of my shoulder reborn, I listened to the light of her caress" (88). Flowing from the cruel grace of vulnerability, Leduc's writing, like Isabelle's caresses, creates another world in the very place of the unseizable real.

La Bâtarde incarnates and celebrates the disquieting, painful, and unpredictable freedom of the illegitimate birth of the subject in the speech of the Other. As Leduc says at the opening of the book, "My case is not unique." Indeed, we are all of us illegitimate; we are all of us bastard children.

Between the real body and the body of desire, between the world and the text, between the end of this book and its beginning, as between the thumb and forefinger of Leduc, shimmers that "long, long scarf of silk" marking the breach that precludes the closing of the circle, excludes the legitimacy of birth, and bars off the wholeness of the subject. At once excrescence and emptiness, excess and lack, generosity and despair, this separation where silence trembles, where a halo shines, is the place of difference, painful and glorious zone of liberty: "Strong with the silence of the pines and chestnut trees, I cross without flinching through sum-mer's burning cathedral. My path of wild grass is grandiose and full of music. It is the fire that solitude places on my mouth" (462). At the closing of her book, Leduc receives, like an apostle at Pentecost, the gift of tongues. Neither father nor mother but the difference that en-genders them, neither presence nor absence but the solitude that founds them, the words of Violette Leduc emerge from the domain of silence to lead us in the dance of her desire to write her life.

14

"Women Together" in Virginia Woolf's *Night and Day*

SHIRLEY NELSON GARNER

Virginia Woolf's *Night and Day* is generally seen as a comic novel, traditional in form and vision.[1] It begins as a story of romantic mismatching and moves toward a "happy" ending in which "true" lovers are paired in marriage. But Woolf's novel is marked by ambiguity. Since Woolf created her art within a cultural milieu even more bent than our own on fostering what Adrienne Rich has called "compulsory heterosexuality,"[2] she moved toward the harmonious heterosexual coupling of her characters. Yet she emphasized the tenuousness of the bonds between women and men and presented the heterosexual alliance as painful in its rupturing of women's bonds with each other. Woolf's novel encodes a perception that many psychoanalysts and feminists have come to share: that women, because they have been mothered by women in infancy, retain primary emotional bonds with

---

1. See, for example, Herbert Marder, *Feminism and Art: A Study of Virginia Woolf* (Chicago: University of Chicago Press, 1968), 21–22. More recently, in "Enchanted Organs, Magic Bells: *Night and Day* as Comic Opera," in *Virginia Woolf: Revaluation and Continuity*, ed. Ralph Freedman (Berkeley: University of California Press, 1980), 97–122, Jane Marcus compares the novel with *The Magic Flute* and views it as comic opera. Finding the conflicts that accompany the approach to marriage a dramatization of "the struggle against the fears of death," she sees in *Night and Day* "as brave and affirmative an act as marriage itself was in Virginia Woolf's eyes" (121).

2. "Compulsory Heterosexuality and Lesbian Existence," *Signs*, 5 (1980), 631–60.

each other even though their adult sexual orientation may be toward men.[3] The significant story of *Night and Day* is the one told indirectly: a tale of "women together."[4] Woolf's first version of "Chloe liked Olivia," the story denied is the one most deeply felt.[5]

Woolf's novel is set against a tradition of romantic love fictions in which women are generally idealized, unattainable, and alone. The pattern is prevalent in various genres and cuts across time; we find it in works that make claims upon us as great art as well as those that are merely popular. We see it, for example, in Chaucer's *Troilus and Criseyde*, Shakespeare's *Romeo and Juliet*, Fitzgerald's *Great Gatsby*, Barth's *End of the Road*, and Erich Segal's *Love Story*. As Denis de Rougemont describes it, its quintessential story is that of Tristan and Iseult.[6] Male authors established the tradition and follow it more often than female authors, though the latter occasionally work within it.

Love, as presented in this tradition, is exciting, painful, and wholly involving because it is fixed on the possession of a fantasy, a consummation promising ecstasy akin to that of a mystic vision. The character that must embody this burdensome fantasy can bear little resemblance to a living woman, who would be much too ordinary to command the lover's complete absorption, the intensity of his passion. If the beloved were ever attained, her lover could not sustain his idealization or, consequently, his exuberant love. Therefore, she tends to be out of reach. If the lover does win her, she immediately dies or deserts. The psychological underpinnings of this oft-told story are to be found in the desires and fears of the male psyche. The tale reflects the desire for union with an idealized and nurturing mother and at the same time the fear of engulfment by her.[7]

---

3. Nancy Chodorow, *The Reproduction of Mothering: Psychoanalysis and the Sociology of Gender* (Berkeley: University of California Press, 1978), 138–40.

4. Virginia Woolf, *Night and Day* (New York: Harcourt, Brace, 1948), 101. Subsequent quotations from *Night and Day* are from this edition.

5. In *A Room of One's Own* (New York: Harcourt, Brace, 1929), Woolf writes that she was struck by the sentence "Chloe liked Olivia" when she supposedly encountered it in the first novel of a fictitious author, Mary Carmichael. She used the statement to initiate a discussion of the limited vision of women traditionally presented in literature. Generally they are "not only seen by only the other sex, but seen only in relation to the other sex," at least until Jane Austen's time (85–89).

6. Denis de Rougemont, *Love in the Western World* (1956; rpt. New York: Harper & Row, 1974), 15–55.

7. See Murray Schwartz's analysis of *The Winter's Tale*, in which he argues that Leontes' fear of and desire for union with an idealized mother are at the root of his

The beloved in the stories of this tradition never has a woman friend who is her equal. Besides her lover, her only companion is usually her lover's male friend, who is often a voyeur, like Pandarus, or a hanger-on at the edges of life, like Nick Carraway, or her maid, who becomes her confidante and counselor. The author need not flesh out the beloved's life, for however vivid a Criseyde or a Daisy Buchanan may remain in our memories, she is often peripheral to the story. The beloved has no woman friend because the author is principally interested in the male lover's passion and suffering and elaborates the experience of the beloved only insofar as it enhances that interest. Another, probably more important, reason for her isolation is that any effort to imagine friendships between women who are peers and to create convincing dialogue and action between them would destroy the notion of romantic love that thrives on an idealized and unattainable woman.

In *Night and Day*, Virginia Woolf illustrates how friendship between women may subvert the romantic tale we have heard so often.[8] Woolf depicts romantic love in the novel, but departs from the conventional treatment of women that I have described. She does so because wom-

jealousy of Hermione and hence the ultimate cause of his efforts to separate himself from her ("Leontes' Jealousy in *The Winter's Tale*," *American Imago*, 30 [1973], 250–73; "*The Winter's Tale*: Loss and Transformation," *American Imago*, 32 [1975], 145–99). In " 'This Is and Is Not Cressida': The Characterization of Cressida," in this volume, Janet Adelman finds the same fear and desire underlying Troilus' fantasies in Shakespeare's *Troilus and Cressida* and argues that Shakespeare shaped the play in a way that suggests that he shared Troilus' fantasies.

8. In "(E)Merging Identities: The Dynamics of Female Friendship in Contemporary Fiction by Women," *Signs*, 6 (1981), 413–35, Elizabeth Abel differentiates between the presentations of female friendships in nineteenth- and twentieth-century fiction. Abel concentrates on twentieth-century novels that pattern friendships between their female characters after "actual friendships of women," which suggest, she asserts, that "identification" rather than "complementarity" is "the psychological mechanism that draws women together" (415). Woolf's portrayal of Katharine and Mary depicts them as feeling strong identifications with each other; but it also conforms in some of its features to what Abel describes as "traditional novelistic use of female friendships." Like nineteenth-century writers of fiction, who fit the portrayal of friendship "into the narrative progression toward the marriage of the heroine(s)" (414 n. 2), Woolf presents the friendship of Mary and Katharine within a framework of Katharine's progression toward marriage. In the vein of major turn-of-the-century American writers, in whose works "the protagonist's relation to her friends is less significant than the rather schematic options these friendships often represent" (414 n. 3), Woolf depicts Mary as representing certain possibilities of life for Katharine. As my discussion of Mary and Katharine's friendship will make clear, however, Woolf's characterization of it resists all of Abel's categories. It is particular.

en's experience and their friendships with each other are central to her vision. From her own life, she knew that women have rich and complicated relationships with each other, and she brought that knowledge to her art. The women in *Night and Day* know, talk to, respect, like, and even love each other. Consequently, their experience of love is different from that of an isolated heroine, and the story of romantic love at the heart of the novel is radically different from that in the mainstream of romantic love fictions.

Woolf's emphasis represents a shift in interest from the male to the female psyche. Her female characters are not merely objects of male desire, and their fantasies and desires do not focus wholly on the men they love. Woolf stresses particularly the primacy of women's bonds with each other and the fragility of their bonds with men. In so doing, she illustrates a view of women's friendships and sexuality that contemporary feminists and psychoanalysts who depart from Freud articulate and give a theoretical basis. Both insist that the cost of achieving heterosexuality is different for women and men. Since a heterosexual man gives his love to a woman, who is of the same sex as his mother, his deepest, most elemental feelings are engaged. On the other hand, a heterosexual woman turns to a man, whose sex is different from her mother's. Freud's early view was that the change of a woman's love object from mother to father was normally achieved in the oedipal phase. But Helene Deutsch argued that the change was never completely accomplished.[9] Following Deutsch, Nancy Chodorow has more recently insisted that "girls cannot and do not 'reject' their mother and women in favor of their father and men, but remain in a bisexual triangle into puberty." They always retain an "internal emotional triangle." Though their father and men may become "primary *erotic* objects ... heterosexual love and emotional commitment are less exclusively established. Men tend to remain *emotionally* secondary."[10] Woolf, however, does not draw a hard line between erotic and emotional attachment; the two are not always separable and are never clearly so.[11] She suggests in *Night and Day*, as she affirms more strongly in *Mrs. Dalloway* later, that love between women may threaten heterosexual love.

9. Helene Deutsch, *Psychology of Women: A Psychoanalytic Interpretation* (New York: Grune & Stratton, 1944), I, 20.

10. Chodorow, *Reproduction of Mothering*, 138–40, 167.

11. In considering female friendship, Abel seems to separate emotional from erotic attachment ("[E]Merging of Identities," 418).

For Woolf to write about sexual attraction and love between women was to confront the sexual ambivalence at the heart of her own life. Though she was committed to her marriage to Leonard Woolf, it had been passionless at the outset and evidently remained so.[12] Her strongest attachments and her greatest emotional responsiveness seem always to have been to women and continued to be so throughout her life.[13] The questions about love posed in *Night and Day* seem to reflect Woolf's uncertainties about her own sexuality as well as about love and marriage. By the time she wrote *Mrs. Dalloway*, she had fallen in love with Vita Sackville-West and was able to depict more clearly and strongly the pull that love between women exerted against heterosexual love and marriage aᵢ ' the costs of denying the former and choosing the latter.

The effect of *Night and Day* is comparable to anamorphosis in painting, which renders a view from an oblique angle, a vision that is often more compelling than the one most obvious. Though the novel works toward a conventional ending in which lovers are paired and marriages are imminent, the most deeply felt relationship is not between the engaged couples, but rather between Mary and Katharine. In a work in which there is a great deal of talk, indeed almost nothing but talk, where vision becomes action in the Jamesian sense, the strength of the two women's friendship strikes us most powerfully as it is presented through their silence.

The main action of the novel involves Katharine Hilbery's and Ralph Denham's recognizing and admitting that they love each other. At its center is the effort to understand the meaning of love. Katharine thinks of her mother and father and asks, "What is love?" "Splendid . . . was the presence of love she dreamt. . . . But waking, she was able to contemplate a perfectly loveless marriage" (107). Brooding over her impending marriage to William Rodney, she decides that she can "satisfy" him as her aunt and mother had satisfied their husbands:

12. For a discussion of Virginia and Leonard Woolf's sexual relationship, see Roger Poole, *The Unknown Virginia Woolf* (Cambridge: Cambridge University Press, 1978), especially 33–53.

13. Phyllis Rose, *Woman of Letters: A Life of Virginia Woolf* (New York: Oxford University Press, 1978), 109–25, 175–93. Rose treats at length Woolf's early friendships with women as well as her passion for Vita Sackville-West. See also Joanne Trautmann, *The Jessamy Brides: The Friendship of Virginia Woolf and V. Sackville-West*, Pennsylvania State University Studies, no. 36 (University Park: Pennsylvania State University, 1973), and Blanche Wiesen Cook, " 'Women Alone Stir My Imagination': Lesbianism and the Cultural Tradition," *Signs*, 4 (1979), 718–39.

"She could pretend to like emeralds when she preferred diamonds" (216). After Mary rejects Ralph, he asks her, "Love—don't we all talk a great deal of nonsense about it? What does one mean?" (253). William is haunted by Katharine's conviction that their marriage would be a "farce" (244, 246) and continually ponders her meaning. Mary says of love to Katharine, "I think you underrate the value of that emotion" (361).

The characters' efforts at understanding are continually baffled. In the first place, they find no patterns of love among the older generation. When old and young attempt to communicate with each other about love and marriage, it is all too apparent how far apart they are and how much cannot or must not be said. Katharine's gossiping and interfering aunt Celia and her rigid, emotionally reticent father actively work against anything that appears to offend convention in the relationships of the young people. Social pressures from without and the internalization of those pressures also exert themselves heavily on William and Katharine to make them keep their initial contract and avoid the truth of their feelings. But most important, the characters' own reserve, need for order, and fear of risk keep them from plunging into the depths of emotion and uncertainty. The difficulty of awareness and the instability of feeling and circumstance also make it hard for any of them to know themselves except fitfully.

Though the novel does not define love explicitly, its meaning is implied. Woolf presents it as a clear, though unstable, feeling that proceeds from the unconscious. At a moment when Katharine and Ralph clearly feel love for each other, Woolf writes, "From the heart of his darkness he spoke this thanksgiving; from a region as far, as hidden, she answered him" (507). We can find "reasons" for Katharine's failing to love William or Ralph's failing to love Mary, but finally, love does not yield to reason. It is or it is not. When one is in love, he or she is enraptured and may be forgetful, brood, or act foolishly. Perhaps most significant, one can let oneself be vulnerable to another.

It is mainly through Mary Datchet and the friendship that springs between her and Katharine that the characters in *Night and Day* work their way out of mismatches, self-deception, and emotional disconnectedness, for which they seem marked at the beginning of the novel. Mary and Katharine are opposites in many respects. The wealthy granddaughter of a famous poet, Katharine does not have a career. She reluctantly lives at home, helping her charming but zany mother write the poet's biography, which, given her mother's work habits, will never be seriously started, much less finished. Ralph admires Katharine for her "charm," "beauty," "character," and "aloofness" (24); Mary sees her as "what one calls a 'personality' " (51). Having beauty and the practical skills to manage a household, she seems perfectly suited to marry well and live conventionally and comfortably, as women of her social class might be expected to do. Her single apparent aberration is her secret passion for mathematics, which "she rose early in the morning or sat up late at night" to work at, hiding her papers in her father's huge Greek dictionary (45).

Though Mary is young and "full of the promise of womanhood" (263), is "well-proportioned" and dresses becomingly (47), her virtues are not beauty and charm:

> She was some twenty-five years of age, but looked older because she earned, or intended to earn, her own living, and had already lost the look of the irresponsible spectator, and taken on that of a private in the army of workers. Her gestures seemed to have a certain purpose, the muscles round eyes and lips were set rather firmly, as though the senses had undergone some discipline, and were held ready for a call on them. She had contracted two faint lines between her eyebrows, not from anxiety but from thought, and it was quite evident that all the feminine instincts of pleasing, soothing, and charming were crossed by others in no way peculiar to her sex. For the rest she was brown-eyed, a little clumsy in movement, and suggested country birth and a descent from respectable hard-working ancestors, who had been men of faith and integrity rather than doubters or fanatics. [48]

The daughter of a clergyman, Mary has left her family to live alone in London to work for women's suffrage. Seeing Mary and Katharine together, Ralph thinks, "Two women less like each other could scarcely be imagined" (92).

Yet despite their opposition, or probably because of it, they are drawn to each other. Feeling that Katharine is a "personality" (57), Mary wants to know her, and she comes to like, trust, and respect her. Lacking a profession and feeling that everyone should have one, Katharine both admires and envies Mary her devotion to work. She envies Mary's living alone as well. At the end of the novel, when Katharine and Ralph's happiness is as complete as we imagine it ever will be, Katharine still looks up from the dark London street to Mary's lighted window, which swims "like an ocean of gold behind her tears" (505).

Mary and Katharine feel immediately a bond between themselves as women. Woolf alludes several times in *Night and Day* to the tensions between the sexes and the feelings of oneness and comfortableness between people of the same sex. She once describes Katharine in a mood "perhaps not uncommon with either sex, when the other becomes very clearly distinguished, and of contemptible baseness, so that the necessity of association is degrading, and the tie, which at such moments is always extremely close, drags like a halter round the neck. William's exacting demands and his jealousy had pulled her down into some horrible swamp of her nature where the primeval struggle between man and woman still rages" (370). Katharine and her mother have their most meaningful conversations after dinner, when they leave Mr. Hilbery to enjoy his cigar and port: "These short, but clearly marked, periods of separation between the sexes were always used for an intimate postscript to what had been said at dinner, the sense of being women together coming out most strongly when the male sex was, as if by some religious rite, secluded from the female" (101). On another occasion, Woolf comments on William's need for masculine companionship: "After the mystery, difficulty, and uncertainty of dealing with the other sex, intercourse with one's own is apt to have a composing and even ennobling influence, since plain speaking is possible and subterfuges of no avail" (397). When Mary and Katharine first meet, Woolf writes that Katharine "was conscious of Mary's body beside her, but, at the same time, the consciousness of being both women made it unnecessary to speak to her" (57). Later, Woolf tells us that the "tremendous fact" that manifests itself as Mary stands alone with Katharine "may have been their common womanhood" (359).

The moments between the two women are as portentous as those between any other figures in the novel. When they are together, the manner and intensity of their responses to each other suggest that they feel the affection and attraction of lovers, not merely of friends. Woolf portrays them as having sexual feelings for each other, even though when they "fall in love," they do so with a man, Ralph. Mary and Katharine never kiss each other on the lips, as do Clarissa Dalloway and Sally Seton. They never say even to themselves, "I love Katharine" or "I love Mary." Their love for each other is most often inferred rather than known, understood rather than stated, shown indirectly rather than directly. As narrator, Woolf often treats their friendship ambiguously, evasively, even teasingly.

Woolf's handling of their relationship at their first meeting illustrates her treatment of it throughout. From the beginning, each moves the other emotionally. Mary notices that "Katharine possessed a curious power of drawing near and receding, which sent alternate emotions through her far more quickly than was usual, and kept her in a condition of curious alertness" (60). When Mary laughs at Katharine's calling her "Miss Datchet," she replies, " 'Mary, then, Mary, Mary, Mary,' " and Woolf adds, "So saying, Katharine drew back the curtain in order, perhaps, to conceal the momentary flush of pleasure which is caused by coming perceptively nearer to another person." After several moments of familiar conversation, Mary sees Katharine "raise her eyes again to the moon, with a contemplative look in them, as though she were setting that moon against the moon of other nights, held in memory." Watching them together, someone in the room behind interrupts by making a joke about stargazing, which Woolf tells us "destroyed their pleasure in it" (61). Then Ralph intervenes, causing Mary to exclaim almost aloud, " 'Oh, you idiot!' "

The structure of this scene—the intimacy between Mary and Katharine, their separateness, and the hostility and intervention of those around them—recalls a similar scene in *Mrs. Dalloway*, where the sexual feelings between Sally Seton and Clarissa are clear:

> She and Sally fell a little behind. Then came the most exquisite moment of her whole life passing a stone urn with flowers in it. Sally stopped; picked a flower; kissed her on the lips. The whole world might have turned upside down! The others disappeared; there she was alone with Sally. And she felt that she had been given a present, wrapped up, and told just to keep it, not to look at it—a diamond, something infinitely precious, wrapped up, which, as they walked (up and down, up and down), she uncovered, or the radiance burnt through, the revelation, the religious feeling!—when old Joseph and Peter faced them:
> "Star-gazing?" said Peter.
> It was like running one's face against a granite wall in the darkness! It was shocking; it was horrible!
> Not for herself. She felt only how Sally was being mauled already, maltreated; she felt his hostility; his jealousy, his determination to break into their companionship.[14]

The similarities between the two scenes affirm that Woolf certainly intended to describe an incipient love between Katharine and Mary.

14. *Mrs. Dalloway* (New York: Harcourt, Brace, 1925), 52–53.

But the greater clarity with which Woolf presents the love of Sally and Clarissa also reveals the narrative ambiguities of her treatment of Katharine and Mary.

Whenever Mary and Katharine are together, Woolf takes a narrative stance different from the one she takes in most of *Night and Day*. She is most often an omniscient narrator, who sees into her characters' thoughts, feelings, or motives whenever she wishes. Assuming the voice of wisdom or experience, she does not hesitate to comment upon or assess them. As the scene I have described above shows, Woolf is much more hesitant as narrator when she draws Mary and Katharine. To begin with, she does not tell us but leaves us to infer that Mary and Katharine are particularly attracted to each other. We assume that Katharine attributes something special to the evening since she sets "that moon against the moon of other nights"; since Woolf uses "moon" instead of "night" or "evening," we associate the moment with desire and romance. In the particular situation, Mary is the only person for whom Katharine can feel desire. Compare the directness of a similar moment in the scene from *Mrs. Dalloway*: "Then came the most exquisite moment of her whole life . . ."

But so far, *Night and Day* seems merely indirect, not ambiguous. Then we reread the sentence: "Mary then saw Katharine raise her eyes again to the moon, with a contemplative look in them, as though she were setting that moon against the moon of other nights, held in memory." Is Woolf describing what Katharine does or what Mary imagines she does? Why it is "*as though* she were setting . . ."? Was Katharine measuring that night against others or wasn't she? Since elsewhere Mary evidences stronger love for Katharine than Katharine for Mary, is this Mary's projection onto Katharine of her own feelings? (In another instance, we are told that Mary "could not help believing" [278] that Katharine shared her feelings.) Then if we go back over the entire scene, we notice that "Katharine drew back the curtain in order, perhaps, to conceal the momentary flush of pleasure which is caused by coming perceptively nearer to another person." Why *perhaps*? Does Katharine need to conceal her "flush of pleasure" or not?

Despite such hesitations, Woolf continues to develop Katharine and Mary's friendship to emphasize, rather than deny, its sexual undercurrents. Katharine's feelings for Mary are elusive, and if they come clearly into her consciousness, it is only once, and they are more strongly repressed than Mary's feelings for her. On one occasion, when Katharine wishes to talk and also to perserve a momentary "queer sense of heightened existence," Woolf tells us that she seeks out Mary Datchet's office "with a sense of adventure that was out of all proportion to the deed itself" (84). Another time, upon leaving Mary and William, she forgets her purse, suggesting that she wants an opportunity to return to Mary's and see her alone. Once there, she takes a tone that excludes William and seems to express hostility toward him: " 'I think being engaged is very bad for the character' " (176). Katharine suggests as well that a sexual relationship with a man may have an adverse effect on a woman. Watching Cassandra and William fall more deeply in love, she wants to leave her drawing room and rush to Mary: "She wished inconsistently enough that she could find herself driving rapidly through the streets; she was even anxious to be with some one who, after a moment's groping, took a definite shape and solidified into the person of Mary Datchet" (352–53).

Mary's love for Katharine is much nearer the surface of her consciousness. In a novel where there is scarcely any touching, she continually touches Katharine.[15] After Katharine tells Mary that she has seen Ralph and that they have "agreed to be friends" (359), Mary must tear herself away from Katharine: "Mary mounted the stairs step by step, as if she had to lift her body up an extremely steep ascent. She had had to wrench herself forcibly away from Katharine, and every step vanquished her desire" (361). Though she is in love with Ralph, she never surrenders herself to tell him she loves him or to reveal the pain he causes her. She gives away to her deepest feelings only once, with Katharine.

The feelings between Mary Datchet and Katharine Hilbery culminate in what is surely one of the most remarkable scenes between two women ever created, one that disappoints every conventional expectation. After rejecting Ralph's proposal, Mary feels compelled to tell Katharine that Ralph is really in love with her. Ralph has not told Mary that he is in love with Katharine, but knowing him as she does, Mary has intuited it. She must overcome overwhelming reticence to reveal to Katharine a truth that bares her pain:

> She flinched from the thought. It asked too much of one already stripped bare. Something she must keep of her own. But if she did keep something of her own? Immediately she figured an immured life, continuing for an immense period, the same feelings living for ever, neither dwin-

15. See 278, 359, 450.

dling nor changing within the ring of a thick stone wall. The imagination
of this loneliness frightened her, and yet to speak—to lose her loneliness, for it had already become dear to her, was beyond her power.

Her hand went down to the hem of Katharine's skirt, and, fingering
a line of fur, she bent her head as if to examine it.

"I like this fur," she said, "I like your clothes. And you mustn't think
that I'm going to marry Ralph," she continued, in the same tone, "because he doesn't care for me at all. He cares for some one else." [274–
75]

She does not protect herself, telling Katharine, " 'I *am* in love. There's
no doubt about that. . . . I'm tremendously in love . . . with Ralph,' "
and insisting, " 'I haven't any authority from Ralph to say it; but I'm
sure of this—he's in love with you' " (276). And she goes on: " 'I've
told you . . . because I want you to help me. I don't want to be jealous
of you. And I am—I'm fearfully jealous. The only way, I thought, was
to tell you' " (276–77).

In this moment, Mary and Katharine love each other intensely. And
it is Mary's awareness and courage as well as her need that bring their
love into being:

[Mary] seemed to have lost her isolation; she was at once the sufferer
and the pitiful spectator of suffering; she was happier than she had ever
been; she was more bereft; she was rejected; she was immensely loved.
Attempt to express these sensations was vain, and moreover, she could
not help believing that, without any words on her side, they were
shared. Thus for some time longer they sat silent, side by side, while
Mary fingered the fur of the skirt of the old dress. [278]

From knowing Mary and sharing this moment of intimacy, Katharine
recognizes the pallor of her feelings for William and begins to work
her way out of her unfortunate engagement to him: "Katharine perceived far too vividly for her comfort the mediocrity, indeed the entirely fictitious character of her own feelings so far as they pretended
to correspond with Mary's feelings. She made up her mind to act
instantly upon the knowledge thus gained" (279). Katharine's awareness ultimately leads William and Cassandra to the truth of theirs and
to her own recognition that she loves Ralph. For Mary, the consequences are less dramatic but equally significant. She establishes con-
nectedness and transcends her aloneness outside of her romantic
relationship with Ralph.

Mary contains her jealousy of Katharine in this moment, but it is clear that she will have to struggle to keep it under control, for she feels it again at their next meeting and tells Mary, " 'I believe I'm jealous' " (359). Yet the relationship among Mary, Katharine, and Ralph will not degenerate into the ordinary triangle; nor will it become a simple and easy friendship. This conclusion is apparent from the fact that after Ralph and Katharine decide to marry, neither of them can see Mary though earlier both have sought her out to confide in. Leaving Katharine in the street below, Ralph goes to Mary's door, but stands outside, "unable to bring himself to knock; if she had come out she would have found him there, the tears running down his cheeks, unable to speak" (506).

Both Katharine and Ralph cry out at the end of the novel as they contemplate Mary. We are not told their precise feelings but are left to infer them. Since they talk of regrets and Mary's happiness, we are led to believe that they are sorry that their love has caused Mary pain. But Mary also calls into question the completeness of Ralph and Katharine's love. When Ralph mentions going to see Mary, Katharine does not want to: "She held in her hands for one brief moment the globe which we spend our lives in trying to shape, round, whole, and entire from the confusion of chaos. To see Mary was to risk the destruction of this globe" (503). As she looks up at Mary's light, it swims behind her tears "like an ocean of gold" (505).

Mary stands as a reminder of the "lapses" between Ralph and Katharine. On Ralph's side, the truth and reality of Mary must remind him of his need to romanticize Katharine, his part in the lapses between them. Woolf presents Ralph's need to be the romantic lover, to put Katharine on a pedestal so that he may worship her, as destructive, the cause of lapses in feeling:

> Either because Katharine looked more beautiful, or more strange, because she wore something different, or said something unexpected, Ralph's sense of her romance welled up and overcame him either into silence or into inarticulate expressions, which Katharine, with unintentional but invariable perveristy, interrupted or contradicted with some severity or assertion of prosaic fact. Then the vision disappeared, and Ralph expressed vehemently in his turn the conviction that he only loved her shadow and cared nothing for her reality. [473]

Katharine's part in the lapses, the "fragmentary nature" of her relationship with Ralph, has to do with her "detachment" and self-absorption, her desire to be left to herself. There were moments when she had no need of Ralph and "was very loath to be reminded of him" (473). This side of her is most manifest in her secret preoccupation with mathematics; it is private and resists intrusion or relationship. When she accidentally drops some sheets containing her mathematical figures and allows Ralph to pick them up and read them, she blushes and has "the appearance of some one disarmed of all defences." She has to adjust to the idea "that some one shared her loneliness" (492). Mary's light reminds Katharine of Mary's aloneness and her single life, which have always compelled Katharine and which her marriage to Ralph puts forever out of reach. The clarity of her love for Ralph and her certainty of the rightness of her decision to marry him are very fragile, and Mary's presence makes her aware of that fragility.

The love that Virginia Woolf presents in *Night and Day* is more perilous—and more interesting—than the love of a man for a fantasy woman that is unfulfilled or that culminates in death or desertion. Because of Katharine's need for aloneness, Ralph's need for illusion, and the sexual opposition that both of them will occasionally feel, they must inevitably doubt at times that their love is "worth it," to use Mary's phrase. Woolf's version of love does not hold out the promise of an eternal, pure white flame, which, after all, burns only on graves; it promises instead a bright but flickering fire.

Most significant, Woolf forces us to see that romantic fulfillment coincides with loss for Katharine. Choosing Ralph, Katharine gives up aloneness as well as cuts herself off from Mary. Woolf saw that singleness offers possibilities for a woman that love and marriage close off. She also viewed love and friendship between women as unique, as offering an emotional bond that love between women and men cannot. At this point in time, Woolf was just beginning to recognize the limitations of heterosexual love and to explore them in her art. She was just starting to elaborate stories of "Chloe liked Olivia." She was beginning to realize that "women together," implying the possibility of sexual love between women, seriously threatened patriarchal order with its insistence on heterosexual alliances, especially for women.

Woolf's need to treat Mary and Katharine's friendship with ambiguity and evasion may derive from the subversiveness of her viewpoint—in her art, her society, and her personal life. Woolf surely understood the social attitudes that caused Radclyffe Hall's novel *The Well of Loneliness* to be banned for obscenity in 1928 because of its open treatment of lesbianism. Though the Bloomsbury group was tolerant of homosexuality and contained at least as many, and perhaps

more, homosexual than heterosexual members, it regarded lesbianism
with suspicion. Though E. M. Forster was himself homosexual, he
told Woolf that he "thought Sapphism disgusting: partly from convention, partly because he disliked that women should be independent
of men."[16] To be a lesbian or to find lesbianism attractive was un-
doubtedly to risk Forster's friendship as well as his good critical opinion, and Woolf cared very much about both. When she received his
unenthusiastic response to *Night and Day*, after receiving praise from
many, she wrote in her diary that Forster's comments "rubbed out
all the pleasure of the rest" and remarked, "I suppose I value Morgan's
opinion as much as anybodies."[17]

In *Night and Day* Woolf can carry her exploration of love between
women only so far. She is stopped by the limits her society poses as
well as by her own fears. To imagine the possibility that Katharine
and Mary might become lovers would have meant imagining a new
world, for Woolf's society offered lesbian love no place. Furthermore,
her portrayal of Mary suggests that she had internalized a vestige of
her society's homophobia. Mary has stronger sexual feelings for Katharine than Katharine for Mary; for that reason Woolf may have
depicted Mary as the less attractive of the two and from a lower social
class than Katharine. By the time Woolf wrote *Mrs. Dalloway*, she
could draw Sally Seton as a social peer of Clarissa and as wholly
attractive, even more compelling than Clarissa.

It is hard to tell how aware Woolf was of her own tentativeness as
she presented the friendship of Mary and Katharine. Yet she may have
quite consciously adopted a double perspective that she expected some
to perceive. In *The Voyage Out*, Woolf's first novel and the predecessor of *Night and Day*, Hewet, a novelist, tells Rachel Vinrace, " 'I
want to write a novel about Silence . . . the things people don't say.' "[18]
The most important moment between Mary and Katharine is rendered
through silence: "For some time longer they sat silent, side by side,
while Mary fingered the fur on the skirt of the old dress" (278). Perhaps
she expected Janet Case to understand, for she wrote her concerning
Night and Day, "And then there's the whole question, which inter-

16. Quentin Bell, *Virginia Woolf: A Biography*, 2 vols. (New York: Harcourt Brace
Jovanovich, 1972), II, 138.
17. *The Diary of Virginia Woolf*, ed. Anne Olivier Bell, 4 vols. (New York: Harcourt
Brace Jovanovich, I, 1977), 308.
18. *The Voyage Out* (1920; rpt. New York: Harcourt, Brace, 1948), 216.

ested me, again too much for the books sake, I daresay, of the things one doesn't say; what effect does that have?"[19] The picture glimpsed obliquely, the one conveyed through silence, illuminates a story Woolf will tell and retell in the novels to come.

19. *The Letters of Virginia Woolf*, ed. Nigel Nicholson and Joanne Trautmann, 6 vols. (New York: Harcourt Brace Jovanovich, II, 1976), 400.

15

The Gothic Mirror

CLAIRE KAHANE

Within an imprisoning structure, a protagonist, typically a young woman whose mother has died, is compelled to seek out the center of a mystery, while vague and usually sexual threats to her person from some powerful male figure hover on the periphery of her consciousness. Following clues that pull her onward and inward—bloodstains, mysterious sounds—she penetrates the obscure recesses of a vast labyrinthean space and discovers a secret room sealed off by its association with death. In this dark, secret center of the Gothic structure, the boundaries of life and death themselves seem confused. Who died? Has there been a murder? Or merely a disappearance? This is the conventional plot of the Gothic novel, first popularized by Ann Radcliffe in the late eighteenth century and still being dispensed over the counter in drugstores across the country. Its confusions—its misleading clues, postponements of discovery, excessive digressions—are inscribed in the narrative structure itself.

Looking more closely, however, one finds a curious thread running through this labyrinth. In *The Mysteries of Udolpho*, for example, although a corpse discovered in a hidden room turns out to be an

This essay is a revised version of "Gothic Mirrors and Feminine Identity," which first appeared in *Centennial Review*, 24, no. 1 (Winter 1980), 43–64. Reprinted by permission of *Centennial Review*.

anonymous soldier, for pages we are encouraged to believe that the heroine's aunt, who functions as her surrogate mother, was murdered there. Stranger still, later we discover that a woman hinted to be the heroine's real mother—but in fact another aunt—was indeed murdered. In *The Monk*, the underground vaults of a convent reveal the corpse of an infant clasped in the arms of its naively inadequate mother; but the text that leads to this eventual discovery first misleads by implying that it is the mother, a "fallen" nun, that has been killed— by *her* mother superior. In *Frankenstein*, Victor first creates life from the relics of death, plays a macabre mother, as several critics have noted,[1] and then, about to "birth" a second, more terrible—and female—monster, aborts that prospective "child." Mrs. Reed, another surrogate mother, locks Jane Eyre into a red room, a bedroom whose secret, as Brontë calls it, is its having been the death chamber of Jane's maternal uncle. And locked into the novel's center is another woman, Rochester's mad wife, who must die—whom Jane must displace to assume her own place. Even in a parody of the Gothic novel, Jane Austen provides the quasi heroine of *Northanger Abbey* with a secret bedroom in which a mother has died, a space that Austen must demystify for Catherine.

What I hope to suggest by my particular focus on dead or displaced mothers is another angle of vision on the Gothic which has been virtually ignored. Most interpretations of Gothic fiction, written primarily by male critics, attribute the terror that the Gothic by definition arouses to the motif of incest within an oedipal plot.[2] From this perspective, the latent configuration of the Gothic paradigm seems to be that of a helpless daughter confronting the erotic power of a father or brother, with the mother noticeably absent. More typically, however, male critics of the Gothic choose to focus on male authors and male protagonists in order to elaborate the oedipal dynamics of a Gothic

1. See, for example, Ellen Moers, *Literary Women* (Garden City, N.Y.: Doubleday, 1976), 90–99, and Marc Rubenstein, " 'My Accursed Origin': The Search for the Mother in *Frankenstein*," *Studies in Romanticism*, 15 (Spring 1976), 165–94.

2. See Devendra Varma, *The Gothic Flame* (New York: Russell & Russell, 1964); Mario Praz, *The Romantic Agony* (New York: Meridian, 1967); Elino Railo, *The Haunted Castle* (New York: Humanities Press, 1964); Morton Kaplan and Robert Kloss, "Fantasy of Paternity and the Doppelgänger: Mary Shelley's *Frankenstein*," in *The Unspoken Motive* (New York: Free Press, 1973). In the last work, Kaplan and Kloss, while writing that "the Gothic genre . . . depicts in varying degrees of explicitness the passions of the oedipal child," acknowledge that they interpret Mary Shelley's work "in the light of male psychology" (145).

text, and effectively restrict if not exclude female desire even from texts written by women. Leslie Fiedler, for example, defining the Gothic mystery as "incest of mother and son, the breach of the primal taboo and the offense against the father," locates the Gothic experience in the villain, and interprets even the ubiquitous "maiden in flight" as "the spirit of the man who has lost his moral home."[3] Thus Fiedler discusses the Gothic as representing the son's rebellious confrontation with paternal authority.

Yet as Fiedler himself points out, "beneath the haunted castle lies the dungeon keep: the womb from whose darkness the ego first emerged, the tomb to which it knows it must return at last. Beneath the crumbling shell of paternal authority, lies the maternal blackness, imagined by the gothic writer as a prison, a torture chamber."[4] Although he quickly drops this chilling perception of the maternal space, that space is central to my experience of the Gothic. Indeed, from my perspective the oedipal plot seems more a surface convention than a latent fantasy exerting force, more a framework that houses another mode of confrontation even more disquieting. What I see repeatedly locked into the forbidden center of the Gothic which draws me inward is the spectral presence of a dead-undead mother, archaic and all-encompassing, a ghost signifying the problematics of femininity which the heroine must confront.

That both men and women maintain an uneasy relation to female-ness is by now a truism. Certainly the prevailing social situation of female rule over infancy promotes ambivalence toward all women, as Nancy Chodorow and Dorothy Dinnerstein have so forcefully argued.[5] As psychoanalysts describe this critical period of early infancy, mother and infant are locked into a symbiotic relation, an experience of one-ness characterized by a blurring of boundaries between mother and infant—a dual unity preceding the sense of separate self. Because the mother-woman is experienced as part of Nature itself before we learn her boundaries, she traditionally embodies the mysterious not-me world, with its unknown forces. Hers is the body, awesome and pow-

3. Leslie Fiedler, *Love and Death in the American Novel* (New York: Dell, 1966), 129–33.

4. Fielder, *Love and Death*, 132.

5. The consequences of women's monopoly of child rearing are persuasively elaborated in Dorothy Dinnerstein, *The Mermaid and the Minotaur* (New York: Harper & Row, 1977), and Nancy Chodorow, *The Reproduction of Mothering* (Berkeley: University of California Press, 1979).

erful, which is both our habitat and our prison, and while an infant gradually becomes conscious of a limited Other, the mother remains imaginatively linked to the realm of Nature, figuring the forces of life and death. While the male child can use the very fact of his sex to differentiate himself from this uncanny figure, the female child, who shares the female body and its symbolic place in our culture, remains locked in a more tenuous and fundamentally ambivalent struggle for a separate identity. This ongoing battle with a mirror image who is both self and other is what I find at the center of the Gothic structure, which allows me to confront the confusion between mother and daughter and the intricate web of psychic relations that constitute their bond.

Perhaps for this reason Gothic literature has always seemed especially congenial to the female imagination and has attracted so many women readers. In their discussion of the gender-related appeal of the Gothic, Norman Holland and Leona Sherman focus on the early mother-child relationship in both the Gothic text and their response to it.[6] Both experience the castle as a pivotal image, a nighttime house that admits various projections. "It becomes all the possibilities of a parent or a body," they write, "a total environment in one-to-one relation with the victim, like the all-powerful mother of early childhood." Significantly, however, their responses toward this characteristically untrustworthy environment break down along gender lines. Uncomfortable with the Gothic plot, Holland concentrates on developing strategies for avoiding vulnerability to that environment, which he associates with the feminine, while Sherman seeks confirmations in the midst of Gothic threats. Not only does she experience pleasure in the active role taken by the intrusive and questing heroine, but she insists on the power inherent in the conventional feminine mode of passive resistance, the power of mere but absolute being. Thus she points to the heroine of The Mysteries of Udolpho, who opposes the villain "only by the mild dignity of a superior mind."

Paradoxically, however, when Sherman attempts to locate the source of her response, she writes: "For me, the primary motivating fear is of nothingness or nonseparation." From an emphasis on the power of absolute being to the fear of nothingness, Sherman's shift dramatically demonstrates the polar oppositions of experience within the symbiotic

6. Norman Holland and Leona Sherman, "Gothic Possibilities," *New Literary History*, 8 (1976–77), 279–94. Subsequent quotations are from 283, 293, and 284, respectively.

bond: the illusion of being all or nothing in which the fledgling psyche participates. Her subsequent association to the Gothic secret points to its special resonance for women: "I find myself harking back to the ultimate mystery, the maternal body with its related secrets of birth and sexuality." If nonseparation from the castle as mother—"mother as nurturer, as sexual being, as body, as harboring a secret"—is a primary Gothic fear, women, whose boundaries from the maternal are at the very least ambiguous because of their own femaleness, must find that fear dramatically rendered in the secret center of the Gothic structure, where boundaries break down, where life and death become confused, where images of birth and sexuality proliferate in complex displacements. Sherman's own discourse increasingly reflects this Gothic confusion as she concludes: "I find myself recreating from Gothic my ambivalence toward a femaleness which is my mother in me: nurturing and sexuality, mother and woman and child, conflicted between her and me and therefore in me as me."

In this light, the heroine's active exploration of the Gothic house in which she is trapped is also an exploration of her relation to the maternal body that she shares, with all its connotations of power over and vulnerability to forces within and without. In *Udolpho*, for example, Ann Radcliffe's initial representation of the castle Udolpho both suggests a version of the maternal body and establishes the terms of Emily's subsequent exploration of this "sovereign frowning defiance on all who dared to invade its solitary reign."[7] As if from a child's perspective on this giant house, moving first from eye level upward and then downward, Radcliffe focuses attention on the castle's body parts in terms that allude to defense, penetration, and entrapment. From "the gateway ... of gigantic size" the eye sweeps up to "two round towers ... united by a curtain pierced and embattled" and then down again to "the pointed arch of a huge portcullis surmounting the gates" (227). Once inside, Emily finds that the space relegated to her is controlled not from within but from without: in this suggestive representation of female space, the door of her room "had no bolts on the chamber side, though it had two on the other" (235). Yet while her own chamber is "liable to intrusion" (242) by threatening male figures who control her environment, she herself aggressively intrudes into the secret chambers of the castle; in spite of her vulnerable sit-

---

7. Ann Radcliffe, *The Mysteries of Udolpho* (New York: Oxford University Press, 1970), 227. All subsequent page references to this edition appear in the text.

uation, or rather, and this is the important fact, because of it, she must explore and penetrate the mysteries of Udolpho, locate and tap its secret center of that knowledge which is power.

Transgressing the boundaries of her role as a conventional heroine, Emily wanders through both a physical and historical labyrinth, discovering in both space and time, as does the reader, first at Udolpho and later at its protective counterpart, the Château Blanc, her relations to the women who are the original owners of "the castle." These women are specifically represented by the text as her doubles, her own originals. At the center of Udolpho, the text uncovers the ghost of Laurintini, its true owner, a strong-willed and sexually voracious woman who has disappeared and is presumed dead. Radcliffe alludes to a connection between Laurintini's disappearance and a secret horror, which Emily unveils early in the novel but which Radcliffe keeps tauntingly veiled until the conclusion. When that horror is finally revealed to have been a waxen figure of a decaying corpse, it becomes for me a primary trope for understanding the horror of the text. Although Emily has mistakenly assumed the figure to be literally Laurintini's corrupted body, her misapprehension is itself a constitutive metaphor of the novel's secret. It is precisely Laurintini's corruption through the flesh, through the strength of her sexual desire, that the penultimate chapter affirms in its disclosure of her story. Having been allowed from childhood to indulge her impulses, Laurintini yielded to her passion for a marquis. When he married another, Laurintini, obsessed with desire, designed with him the murder of the innocent marchioness (who turns out to be Emily's aunt). Abandoned by her repentant lover, Laurintini becomes the deranged nun Sister Agnes, and in a final interview with Emily years later she spies her own corruption reflected in Emily. As a victimizer victimized by her own desire, Laurintini is presented as Emily's potential precursor, a mad mother-sister-double who mirrors Emily's own potential for transgression and madness.

But the murdered marchioness, whose innocence lies at the historical center of the other Gothic house, the Château Blanc, is also Emily's precursor. Emily is literally told to look into a mirror to see the marchioness, is identified mistakenly both as the marchioness and as her daughter—a mistake that is nevertheless a metaphorical take— and, draped in the veil of the dead marchioness, is named by the text as her living embodiment: the *passive* victim of desire. Although Emily struggles to throw off that veil, refusing that identification, mirror images and mother-daughter confusions continue to haunt her in this paradigmatic Gothic novel, creating that labyrinth of relations through which both she and I as reader thread our way.

After Emily has explored this hall of mirrors, however, after she has allowed her imagination full sway so that at least one critic places the dangers of Udolpho within Emily's mind,[8] after Radcliffe herself has confused me about what is inside Emily's mind and what outside, has aroused my prurient imagination by titillating and obscuring innuendo, has indulged in every excess of sensibility against which she explicitly warns the reader, Emily is returned to the happy valley of La Vallée. No Gothic castles or transgressions of boundaries here, but an innocent pastoral paradise that denies the Gothic experience. Thus the novel allows me first to enjoy and then to repress the sexual and aggressive center of Udolpho, which, as the mad nun has warned, leads to madness and death, and leaves me safely enclosed—but, significantly, socially secluded—in an idealized nurturing space, the space provided for heroines by patriarchal narrative convention.

This disjunction between the Gothic experience and the novel's conclusion illustrates a pervasive ambivalence for the female reader in the Gothic paradigm. It allows me a vital imaginary space in which I can reexperience the more aggressive, less inhibited pleasures of an earlier, less gender-constricted childhood, in which I can confront those perilous extremes usually reserved for male adventurers. But once in that space, I am dangerously seduced by the very experience of terror; I delight in the dizzying verge of that ubiquitous Gothic precipice on the edge of the maternal blackness to which every Gothic heroine is fatefully drawn. Ultimately what I confront are the mysteries of identity and the temptation to lose it by merging with a mother imago who threatens all boundaries between self and other.

To this confrontation the characteristic response of the Gothic heroine is escape; as Holland and Sherman put it, "I will not let the castle force itself into me. I will put myself outside it." But for women this is no easy task. Putting herself outside it, the conventional Gothic heroine puts herself outside female desire and aggressivity. In thus excluding a vital aspect of self, she is left on the margin both of identity and society. Thus as in *Udolpho* and *Jane Eyre*, while the heroine ultimately moves into a space that she seemingly controls, that control

8. See, for example, Robert Kiely, *The Romantic Novel in England* (Cambridge: Harvard University Press, 1972).

is illusory, based as it is on social withdrawal and psychological repression, on an ultimate submission to patriarchal constructs of the feminine. Emily returns to her childhood home with a chaste and chastened hero; Jane at Ferndean rules over an isolated domesticity as mother with a debilitated male. Both conclusions excise the Gothic terrors, idealizing the mother and the heroines as well. Yet beneath the pedestal lies an abyss; at the Gothic center of the novels, a fearsome figure in the mirror still remains, waiting to be acknowledged.

In the more radical modern Gothic fictions, that figure emerges from the obscure background and dominates; typically, in modern Gothic, there is no escape. Here I am referring not to those contemporary popular Gothic romances that conform to the conventional paradigm, repeating its evasions in less interesting ways, but to those contemporary fictions that I find truly terrifying. In Shirley Jackson's *Haunting of Hill House*, for example, the heroine, recently freed from an ostensibly odious servitude to her domineering invalid mother by her death, joins a group interested in occult phenomena at Hill House. From the very beginning the house itself is presented as the overt antagonist, specifically through its images as a maternal antagonist, a diseased presence "seeking whom it may devour" and singling out Eleanor as its destined inhabitant. Yet also from the very beginning, Jackson dislocates me in typical Gothic fashion by locating me in Eleanor's point of view, confusing outside and inside, reality and illusion, so that I cannot clearly discern the acts of the house—the supernatural—from Eleanor's own disordered acts—the natural. But whether the agency of the house is inside Eleanor's mind or outside it, in either location it clearly functions as a powerful maternal imago.[9]

Eleanor's most intimate relationship in the group is with the androgynous Theodora, a lesbian who is perceived by Eleanor as alternately protective and tormenting. Jackson's portrayal of their relation recreates the terms of Eleanor's relation with her mother, making overt the hidden force of her longing and her hatred. Compelled ostensibly by the house to share the same bed, the same room, the same clothes as Theodora, Eleanor both fears and delights in their confusion of identity. Yet Theodora's lesbianism demonstrates the adult

9. In her textual references, Jackson leaves no doubt that the house is an image of the mother. Once inside, the characters become infantilized, play, giggle, worry about dirty fingernails, and call one another babies. The nursery is designated the most haunted room (*The Haunting of Hill House* [New York: Popular Library, 1959]).

implications of remaining bound within a mother-daughter relation-ship—erotically bound, that is, to a woman, a transgression of het-erosexual convention by which the novel titillates and disturbs its readers. Whereas in the eighteenth-century Gothic, the erotic bond between mother and daughter is displaced—the heroine explores the secret rooms of a house—in this post-Freudian novel the sexual over-tones of Eleanor's ambivalent wish to remain at Hill House are ex-pressed directly in the text. Whereas the eighteenth-century Gothic ended with an idealized romance between hero and heroine (and interestingly, the hero of the first Gothic novel, *The Castle of Otranto*, is named Theodore), here the book's refrain, "journeys end in lovers meeting," points first toward Eleanor's desire to live with Theodora after they leave Hill House and then to the climax, in which mother and daughter are symbolically reunited.

After a series of supernatural occurrences that serve Eleanor as re-cognitions of her past, after seeing her name literally inscribed on the walls of the house, after being rejected by Theodora, who insists on their separation, Eleanor surrenders to the house, surrenders her illusory new autonomy to remain the child, dependent on the mater-nal, on Hill House as protector, lover, and destroyer. Asked to leave by the group because of her unstable behavior, she crashes her car into a tree. By destroying herself physically, she escapes the carnal consequences of her desire, committing herself instead to the maternal space as one of the ghosts of Hill House, now forever incorporated into its powerful history. Yet to the very end, that submission is ambivalent: moments before her crash, she first exults: "I am really doing it, I am doing this all by myself, now, at last; this is me, I am really doing it by myself" and then thinks, "Why don't they stop me."

As Jackson's novel insists, the female Gothic depends as much on longing and desire as on fear and antagonism. Yet if it frequently indulges some of the more masochistic components of female fantasy, representing the pleasure of submission, it also encourages an active exploration of the limits of identity. Ultimately, however, in this es-sentially conservative genre—and for me this is the real Gothic hor-ror—the heroine is compelled to resume a quiescent, socially acceptable role or to be destroyed.

In moving from eighteenth-century Gothic to a twentieth-century counterpart, I have stressed similarities. Yet I see a significant differ-ence between the old and the new Gothic. The conventional Gothic novel, it should be remembered, followed Edmund Burke's prescription that terror depends on *not* seeing clearly, and created an effective obscurity or mystery that allowed for maximum projection of the reader's fantasies. In this sense, *Hill House*, with its dislocations and indeterminate agents, conforms to the Gothic conventions. But in her provocative study of Female Gothic, Ellen Moers has redefined the Gothic to include any work that gives "visual form to the fear of self."[10] Implicit in this definition is the notion that what was once veiled in the pre-Freudian darkness is now unveiled and even more terrifying for being seen. What is it that is seen? According to Moers, what is seen is images of self-hatred, which take the form of freaks of all kinds, and thus lead to a grotesque tradition in Female Gothic. I would like to complicate that answer; for if the older Gothic tradition involved an obscure exploration of female identity through a confrontation with a diffuse spectral mother, in modern Gothic the spectral mother typically becomes an embodied actual figure. She, and not some threatening villain, becomes the primary antagonist. With that shift, the heroine is imprisoned not in a house but in the female body, which is itself the maternal legacy. The problematics of femininity is thus reduced to the problematics of the female body, perceived as antagonistic to the sense of self, as therefore freakish. Repeatedly, as so much of what we call modern Gothic illustrates, when the unseen is given visual form, when we lose the obscurity of the Gothic darkness, the Gothic focuses on distorted body images and turns into the grotesque.

Perhaps the most exemplary writer of the Gothic-grotesque in recent times is Flannery O'Connor, whose insistence on "staring at the Unnameable," as she pharsed it, produced in her fiction a sideshow of freakish figures.[11] What ties O'Connor's fiction to the conventional Gothic paradigm is the pervasive issue of discovering a truth at "the dark secret center"; what distinguishes it as modern Gothic is her giving that truth grotesque visual form. "What have you seen?" asks the protagonist's mother in O'Connor's first novel, *Wise Blood*, and that question reverberates throughout her work. Significantly, in *Wise Blood*, the name of her protagonist, Hazel Motes, is androgynous, for while he is male, his major conflict—to separate himself from an over-

10. Moers, *Literary Women*, 107.

11. Flannery O'Connor, *Mystery and Manners* (New York: Noonday, 1970), 84. "The writer should never be ashamed of staring." O'Connor repeatedly stresses the importance of visual images.

whelming maternal image haunting his memory—is the familiar one I have been arguing as being particularly female, and is represented in the novel by a sequence of terrifying mirror scenes. What Haze (his nickname reveals O'Connor's insistent pun on his blurred vision) has seen in *Wise Blood*, the answer to his mother's question, is a forbidden carnival sideshow, a naked woman squirming in a coffin and exposed for the delectation of lustful men, a memory that gets confused with his mother's burial, and with his own. O'Connor blurs the line between sexuality and death, just as, in this passage, she slides from Haze's vision of his mother's burial to his vision of his own:

> He had seen her face through the crack when they were shutting the top on her ... He had seen the shadow that came down over her face and pulled her mouth down as if she wasn't any more satisfied dead than alive, as if she were going to spring up and shove the lid back and fly out of there, she might have been going to spring. He saw her in his sleep, terrible, like a huge bat, dart from the closing, fly out of there but it was falling dark on top of her, closing down all the time. *From the inside he saw it closing, coming closer, closer down* and cutting off the light and the room.[12]

This vision is repeated in somewhat different images when Enoch Emory, his comic foil, discovers a "mystery at the dark secret center of the city"—a mummy (mommy) in a museum, which he shows to Haze. Looking at this shrunken man lying in a coffin-like glass case, "naked and dried yellow color" with eyes "drawn almost shut as if a giant block of steel were falling down on top of him," Haze first sees his own face reflected in the glass, and then overlaying his, the grinning face of a woman, who "snickered and put two fingers in front of her teeth.... When Haze saw her face on the glass, his neck jerked back and he made a noise. It might have come from the man inside the case" (57).

Psychoanalytically speaking, the precursor of the mirror is the mother's face, in which the child first sees itself reflected.[13] For Haze, the mother's face is so threatening that instead of finding himself reflected, he loses himself; he becomes a shrunken man, mutilated by visual images of a devouring mother. In a parallel scene, Haze looks in the

---

12. Flannery O'Connor, *Wise Blood* (New York: Farrar, Straus & Giroux, 1978), 27; italics mine. Subsequent references to this edition appear in the text.

13. See D. W. Winnicott, "Mirror-Role of Mother and Family in Child Development," in *Playing and Reality* (New York: Basic Books, 1971).

mirror and sees "his mother's face in his, looking at the face in the mirror" (102). Only when he blinds himself and can no longer see the various mother-women in this unsettling novel do they lose their power over him. The mirror shattered, he is released from that imprisonment by the body which they signify to him. Thus just as in the nineteenth century Victor Frankenstein obsessively attempts to "penetrate the secrets of Nature"—and Shelley's language points to Nature as a disseminated mother—O'Connor's characters feel compelled to peep at a forbidden sideshow that turns into an annihilating maternal image.

Perhaps the most radical terror that is given visual form in O'Connor's fiction concerns procreation. That women writers should find in pregnancy and childbirth primary Gothic metaphors is not surprising, for both can arouse fears about bodily integrity that are intimately related to one's sense of self. In these most definitively female of conditions thus lie the most extreme apprehensions. In pregnancy the woman's very shape changes as she feels another presence inside her, growing on her flesh, feeding on her blood.[14] Moreover, pregnancy also confirms a woman's identification with her own mother, and becoming prey to that intricate network of fears and wishes, rage and love, that informs her relation to her mother, she may be led to fear the fetus as an agent of retaliation, a mirror of her own infantile negativity.

In an early O'Connor story, "A Stroke of Good Fortune," pregnancy become just such a Gothic horror stalking its unwilling victim. Because Ruby Hill refuses to understand her very obvious symptoms and to acknowledge her pregnant condition, O'Connor establishes the reader's ironic distance from Ruby's terror. Yet she simultaneously undermines that distance by a series of disquieting Gothic images that insistently link childbirth to some undefined but terrifying doom. "All those children were what did her mother in—eight of them," Ruby

---

14. It is not too far a metaphorical leap to the Vampyre, to Dracula as fetus draining its mother's vital fluids. In Bram Stoker's novel, this image and its reversal, an infant being force-fed by its mother, are powerfully condensed when Mina Harker's face is forced onto Dracula's bosom; by this act of feeding, she herself becomes a vampire: "Her white nightdress was smeared with blood, and a thin stream trickled down the man's bare breast, which was shown by his torn open dress. The attitude of the two had a terrible resemblance to a child forcing a kitten's nose into a saucer of milk to compel it to drink." (*Dracula* [New York: New American Library, 1965], 288).

thinks. "Her mother had gotten deader with every one of them."[15] Recalling the horror of her baby brother's birth, she remembers that "she walked all the way in to Melsy, in the hot sun ten miles to the picture show to get clear of the screaming, and had sat through two westerns and a horror picture and a serial and then had walked all the way back and found it was just beginning, and she had to listen all night" (97).[16] In O'Connor's version of the Gothic, the villain's work is already done, and only the bloody consequence, marked by screaming in the night, constitutes the horror. Significantly, the actual childbirth is never presented directly, so that the indeterminacy of the horror can have its Gothic effect. But it continues to resonate throughout the story, displaced into images—cancer, poisonous seeds, teeth being pulled—which maintain a tension between body wholeness and mutilation.

At the end of the story the images confuse a fantasy of giving birth with Ruby's own birth. Pausing on the staircase of her apartment house, Ruby looks down into the stairwell, which becomes "a stair cavern . . . dark green and mole colored" (106). She "wails" like a baby; "the wail sounded at the very bottom like a voice answering her." That answering voice becomes incarnate, as "little Mr. Good Fortune"—the child antagonist—erupts from the stairwell as if bursting from the womb and knocks her down. Finally doomed to become the mother, to be sacrificed in turn to the waiting child, Ruby sits on the stair gazing "down into the dark hold, down to the very bottom where she had started up so long ago." Although O'Connor has taken a fantasy of entrapment by the maternal body out of the Gothic obscurity and made it the manifest theme of her story, her multivalent images still reverberate in my own dark secret center.

O'Connor's question, "What have you seen?"—a question I hear throughout modern Gothic—is answered in her fiction by images of the womb as the mummy's tomb, of penetration, impregnation, and

15. Flannery O'Connor, *The Complete Stories* (New York: Farrar, Straus & Giroux, 1971), 97. Subsequent page references appear in the text.

16. Karen Horney records an actual case history that uncannily parallels Ruby's situation, that of a woman, "the oldest of eight children, [whose] most frightening memories concerned the time when a new child was born. She had heard her mother scream and had seen bowls of blood carried out of her mother's room. The early association between childbirth, sex and blood" was revived during her menstruation ("Psychogenic Factors in Functional Disorders," in *Feminine Psychology* [New York: Norton, 1967], 173).

childbirth as female Gothic terrors, committing women to an imprisoning biological destiny that denies the autonomy of the self. The Gothic fear is revealed as the fear of femaleness itself, perceived as threatening to one's wholeness, obliterating the very boundaries of self. Although her various female characters continually attempt to escape by repudiating their womanhood, their flight invariably proves to be circular, nightmarishly bringing them face to face with the danger inherent in female identity—face to face, that is, with mothers.

But let me turn the Gothic screw one last time. For I see another image in what has by now become for me a Gothic mirror: the hermaphrodite. Although Ellen Moers identifies the hermaphrodite as a grotesque image of self-hatred, I think it occupies a more ambiguous position. If it is a grotesque image when it is visually described, it is also—or can be—in its symbolic dimension a Gothic emblem of that desired transgression of boundaries I experience within the Gothic space. For my response to the hermaphrodite as a literary image derives from ambiguity: from what is visually obscure yet demands to be seen, from what is impossible but true, from what is wished for and feared. Especially in a time when the traditional boundaries of sexual identity are in flux, the hermaphrodite, challenging those boundaries by its existence, mirrors both the infantile wish to destroy distinction and limitation and be both sexes—a power originally attributed to the primal mother—and the fear of that wish when it is physiologically realized as freakishness. Leslie Fiedler speaks to this response when he says that "no category of Freaks is regarded with such ferocious ambivalence as the hermaphrodites, for none creates in us a greater tension between physical repulsion and spiritual attraction."[17]

This duplicitous significance emerges in two contrasting modern Gothics. In Carson McCullers' *Ballad of the Sad Café*, the self-hatred of the grotesque predominates primarily because McCullers insists on presenting me with visual descriptions of the hermaphroditic Miss Amelia which cumulatively contrast with the gender location she increasingly assumes. Initially Miss Amelia—feisty, muscular, and an exceptionally good nurse, prosperous and skilled in both the masculine and feminine crafts—maintains a powerful authority over her town because she is both sexually ambiguous and completely independent. Yet her name itself locates her within a cultural conception of fe-

17. Leslie Fiedler, *Freaks* (New York: Simon & Schuster, 1978), 179.

maleness against which her masculine physicality appears inappropriate, if not grotesque. When her cousin Lyman, a hunchbacked dwarf, appears, he is uncannily taken up by Miss Amelia as the object of her desire, functioning as both her child and her beloved. As if she has been waiting for an external object with which to re-present herself, she places her authority in him. But in doing so she becomes vulnerable and loses her hermaphroditic independence. Effectively he becomes her phallus, an object signifying her power—though significantly, a grotesque phallus—and she becomes increasingly "female"—even wearing, notes McCullers, a dress on special occasions. When her antagonist, Marvin Macy, breaks into their almost symbiotic dyad, she "put aside her overalls and wore always the red dress."[18] When Macy moves into her house at Lyman's insistence, McCullers pointedly describes Miss Amelia warming herself before a stove: "The red dress was pulled up quite high in the back so that a piece of her strong hairy thigh could be seen" (60). Although I am relieved that the dress is not pulled up "quite high in the front"—(what could I see?)—the grotesque disjunction between the strong hairy thigh that signifies male power and the red dress that signifies her femaleness within a context of her increasing loss of power both dramatizes her indeterminate location and foreshadows the conclusion. Finally betrayed by the dwarf, who attaches himself to the "real" man, Miss Amelia goes through a physical metamorphosis; or, as the story suggests, she is unmasked: "the great muscles of her body shrank until she was thin as old maids are thin when they go crazy" (70). At the end, she is left a woman, gender-locked in a decaying house. If the image of the hermaphrodite recalls a fantasy of an omnipotent primal mother, McCullers' story effectively castrates her.

But in Flannery O'Connor's "A Temple of the Holy Ghost," the imprisoning physicality of the Gothic house is transformed into the spiritual temple as O'Connor explores the transcendent, unseen possibilities of hermaphroditic power. Thus this story moves away from the grotesque and toward the sublime through the mediation of a carnival hermaphrodite, whose freakishness is a sign of grace precisely because it is never visually defined. Told from the point of view of an ugly twelve-year-old girl who is significantly unnamed and as yet un-

18. Carson McCullers, *The Ballad of the Sad Café and Other Stories* (New York: Bantam, 1971), 53. Subsequent page references appear in the text.

feminized, the story resonates with adolescent concerns about the female body, about its limitations, its defilement, its mysteries.

The crux of the story is a conversation between the girl and her two cousins, who taunt her with their having seen something forbidden at a fair. " 'There are some things,' Susan said, 'that a child of your age doesn't know,' and they both began to giggle."[19] Their mysterious hint immediately triggers the girl's association to the mystery of birth, and she attempts to tease them into disclosing their secret. " 'One time,' she said, her voice hollow-sounding in the dark, 'I saw this rabbit have rabbits.' " Her ploy effective, the cousins tell of the "freak" they have seen, a hermaphrodite who had exhibited itself saying,

"God made me this way and if you laugh, He may strike you the same way. This is the way He wanted me to be and I ain't disputing His way. I'm showing you because I got to make the best of it . . . I never done it to myself nor had a thing to do with it, but I'm making the best of it. I don't dispute it." [245]

Although in light of the girl's reluctance to be "feminine," the spiel of the hermaphrodite suggests that she should submit to her fate as a woman, it is the common fact of their freakishness on which the story turns. What is psychologically most significant is that the double sex of the hermaphrodite—the sign of the freak—is never exhibited to the girl or to the reader directly. Even in the one allusion to its physical appearance, when the cousin states, "It was a man and woman both. It pulled up its dress and showed us. It had on a blue dress," we do not know what it is that is seen. Had O'Connor, like McCullers, presented a visual image, the story would remain within the grotesque tradition of the Gothic; but she transforms the grotesque into the sublime, self-hatred into awe, by means of indirection and ambiguity: the girl's identification with the hermaphrodite is made not through a mirroring physical image but through the symbolic medium of language, through an imagined dialogue in which she and the hermaphrodite merge through the phrase that has haunted the girl throughout the story: "I am a temple of the Holy Ghost." This symbolic identification suggests to me not only that the girl fantasizes that she, too, like the hermaphrodite, has both male and female sexual power, but that as temples of the Holy Ghost, both are associated with the Virgin

19. O'Connor, *Complete Stories*, 245. Subsequent references appear in the text.

Mary, who was impregnated by the Holy Ghost ("God made me this way. . . . I never done it to myself nor had a thing to do with it . . ."). By this line of association (confirmed for me by the hermaphrodite's blue dress, the Virgin's color), the Holy Mother becomes a herma-phrodeity, her androgynous power providing a symbolic resolution to the problem of gender limitation.

Only in this context can I understand O'Connor's introduction, near the close of the story, of an uncanny figure, a "big, moon-faced nun" who "swooped down" on the girl and nearly "smothered her in the black habit, mashing her face into the crucifix hitched onto her belt" (248). I am reminded of a remark once made to me by a Catholic student, that what had frightened him about nuns in primary school was that he "didn't know what they were like under that big black habit." His remark, O'Connor's description, and the ubiquitous pres-ence of nuns in Gothic fiction all point to the awesome power of sexual ambiguity which the unseen allows. For women, that ambiguity pre-sents a symbolic means of transcending the limitations placed on fem-inine identity. In a culture that defines the true woman in predominantly biological terms, locating feminine identity within the straits of passive sexuality and selfless maternity, it seems especially apt that the es-sentially biological image of the hermaphrodite has been extended to signify the range of human identity, has become a core symbol of androgyny for contemporary women. Recalling the illusion of the on-mipotent magic mother before her powers are culturally curtailed, before disillusion sets in, with its attendant fear, rage, and guilt, the unseen hermaphrodite serves as a symbolic way out of women's sense of Gothic imprisonment, restoring to women at least conceptually the breadth of human potential.

In exploring the movement of the Gothic from the paradigm most clearly established by Radcliffe to the redefined modern Gothic fiction of O'Connor and McCullers, I have been led from an external Gothic structure in which a woman is trapped to the body as an imprisoning Gothic structure whose secret center contains a mystery that the her-oine must confront. Ultimately, because of my own location as a woman and as a feminist-psychoanalytic critic, because of my understanding of femaleness, my sensitivity to its terrors and longings, I discover— or recreate—in the Gothic center the mystery of female identity, teeming with archaic fantasies of power and vulnerability, which a patriarchal society encourages by its cultural divisions. Especially in a time when these divisions themselves are being weakened, issues of identity, and especially gender identity, converge for me within the center of modern Gothic, where boundaries are explored and transgressions allowed expression. There, however, a spectral mother, the original Other, reveals herself as the antagonist in our common struggle to locate a self. Explored obscurely in the conventional Gothic novel because of the force of social and psychological repression, that presence is brought to light in the modern Gothic, which, by its transformation of the unseen to the seen, moves the Gothic toward the grotesque. What is seen depends on how women are seen, but that in turn depends on our vision of the mother, a vision that in Gothic fiction is dominated by the uncanny mother of infancy, who will continue to haunt us as long as women remain, on the one hand, the sole custodians of infantile identity, and on the other, on the margin of social power.

16

Writing and Motherhood

SUSAN RUBIN SULEIMAN

> With the approach of the climacterium, new motherhood
> is impossible, and the frustrated activity is directed to-
> ward other goals. Simply expressed, this attitude is: "If I
> cannot have any more children, I must look for some-
> thing else."
>
> —Helene Deutsch

> ... que savons-nous du discours que (se) fait une mère?
>
> —Julia Kristeva

My epigraphs define the space I shall explore in this essay. At one
end, the confident assertion of a psychoanalyst who not only knows
what mothers want and feel, but does not hesitate for more than an
instant ("simply expressed"—a pause) in formulating the very words
that mothers speak to themselves. At the other end, a simple yet
insidious question. Does the question demolish the psychoanalyst's
certitudes? That is not the point. My purpose here is not to discredit
psychoanalysis but, in the literal sense of the term, to put it in its
place. It is a question not of distributing praise or blame but of seeing
more clearly, of "knowing where it's at."

First, however, where am I at? Why did I choose to write about
writing and motherhood? Is that a valid subject, is there really a
connection there? Or am I indulging in a purely private pleasure,

tracking a private mania, exorcizing private ghosts? I am the mother of two children, boys, aged 9 and 2 (or so they were in 1979, when these words were first written). I have written learned books and essays about fiction and the theory of literature. My first impulse, when faced with a problem or a text, is to analyze it, understand it.

I am not the first to write about writing and motherhood, their conjunction or disjunction; I need not seek justifications for doing so. But necessarily, for better or for worse, I shall write about them in my own way.

Mothers/Writing: The Psychoanalytic Projection

The traditional psychoanalytic view of motherhood is indissociable from the more general theory of normal female development and female sexuality. According to Freud and his orthodox followers, the little girl's problem is to effect a satisfactory transition from the preoedipal phase of "masculine" (i.e., clitoral) eroticism to the properly feminine, vaginal eroticism that will prepare her for her role as a mother. In the process of this transition, the little girl must reject her own mother in favor of the father, whose child she longs to bear. She must reconcile herself to the "fact" of her castration, and must give up the active-sadistic impulses of the preoedipal phase in favor of the passive-masochistic gratifications appropriate to her female role. In the words of Karl Abraham, "The normal adult woman becomes reconciled to her own sexual role.... She desires passive gratification and longs for a child."[1] According to Helene Deutsch, the sine qua non of normal motherhood is "the masochistic-feminine willingness to sacrifice"—a sacrifice made easy by the impulse of maternal love, whose "chief characteristic is tenderness. All the aggression and sexual sensuality in the woman's personality are suppressed and diverted by this central emotional expression of motherliness."[2] The mother's sacrifice is also made easy by the fact that through the child, especially if it is a male child, she compensates for the one great lack of her life, the lack of a penis.

1. Quoted in Joel Kovel, "The Castration Complex Reconsidered," in *Women and Analysis*, ed. Jean Strouse (New York: Viking, 1974), 136.
2. Helene Deutsch, *The Psychology of Women* (1945; rpt. New York: Bantam, 1973), II, 411–12, 20.

Feminine masochism, feminine passivity, feminine castration, feminine penis envy—every one of these notions has been challenged, both by contemporary feminists and by such earlier revisionists as Karen Horney and Clara Thompson. Significantly, however, their arguments have not borne on the *fact* of feminine masochism, passivity, or penis envy in our society, but rather on their innateness versus their culturally conditioned character. More recently, such feminists as Juliet Mitchell and Elizabeth Janeway have salvaged Freud's insights by relativizing them: whereas for Freud the course of female development was a physiologically determined process and therefore inevitable (despite his well-known demurrals, his famous statements about not knowing what women are and what women want), for Mitchell and Janeway, as for Horney and Thompson before them, the fact of feminine masochism or penis envy reflects the devalued position of women in patriarchal society. The facts are there, it is their explanation that must be corrected and their inevitability that must be challenged. As Juliet Mitchell has written: "Freud's psychoanalytic theories are about sexism; that he himself propagated certain sexist veiws and that his work has been the bulwark of the ideological oppression of women are doubtless of great importance. But we can understand its significance only if we first realize that it was precisely the psychological formations produced within patriarchal societies that he was revealing and analysing."[3]

By and large I agree with this view, which also informs (by and large) Nancy Chodorow's important book *The Reproduction of Mothering*. As Chodorow shows, neither a biological-anthropological nor a behavioral role-socialization model is adequate to account for the permanence of women's mothering function: "Women's capacities for mothering and abilities to get gratification from it are strongly internalized and psychologically enforced, and are built developmentally into the feminine psychic structure. Women are prepared psychologically for mothering through the developmental situation in which they grow up, and in which women have mothered them."[4] This being the case, Chodorow argues that only a radical change in modes of parenting, so that fathers and men also "mother," can effect a change in

3. Juliet Mitchell, "On Freud and the Distinction between the Sexes," in *Women and Analysis*, ed. Strouse, 32.

4. Nancy Chodorow, *The Reproduction of Mothering: Psychoanalysis and the Sociology of Gender* (Berkeley: University of California Press, 1978), 39.

the feminine psyche. If such a change should ever occur on a large enough scale to make a difference, the conjunction of writing and motherhood, like most other conjunctions involving motherhood, will become an altogether different subject. In the meantime, I shall argue that that particular conjunction is (1) a problem, (2) a woman's problem, and (3) a problem that must be considered as much in psychological as in sociological terms, if not more so.

Let me return, however, to the psychoanalytic view of motherhood as it exists in the traditional literature. The good and even the good-enough (Winnicott) mother is characterized according to this literature, not only by tenderness and the "masochistic-feminine willingness to sacrifice" but above all by her exclusive and total involvement with her child. Chodorow quotes the psychoanalyst Alice Balint as representative in this respect. Balint states: "The ideal mother has no interests of her own. . . . For all of us it remains self-evident that the interests of mother and child are identical, and it is the generally acknowledged measure of the goodness or badness of the mother how far she really feels this identity of interests." Chodorow comments: "This statement does not mean that mothers have no interests apart from their children—we all know that this kind of overinvestment is 'bad' for children. But social commentators, legislators, and most clinicians expect women's interests to enhance their mothering and expect women to want only interests that do so." Good mothering, in other words, "requires both a constant delicate assessment of infantile needs and wants and an extreme selflessness. Analysts do not consider their prescription difficult for most 'normal' mothers to fulfill."[5]

Melanie Klein speaks with great sympathy and understanding about the murderous impulses that every child feels toward its beloved mother; she does not speak about the murderous impulses that a mother may feel toward her beloved child.[6] According to Helene Deutsch, the one permanent tragedy of motherhood is that children grow up: "Every phase of the child's development ends with intensified tendencies to liberate himself. The mother—every mother—tries to keep him attached to herself and opposes the actions that tend to dissolve the tie."[7] The notion that another tragedy of motherhood may

5. Chodorow, *Reproduction of Mothering*, 77, 82, 84–85.
6. See in particular Klein's 1937 essay, "Love, Guilt, and Reparation," reprinted in *Love, Guilt, and Reparation and Other Works, 1921–1945* (New York: Doubleday, 1977), 306–43.
7. Deutsch, *Psychology of Women*, 331.

lie in the conflict between the mother's desire for self-realization—a self-realization that has nothing to do with her being a mother—and the child's need for her selflessness seems never to have entered the psychoanalysts' mind.[8] Even Karen Horney, herself a mother and a writer, could devote a paper to the subject of "maternal conflicts" whose entire emphasis was on the harm a mother could do to her son if her own relations to her parents were not properly worked out.[9] It is as if, for psychoanalysis, the only self worth worrying about in the mother-child relationship were that of the child. How this exclusive focus affects the mother is something we are only beginning to become aware of, as mothers begin to speak for themselves. "Most of the literature of infant care and psychology has assumed that the process toward individuation is essentially the *child's* drama, played out against and with a parent or parents who are, for better or worse, givens. Nothing could have prepared me for the realization that I was a mother, one of those givens, when I knew I was still in a state of uncreation myself."[10] That is Adrienne Rich's testimony; the feelings it describes are not unique to her.

Mothers don't write, they are written. Simply expressed (to quote Helene Deutsch), this is the underlying assumption of most psychoanalytic theories about writing and about artistic creation in general. According to Freud, the poet is a superior daydreamer, endowed with the gift of transforming his personal fantasies into aesthetically pleasing creations. The fantasies themselves, however, are always derived from

8. It will certainly be noticed that almost all of the analysts I have been quoting are women. Their statements show either a remarkable alienation from their own experience (surely they did not become analysts and writers by adapting without problems to the "passive-masochistic gratifications" of femininity) or else a remarkable degree of self-hate (their own development was "abnormal," since they chose the route of the masculinity complex in their own lives). What seems astonishing is that Helene Deutsch recently declared herself to be a long-standing feminist, whose greatest hope for her women patients was that they would "have a passionate interest in something other than the possible man and children in [their lives]." That is a curious statement to come from the most orthodoxly Freudian theorist of "normal" femininity. As Marcia Cavell rightly points out, the statement suggests at the very least a deep split between Deutsch the therapist and Deutsch the theorist. (See Cavell, "Since 1924: Toward a New Psychology of Women," *Women and Analysis*, ed. Strouse, 167.)

9. Karen Horney, "Maternal Conflicts," in *Feminine Psychology* (New York: Norton, 1973), 175–81.

10. Adrienne Rich, *Of Woman Born: Motherhood as Experience and Institution* (New York: Bantam, 1977), 17.

the poet's childhood self: "a piece of creative writing, like a daydream, is a continuation of, and a substitute for, what was once the play of childhood."[11] D. W. Winnicott enlarged this view with his theory of transitional objects, which function essentially as substitutes for the mother. According to Winnicott, transitional objects exist in an intermediate area between the purely subjective world of the child and the external reality of the "not-me"—more exactly, in the "potential space between the baby and the mother."[12] Artistic creation, indeed all cultural experience, belongs to the realm of transitional phenomena. Successful creation, like all creative living, depends on the trust and self-confidence first developed in the child's earliest relationship to his mother.

In Melanie Klein's theory of artistic creation, the mother—or rather, the mother's body—functions as a "beautiful land" to be explored. The creative writer, like the explorer, the scientist, the artist in general, is impelled by the "desire to re-discover the mother of the early days, whom [he] has lost actually or in [his] feelings."[13] The work of art itself stands for the mother's body, destroyed repeatedly in fantasy but restored or "repaired" in the act of creation.

The fact that for Klein, as for Freud, the poet is always a "he" is worth remarking, but it is not the point I wish to stress here. For me it is more significant that psychoanalytic theory invariably places the artist, man or woman, in the position of the child. Just as motherhood is ultimately the child's drama, so is artistic creation. In both cases the mother is the essential but silent Other, the mirror in whom the child searches for his own reflection, the body he seeks to appropriate, the thing he loses or destroys again and again, and seeks to recreate. A writer, says Roland Barthes, is "someone who plays with the body of his [her?—the French is conveniently ambiguous on this point, but Barthes' own meaning seems clear enough] mother."[14]

This is an extremely suggestive idea, one that is capable of renewing our understanding of a host of writers, such as Proust, Poe, Stendhal, Woolf (see *To the Lighthouse*), Robbe-Grillet (as I have tried to show

---

11. Sigmund Freud, "Creative Writers and Day-Dreaming" (1908), in *Standard Edition*, IX, 152.

12. See D. W. Winnicott, *Playing and Reality* (New York: Basic Books, 1971), 107 and *passim*.

13. Klein, "Love, Guilt, and Reparation," 334.

14. Roland Barthes, *Le Plaisir du texte* (Paris, 1973), 60. All translations from the French are my own.

elsewhere),[15] and many others. And yet ... what about the writer who *is* "the body of the mother"? Is this a foolish question, since mothers too have mothers? Does the mother who writes write exclusively as her own mother's child?

Perhaps. Yet I contend that we know too little about what and how and why mothers write to answer the question one way or the other. We may even know too little to have asked the right questions. As Tillie Olsen has pointed out, mothers who have been "full-time" writers have been rare until our own century, and the great women writers have been, with very few exceptions, childless during all or most of their writing lives.[16] Kristeva is right, we know very little about the inner discourse of a mother; and as long as our own emphasis, encouraged by psychoanalytic theory and by the looming presence of (mostly male) mother-fixated writers, continues to be on the-mother-as-she-is-written rather than on the-mother-as-she-writes, we shall continue in our ignorance.

There are consistent reasons for psychoanalysis' failure to see mothers writing (*as* mothers). First of all, psychoanalysis is nothing if not a theory of childhood. We should not be surprised if it locates artistic creativity, as it does every other aspect of adult personality, in the child the adult once was, and often continues to be. A second and more specific reason lies, as I suggested earlier, in the psychoanalytic theory of normal female development: mothers don't create works of art because all of their creative, aggressive drives find an outlet in the production of children. As Helene Deutsch put it: "The urge to intellectual and artistic creation and the productivity of motherhood spring from common sources, and *it seems very natural that one should be capable of replacing the other.*" As long as her motherly capacities are put to use, a mother does not need to write: "A motherly woman can give up her other interests in favor of the reproductive function, and she returns to the former when she feels the biologic restriction approaching." This might be called the menopausal theory of artistic creation (although when one reads Deutsch's description of the woman at menopause, one wonders what sort of creation she could possibly undertake: "With the lapse of the reproductive service, her beauty

15. Susan Suleiman, "Reading Robbe-Grillet: Sadism and Text in *Projet pour une révolution à New York*," *Romanic Review*, 68 (January 1977), 43–62.
16. Tillie Olsen, *Silences* (New York: Doubleday, 1979), 16, 31.

vanishes, and usually the warm, vital flow of feminine emotional life as well"—the grave is not far off, it would seem), itself a subcategory of the more general "either/or" theory that can be summed up as follows: writing or motherhood, work or child, never the two at the same time.[17]

The either/or theory is, of course, older than psychoanalysis. As Elaine Showalter has documented, it was already invoked by the early Victorians. Victorian critics were on the whole more kind to women writers who were mothers than to their childless sisters, but with the clear understanding that "mothers must not dream of activity beyond the domestic sphere until their families are grown."[18] This line of argument, adopted even by such writers as Mrs. Gaskell, who was the mother of four children (she published her first novel at age 38), was based on the moral obligations of the good wife and mother. "What most women rejected as unacceptable and unchristian," writes Showalter, "was the use of literary vocation to avoid the responsibilities of home life."[19] It took psychoanalysis to transform moral obligation into a psychological "law," equating the creative impulse with the procreative one and decreeing that she who has a child feels no need to write books.

By means of this "law," psychoanalytic theory not only offered an elegant explanation for and justification of the mother's silence (making any mother who did not wish to wait until menopause to write books feel "abnormal") but provided an equally elegant explanation for why some childless women (and men) did write books: books were obviously substitutes for children. Once the "law" was properly internalized by women (in a way it could not possibly be by men, since men cannot *choose* to bear children), its capacities for generating guilt and anguish were infinite: corresponding to the writing mother's sense of "abnormality" was the childless woman writer's sense of "unnaturalness." Not for nothing did Virginia Woolf, who knew her Freud, "fear that writing was an act that unsexed her, made her an unnatural woman."[20] Whereas the male writer, in comparing his books to tend-

17. Deutsch, *Psychology of Women*, 479, 481.

18. Elaine Showalter, "Women Writers and the Double Standard," in *Woman in Sexist Society*, ed. Vivian Gornick and Barbara Moran (New York: Basic Books, 1971), 333.

19. Elaine Showalter, *A Literature of Their Own: British Women Novelists from Brontë to Lessing* (Princeton: Princeton University Press, 1977), 65.

20. Phyllis Rose, as paraphrased in Elaine Showalter, *Literature of Their Own*, 270.

erly loved children (a common metaphor, at least until the recent emphasis on writing as an autoerotic activity), could see his metaphorical maternity as something *added* to his male qualities, the childless woman whose books "replaced" real children too often thought (was made to feel) that she had less, not more.

Here again, psychoanalysis cannot be held entirely responsible, since the derogation of childless and/or unmarried women writers was already common in the days of Austen and the Brontës. My point, however, is that psychoanalysis lent scientific prestige to a widespread cultural prejudice, reinforcing it and elevating it to the status of a "natural" law.

It is in this context that the protest against the "motherhood myth" perpetrated by psychoanalysis and against the fact of motherhood itself, which has characterized one branch of contemporary feminist writing and criticism, must be understood. We should also understand, however, that this protest is itself in a sense a victim of the either/or theory. The only difference is that the values attributed to book and child have been reversed. Thus Nina Auerbach, in an article significantly titled "Artists and Mothers: A False Alliance," declares that "far from endowing Austen with second-hand motherhood, her identity as an artist represented an escape from confinement into a child-free world with space for mind and spirit, time for change, and privacy for growth." Auerbach celebrates Austen and Eliot *because* they "both turned away from motherhood and embraced a creativity they defined as more spacious, more adult, more inclusive."[21]

Is there no alternative to the either/or? Will we ever be forced to write the book and deny the child (not the child we were but the child we have, or might have) or love the child and postpone/renounce the book? Or is Kristeva right in insisting that "while a certain feminism takes its pouting and its isolation for protest and perhaps even for dissidence, genuine feminine innovation . . . will not be possible until we have elucidated motherhood, feminine creation, and the relationship between them"?[22]

It is time to let mothers have their word.

21. Nina Auerbach, "Artists and Mothers: A False Alliance," *Women and Literature*, 6 (Spring 1978), 9, 14.
22. Julia Kristeva, "Un Nouveau Type d'intellectuel: Le dissident," *Tel Quel*, no. 74 (Winter 1977), 6–7.

Writing and Motherhood: As Mothers See It

The picture is not all rosy.

> Try telling a child that Mamma is working, when the child can see with its own eyes that she is just sitting there writing.... I dare not have music on when I am in the basement, writing, lest upstairs they think I am just sitting here loafing. I feel that to be respected I must produce pancakes and homebaked bread and have neat, tidy rooms. [Liv Ullman][23]

> Since I had begun writing, I had sought time alone. That very self I had once sought to flee, ... that dangerous, frightening self was precisely what I had learned to treasure, what I had begun to understand.
> In order to tame [the dangerous self], I had to write, regularly and consistently, and in order to write I had to be alone.
> Now suddenly I was always with Benjamin. [Jane Lazarre][24]

> For me, poetry was where I lived as no-one's mother, where I existed as myself. [Adrienne Rich][25]

> I just started pecking away at this story set during the American Revolution. It wasn't anything I could get completely absorbed in. I had three boys at home, and there were always dishes to put in the dishwasher. [Kathleen Woodiwiss][26]

> Children need one *now*. The very fact that these are real needs, that one feels them as one's own (love, not duty); that there is no one else responsible for these needs, gives them primacy.... Work interrupted, deferred, relinquished, makes blockage—at best, lesser accomplishment. [Tillie Olsen][27]

> Every time I thought something would do, in the old days I'd race to the writing pad ... and really be excited. Now I kept thinking: "Oh no, I don't think that's very good." Then one morning I woke up and I thought: "It's gone ... and I don't want it to come back." [Susan Hill][28]

Guilt, desperation, splitting of the self, alienated role playing ("My

23. Liv Ullman, *Changing* (New York: Bantam, 1978), 36, 37.
24. Jane Lazarre, *The Mother Knot* (New York: Dell, 1977), 55–56.
25. Rich, *Of Woman Born*, 12.
26. Kathleen E. Woodiwiss, interviewed by Judy Klemensrud, *New York Times Book Review*, November 4, 1979, 52.
27. Olsen, *Silences*, 19.
28. Susan Hill, "On Ceasing to Be a Novelist" (interview with Robert Robinson), *The Listener*, February 2, 1978, 154.

writing is not serious, don't be offended by it, just look at my three children"), resignation to lesser accomplishment, renunciation of the writing self—these are some of the realities, some of the possible choices that writing mothers live with.

Kathleen Woodiwiss is a rich woman, the author of historical romances for the "housewife market." Her last book has sold more than two million copies. She calls herself "an ordinary housewife": "I enjoy cooking and cleaning, my family and home. Right now my husband is remodeling one of the bathrooms."[29] She represents what some would call the perfect accommodation between writing and mother-wifehood. Perhaps she has no serious talent or ambition; perhaps she has never allowed herself to ask whether she does.

Susan Hill was a highly respected "younger" British novelist—for the cultivated reader, not the best-seller type. In her late thirties she married, and she became pregnant soon after. She was working on a novel at the time, but never finished it. She no longer writes fiction.

Between these two extremes, each of which is in its own way a renunciation of the writing self, are manifold ways of coping—some we know about because they have been written, others we can only guess at. We need to have more information—more interviews, more diaries, more memoirs, essays, reminiscences by writing mothers. I am sure I have missed many as it is, but exhaustiveness is not what I am aiming for. I wish merely to glimpse the possibilities, the principal recurrent themes in what some contemporary writing mothers have said discursively (poetry and fiction are a later question) about, or out of, their own experience of the relationship between writing and motherhood.

What are the major themes? I see them clustered into two large groups: opposition and integration, motherhood as obstacle or source of conflict and motherhood as link, as source of connection to work and world. The oppositional themes—guilt vs. love, mother's creative self vs. child's needs, isolation vs. commitment—are the ones I emphasized in the above quotations. The daily conflict and self-doubt, the waste of creative energies these oppositions engender cannot be overestimated. What is involved here, furthermore, is not simply an institutional or social problem; alternate nurturers will not necessarily relieve it (although they may eventually help) because the conflicts are *inside* the mother, they are part of her most fundamental experience. One can always argue, as Rich and others have done, that the

29. Woodiwiss, interviewed by Klemesrud.

internal conflicts are the result of institutional forces, the result of women's isolation, women's victimization by the motherhood myth in patriarchal society. But while this argument can help us understand *why* the conflicts are internal, it does not eliminate them. *At the present time*, any mother of young children (and I don't mean only infants, but children of school age and beyond) who wants to do serious creative work—with all that such work implies of the will to self-assertion, self-absorption, solitary grappling—must be prepared for the worst kind of struggle, which is the struggle against herself. Here I am reminded of Karen Horney's description of a certain type of neurotic disturbance in work—the disturbance she sees as typical of the "self-effacing type":

> Without being aware of it, he is up against two kinds of chronic handicaps: his self-minimizing and his inefficiency in tackling the subject matter. His self-minimizing largely results . . . from his need to keep himself down in order not to trespass against the taboo on anything "presumptuous." *It is a subtle undermining, berating, doubting*, which saps the energies without his being aware of what he is doing to himself. . . . As a result he works with the oppressive feeling of impotence and insignificance. . . . His inefficiency in tackling the subject matter is caused mainly by taboos on all that implies assertion, aggression, mastery. . . . His difficulty is not in being unproductive. Good original ideas may emerge, but he is inhibited in taking hold of them, tackling them, grappling with them, wrestling with them, checking them, shaping them, organizing them. We are not usually aware of these mental operations as being assertive, aggressive moves, although the language indicates it; and we may realize this fact only when they are inhibited by a pervasive check on aggression.[30]

Mothers, or women, are of course not the only ones to whom Horney's description applies.[31] She herself obviously had both men and

---

30. Karen Horney, "Neurotic Disturbances in Work," in *Neurosis and Human Growth: The Struggle toward Self-Realization* (New York: Norton, 1970), 319–20 (my emphasis).

31. I am struck, however, by how closely Horney's description corresponds to Simone de Beauvoir's explanation for the lack of audaciousness in women writers:

> To please is her first care; and often she fears she will be displeasing as a woman from the mere fact that she writes. . . . The writer of originality, unless dead, is always shocking, scandalous; novelty disturbs and repels. Woman is still astonished and flattered at being admitted to the world of thought, of art—a masculine world. She is on her best behavior; *she is afraid to disarrange, to investigate, to explode*; she feels she should seek pardon for literary pretensions through her modesty and good taste. She stakes on the reliable values of conformity. . . . [*The Second Sex*, trans. and ed. H. M. Parshley (New York: Bantam, 1961), 666; my emphasis]

women in mind. But I would suggest that in the case of the writing mother, the subtle undermining, the oppressive feeling of impotence and insignificance, the pervasive check on aggression that Horney talks about are intimately linked to a sense of guilt about her child. Jean-Paul Sartre once said in an interview, when asked about the value of literature and of his own novels in particular: "En face d'un enfant qui meurt, *La Nausée* ne fait pas le poids" (freely translated: "When weighed against a dying child, *La Nausée* doesn't count").[32] If this statement reflects the well-known guilt of the bourgeois writer with left-wing sympathies (Sartre being a specialist on *that* question), what are we to say about the guilt of a mother who might weigh her books not against a stranger's dying child but merely against her own child who is crying?

One way to appease the crying child (and my contention is that whether or not the child actually cries while the mother writes, s/he always cries in the mother's nightmares) is to tender her/him the book as a propitiatory offering. Phyllis Chesler's *With Child*, a diary of her first pregnancy and childbirth at the age of 37, is dedicated to her son: "To my son Ariel, this handmade gift to welcome you." (I am a good mother, I make my own presents.) Liv Ullman's autobiography, from which I quoted above, is dedicated to her daughter, Linn, with a frontispiece photograph of mother and child forehead to forehead. The back cover is a close-up photo of Liv, somber, alone. The last pages are a letter to Linn—a series of self-reproaches by the mother, culminating in the astonishing question: "Do you understand that I really have no valid reason not to run out to you and live your life?" This from one of the most serious actresses of our time, who is also a genuine writer.

Another way to propitiate the crying child is not to write the book, or to write it less well than one could. "Almost no mothers—as almost no part-time, part-self persons—have created enduring literature . . . so far." That was Tillie Olsen writing, in 1972.[33]

So much for the dark side. There is also a lighter one.

32. Quoted by Jean Ricardou in Simone de Beauvoir et al., *Que peut la littérature?* (Paris: Union Générale, 1965), 59.
33. Olsen, *Silences*, 19.

Through you, Ariel, I'm enlarged, connected to something larger than myself. Like falling in love, like ideological conversion, the connection makes me *feel* my existence. [Phyllis Chesler][34]

And yet, somehow, something, call it Nature or that affirming fatalism of the human creature, makes me aware of the inevitable as already part of me, not to be contended against so much as brought to bear as an additional weapon against drift, stagnation and spiritual death. [Adrienne Rich][35]

A mother can be any sort of person, great or ordinary, given to moderation or intensity, inclined toward amazonian aggression or receptivity. But whatever type you are, being a mother forces you to accept your limitations. And when you accept your limitations as a mother, you begin to accept your limitations in other areas of life as well. The daily grinding friction of motherhood will give you the chance, at least, of relinquishing some of your egotism. You will finally cease to be a child. [Jane Lazarre][36]

... through the coming of the child and the beginning of a love, perhaps the only genuine feminine love for another ... one has the chance to accede to that relationship so difficult for a woman, the relationship to the Other: to the symbolic and the ethical. If pregnancy is a threshold between nature and culture, motherhood is a bridge between the singular and the ethical. ... [Julia Kristeva][37]

What does it mean to love, for a woman? The same thing as to write. ... WORD/FLESH. From one to the other, eternally, fragmented visions, metaphors of the invisible. [Julia Kristeva][38]

Integration, connection, reaching out; a defense against drift and spiritual death, a way of outgrowing the solipsism of childhood, a way to relate, a way to write—this too is motherhood as seen by mothers, often by the very same mothers who at other times feel torn apart by the conflicting pulls of work and child. Jane Lazarre, at the end of *The Mother Knot*, invents a debate between "the mother" and "the dark lady," the one urging Jane to have a second child, the other

---

34. Phyllis Chesler, *With Child: A Diary of Motherhood* (New York: Crowell, 1979), 246.

35. Rich, *Of Woman Born*, 9.

36. Lazarre, *Mother Knot*, 216.

37. Kristeva, "Nouveau Type d'intellectuel," 6.

38. Julia Kristeva, "Héréthique de l'amour," *Tel Quel*, no. 74 (Winter 1977), 31. Reprinted as "Stabat Mater" in Kristeva, *Histoires d'amour* (Paris: Denoël, 1983). English translation to appear in special issue of *Poetics Today* titled *The Female Body in Western Culture: Semiotic Perspectives*, ed. Susan Rubin Suleiman, forthcoming.

arguing against it. The dark lady says: "I am not speaking about mere details and practical responsibilities. It is the effect of those continuous demands on the spirit to which I commend your attention." The mother counters: "Don't you want the feeling of a baby moving inside you again?" But it turns out that the dark lady is the mother in disguise, the mother the dark lady. And Jane is both of them, they are inside her head.

Have we simply arrived here at the point where Adrienne Rich began? "My children cause me the most exquisite suffering of which I have any experience. It is the suffering of ambivalence: the murderous alternation between bitter resentment and raw-edged nerves, and blissful gratification and tenderness."[39] Yes and no. For Rich, as she expresses it in this diary entry, ambivalence is an *alternation* between resentment and tenderness, negation of the child and reaching out for the child—as if these two impulses were unconnected to each other, locked in an insurmountable opposition, corresponding perhaps to the opposition between the mother's need to affirm her self as writer and the child's need (or her belief in the child's need) for her selflessness. There is something of this struggle in Lazarre's parable, but the parable also suggests a possibility of reconciliation rather than conflict between the warring elements. If the mother is the dark lady and the dark lady the mother, then the energies and aspirations of the one are also those of the other. The mother's tenderness and the dark lady's urge for self-expression may support, not hinder, each other.

This is precisely what is implied by Chesler, by Rich in another diary entry (the one I quoted above), and especially by Kristeva, who goes beyond implication to explicit statement: "Far from being in contradiction with creativity (as the existentialist myth still tries to make us believe), motherhood can—in itself and if the economic constraints are not too burdensome—favor a certain feminine creation. To the extent that it lifts the fixations, makes passion circulate between life and death, self and other, culture and nature . . ."[40] Kristeva is prudent, she makes no absolute claims (motherhood *can* favor creation, it doesn't necessarily do so); she is aware of the material obstacles (how will mother write if there is no one else to care for baby, or if she must work at other jobs to support baby?—Tillie Olsen's ques-

39. Rich, *Of Woman Born*, 1.
40. Kristeva, "Nouveau Type d'intellectuel," 6.

tions). Yet, in an important turn of French feminist theory, which we also see appearing in a less abstract version in current American feminist thinking, Kristeva rejects the either/or dilemma and suggests that motherhood and feminine creation go hand in hand.

Kristeva's argument, as stated in two essays in the Winter 1977 issue of *Tel Quel*, is a very complex one and would deserve a long analysis unto itself. This is not the appropriate place for that, but I wish to pause at least briefly in order to take a closer look.

Kristeva's argument can be summed up approximately as follows: the order of the symbolic, which is the order of language, of culture, of the law, of the Name-of-the-Father (to use Lacan's terminology), is especially difficult for women to accede to, whether for historical or other reasons. Motherhood, which establishes a *natural* link (the child) between woman and the social world, provides a privileged means of entry into the order of culture and of language. This privilege belongs to the mother (if I read Kristeva correctly here) not only in contrast to women who are not mothers but also in contrast to men, whose relationship to the symbolic order is itself problematical, characterized by discontinuity, separation, absence. The symbolic, whether for men or for women, functions as the realm of the (unattainable) Other, the realm of arbitrary signs rather than of things; it is by definition the realm of frustrated relations, of impossible loves. The love of God, that ultimate sign of the Other, is of the order of the impossible. But for the mother, according to Kristeva, the Other is not (only) an arbitrary sign, a necessary absence: it is the child, whose presence and whose bodily link to her are inescapable givens, material facts. If to love (her child) is, for a woman, the same thing as to write, we have in that conjunction a modern, secular equivalent of the word made flesh.

This straightforward summary is in a sense a betrayal, however, for the most interesting thing about Kristeva's argument is its quasi-byzantine indirection. The first of the two essays, placed as an introduction to the special issue of the journal devoted to "*recherches féminines,*" is not ostensibly about motherhood at all, or even about women, but about the possibilities of intellectuals and of intellectual dissidence in Western culture. The remarks about motherhood and its relation to feminine creation form part of a section on the possibly dissident role of women in relation to patriarchal law. Since the more elemental law of the reproduction of the species is essentially in women's hands, Kristeva wonders whether mothers are not, in fact, at the very opposite pole of dissidence—whether by maintaining the species they do not also maintain and guarantee the existing social order. She does not answer this question directly, but my sense is that, if pressed, her answer would be: "Yes and no." The mother's body, being a place of fragmentation, cleavage, elemental pulsations that exist *before* language and meaning, is necessarily a place of exile, a place of dis-order and extreme singularity in relation to the collective order of culture. At the same time, the mother's body is the link between nature and culture, and as such must play a conserving role.

What interests me, however, is another question that Kristeva poses: "After the Virgin [Mary], what do we know about the inner discourse of a mother?" The question is both provocative and bizarre, its bizarreness residing in the opening words. Do we know more about the Virgin's inner discourse than about any other mother's? At best we know the discourse that has been attributed to her, that has in fact *created* her—it is the discourse of Christianity, of the *Fathers* of the Church.

Kristeva is aware of this. Her second and much longer essay ("Héréthique de l'amour") is devoted precisely to the question of how the myth of the Virgin Mother was gradually elaborated by Christian discourse, and how it has functioned in the imagination of the West. Above all, she seeks to answer this question: What is it about the Christian representation of ideal motherhood, as embodied in the Virgin, that was satisfactory to women for hundreds of years, and why is that representation no longer satisfactory today? Her tentative conclusion is that in the image of the Virgin Mother, Christianity provided what for a long time was a satisfactory compromise solution to female paranoia: a denial of the male's role in procreation (virgin birth), a fulfillment of the female desire for power (Mary as Queen of Heaven), a sublimation of the woman's murderous or devouring desires through the valorization of her breast (the infant Jesus suckling) and of her own pain (the *Mater dolorosa*), a fulfilling of the fantasy of deathlessness or eternal life (the Assumption), and above all a denial of other women, including the woman's own mother (Mary was "alone of all her sex")—all of this being granted upon one condition: that the ultimate supremacy and divinity of the male be maintained in the person of the Son, before whom the Mother kneels and to whom she is subservient.

According to Kristeva, the compromise solution represented by the Virgin Mother provided a model that women could, however indirectly, identify with, and at the same time allowed those in charge of the social and symbolic order to maintain their control. (It may be worth noting that the Christian representation of the Virgin Mother has some affinities with, but is much more powerful than, the representation of ideal motherhood in psychoanalytic discourse: in both cases the mother is elevated precisely to the extent that she prostrates herself before her son; for Freud, the mother's greatest satisfaction is to see her favorite son attain glory, which then reflects back on her.) For today's women, however, Kristeva argues, the myth of Mary has lost its positive powers: it leaves too many things unsaid, censors too many aspects of female experience, chief among them the experience of childbirth and of the mother's body in general, the relationship of women to their mothers (and to their daughters), and the relationship of women to men (not to male children, but to adult men). As far as all of these relationships are concerned, motherhood provides a central point from which to ask the questions and to make a first step toward answering them.

As if to demonstrate this very thing, Kristeva intersperses her analytical, discursive text with lyrical, discontinuous fragments of an "other" text—this "other" text being the inner discourse of a mother, Kristeva herself. Since the lyrical fragments are surrounded, enveloped by the discursive text, it is tempting to see the two as "mother" and "child," with the lyrical fragments representing the child. (This idea was suggested to me by Carolyn Burke). But paradoxically, in the "child-text" it is a *mother* who writes of her experiences: childbirth, playing with her infant, watching over the child sick for the first time, feeling separated from and at the same time united with the child, memories of her own mother (the "other woman"), her relationship to language, to the Law. The lyrical fragments are thus in counterpoint, both stylistically and on the level of content, to the discursive text, as the mother's *inner* discourse is in counterpoint to the discourse given to her, constructed about her, by Christianity, the dominant order of Western culture.

These essays by Kristeva seem to me to be especially important for three reasons: she seeks to analyze and show the limitations of Western culture's traditional discourse about motherhood; she offers a theory, however incomplete and tentative, about the relation between motherhood and feminine creation; finally, she *writes* her own maternal text as an example of what such creation might be. This ambitious undertaking is part of the much broader context of contemporary

French feminist theory, which over the past several years has been trying both to elaborate a theory of and to exemplify the specificity of *l'écriture féminine*. Luce Irigaray and Hélène Cixous (who is a mother) have insisted on the essentially subversive, dis-orderly nature of women's writing in patriarchal culture, without attempting to differentiate between the feminine and the maternal. This may be because—at least for Cixous—the very fact of being a woman means that one is "never far from the 'mother,' " that is, from a force of reparation and nourishment that is fundamentally "other" in relation to the desiccated rationalism of male discourse.[41]

Chantal Chawaf, on the other hand, much more radically than Kristeva, has tied the practice of feminine writing to the biological fact of motherhood. Chawaf is the mother of two children and the author of several books written in a lyrical autobiographical mode. The central experience around which all her writing turns is the physical and emotional experience of motherhood and of maternal love, which she endows with quasi-cosmic significance. One of her recent books, *Maternité*, is a series of sensuous prose poems celebrating the love between a mother who is on the verge of emotional breakdown and her two children, whom she perceives as her only link to communication and light, in opposition to solitude and eternal darkness. Chawaf has stated in interviews and in commentaries on her work that for her motherhood is the only access to literary creation. In *Maternité* she speaks of a "new syntax with fatty nouns, infinitive thighs," a language so physical that it would be a nourishment and "would make every sentence the close relative of the skin and of the mucous membranes. . . ."[42]

The work of the French radical feminists represents without a doubt the most ambitious attempt so far to theorize the relationship between writing and femininity, and more or less directly between writing and motherhood. Personally, my one reservation about their work—which is clearly a work in progress, and therefore too early to make definitive pronouncements about—concerns its exclusionary aspects. To recognize that women, mothers, have been excluded from the order of patriarchal discourse, and to insist on the positive difference of maternal and feminine writing in relation to male writing, can only be beneficial at this time. But it would be a pity if the male gesture of

41. See Cixous's essay "Sorties," in Catherine Clément and Hélène Cixous, *La Jeune Née* (Paris: Union Générale, 1975), esp. 169–80.
42. Chantal Chawaf, *Manternité* (Paris, 1979), 20.

exclusion and repression of the female "other" were to be matched by a similar gesture in reverse. I do not mean by that only the obvious exclusion of men, for some French feminists (Hélène Cixous among them) are willing to admit that certain male poets have attained a "feminine" status in their writing. Rather, I mean the exclusion of a certain *kind* of writing and discourse arbitrarily defined as "male," repressive, logical, the discourse of power, or what have you. Such a gesture necessarily places "feminine" writing in a minority position, willfully ex-centric in relation to power. I am not wholly convinced that that is the best position for women to be in.

I also have reservations about what might be called that fetishization of the female body in relation to writing. It may be true that femininity and its quintessential embodiment, motherhood, can provide a privileged mode of access to language and the mother tongue. What would worry me would be the codification, on the basis of this insight, of women's writing and writing style. In recent French feminist theory and practice, one sees tendencies toward just such codification, both on the level of themes and on the level of style: the centrality of the woman's body and blood, her closeness to Nature, her attunement to the quality of *voice* rather than to "dry" meaning; elemental rhythms, writing as flow (of menstrual blood, of mother's milk, of uterine fluid), "liquid" syntax, lyricism at all costs, receptivity, union, nonaggression.... We are reaching the point where a new genre is being created, and that may be all to the good. But to see in this genre the one and only genuine mode of feminine writing would, I think, be a mistake.[43]

Writing and Motherhood: The Mother's Fictions

After that ascent into theory, I want to return to more concrete ground. Mothers write, and they write fiction as well as personal

---

43. The debate over *l'écriture féminine*, whose implications have properly been seen as political rather than merely stylistic, has been long and sometimes acrimonious among French feminists. The issues are clearly defined in the dialogue that concludes Cixous's and Clément's *Jeune Née*, as well as in Clément's essay "Enslaved Enclave" and Cixous's "Laugh of the Medusa," in *New French Feminisms*, ed. Elaine Marks and Isabelle de Courtivron (New York: Schocken, 1981). Like Clément, but from a different perspective, Kristeva has criticized the concept of *l'écriture féminine*; see in particular "A partir de *Polylogue*," *Revue des sciences humaines*, no. 168 (December 1977), 495–501.

statements. Tillie Olsen remarked about contemporary (British and American) novelists who are mothers that "not many have directly used the material open to them out of motherhood as central source of their work."[44] An interesting question is implied here. What fascinates me, however, is a more specific question: whether, and how, the conjunction of writing and motherhood is refracted in the fictions— as opposed to the more direct statements where the mother says "I"— of mothers who write. Here psychoanalysis may be of help, if only by analogy. Using as a starting point Freud's contention that the work of fiction is a distantiated, formally "disguised" version of the writer's fantasy, we can ask: Is there such a thing as the writing mother's fantasy? And if so, what transformations does the fantasy undergo in the process of its fictionalization? To put it somewhat differently, what happens to the mother's discourse when it chooses not direct expression but the indirections of fiction?

Having asked the question, I am not quite sure just how to go about answering it. But no matter. I shall assume that mothers' fantasies exist, that they are formulatable, and that they can (can, not must) provide the impetus for fictional elaboration. I shall further assume that they are to be found, if anywhere, in the fictions of women writers who are mothers. To demonstrate the literary-critical, if not scientific, usefulness of these assumptions, I shall propose readings of two works by a single writer. The writer is the American poet and novelist Rosellen Brown. The works are a three-page short story titled "Good Housekeeping" and a novel titled *The Autobiography of My Mother*.[45]

"Good Housekeeping"—the title is double-edged. A mother puts her baby down for a nap, first photographing his behind from close up. She is a photographer, working now after an interval long enough for all the chemicals in her darkroom to have dried up. But she is a professional, already imagining how she will hang the pictures in her next show ("utterly random, on flat matte. No implicit order, no heavy ironies"), and she works fast. After the baby's rear come the sludge-covered coffeepot, the inside of the toilet bowl, the mountain of laundry seen from the inside looking out, a bunch of peeled vegetables

44. Olsen, *Silences*, 32.

45. "Good Housekeeping" first appeared in *American Review*, no. 18 (1973), and was reprinted in *Bitches and Sad Ladies: An Anthology of Fiction by and about Women*, ed. Pat Rotter (New York: Dell, 1976), 68–70. *The Autobiography of My Mother* was published in 1976 (New York: Doubleday). Rosellen Brown is the mother of two young daughters.

strewn among the peels, the rumpled bedsheets, her own vagina (seen only by the viewfinder of the camera), a handful of condoms found in a box and randomly arranged, the dirty window, fresh soil in which seedlings of vegetables are buried, a drawerful of household odds and ends, cigarette paper and the marijuana hidden in a spice jar, the inside of a pencil sharpener, a stretch of ugly wallpaper left uncovered, the welcome mat caked with mud. She rejects a row of lined-up cans and an omelet made for the occasion as inappropriate—"too much like *Good Housekeeping*"—and also a pile of bird feathers left by the cat: their function is not clear without the cat, and besides, "are murdered birds a part of every household?"

Then the baby wakes, screaming. With the shades up it is so light "you could see the baby's uvula quivering like an icicle about to drop." When he sees the camera, the baby stops crying, fascinated. "Eyes like cameras. His mother looked back at herself in them, a black box in her lap with a queer star of light in its middle." The baby smiles, reaching for his mother (or for the camera?) through the slats of the crib. The mother's next action (and the story's final paragraph):

> She put her head in her hands. Then she reached in and, focusing as well as she could with one hand, the baby slapping at her through the bars, wheezing with laughter, she found one cool bare thigh, the rosy tightness of it, and pinched it with three fingers, kept pinching hard, till she got that angry uvula again, and a good bit of very wet tongue. Through the magnifier it was spiny as some plant, some sponge, maybe, under the sea.

I find this an extraordinarily powerful story, even after several readings. In trying to account for its power (its powerful effect on me), I invariably return to this last paragraph: the mother looking at her child not directly but through the camera, transforming him into an object; feeling his thighs not as flesh, her flesh, but professionally as a "rosy tightness"; then pinching until the cry comes, and with it the thing she wants to capture, the quivering uvula—the clinicalness of it, and at the same time its possiblity for endless metaphorization: icicle, spiny plant, sponge under the sea. The rosy thigh, sentimental and cloying, would be at best good for *Good Housekeeping*; the angry uvula, like the other exemplary objects ("part of every household") that preceded it, will hang in random order on flat matte. It is not propaganda (Let us all be good housekeepers and have rosy babies) but art.

Art? And what about the crying child? The power of the story, for

373

me, lies in the fantasy that I read in (or perhaps into) it: "With every word I write, with every metaphor, with every act of genuine creation, I hurt my child."

Surely I am overreacting? Perhaps not. To me this is not only a story about the inner world of motherhood *as it is felt*, not as it is mythologized in women's magazines (think of the mess and the jumble, the receptacles of every kind, the insides so carefully observed, the hidden things growing); it is also a story about the *representation* of motherhood by a mother, "seeing herself from a great distance, doing an assignment on herself doing an assignment"; and it is a story about the specular relation between mother-as-artist and her child: seeing herself reflected, *as artist* (holding the camera), in his eyes, she reacts by pinning him down, turning him into an image, a metaphor, a text. Portrait of the artist as mother; or, the momentary triumph of aggression over tenderness.

I say momentary triumph, because the anguish and guilt that inevitably attend the real-life mother's fantasy of writing as aggression against her child are absent. The story ends at the precise moment when the artist affirms herself against both the child and her own maternal feelings, before guilt (or madness—for if she were to go on hurting the child, we would have to call her mad) has a chance to appear. The result, both in the fiction and in the effect its language produces, is a sense of freedom, of formal control, which blocks any possibility of sentimentalization or self-pity. This becomes clearer if one compares Brown's story to, say, Alta's long poem, *Momma*, which recounts a similar experience—the poet-mother chasing her child out of the room so that she can write about her, negating her physical presence in order to capture her as a name, a text. In *Momma* the tone is one of anguish, since the mother *feels* the child's pain and expresses, retrospectively, her own sense of guilt and self-reproach in the poem. By opting for a simultaneous rather than a retrospective point of view, Brown's story refuses, I think quite consciously, the relief—but also the sentimentalization—that comes from self-reproach. We do not know how the mother in the story felt about her action afterward; when she focuses her camera on the crying child (but significantly she does not *see* the child, she sees only the "angry uvula"), we know only the cool concentration with which she snaps the picture. The language of the story "doubles" her own activity by means of the concluding metaphors.

Katherine Anne Porter once said about her own work that at the moment of writing "a calculated coldness is the best mood."[46] It is the dialectic between calculated coldness and intensity of feeling—a dialectic that characterizes the mother's problematic position between work and child—which is thematized in Brown's short story and which, present in the very language of the story, gives it its particular power.

Brown's novel *The Autobiography of My Mother* is a more extended and more complex treatment of the same theme. The novel consists of the alternating narratives of a mother and a daughter, herself the mother of a very young girl child. The mother is a woman in her seventies, still actively involved in her work as a civil liberties lawyer, a public figure. The daughter is an ex-flower child of the late sixties, an escapee of various communes and the California scene, who does nothing. She and her baby daughter return to New York, to her mother's Upper West Side apartment, after a ten-year absence.

Through the mother's narrative we learn about her own disturbed and loveless childhood, her conscious repression of passion and tenderness in favor of extreme self-control and rational action; we also learn of her solitude, her emotional sterility, her inability to make contact with people on any but the most abstract level. Through the daughter's narrative we learn about her feeling of abandonment, her pathological sense of failure and worthlessness, her inability to relate to others except on the most debased sexual level, and her deep hatred of as well as emotional dependence on her mother. During a televised mother-daughter talk show, she refuses to utter a single word. Her revenge on her mother, who is never at a loss for words, takes the form of total passivity and silence.

Between these two women, too much hurt and misunderstanding have accumulated to make any renewal possible. There is the granddaughter, however: stubborn and strong-willed like her grandmother, vulnerable like her mother, she appears to hold out the possibility of a reconciliation of sorts, or at least of a new start. She even manages to awaken her grandmother's seemingly nonexistent maternal feelings.

But it doesn't work out that way. The grandmother plans to take the child away from her mother by legal force. At a picnic where she intends to announce her intentions, she and the child walk down to a waterfall, while the child's mother watches from above. The old woman is not holding on to the child, the child is suddenly no longer

---

46. Katherine Anne Porter, "Notes on Writing," in *The Creative Process*, ed. Brewster Ghiselin (1952; rpt. New American Library, n.d.), 199.

there. She has been swept away, drowned. Earlier, the grandmother had stated: "In life there are no accidents."

What is one to make of this very disturbing book? I begin with the title: of which mother is this the autobiography? And who is its author? Gertrude Stein, I recall, wrote *The Autobiography of Alice B. Toklas*. The grandmother's name in this novel is Gerda Stein, and at one point, in an extended allusion to Shakespeare, she refers to herself as Gertrude. She also mentions that her decision to be a lawyer came after her first desire, which was to be a writer. Is the fictional Gertrude a stand-in for the real one? Possibly. But it is Rosellen Brown who is the signed author of this "autobiography," just as Gertrude Stein was of the other one. Structurally, it is Rosellen Brown that is the stand-in for Gertrude Stein—authors both. Yet if one takes the title seriously, then one must consider (the fictional) Gerda/Gertrude Stein to be Rosellen Brown's mother. Rosellen is thus both daughter to a Gertrude and a Gertrude herself, both author and author's daughter. The two narratives in the novel perhaps reflect this split, as does the fact that in the fiction, mother and daughter manage about equally to attract (and occasionally to repel) our sympathy.

But the question that plagues me is this: Why does the granddaughter, the beautiful and innocent child, have to die? And who is it that kills her?

I will propose a reckless interpretation. The child dies as a punishment to the "unnatural" mother—not her own mother, but her mother's mother, Gerda Stein. It is a self-inflicted punishment, for Gerda loves the child and "in life there are no accidents." It is also a punishment inflicted on Gerda by her daughter, whose own life has been a slow suicide and a permanent reproach to her mother. By not intervening in time, she allows her own daughter to perish as the ultimate reproach (thereby proving herself an "unnatural" mother too).[47] And she finally gets what she wants: for the first time ever, she sees her mother cry.

But of course it is neither Gerda nor her daughter that kills the child; it is the one who is both of them, Rosellen Brown. I read the ending of this novel as a gesture of self-punishment by the writing

47. There is an interesting contrast between this scene and one of the culminating scenes in Margaret Drabble's novel *The Garrick Year* (1964), where the heroine sees her young daughter fall into a river and immediately jumps in to save her. In Drabble's fiction, as I suggest below, the mother-child bond is never problematic.

376

mother, and the novel itself as a dark companion piece to "Good Housekeeping." Here the aggressive impulse of the mother as artist is turned in on herself. Gerda is a writer *manquée*, and a failed mother as well. In her relationship to her daughter, she embodies the writing mother's most nightmarish fantasy: "I had not known we were to share but one life between us, so that the fuller mine is, the more empty hers."

Brown is the only contemporary novelist I know of who has explored, in fully rendered fictional forms, the violence and guilt as well as the violent energy that attend the artistic creations of mothers. Compared to Brown on this particular subject, I find Margaret Drabble, who has been called "the novelist of maternity,"[48] surprisingly simple. In Drabble's novels, the mothers who write or pursue a creative career (the older, famous novelist in *Jerusalem the Golden*, the thesis-writing heroine of *The Millstone*, the poet protagonist of *The Waterfall*, the archaeologist heroine of *The Realms of Gold*) all have an unproblematic, quasi-idealized relationship to their children. In *Jerusalem the Golden*, where the novelist's children are already grown, we see her mothering a stranger's baby. In *The Millstone*, the heroine writes better after her child is born. In *The Waterfall*, the narrator-heroine speaks of her feelings of ambivalence during pregnancy, but these feelings miraculously evaporate once the child arrives; her problems with writing are tied up not with her children but with her husband and her lover. As for the heroine of *The Realms of Gold*, she has no problems at all, once her love life is straightened out. Indeed, if the complexity of exploration is any criterion to judge by, Drabble seems to me to be more the novelist of adult love than anything else. Her heroines are almost without exception mothers, but their motherhood is relevant above all to their relations—whether fulfilling or frustrating—with men. The question that I think underlies Drabble's novels is this: Can a creative woman with children have a satisfying, permanent relationship with a man? This question is fascinating in its own right, but it is *another* question.

As far as writing and motherhood goes, Drabble perhaps gives us the wish-fulfillment fantasies that correspond, in reverse, to the nightmare fantasies of Brown. In between, there remains a great deal of space to explore—in fiction and in life.

48. Showalter, *Literature of Their Own*, 305.

Contributors

JANET ADELMAN is Professor of English at the University of California, Berkeley. She is author of *The Common Liar: An Essay on Antony and Cleopatra* and editor of *Twentieth-Century Interpretations of King Lear* and has published essays on Chaucer, Milton, *Coriolanus*, *King Lear*, and *Measure for Measure*. She is working on a psychoanalytic interpretation of the figure of the mother in Shakespeare.

WENDY DEUTELBAUM has published essays and reviews on psychoanalysis, reader theory, feminist philosophy, and epistolary partners in *Sub-stance*, *Genre*, and *Bucknell Review*. She is completing a book, "Epistolary Systems: A Study of Five Correspondences." Assistant Professor of French at the University of Iowa, she is making a transition from teaching to the practice of psychotherapy.

MARGERY DURHAM is Associate Professor of English at the University of Minnesota. She has published articles on Tennyson and Newman and reviews of contemporary poetry. She is working on a study of the family as an image of culture in Victorian literature.

MARTHA NOEL EVANS has published articles on nineteenth- and twentieth-century French literature as well as on psychoanalysis in *Romanic Review*, *Symposium*, *La Revue des sciences humaines*, *Littérature*, *Sub-stance*, and *Psychoanalytic Quarterly*. A translator of

Jacques Lacan, she has also translated Shoshana Felman's *Folie et la chose littéraire*. She teaches at Mary Baldwin College in Staunton, Virginia, where she is Associate Professor of French, and is working on a book on women's writing in contemporary France.

JANE GALLOP is the author of *Intersections: A Reading of Sade with Bataille, Blanchot, and Klossowski* and *The Daughter's Seduction: Feminism and Psychoanalysis* as well as numerous articles. An Associate Professor of French at Miami University, Ohio, she is writing a book on Lacan's *Ecrits*.

SHIRLEY NELSON GARNER, Associate Professor of English at the University of Minnesota, has published articles on Shakespeare and various women writers. She is a founder of *Hurricane Alice*, a feminist review, and is currently writing a series of autobiographical essays.

GAYLE GREENE is Associate Professor of English at Scripps College, Claremont, California. She has published numerous articles on Shakespeare, has co-edited *The Woman's Part: Feminist Criticism of Shakespeare*, and is currently co-editing *Feminist Theory and Criticism*, Methuen New Accents Series. She is also working on a book, "Re-Visions: Contemporary Women Writers and the Tradition," which examines the works of Doris Lessing, Margaret Drabble, Margaret Atwood, Margaret Laurence, Beryl Bainbridge, and Gail Godwin.

CYNTHIA HUFF received a Fulbright Grant in 1981–82 to research nineteenth-century British women's diaries, the subject of her dissertation at the University of Iowa. She has presented papers on women's diaries and on George Sand's autobiography and is soon to publish *A Descriptive Bibliography of Selected Nineteenth-Century British Women's Manuscript Diaries*.

DIANNE HUNTER is Associate Professor of English at Trinity College in Hartford, Connecticut, where she teaches psychoanalytic and feminist criticism of literature. She has published essays on LeRoi Jones, Juliet Mitchell, and Shakespeare.

CLAIRE KAHANE, Associate Professor of English at the State University of New York at Buffalo, directs the Literature and Psychology Program and is a member of the Center for the Psychological Study of the Arts. She has published articles on Gothic fiction, the comic-grotesque, Virginia Woolf, and Flannery O'Connor; is the editor of

Psychoanalyse und das Unhaimliche; and is co-editor, with Charles Bernheimer, of *In Dora's Case: Freud, Hysteria, Feminism.*

COPPÉLIA KAHN is Associate Professor of English at Wesleyan University. She has published *Man's Estate: Masculine Identity in Shakespeare* and, with Murray Schwartz, co-edited *Representing Shakespeare: New Psychoanalytic Research.*

ANNETTE KOLODNY is the author of *The Lay of the Land: Metaphor as Experience and History in American Life and Letters* and *The Land before Her: Fantasy and Experience of the American Frontiers, 1630–1860.* She is Professor of Literature at Rensselaer Polytechnic Institute.

DAVID LEVERENZ is Associate Professor of English at Rutgers University, where he chaired the Livingston College English Department from 1975 to 1981. He is author of *The Language of Puritan Feeling: An Exploration in Literature, Psychology, and Social History* and has published numerous essays. He is also co-editor, with George Levine, of *Mindful Pleasures: Essays on Thomas Pynchon.* At present he is writing on manhood and womanhood in the American Renaissance.

NAOMI SCHOR, Associate Professor of French Studies at Brown University, is author of *Zola's Crowds* and *Breaking the Chain: Woman, Realism, and the French Novel* and co-editor, with Henry Majewski, of *Flaubert and Postmodernism.* She is writing a book on the detail as aesthetic category, tentatively titled "Sublime Details: From Reynolds to Barthes."

MADELON SPRENGNETHER, Associate Professor of English at the University of Minnesota, has published, under the name Madelon S. Gohlke, several articles on Renaissance literature, including Shakespeare. She is also the author of a book of poetry, *The Normal Heart,* and a book of personal essays, *Rivers, Stories, Houses, Dreams.*

SUSAN RUBIN SULEIMAN is Professor of Romance Languages and Literatures at Harvard University. She is the author of *Authoritarian Fictions: The Ideological Novel as a Literary Genre* and co-editor, with Inge Crossman, of *The Reader in the Text: Essays on Audience and Interpretation,* and has published numerous articles on modern French literature and literary theory. She is working on problems of avant-garde writing from surrealism to "new French feminism."

JIM SWAN is Associate Professor of English at the State University

Contributors

of New York at Buffalo, where he is a member of the graduate
program in Literature and Psychology and the Group for Applied
Psychoanalysis. He has published articles on Renaissance literature,
Freud, and psychoanalytic criticism. At present he is working on
several projects in Renaissance literature and culture, under the
general title "The Poetics of Identity."

Index

Abbott, Anne, 196, 213, 216n
Abel, Elizabeth, 320n, 321n
Abraham, Karl, 353
Alta, 374
Anal phase (Freud), 40
Anna O. *See* Pappenheim, Bertha
Antigone, 25
Arendt, Hannah, 149
Asp, Carolyn, 124n
Auerbach, Nina, 360
Austen, Jane: *Northanger Abbey*, 335
Autobiography, 307–8, 316–17

Balint, Alice, 355
Balzac, Honoré de: *Illusions perdues*, 237; *Peau de chagrin*, 222; *Splendeurs et misères des courtisanes*, 237
Barthes, Roland, 357
Basler, Roy, 171n
Bauer, Ida, 54. *See also* Dora
Bayley, John, 119n
Baym, Nina, 199, 205, 206, 210n, 211n, 215, 245
Beauvoir, Simone de, 292n, 363
Beer, John, 191n
Bell, Michael Davitt, 211n, 213n
Berger, John, 225
Bersani, Leo, 237

Bettelheim, Bruno, 182
Bloom, Harold, 251, 252, 258–59; *Anxiety of Influence*, 241–42; *Kaballah and Criticism*, 242, 243n, 252–53; *Map of Misreading*, 241–44, 259n; *Poetry and Repression*, 242n
Breuer, Josef, 17, 90–103, 105–6, 111
Brodhead, Richard, 203n, 210, 211n
Brontë, Charlotte: *Jane Eyre*, 335
Brooks, Ellen, 282n
Brown, Rosellen: *Autobiography of My Mother*, 375–77; "Good Housekeeping," 372–74

Cameron, Sharon, 203n
Castration: for both sexes, 19; and femininity, 69; of girls, 353; and maternal engulfment, 136; perception of, 75–76, 79; and sexual difference, 218n; and signification, 21–22; of woman, 36, 41, 228n. *See also* Penis; Phallus
Castration anxiety, 41, 42, 70, 163, 170
Cavell, Marcia, 356
Charcot, Jean Martin, 90, 98, 109
Chawaf, Chantal, 370
Chesler, Phyllis, 364–65
Chodorow, Nancy, 20, 160n, 162n; *Reproduction of Mothering*, 20n, 73–79,

Chodorow, Nancy (*cont.*) 201, 221, 281, 288–89, 321, 336, 354–55
Chopin, Kate: *Awakening*, 246–47
Cixous, Hélène, 23, 114n, 214n, 370–71
Coburn, Kathleen, 180
Cohen, Mary, 285n
Colacurcio, Michael, 206
Coleridge, Samuel Taylor: *Ancient Mariner*, 192; *Notebooks*, 169–70, 176–80, 188, 192; "Pains of Sleep," 170–71
Collins, Jerre, 52n, 58n, 60n, 69n
Crews, Frederick, 210

Daly, Mary, 61n, 114n
Dauber, Kenneth, 211n
Demeter, 24
Derrida, Jacques, 23–24, 63n, 307
Deutsch, Felix, 59n
Deutsch, Helene, 321, 352–53, 355–56, 358
Diehl, Joanne Feit, 243n
Dinnerstein, Dorothy, 72–73, 77–79, 290, 336
Dora: and fantasy of fellatio, 56–57, 61–62, 65–66, 69; and Frau K., 55, 81–82; and Herr K., 17, 58–60, 81; and homosexuality, 58, 69, 70; and masturbation, 63–64, 68; naming of, 52–53; and preoedipal fantasy, 58, 63. *See also* Bauer, Ida
Drabble, Margaret, 283, 376n, 377
Dryden, Edgar A., 208n

Eagleton, Terrence, 130n
Ego boundaries: fluidity of, 20; loss of, 88, 131, 338, 340, 347. *See also* Imaginary; Preoedipal period; Symbiosis
Enscoe, Gerald E., 191n
Erikson, Erik, 86n, 102
Erlich, Iza, 54n, 80, 82

Farrell, Warren, 291n
Felman, Shoshona, 218–19, 229
Female sexuality, theory of, 34. *See also* Freud, Sigmund; Preoedipal period; Sexual difference
Feminism: French, 22–25, 367, 370–71; and hysteria, 16, 113; of Doris Lessing, 283–84, 304–5; and literary criticism, 88; and philosophy, 34–35; and psychoanalysis, 25; of George Sand, 262–64, 277–79; in *Scarlet Letter*,
195–96, 198–200; and separatism, 252n. *See also* Patriarchy; Phallocentrism
Feminist criticism: and feminine specificity, 218; of *Scarlet Letter*, 196–97, 215
Fetterley, Judith, 257n
Fiedler, Leslie, 213, 336, 347
Fineman, Joel, 132
Firestone, Shulamith, 298n
Fitzgerald, F. Scott: *Great Gatsby*, 320
Fliess, William, 79–80, 84
Forster, E. M., 332
Franzosa, John, 215n
Freud, Sigmund: and Anna O., 98, 109–11; and female castration, 228n; and feminine development, 321, 353–54; and gender difference, 75, 79; and Lacan, 218n; and narcissism, 224n; and preoedipal period, 74; as storyteller, 15–16; and superego formation, 76; and talking cure, 96; and transference theory, 97
—, works of: *Civilization and Its Discontents*, 24, 271; "Creative Writers and Day-Dreaming," 356–57; *Dora*, 17–18, 81–82; "Female Sexuality," 88; "Femininity," 33, 37, 40, 228; *Inhibitions, Symptoms and Anxiety*, 163; *Interpretation of Dreams*, 85, 88, 111; "Leonardo da Vinci," 82–84; *Little Hans*, 81; "Moses of Michelangelo," 82–83, 85–87; "Mourning and Melancholia," 88, 186, 228, 232; *New Introductory Lectures*, 35, 37–41, 43, 46; "On Narcissism," 221–22, 236; "On the Universal Tendency to Debasement," 134n; "Prevalent Form of Degradation," 84; "Psychopathology of Everyday Life," 53; *Rat Man*, 81; "Special Type of Object Choice," 84; *Studies on Hysteria*, 89; "Theme of the Three Caskets," 234–36
Fryer, Judith, 199n
Furman, Nelly, 253
Fuseli, Henry, 113n

Gale, John, 227n
Gallop, Jane, 55n, 58n, 61n, 69n
Gardiner, Judith Kegan, 297
Genette, Gérard, 231n
Gilbert, Sandra, 203, 243n

Gilligan, Carol, 76, 290n
Gilman, Charlotte Perkins: "Yellow
  Wallpaper," 247–52, 256–57
Gilman, Sander, 61n
Glaspell, Susan Keating: "Jury of Her
  Peers," 253–57
Goldberg, Herb, 289n, 291n
Greene, Gayle, 120n, 122n, 123n, 134n
Gregson, Linda, 168n
Griggs, Kenneth, 55n
Gubar, Susan, 203, 243n

Hall, Radclyffe, 331
Harding, Anthony John, 191n
Hartley, David, 173–74
Hertz, Neil, 52n, 56n, 58n
Heterosexuality: and boy's oedipal love,
  77; compulsory, 318; cost of, 321; and
  female desire, 17–18, 42; and interpretation, 67; in literature of romantic
  love, 319–21; male, 60, 290–91; and
  nuclear family, 74–75; and patriarchy,
  331; and phallic aggressiveness, 68;
  and seduction in Dora, 58, 82
Hill, Susan, 361–62
Holland, Norman, 337, 340
Homosexuality: in Bloomsbury group,
  331–32; in Dora, 69; and feminine position, 58; genesis of, 82; and homoerotic friendship, 145; and homoerotic
  mirror relationship, 148; in "Leonardo
  da Vinci," 83n; and mirror stage,
  233n; in Mrs. Dalloway, 326; and
  Oedipus complex, 88; of Virginia
  Woolf, 322. See also Lesbianism
Horney, Karen, 79, 345n, 354, 356, 363
Howells, William Dean, 248
Hutchinson, Anne, 198, 201, 205n
Hysteria: and altruism, 105; and Dora,
  17–18, 58, 63; as failed feminism, 113;
  and language, 98–100, 102, 114–15;
  male, 114; and masturbation, 65n;
  and narrative, 67; and Bertha Pappenheim, 89–95; and patriarchy, 114;
  and seduction, 45, 47; sociology of,
  95; and surrealism, 109, 114. See also
  Dora; Pappenheim, Bertha

Identity, in Milton, 158–59
Imaginary, 217–19, 224, 227–28, 237.
  See also Lacan, Jacques; Mother;
  Preoedipal period; Symbiosis

Irigaray, Luce, 23, 114n, 278, 370; and
  Imaginary, 219; Ce Sexe qui n'en est
  pas un, 34, 36, 39, 50, 223–24; Spe-
  culum de l'autre femme, 33–36, 38–
  39, 42–50, 223, 228
Irwin, John, 203n, 210
Iser, Wolfgang, 253
Israel, Lucien, 105, 113

Jackson, Shirley: Haunting of Hill
  House, 341
James, Henry, 196
Jameson, Fredric, 260n
Janet, Pierre, 98
Janeway, Elizabeth, 354
Jones, Ernest, 172
Jonson, Ben: "Ode to Cary and Mori-
  son," 146–47
Jung, Carl, 300n

Kaufmann, R. J., 133n
Kerrigan, William, 149n
Klein, Melanie: depressive position,
  184; infant's rage, 355; manic evasion,
  186; paranoid-schizoid position, 182–
  83; reparation, 172–73, 191–92, 357;
  symbolization, 172–74. See also
  Mother; Preoedipal period
Knights, L. C., 120n, 125n, 139n
Krafft-Ebing, Richard, 65n
Kristeva, Julia, 352, 358, 360, 365–69

Lacan, Jacques: and hysteria, 16, 109;
  and Imaginary, 21, 217–19; and law of
  father, 217; and mirror stage, 217,
  222–24; and name of father, 367; and
  Symbolic, 22, 217–19, 235–36, 367.
  See also Imaginary; Law of father;
  Phallocentrism; Phallus; Symbolic
La Fayette, Madame de: Princesse de
  Clèves, 220–21, 227, 236
Laing, R. D., 265–66, 268, 273, 275,
  285, 299, 303
Landy, Marcia, 153n
Laplanche, Jean, 217n
Law of father: and daughter's identity,
  49; in Eugénie Grandet, 226; and
  feminine desire, 50; and patriarchy,
  43, 46–48. See also Lacan, Jacques;
  Patriarchy
Lawrence, D. H., 195
Lazarre, Jane, 361, 365–66

Leduc, Violette: *L'Asphyxie*, 306–7, 310
Lesbianism, 331–32, 341–42; in *Eugénie Grandet*, 221; in *Haunting of Hill House*, 341–42; in *Mrs. Dalloway*, 326; of Virginia Woolf, 322. *See also* Homosexuality
Lessing, Doris: *Canopus in Argos*, 304; *Four-Gated City*, 304; *Memoirs of a Survivor*, 304; *Proper Marriage*, 288n, 303n; *Summer before the Dark*, 304
Lewis, M. G.: *The Monk*, 335
Lichtenstein, Heinz, 99
Low, Anthony, 153n
Lyons, Charles, 133n, 140n

McCullers, Carson: *Ballad of the Sad Café*, 347–48
Mailloux, Steven, 197n
Main, William, 120n
Malcolm, Janet, 52n, 71, 98
Mantegazza, Paolo, 56, 65n, 69n
Marcus, Jane, 318n
Marcus, Steven, 52n, 53, 59n
Marvell, Andrew, 147; "Mower's Song," 148–52; "On Mr. Milton's *Paradise Lost*," 157
Marxism: and feminist criticism, 260, 264–65; of Doris Lessing, 284n; and literary criticism, 278–79; of Flora Tristan, 264n
Mary (Virgin), 368–69
Maternal figure: Cressida as, 130, 132–34, 136–38; in *Dora*, 58. *See also* Mother; Motherhood; Preoedipal period
Mauron, Charles, 278
Melancholia: in *Eugénie Grandet*, 228–34, 236. *See also* Freud, Sigmund
Miller, J. Hillis, 139n
Miller, Jean Baker, 72–73
Milton, John: *Areopagitica*, 158; "How soon hath time," 165–67; "Il Penseroso," 164–65; "L'Allegro," 164–65; "Lycidas," 167; *Paradise Lost*, 143, 159–62, 167–68, 191; *Reason of Church Government*, 167; *Samson Agonistes*, 144, 150–57, 161–64
Mirror: in Dimmesdale–Chillingworth relationship, 210; in *Eugénie Grandet*, 224–26; fantasy, 147; in Gothic fiction, 339–40, 344–47; in homoerotic relationship, 148

Mirror stage, 21, 217, 233
Misogyny: Milton's, 143; in Renaissance poetry, 168
Mitchell, Juliet, 16, 162n, 223, 278, 354
Moers, Ellen, 343, 347
Moi, Toril, 52n, 54n, 56n, 59n, 62n, 63n
Montrelay, Michèle, 219n
Mother: ambivalence of, 355–56; ambivalence toward, 173, 336; in *Bâtarde*, 310–11, 315; boy's separation from, 289; and civilization, 193; dependence on, 180; discourse of, 358, 372; fantasies about, 290; in French feminism, 23; in Gothic fiction, 335, 338, 341–47; and Hawthorne, 201, 209, 215; ideal, 319, 355, 368; in Lacan's theory, 21; in "Leonardo da Vinci," 83–84; as Nature, 178, 336–37, 345; in object relations theory, 19–20; omnipotence of, 348, 350; as Other, 337, 351; as poet, 259; separation from, 175–77, 181; spectral, 336, 343; splitting of, 182–83; symbolic re-creation of, 186; and symbolization process, 172–74; woman as, 296–98; as writer, 25, 361–71. *See also* Imaginary; Mother-daughter relationship; Motherhood; Preoedipal period; Symbiosis
Mother-daughter relationship, 20, 75–76, 219–21, 271, 281, 318–19, 321, 337, 342
Motherhood: and altruism, 77–78; and childbirth, 345–47; in contemporary literature, 371–77; and female ego, 78; in Freud's theory, 87; institution of, 73, 336; and power, 75; psychoanalytic theory of, 352–58; viewed by women writers, 361–70; and writing, 358–60. *See also* Imaginary; Preoedipal period

Narcissism: in *Eugénie Grandet*, 221–22, 229–34, 236; in *Scarlet Letter*, 210–12

O'Connor, Flannery: "Stroke of Good Fortune," 345–46; "Temple of the Holy Ghost," 348–50; *Wise Blood*, 343–45
Oedipal conflict: in *Eugénie Grandet*, 219; in Gothic fiction, 335–36; in *Scarlet Letter*, 213–15

Index

Oedipal period, 191, 321
Oedipus, 15–16, 37, 189, 191–92, 218n
Oedipus complex: aggression of, 186;
and female desire, 18; of Freud, 79;
and gender difference, 75–77; and
homosexuality, 88; and image of
woman, 84; and phallic phase, 37;
and reality principle, 74; and seduction, 46
Olsen, Tillie, 358, 361, 364, 366, 372
Ornstein, Robert, 122n, 139n

Pappenheim, Bertha, 91; and feminism,
104–6, 114; and language, 99–100,
102, 109, 114; and seduction of
Breuer, 96–97; and social work, 103–
4; symptoms of, 91–95, 106–7; and
talking cure, 16–17, 89–90, 98, 102.
See also Hysteria
Patriarchy: discourse of, 370; and Dora,
54; and family systems, 260, 265, 267,
277–79; and female narcissism, 225–
26; and feminine identity, 350; and
masculine behavior, 88; and motherhood, 73–75, 363, 367; and psychoanalytic theory, 354; reversal of, 49; and
role of father, 99; in *Scarlet Letter*,
198–99, 214; unconscious structure of,
16; woman under, 237; and women's
bonds, 331. *See also* Feminism; Law
of father; Phallocentrism
Penis: envy of, 75–76, 79, 354; lack of,
18, 353; overvaluation of, 47. *See also*
Phallus
Phallic phase, 40, 41, 47
Phallocentrism: of Freud, 34, 36, 75; of
Lacan, 22; and matrophobia, 79; and
philosophy, 50; as primacy of One,
40. *See also* Law of father; Patriarchy
Phallus: absence of, 36; domination of,
34; and law of father, 21; overvaluation of, 278; rule of, 38–39; as sexual
standard, 223; as signifier, 22, 348; as
standard of value, 42; transmission of,
236. *See also* Lacan, Jacques; Penis
Poe, Edgar Allen, 247–48
Pontalis, J.-B., 217n
Porter, Katherine Anne, 374–75
Preoedipal period: and Dora, 58; fantasies in, 182–83; father's exclusion
from, 74; and female desire, 22; and
feminine development, 353; in

Freud's theory, 82; and gender difference, 84, 281; and gender identity,
19, 20; in Lacan's theory, 217–18; and
language, 169–70; and mirroring, 99;
and mother-daughter bond, 271; and
sexual difference, 223, 289; and symbiosis with mother, 98–99, 336–38;
symbolization in, 183. *See also* Imaginary; Mother; Motherhood; Symbiosis
Primal scene, 55, 99

Rabkin, Norman, 125n
Radcliffe, Ann: *Mysteries of Udolpho*,
334–35, 338–40
Ramas, Maria, 52n, 54n, 59n, 65n
Rapping, Elayne Antlar, 282n
Reid, Stephen, 125n, 138n
Ricardou, Jean, 250
Rich, Adrienne: "Compulsory Hetero-
sexuality," 65n, 318; *Dream of a
Common Language*, 114; *Of Woman
Born*, 72–75, 77–79, 356, 361, 365–
66; *On Lies, Secrets, and Silence*,
284; "When We Dead Awaken," 258
Rieff, Philip, 51n, 54n, 59n
Rogow, Arnold, 52n, 54n
Rose, Jacqueline, 52n
Rose, Phyllis, 322n
Roy, Emil, 124n, 133n, 137
Rubenstein, Roberta, 284n, 295n, 299n,
300n, 305n

Sachs, Maurice, 306, 309
Sand, George: *Histoire de ma vie*, 266–
67, 270–72; *Indiana*, 276–78; *Mademoiselle la Quintinie*, 261; *Marquis de
Villemer*, 261; *My Convent Life*, 273–
78
Sartre, Jean-Paul, 364
Schwartz, Murray, 139n, 319n
Seduction: and Freud in *Dora*, 60; and
hysteria, 115; and illness, 52; and
interpretation, 60; scene of, 55, 57
Sexual difference: in *Bâtarde*, 308–10;
in female Gothic, 343; in feminine development, 18–20; and hermaphrodites, 347–50; and heterosexuality,
321; in Imaginary and Symbolic, 218;
and individuation, 160–62; in interpretation, 243, 248, 251, 253, 256–57,
259; and mirror stage, 222–23; and
poetic identity, 168; in preoedipal

Sexual difference, (*cont.*) period, 289; in reader response, 337–38, 340, 350–51; in relation to mother, son, 290, 337; in *Samson Agonistes*, 144. *See also* Freud, Sigmund; Mother; Preoedipal period

Shakespeare, William: *King Lear*, 141, 145; *Othello*, 140; *Sonnets*, 145; *Winter's Tale*, 139

Shelley, Mary: *Frankenstein*, 335, 345

Sherman, Leona, 337, 340

Showalter, Elaine, 282, 283n, 284, 294n, 359

Spatz, Jonas, 171n, 191n

Spenser, Edmund: *Faerie Queene*, 145, 153n

Stein, Arnold, 120n

Stein, Gertrude, 376

Stewart, Randall, 194

Stoehr, Taylor, 196n

Stoker, Bram: *Dracula*, 345n

Sukenick, Lynn, 282n, 283n

Suleiman, Susan, 74

Swan, Jim, 54–55n, 79–80, 88

Symbiosis: in adult personality, 77; in *Bâtarde*, 311; defense against, 290; and gender difference, 281; in infancy, 19, 132, 160, 336; in mother-daughter relationship, 75, 227; in mother-son relationship, 88; oral, 99; and poetic identity, 168; in *Samson Agonistes*, 155; in *Scarlet Letter*, 214; Troilus' desire for, 130. *See also* Imaginary; Mother; Motherhood; Preoedipal period

Symbolic, 217–18, 226–28, 235–37. *See also* Lacan, Jacques

Thompson, Clara, 354

Tolson, Andrew, 288n, 289n

Tompkins, Jane, 197n

Transference, 45, 47, 97–98

Traversi, Derek, 119n, 125n, 134n

Trilling, Diana, 294n

Tristan, Flora, 264

Trollope, Anthony, 196

Ullman, Liv, 361, 364

Wagenknecht, Edward, 200

Waggoner, Hyatt, 199

Walpole, Horace: *Castle of Otranto*, 342

Whipple, E. P., 197

Willbern, David, 88n

Willis, Sharon, 56n, 67n, 69n

Winnicott, D. W., 19, 111–13, 185–86, 192, 355, 357

Womb: envy of, 79; as tomb, 336

Woodiwiss, Kathleen, 361–62

Woolf, Virginia: marriage of, 322; *Mrs. Dalloway*, 321–22, 326–27, 332; *Room of One's Own*, 244, 319n; *Voyage Out*, 332; and writing and femininity, 359

Yarlott, Geoffrey, 191n

Yoder, Carol, 121n, 126n

Library of Congress Cataloging in Publication Data

Main entry under title:

The (M)other tongue.

    Includes index.
      1. Psychoanalysis and literature—Addresses, essays,
lectures. 2. Psychoanalysis—Addresses, essays, lectures.
3. Sex differences (Psychology) in literature—Addresses,
essays, lectures. 4. Feminism and literature—Addresses,
essays, lectures. I. Garner, Shirley Nelson, 1935–
II. Kahane, Claire. III. Sprengnether, Madelon.
IV. Title: (M)other tongue.
PN98.P75M67 1985   809′.93353   84-17560
ISBN 0-8014-1693-0 (alk. paper)